The fine

911FO

Modeling Techniques in Predictive Analytics

Business Problems and Solutions with R

Thomas W. Miller

Vice President, Publisher: Tim Moore
Associate Publisher and Director of Marketing: Amy Neidlinger
Executive Editor: Jeanne Glasser
Operations Specialist: Jodi Kemper
Cover Designer: Alan Clements
Managing Editor: Kristy Hart
Project Editor: Sara Schumacher
Senior Compositor: Gloria Schurick
Manufacturing Buyer: Dan Uhrig

Published by Pearson Education, Inc.
Upper Saddle River, New Jersey 07458

Pearson offers excellent discounts on this book when ordered in quantity for bulk purchases or special sales. For more information, please contact U.S. Corporate and Government Sales, 1-800-382-3419, corpsales@pearsontechgroup.com. For sales outside the U.S., please contact International Sales at international@pearsoned.com.

Printed in the United States of America

Second Printing December 2013

ISBN-10: 0-13-341293-8
ISBN-13: 978-0-13-341293-2

Pearson Education LTD.
Pearson Education Australia PTY, Limited.
Pearson Education Singapore, Pte. Ltd.
Pearson Education Asia, Ltd.
Pearson Education Canada, Ltd.
Pearson Educacin de Mexico, S.A. de C.V.
Pearson Education—Japan
Pearson Education Malaysia, Pte. Ltd.

Library of Congress Control Number: 2013946325

Contents

Preface   v

Figures   ix

Tables   xiii

Exhibits   xv

1   Analytics and Data Science   1

2   Advertising and Promotion   15

3   Preference and Choice   29

4   Market Basket Analysis   37

5   Economic Data Analysis   53

6   Operations Management   67

7   Text Analytics   83

8   Sentiment Analysis   113

9   Sports Analytics   149

10 Brand and Price   **173**

11 Spatial Data Analysis   **209**

12 The Big Little Data Game   **231**

A There's a Pack' for That   **237**

   A.1 Regression 238

   A.2 Classification 240

   A.3 Recommender Systems 242

   A.4 Product Positioning 244

   A.5 Segmentation and Target Marketing 246

   A.6 Finance and Risk Analytics 249

   A.7 Social Network Analysis 250

B Measurement   **253**

C Code and Utilities   **267**

Bibliography   **297**

Index   **327**

Preface

"Toto, I've got a feeling we're not in Kansas anymore."

—JUDY GARLAND AS DOROTHY GALE IN *The Wizard of Oz* (1939)

Data and algorithms rule the day. Welcome to the new world of business, a fast-paced, data-intensive world, an open-source world in which competitive advantage, however fleeting, is obtained through analytic prowess and the sharing of ideas.

Many books about predictive analytics talk about strategy and management. Some focus on methods and models. Others look at information technology and code. This is that rare book that tries to do all three, appealing to modelers, programmers, and business managers alike.

We recognize the importance of analytics in gaining competitive advantage. We help researchers and analysts by providing a ready resource and reference guide for modeling techniques. We show programmers how to build upon a foundation of code that works to solve real business problems. We translate the results of models into words and pictures that management can understand. We explain the meaning of data and models.

Growth in the volume of data collected and stored, in the variety of data available for analysis, and in the rate at which data arrive and require analysis, makes analytics more important with every passing day. Achieving competitive advantage means implementing new systems for information management and analytics. It means changing the way business is done.

Covering a variety of applications, this book is for people who want to know about data, modeling techniques, and the benefits of analytics. This book is for people who want to make things happen in their organizations.

Predictive analytics is data science. The literature in the field is massive, drawing from many academic disciplines and application areas. The relevant code (even if we restrict ourselves to R) is growing quickly. Indeed, it would be a challenge to provide a comprehensive guide to predictive analytics. What we have done is offer a collection of vignettes with each chapter focused on a particular application area and business problem.

Our objective is to provide an overview of predictive analytics and data science that is accessible to many readers. There is scant mathematics in the book—statisticians and modelers may look to the references for details and derivations of methods. We describe methods in plain English and use data visualization to show solutions to business problems.

Given the subject of the book, some might wonder if I belong to either the classical or Bayesian camp. At the School of Statistics at the University of Minnesota, I developed a respect for both sides of the classical/Bayesian divide. I regard highly the perspective of empirical Bayesians and those working in statistical learning, an area that combines machine learning and traditional statistics. I am a pragmatist when it comes to modeling and inference. I do what works and express my uncertainty in statements that others can understand.

What made this book possible is the work of thousands of experts across the world, people who contribute time and ideas to the R community. The growth of R and the ease of growing it further ensures that the R environment for modeling techniques in predictive analytics will be around for many years to come. Genie out of the lamp, wizard from behind the curtain—rocket science is not what it used to be. Secrets are being revealed. This book is part of the process.

Most of the data in the book were obtained from public domain data sources. Bobblehead promotional data were contributed by Erica Costello. Computer choice study data were made possible through work supported by Sharon Chamberlain. The call center data of "Anonymous Bank" were provided by Avi Mandelbaum and Ilan Guedj. Movie information was obtained courtesy of The Internet Movie Database, used with permission.

IMDb movie reviews data were organized by Andrew L. Mass and his colleagues at Stanford University. Some examples were inspired by working with NCR Comten, Hewlett-Packard Company, Union Cab Cooperative of Madison, Site Analytics Co. of New York, and Sunseed Research LLC of Madison, Wisconsin.

As with vignettes under the Comprehensive R Archive Network, program examples in the book show what can be done with R. We work in a world of open source, sharing with one another. The truth about what we do is in programs for everyone to see and for some to debug. The code in this book contains step-by-step comments to promote student learning. Each program example ends with suggestions to build on the analysis that has been presented.

Many have influenced my intellectual development over the years. There were those good thinkers and good people, teachers and mentors for whom I will be forever grateful. Sadly, no longer with us are Gerald Hahn Hinkle in philosophy and Allan Lake Rice in languages at Ursinus College, and Herbert Feigl in philosophy at the University of Minnesota. I am also most thankful to David J. Weiss in psychometrics at the University of Minnesota and Kelly Eakin in economics, formerly at the University of Oregon. Good teachers—yes, great teachers—are valued for a lifetime.

Thanks to Michael L. Rothschild, Neal M. Ford, Peter R. Dickson, and Janet Christopher who provided invaluable support during our years together at the University of Wisconsin–Madison and the A. C. Nielsen Center for Marketing Research.

Those who know me well are not surprised by my move to the Los Angeles area. Two Major League Baseball teams, movies, and good weather is a hard combination to beat. I am most fortunate to be involved with graduate distance education at Northwestern University's School of Continuing Studies. Distance learning faculty and students at this school can live and work anywhere they like.

Thanks to Glen Fogerty who offered me the opportunity to teach and take a leadership role in the Predictive Analytics program at Northwestern University. Thanks to colleagues and staff who administer this exceptional graduate program. And thanks to the many students and fellow faculty from whom I have learned.

Amy Hendrickson of TeXnology Inc. applied her craft, making words, tables, and figures look beautiful in print—another victory for open source. Thanks to Donald Knuth and the TeX/LaTeX community for their contributions to this wonderful system for typesetting and publication.

Thanks to readers and reviewers who provided much needed assistance, including Suzanne Callender, Philip M. Goldfeder, Melvin Ott, and Thomas P. Ryan. Jennifer Swartz provided proofreading assistance. Candice Bradley served dual roles as a reviewer and copyeditor. I am most grateful for their feedback and encouragement. Thanks to my editor, Jeanne Glasser Levine, and publisher, Pearson/FT Press, for making this book possible. Any writing issues, errors, or items of unfinished business, of course, are my responsibility alone.

My good friend Brittney and her daughter Janiya keep me company when time permits. And my son Daniel is there for me in good times and bad, a friend for life. My greatest debt is to them because they believe in me.

Thomas W. Miller
Glendale, California
July 2013

Figures

1.1	Data and models for research	3
1.2	Training-and-Test Regimen for Model Evaluation	6
1.3	Training-and-Test Using Multi-fold Cross-validation	7
1.4	Training-and-Test with Bootstrap Resampling	8
1.5	Importance of Data Visualization: The Anscombe Quartet	10
2.1	Dodgers Attendance by Day of Week	18
2.2	Dodgers Attendance by Month	18
2.3	Dodgers Weather, Fireworks, and Attendance	19
2.4	Dodgers Attendance by Visiting Team	21
2.5	Regression Model Performance: Bobbleheads and Attendance	22
3.1	Spine Chart of Preferences for Mobile Communication Services	31
4.1	Market Basket for One Shopping Trip	38
4.2	Market Basket Prevalence of Initial Grocery Items	41
4.3	Market Basket Prevalence of Grocery Items by Category	43
4.4	Market Basket Association Rules: Scatter Plot	44
4.5	Market Basket Association Rules: Matrix Bubble Chart	45
4.6	Association Rules for a Local Farmer: A Network Diagram	47
5.1	Multiple Time Series of Economic Data	55
5.2	Horizon Plot of Indexed Economic Time Series	57
5.3	Forecast of National Civilian Employment Rate (percentage)	59
5.4	Forecast of Manufacturers' New Orders: Durable Goods (billions of dollars)	59
5.5	Forecast of University of Michigan Index of Consumer Sentiment (1Q 1966 = 100)	60
5.6	Forecast of New Homes Sold (millions)	60
6.1	Call Center Operations for Monday	69
6.2	Call Center Operations for Tuesday	69
6.3	Call Center Operations for Wednesday	70

6.4	Call Center Operations for Thursday	70
6.5	Call Center Operations for Friday	71
6.6	Call Center Operations for Sunday	71
6.7	Call Center Arrival and Service Rates on Wednesdays	72
6.8	Call Center Needs and Optimal Workforce Schedule	75
7.1	Movie Taglines from The Internet Movie Database (IMDb)	84
7.2	Movies by Year of Release	86
7.3	A Bag of 200 Words from Forty Years of Movie Taglines	88
7.4	Picture of Text in Time: Forty Years of Movie Taglines	89
7.5	Text Measures and Documents on a Single Graph	90
7.6	Horizon Plot of Text Measures across Forty Years of Movie Taglines	92
7.7	From Text Processing to Text Analytics	93
7.8	Linguistic Foundations of Text Analytics	94
7.9	Creating a Terms-by-Documents Matrix	96
7.10	An R Programmer's Word Cloud	100
8.1	A Few Movie Reviews According to Tom	114
8.2	A Few More Movie Reviews According to Tom	115
8.3	Fifty Words of Sentiment	117
8.4	List-Based Text Measures for Four Movie Reviews	119
8.5	Scatter Plot of Text Measures of Positive and Negative Sentiment	120
8.6	Word Importance in Classifying Movie Reviews as Thumbs-Up or Thumbs-Down	124
8.7	A Simple Tree Classifier for Thumbs-Up or Thumbs-Down	125
9.1	Predictive Modeling Framework for Picking a Winning Team	150
9.2	Game-day Simulation (offense only)	156
9.3	Mets' Away and Yankees' Home Data (offense and defense)	157
9.4	Balanced Game-day Simulation (offense and defense)	158
9.5	Actual and Theoretical Runs-scored Distributions	160
9.6	Poisson Model for Mets vs. Yankees at Yankee Stadium	162
9.7	Negative Binomial Model for Mets vs. Yankees at Yankee Stadium	163
9.8	Probability of Home Team Winning (Negative Binomial Model)	165
10.1	Computer Choice Study: One Choice Set	176
10.2	Computer Choice Study: A Mosaic of Top Brands and Most Valued Attributes	179
10.3	Framework for Describing Consumer Preference and Choice	181
10.4	Ternary Plot of Consumer Preference and Choice	181
10.5	Comparing Consumers with Differing Brand Preferences	182
10.6	Potential for Brand Switching: Parallel Coordinates for Individual Consumers	184

10.7 Potential for Brand Switching: Parallel Coordinates for Consumer
Groups 185
10.8 Market Simulation: A Mosaic of Preference Shares 188
11.1 California Housing Data: Correlation Heat Map for the Training Data 213
11.2 California Housing Data: Scatter Plot Matrix of Selected Variables . . . 214
11.3 Tree-Structured Regression for Predicting California Housing Values . 216
11.4 Random Forests Regression for Predicting California Housing Values . 217
12.1 From Data to Explanation 232
A.1 Evaluating Predictive Accuracy for a Binary Classifier 241
B.1 Hypothetical Multitrait-Multimethod Matrix 255
B.2 Conjoint Degree-of-Interest Rating 258
B.3 Conjoint Sliding Scale for Profile Pairs 258
B.4 Paired Comparisons 259
B.5 Multiple-Rank-Orders 259
B.6 Best-worst Item Provides Partial Paired Comparisons 260
B.7 Paired Comparison Choice Task 262
B.8 Choice Set with Three Product Profiles 262
B.9 Menu-based Choice Task 264
B.10 Elimination Pick List 265

Tables

1.1	Data for the Anscombe Quartet	9
2.1	Bobbleheads and Dodger Dogs	17
2.2	Regression of Attendance on Month, Day of Week, and Bobblehead Promotion	23
3.1	Preference Data for Mobile Communication Services	30
4.1	Association Rules for a Local Farmer	46
6.1	Call Center Shifts and Needs for Wednesdays	73
6.2	Call Center Problem and Solution	74
8.1	List-Based Sentiment Measures from Tom's Reviews	118
8.2	Accuracy of Text Classification for Movie Reviews (Thumbs-Up or Thumbs-Down)	122
8.3	Random Forest Text Measurement Model Applied to Tom's Movie Reviews	123
9.1	New York Mets' Early Season Games in 2007	153
9.2	New York Yankees' Early Season Games in 2007	154
10.1	Computer Choice Study: Product Attributes	175
10.2	Computer Choice Study: Data for One Individual	177
10.3	Contingency Table of Top-ranked Brands and Most Valued Attributes	180
10.4	Market Simulation: Choice Set Input	187
10.5	Market Simulation: Preference Shares in a Hypothetical Four-brand Market	189
11.1	California Housing Data: Original and Computed Variables	211
11.2	Linear Regression Fit to Selected California Block Groups	215
11.3	Comparison of Regressions on Spatially Referenced Data	218

Exhibits

1.1 R Program for the Anscombe Quartet 13

2.1 Shaking Our Bobbleheads Yes and No 26

3.1 Measuring and Modeling Individual Preferences 34

4.1 Market Basket Analysis of Grocery Store Data 50

5.1 Working with Economic Data 62

6.1 Call Center Scheduling Problem and Solution 77

7.1 Text Analytics of Movie Taglines 101

8.1 Sentiment Analysis and Classification of Movie Ratings 129

9.1 Winning Probabilities by Simulation (Negative Binomial Model) 171

10.1 Computer Choice Study: Training and Testing with Hierarchical Bayes 192

10.2 Preference, Choice, and Market Simulation 197

11.1 California Housing Values: Regression and Spatial Regression Models 220

C.1 Conjoint Analysis Spine Chart 268

C.2 Market Simulation Utilities 276

C.3 Split-plotting Utilities 277

C.4 Wait-time Ribbon Plot 280

C.5 Word Scoring Code for Sentiment Analysis 292

C.6 Utilities for Spatial Data Analysis 296

1

Analytics and Data Science

Mr. Maguire: "I just want to say one word to you, just one word."

Ben: "Yes, sir."

Mr. Maguire: "Are you listening?"

Ben: "Yes, I am."

Mr. Maguire: "Plastics."

—WALTER BROOKE AS MR. MAGUIRE AND DUSTIN HOFFMAN
AS BEN (BENJAMIN BRADDOCK) IN *The Graduate* (1967)

While earning a degree in philosophy may not be the best career move (unless a student plans to teach philosophy, and few of these positions are available), I greatly value my years as a student of philosophy and the liberal arts. For my bachelor's degree, I wrote an honors paper on Bertrand Russell. In graduate school at the University of Minnesota, I took courses from one of the truly great philosophers, Herbert Feigl. I read about science and the search for truth, otherwise known as epistemology. My favorite philosophy was logical empiricism.

Although my days of "thinking about thinking" (which is how Feigl defined philosophy) are far behind me, in those early years of academic training I was able to develop a keen sense for what is real and what is just talk.

When we use the word *model* in predictive analytics, we are referring to a representation of the world, a rendering or description of reality, an attempt to relate one set of variables to another. Limited, imprecise, but useful, a model helps us to make sense of the world.

Predictive analytics brings together management, information technology, and modeling. It is for today's data-intensive world. Predictive analytics is data science, a multidisciplinary skill set essential for success in business, nonprofit organizations, and government. Whether forecasting sales or market share, finding a good retail site or investment opportunity, identifying consumer segments and target markets, or assessing the potential of new products or risks associated with existing products, modeling methods in predictive analytics provide the key.

Data scientists, those working in the field of predictive analytics, speak the language of business—accounting, finance, marketing, and management. They know about information technology, including data structures, algorithms, and object-oriented programming. They understand statistical modeling, machine learning, and mathematical programming. Data scientists are methodological eclectics, drawing from many scientific disciplines and translating the results of empirical research into words and pictures that management can understand.

Predictive analytics, like much of statistics, involves searching for meaningful relationships among variables and representing those relationships in models. There are response variables—things we are trying to predict. There are explanatory variables or predictors—things we observe, manipulate, or control that could relate to the response.

Regression and classification are two common types predictive models. Regression involves predicting a response with meaningful magnitude, such as quantity sold, stock price, or return on investment. Classification involves predicting a categorical response. Which brand will be purchased? Will the consumer buy the product or not? Will the account holder pay off or default on the loan? Is this bank transaction true or fraudulent?

Predictive modeling involves searching for useful predictors. Prediction problems are defined by their width or number of potential predictors and their depth or number of observations or cases in the data set. It is the number of potential predictors in business, marketing, and investment analysis

Figure 1.1. *Data and models for research*

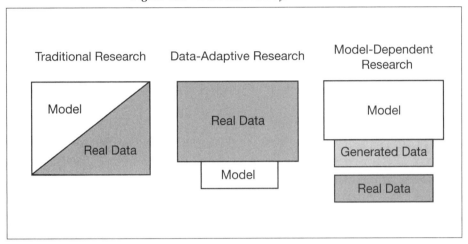

that causes the most difficulty. There can be thousands of potential predictors with weak relationships to the response. With the aid of computers, hundreds or thousands of models can be fit to subsets of the data and tested on other subsets of the data, providing an evaluation of each predictor.

Predictive modeling involves finding good subsets of predictors or explanatory variables. Models that fit the data well are better than models that fit the data poorly. Simple models are better than complex models. Working with a list of useful predictors, we can fit many models to the available data, then evaluate those models by their simplicity and by how well they fit the data.

Consider three general approaches to research and modeling as employed in predictive analytics: traditional, data-adaptive, and model-dependent. See figure 1.1. The traditional approach to research and modeling begins with the specification of a theory or model. Classical or Bayesian methods of statistical inference are employed. Traditional methods, such as linear regression and logistic regression, estimate parameters for linear predictors. Model building involves fitting models to data. After we have fit a model, we can check it using model diagnostics.

When we employ a data-adaptive approach, we begin with data and search through those data to find useful predictors. We give little thought to theories or hypotheses prior to running the analysis. This is the world of machine learning, sometimes called statistical learning or data mining. Data-adaptive methods adapt to the available data, representing nonlinear relationships and interactions among variables. The data determine the model. Data-adaptive methods are data-driven.

Model-dependent research is the third approach. It begins with the specification of a model and uses that model to generate data, predictions, or recommendations. Simulations and mathematical programming methods, primary tools of operations research, are examples of model-dependent research. When employing a model-dependent or simulation approach, models are improved by comparing generated data with real data. We ask whether simulated consumers, firms, and markets behave like real consumers, firms, and markets.

It is often a combination of models and methods that works best. Consider an application from the field of financial research. The manager of a mutual fund is looking for additional stocks for a fund's portfolio. A financial engineer employs a data-adaptive model (perhaps a neural network) to search across thousands of performance indictors and stocks, identifying a subset of stocks for further analysis. Then, working with that subset of stocks, the financial engineer employs a theory-based approach (CAPM, the capital asset pricing model) to identify a smaller set of stocks to recommend to the fund manager. As a final step, using model-dependent research (mathematical programming), the engineer identifies the minimum-risk capital investment for each of the stocks in the portfolio.

Data may be organized by observational unit, time, and space. The observational or cross-sectional unit could be an individual consumer or business or any other basis for collecting and grouping data. Data are organized in time by seconds, minutes, hours, days, and so on. Space or location is often defined by longitude and latitude.

Consider numbers of customers entering grocery stores (units of analysis) in Glendale, California on Monday (one point in time), ignoring the spatial location of the stores—these are cross-sectional data. Suppose we work with one of those stores, looking at numbers of customers entering the store each day of the week for six months—these are time series data. Then we look at numbers of customers at all of the grocery stores in Glendale across six months—these are longitudinal or panel data. To complete our study, we locate these stores by longitude and latitude, so we have spatial or spatio-temporal data. For any of these data structures we could consider measures in addition to the number of customers entering stores. We look at store sales, consumer or nearby resident demographics, traffic on Glendale streets, and so doing move to multiple time series and multivariate methods. The organization of the data we collect affects the structure of the models we employ.

As we consider business problems in this book, we touch on many types of models, including cross-sectional, time series, and spatial data models. Whatever the structure of the data and associated models, prediction is the unifying theme. We use the data we have to predict data we do not yet have, recognizing that prediction is a precarious enterprise. It is the process of extrapolating and forecasting.

To make predictions, we may employ classical or Bayesian methods. Or we may dispense with parametric formulations entirely and rely upon machine learning algorithms. We do what works.[1] Our approach to predictive analytics is based upon a simple premise:

The value of a model lies in the quality of its predictions.

We learn from statistics that we should quantify our uncertainty. On the one hand, we have confidence intervals, point estimates with associated standard errors, and significance tests—that is the classical way. On the other hand, we have probability intervals, prediction intervals, Bayes factors, subjective (perhaps diffuse) priors, and posterior probability distributions—the path of Bayesian statistics. Indices like the Akaike information criterion (AIC) or the Bayes information criterion (BIC) help us to to judge one model against another, providing a balance between goodness-of-fit and parsimony.

Central to our approach is a *training-and-test regimen*. We partition sample data into training and test sets. We build our model on the training set and

---

[1] Within the statistical literature, Seymour Geisser (1929–2004) introduced an approach best described as *Bayesian predictive inference* (Geisser 1993). Bayesian statistics is named after Reverend Thomas Bayes (1706–1761), the creator of Bayes Theorem. In our emphasis upon the success of predictions, we are in agreement with Geisser. Our approach, however, is purely empirical and in no way dependent upon classical or Bayesian thinking.

Figure 1.2. *Training-and-Test Regimen for Model Evaluation*

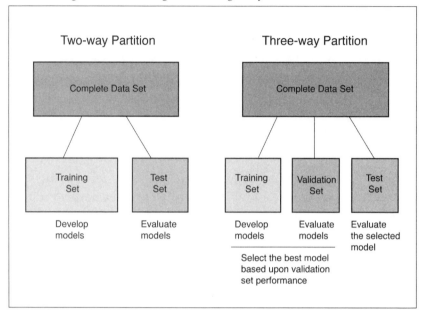

evaluate it on the test set. Simple two- and three-way data partitioning are shown in figure 1.2.

A random splitting of a sample into training and test sets could be fortuitous, especially when working with small data sets, so we sometimes conduct statistical experiments by executing a number of random splits and averaging performance indices from the resulting test sets. There are extensions to and variations on the training-and-test theme.

One variation on the training-and-test theme is multi-fold cross-validation, illustrated in figure 1.3. We partition the sample data into M folds of approximately equal size and conduct a series of tests. For the five-fold cross-validation shown in the figure, we would first train on sets B through E and test on set A. Then we would train on sets A and C through E, and test on B. We continue until each of the five folds has been utilized as a test set. We assess performance by averaging across the test sets. In leave-one-out cross-valuation, the logical extreme of multi-fold cross-validation, there are as many test sets as there are observations in the sample.

Figure 1.3. *Training-and-Test Using Multi-fold Cross-validation*

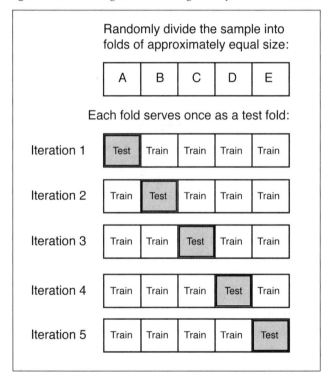

Figure 1.4. Training-and-Test with Bootstrap Resampling

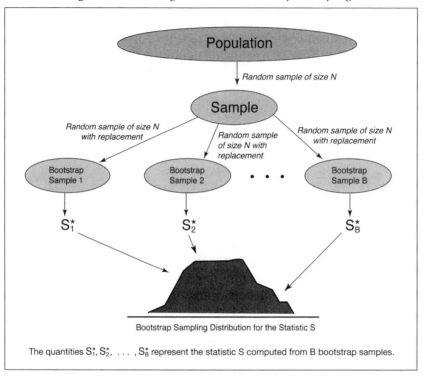

The quantities $S_1^*, S_2^*, \ldots, S_B^*$ represent the statistic S computed from B bootstrap samples.

Another variation on the training-and-test regimen is the class of bootstrap methods. If a sample approximates the population from which it was drawn, then a sample from the sample (what is known as a resample) also approximates the population. A bootstrap procedure, as illustrated in figure 1.4, involves repeated resampling with replacement. That is, we take many random samples with replacement from the sample, and for each of these resamples, we compute a statistic of interest. The bootstrap distribution of the statistic approximates the sampling distribution of that statistic. What is the value of the bootstrap? It frees us from having to make assumptions about the population distribution. We can estimate standard errors and make probability statements working from the sample data alone. The bootstrap may also be employed to improve estimates of prediction error within a leave-one-out cross-validation process. Cross-validation and bootstrap methods are reviewed in Davison and Hinkley (1997), Efron and Tibshirani (1993), and Hastie, Tibshirani, and Friedman (2009).

Table 1.1. *Data for the Anscombe Quartet*

Set I		Set II		Set III		Set IV	
x	*y*	*x*	*y*	*x*	*y*	*x*	*y*
10	8.04	10	9.14	10	7.46	8	6.58
8	6.95	8	8.14	8	6.77	8	5.76
13	7.58	13	8.74	13	12.74	8	7.71
9	8.81	9	8.77	9	7.11	8	8.84
11	8.33	11	9.26	11	7.81	8	8.47
14	9.96	14	8.10	14	8.84	8	7.04
6	7.24	6	6.13	6	6.08	8	5.25
4	4.26	4	3.10	4	5.39	19	12.50
12	10.84	12	9.13	12	8.15	8	5.56
7	4.82	7	7.26	7	6.42	8	7.91
5	5.68	5	4.74	5	5.73	8	6.89

Data visualization is critical to the work of data science. Examples in this book demonstrate the importance of data visualization in discovery, diagnostics, and design. We employ tools of exploratory data analysis (discovery) and statistical modeling (diagnostics). In communicating results to management, we use presentation graphics (design).

There is no more telling demonstration of the importance of statistical graphics and data visualization than a demonstration that is affectionately known as the Anscombe Quartet. Consider the data sets in table 1.1, developed by Anscombe (1973). Looking at these tabulated data, the casual reader will note that the fourth data set is clearly different from the others. What about the first three data sets? Are there obvious differences in patterns of relationship between x and y?

When we regress y on x for the data sets, we see that the models provide similar statistical summaries. The mean of the response y is 7.5, the mean of the explanatory variable x is 9. The regression analyses for the four data sets are virtually identical. The fitted regression equation for each of the four sets is $\hat{y} = 3 + 0.5x$. The proportion of response variance accounted for is 0.67 for each of the four models.

Anscombe (1973) argues that statistical summaries do not tell the story of data. It is not sufficient to look at data tables, regression coefficients, and the results of statistical tests. As the plots in figure 1.5 clearly show, the four Anscombe data sets are very different from one another.

Figure 1.5. *Importance of Data Visualization: The Anscombe Quartet*

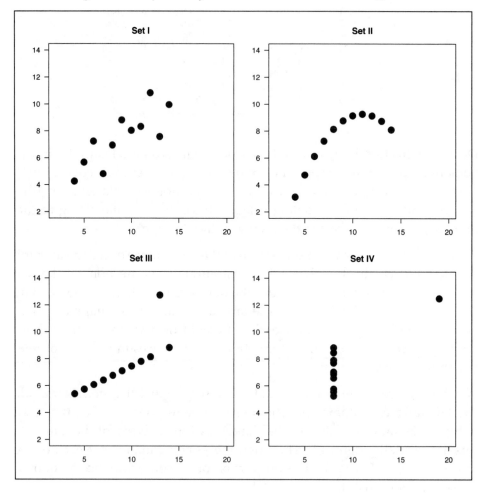

The Anscombe Quartet shows that we must look at data to understand data. The program for the Anscombe Quartet demonstration is provided in exhibit 1.1 at the end of this chapter. The program uses standard R graphics.

Visualization tools help us learn from data . We explore data, discover patterns in data, identify groups of observations that go together and unusual observations or outliers. We note relationships among variables, sometimes detecting underlying dimensions in the data.

Graphics for exploratory data analysis are reviewed in classic references by Tukey (1977) and Tukey and Mosteller (1977). Regression graphics are covered by Cook (1998), Cook and Weisberg (1999), and Fox and Weisberg (2011). Statistical graphics and data visualization are illustrated in the works of Tufte (1990, 1997, 2004, 2006), Few (2009), and Yau (2011, 2013). Wilkinson (2005) presents a review of human perception and graphics, as well as a conceptual structure for understanding statistical graphics. Heer, Bostock, and Ogievetsky (2010) provide a collection of contemporary visualization techniques.

The R programming environment provides a rich collection of open-source tools for data visualization, including interfaces to visualization applications on the World Wide Web. An R graphics overview is provided by Murrell (2011). R lattice graphics, discussed by Sarkar (2008, 2013), build upon the conceptual structure of an earlier system called S-Plus Trellis™ (Cleveland 1993; Becker and Cleveland 1996). Wilkinson's (2005) "grammar of graphics" approach has been implemented in the R ggplot2 package (Wickham and Chang 2013), with programming examples provided by Chang (2013).

Zeileis, Hornik, and Murrell (2009, 2013) provide advice about colors for statistical graphics. Ihaka et al. (2013) show how to specify colors in R by hue, chroma, and luminance.

Specialized techniques for data visualization may be needed when working with very large data sets as we often do in predictive analytics (Unwin, Theus, and Hofmann 2006). Partial transparency techniques can help, and hexbin plots are often better than scatter plots for showing relationships between variables (Carr, Lewin-Koh, and Maechler 2013; Lewin-Koh 2013).

These are the things that data scientists do—things that we discuss in this book:

- **Finding out about.** This is the first thing we do—information search, finding what others have done before, learning from the literature. We draw on the work of academics and practitioners in many fields of study, contributors to predictive analytics and data science.[2]
- **Looking at data.** We begin each modeling project with exploratory data analysis, data visualization for the purpose of discovery. We prepare data for further analysis.
- **Predicting how much.** We are often asked to predict how many units or dollars of product will be sold, the price of financial securities or real estate. Regression techniques are useful for making these predictions. This book begins and ends with regression problems.
- **Predicting yes or no.** Many business problems are classification problems. Predicting whether a person will buy or not, default on a loan or not, click on a Web page or not. We use classification techniques in predicting consumer behavior and in text classification.
- **Testing it out.** We examine models with diagnostic graphics. We see how well a model developed on one data set works on other data sets. We employ a training-and-test regimen with data partitioning, cross-validation, or bootstrap methods.
- **Playing what-if.** We may need to manipulate key variables to see what happens to our predictions. In pricing research we play what-if games in a simulated marketplace. In operations management we employ sensitivity testing of mathematical programming models. We see how new values for input variables affect outcomes or payoffs.
- **Explaining it all.** Data and models help us to understand the world. We turn what we have learned into an explanation that others can understand. We present project results in a clear and concise manner. These presentations benefit from well constructed data visualizations (design with a purpose).

Let us begin.

---

[2] We start with the title of Richard Belew's (2000) book—*Finding Out About*—at the top of the list. This title describes well the task of information search.

Exhibit 1.1. *R Program for the Anscombe Quartet*

```
# The Anscombe Quartet in R

# demonstration data from
# Anscombe, F. J. 1973, February. Graphs in statistical analysis.
#  The American Statistician 27: 1721.

# define the anscombe data frame
anscombe <- data.frame(
    x1 = c(10, 8, 13, 9, 11, 14, 6, 4, 12, 7, 5),
    x2 = c(10, 8, 13, 9, 11, 14, 6, 4, 12, 7, 5),
    x3 = c(10, 8, 13, 9, 11, 14, 6, 4, 12, 7, 5),
    x4 = c(8, 8, 8, 8, 8, 8, 8, 19, 8, 8, 8),
    y1 = c(8.04, 6.95,  7.58, 8.81, 8.33, 9.96, 7.24, 4.26,10.84, 4.82, 5.68),
    y2 = c(9.14, 8.14,  8.74, 8.77, 9.26, 8.1, 6.13, 3.1,  9.13, 7.26, 4.74),
    y3 = c(7.46, 6.77, 12.74, 7.11, 7.81, 8.84, 6.08, 5.39, 8.15, 6.42, 5.73),
    y4 = c(6.58, 5.76,  7.71, 8.84, 8.47, 7.04, 5.25, 12.5, 5.56, 7.91, 6.89))

# show results from four regression analyses
with(anscombe, print(summary(lm(y1 ~ x1))))
with(anscombe, print(summary(lm(y2 ~ x2))))
with(anscombe, print(summary(lm(y3 ~ x3))))
with(anscombe, print(summary(lm(y4 ~ x4))))

# place four plots on one page using standard R graphics
# ensuring that all have the same scales
# for horizontal and vertical axes
pdf(file = "fig_more_anscombe.pdf", width = 8.5, height = 8.5)
par(mfrow=c(2,2),mar=c(3,3,3,1))
plot(x1, y1, xlim=c(2,20),ylim=c(2,14),
  pch = 19, col = "darkblue", cex = 2, las = 1)
title("Set I")
plot(x2, y2, xlim=c(2,20),ylim=c(2,14),
  pch = 19, col = "darkblue", cex = 2, las = 1)
title("Set II")
plot(x3, y3, xlim=c(2,20),ylim=c(2,14),
  pch = 19, col = "darkblue", cex = 2, las = 1)
title("Set III")
plot(x4, y4, xlim=c(2,20),ylim=c(2,14),
  pch = 19, col = "darkblue", cex = 2, las = 1)
title("Set IV")
dev.off()

par(mfrow=c(1,1),mar=c(5.1, 4.1, 4.1, 2.1))  # return to plotting defaults

# suggestions for the student
# see if you can develop a quartet of your own
# or perhaps just a duet...
# two very different data sets with the same fitted model
```

2

Advertising and Promotion

"I'm going to make him an offer he can't refuse."

—MARLON BRANDO AS VITO CORLEONE IN *The Godfather* (1972)

It is a Thursday night in July. I am thinking about going to the ballpark. The Los Angeles Dodgers are playing the Colorado Rockies, and I am supposed to get an Adrian Gonzalez bobblehead with my ticket. Although I am are not excited about the bobblehead, seeing a ball game at Dodger Stadium sounds like great fun. In April and May the Dodgers' record had not been the best, but things are looking better now. I wonder if the bobbleheads will bring additional fans to the park. Dodgers management may be wondering the same thing or perhaps making plans for a Yasiel Puig bobblehead in the future.

Suppose we are working for the Dodgers and want to learn about promotions. Management has questions: *Will bobblehead promotions increase attendance? And will the increased revenues associated with tickets and concessions cover the fixed and variable costs of putting on the promotion?*

We call this example *Bobbleheads and Dodger Dogs* or *Shaking Our Bobbleheads Yes and No*. The example draws upon Major League Baseball data from the 2012 season. Relevant data for Dodgers' home games are shown in table 2.1.

Dodger Stadium, with a capacity of 56,000, is the largest ballpark in the world. From the data, we can see that Dodger Stadium was filled to capacity only twice in 2012.[1] There were two cap promotions and three shirt promotions in 2012, not enough to draw meaningful inferences. Fireworks were used thirteen times on Friday nights, and once on the Fourth of July. The eleven bobblehead promotions occurred on night games, six of those being Tuesday nights.

Exploratory graphics help us find models that might work for predicting attendance and evaluating the effect of promotions on attendance. Figure 2.1 shows distributions of attendance across days of the week, and figure 2.2 shows attendance by month. Box plots like these reveal the overall values of the data, with the boxes covering the middle fifty percent or so of the distribution and with the center line representing the median. The dotted lines or whiskers extend to more extreme values in the distribution.[2] By looking across the box plots, we can make comparisons across the distributions of attendance by day and by month.

We can explore these data further using a lattice of scatter plots. In figure 2.3 we map the relationship between temperature and attendance, conditioning for time of game (day or night) and clear or cloudy skies. On day games with clear skies, we see what appears to be a moderate inverse relationship between temperature and attendance. Day games are usually on Sunday, and in 2012 all but one of those games was played under clear skies—a benefit of being in Los Angeles.

More telling perhaps are strip plots of attendance by opponent or visiting team; these are the univariate scatter plots in figure 2.4. Opponents from the large metropolitan areas (the New York Mets, Chicago Cubs and White Sox, Los Angeles Angels, and Washington D.C. Nationals) are consistently

---

[1] For predicting attendance at Major League Baseball parks other than Dodger Stadium, we would need to consider the fact that ballparks are often filled to capacity. Special models would be needed to accommodate this high-end censoring, as it is sometimes called (Lemke, Leonard, and Tlhokwane 2010).

[2] To determine the length of the whiskers, we first compute the interquartile range, which is the distance between the 25th percentile and the 75th percentile. The end-points of the whiskers are defined by what are called *adjacent values*. The upper whisker extends to the upper adjacent value, a point one-and-a-half times the interquartile range above the upper end of the box. Or, if the maximum value in the distribution is less than that, the upper whisker extends to that maximum value. We often think of outliers as being points outside the whiskers; these outlier points are plotted as open circles. Box plots were the invention of John Tukey (1977).

Table 2.1.   *Bobbleheads and Dodger Dogs*

month	day	attend	day_of_week	opponent	temp	skies	day_night	cap	shirt	fireworks	bobblehead
APR	10	56000	Tuesday	Pirates	67	Clear	Day	NO	NO	NO	NO
APR	11	29729	Wednesday	Pirates	58	Cloudy	Night	NO	NO	NO	NO
APR	12	28328	Thursday	Pirates	57	Cloudy	Night	NO	NO	NO	NO
APR	13	31601	Friday	Padres	54	Cloudy	Night	NO	NO	YES	NO
APR	14	46549	Saturday	Padres	57	Cloudy	Night	NO	NO	NO	NO
APR	15	38359	Sunday	Padres	65	Clear	Day	NO	NO	NO	NO
APR	23	26376	Monday	Braves	60	Cloudy	Night	NO	NO	NO	NO
APR	24	44014	Tuesday	Braves	63	Cloudy	Night	NO	NO	NO	NO
APR	25	26345	Wednesday	Braves	64	Cloudy	Night	NO	NO	NO	NO
APR	27	44807	Friday	Nationals	66	Clear	Night	NO	NO	YES	NO
APR	28	54242	Saturday	Nationals	71	Clear	Night	NO	NO	NO	YES
APR	29	48753	Sunday	Nationals	74	Clear	Day	NO	YES	NO	NO
MAY	7	43713	Monday	Giants	67	Clear	Night	NO	NO	NO	NO
MAY	8	32799	Tuesday	Giants	75	Clear	Night	NO	NO	NO	NO
MAY	9	33993	Wednesday	Giants	71	Clear	Night	NO	NO	NO	NO
MAY	11	35591	Friday	Rockies	65	Clear	Night	NO	NO	YES	NO
MAY	12	33735	Saturday	Rockies	65	Clear	Night	NO	NO	NO	NO
MAY	13	49124	Sunday	Rockies	70	Clear	Day	NO	NO	NO	NO
MAY	14	24312	Monday	Snakes	67	Clear	Night	NO	NO	NO	NO
MAY	15	47077	Tuesday	Snakes	70	Clear	Night	NO	NO	NO	YES
MAY	18	40906	Friday	Cardinals	64	Clear	Night	NO	NO	YES	NO
MAY	19	39383	Saturday	Cardinals	67	Clear	Night	NO	NO	NO	NO
MAY	20	44005	Sunday	Cardinals	77	Clear	Night	NO	NO	NO	NO
MAY	25	36283	Friday	Astros	59	Cloudy	Night	NO	NO	YES	NO
MAY	26	36561	Saturday	Astros	61	Cloudy	Night	NO	NO	NO	NO
MAY	27	33306	Sunday	Astros	70	Clear	Day	NO	NO	NO	NO
MAY	28	38016	Monday	Brewers	73	Clear	Night	NO	NO	NO	NO
MAY	29	51137	Tuesday	Brewers	74	Clear	Night	NO	NO	NO	YES
MAY	30	25509	Wednesday	Brewers	69	Clear	Night	NO	NO	NO	NO
MAY	31	26773	Thursday	Brewers	70	Clear	Night	NO	NO	NO	NO
JUN	11	50559	Monday	Angels	68	Clear	Night	NO	YES	NO	NO
JUN	12	55279	Tuesday	Angels	66	Cloudy	Night	NO	NO	NO	YES
JUN	13	43494	Wednesday	Angels	67	Clear	Night	NO	NO	NO	NO
JUN	15	40432	Friday	White Sox	67	Clear	Night	NO	NO	YES	NO
JUN	16	45210	Saturday	White Sox	68	Clear	Night	NO	NO	NO	NO
JUN	17	53504	Sunday	White Sox	74	Clear	Day	NO	NO	NO	NO
JUN	28	49006	Thursday	Mets	75	Clear	Night	NO	NO	NO	YES
JUN	29	49763	Friday	Mets	72	Clear	Night	NO	NO	YES	NO
JUN	30	44217	Saturday	Mets	78	Clear	Day	NO	NO	NO	NO
JUL	1	55359	Sunday	Mets	75	Clear	Night	NO	NO	NO	YES
JUL	2	34493	Monday	Reds	70	Clear	Night	NO	NO	NO	NO
JUL	3	33884	Tuesday	Reds	70	Cloudy	Night	YES	NO	NO	NO
JUL	4	53570	Wednesday	Reds	70	Clear	Night	NO	NO	YES	NO
JUL	13	43873	Friday	Padres	76	Cloudy	Night	NO	NO	YES	NO
JUL	14	54014	Saturday	Padres	75	Clear	Night	NO	NO	NO	YES
JUL	15	39715	Sunday	Padres	77	Clear	Day	NO	NO	NO	NO
JUL	16	32238	Monday	Phillies	67	Clear	Night	NO	NO	NO	NO
JUL	17	53498	Tuesday	Phillies	70	Clear	Night	NO	NO	NO	NO
JUL	18	39955	Wednesday	Phillies	80	Cloudy	Day	NO	NO	NO	NO
JUL	30	33180	Monday	Snakes	73	Clear	Night	NO	NO	NO	NO
JUL	31	52832	Tuesday	Snakes	75	Cloudy	Night	NO	NO	NO	YES
AUG	1	36596	Wednesday	Snakes	79	Clear	Day	NO	NO	NO	NO
AUG	3	43537	Friday	Cubs	73	Clear	Night	NO	NO	YES	NO
AUG	4	46588	Saturday	Cubs	73	Cloudy	Night	NO	NO	NO	NO
AUG	5	42495	Sunday	Cubs	83	Clear	Day	YES	NO	NO	NO
AUG	6	32659	Monday	Rockies	79	Clear	Night	NO	NO	NO	NO
AUG	7	55024	Tuesday	Rockies	80	Clear	Night	NO	NO	NO	YES
AUG	8	37084	Wednesday	Rockies	84	Clear	Night	NO	NO	NO	NO
AUG	20	36878	Monday	Giants	80	Clear	Night	NO	NO	NO	NO
AUG	21	56000	Tuesday	Giants	75	Clear	Night	NO	NO	NO	YES
AUG	22	40173	Wednesday	Giants	75	Clear	Night	NO	NO	NO	NO
AUG	24	39805	Friday	Marlins	71	Clear	Night	NO	NO	YES	NO
AUG	25	40284	Saturday	Marlins	70	Clear	Night	NO	NO	NO	NO
AUG	26	41907	Sunday	Marlins	81	Clear	Day	NO	NO	NO	NO
AUG	30	54621	Thursday	Snakes	80	Clear	Night	NO	NO	NO	YES
AUG	31	37622	Friday	Snakes	77	Clear	Night	NO	NO	YES	NO
SEP	1	35992	Saturday	Snakes	81	Clear	Night	NO	NO	NO	NO
SEP	2	31607	Sunday	Snakes	89	Clear	Day	NO	NO	NO	NO
SEP	3	33540	Monday	Padres	84	Cloudy	Night	NO	NO	NO	NO
SEP	4	40619	Tuesday	Padres	78	Clear	Night	NO	YES	NO	NO
SEP	5	50560	Wednesday	Padres	77	Cloudy	Night	NO	NO	NO	NO
SEP	13	43309	Thursday	Cardinals	80	Clear	Night	NO	NO	NO	NO
SEP	14	40167	Friday	Cardinals	85	Clear	Night	NO	NO	YES	NO
SEP	15	42449	Saturday	Cardinals	95	Clear	Night	NO	NO	NO	NO
SEP	16	35754	Sunday	Cardinals	86	Clear	Day	NO	NO	NO	NO
SEP	28	37133	Friday	Rockies	77	Clear	Night	NO	NO	YES	NO
SEP	29	40724	Saturday	Rockies	84	Cloudy	Night	NO	NO	NO	NO
SEP	30	35607	Sunday	Rockies	95	Clear	Day	NO	NO	NO	NO
OCT	1	33624	Monday	Giants	86	Clear	Night	NO	NO	NO	NO
OCT	2	42473	Tuesday	Giants	83	Clear	Night	NO	NO	NO	NO
OCT	3	34014	Wednesday	Giants	82	Cloudy	Night	NO	NO	NO	NO

Figure 2.1. *Dodgers Attendance by Day of Week*

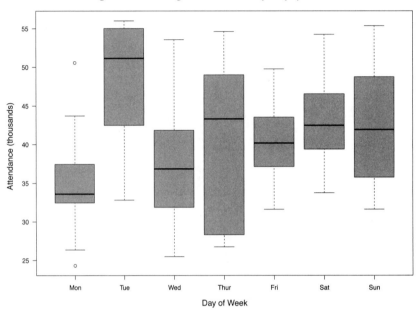

Figure 2.2. *Dodgers Attendance by Month*

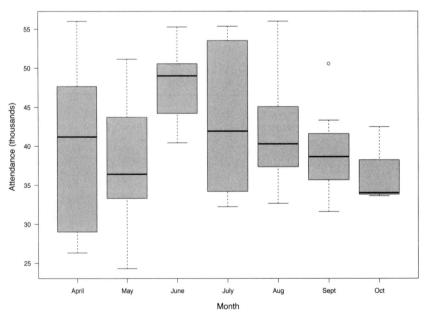

Figure 2.3. Dodgers Weather, Fireworks, and Attendance

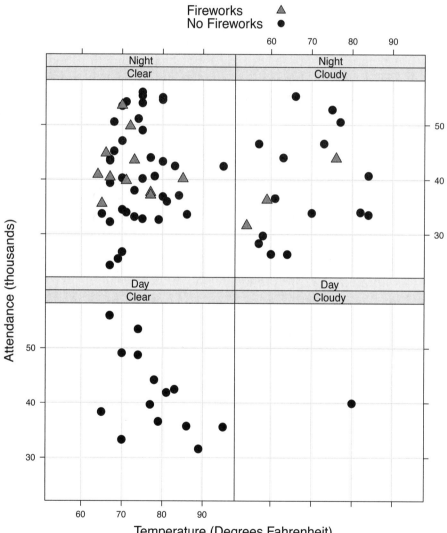

associated with higher attendance. But there are seventeen visiting teams in this study, and only eighty-one games or observations. Accordingly, utilizing the visiting team as a categorical predictor presents problems.

To advise management regarding promotions, we would like to know if promotions have a positive effect upon attendance, and if they do have a positive effect, how much that effect might be. To provide this advice we build a linear model for predicting attendance using month, day of the week, and an indicator variable for the bobblehead promotion, and then we see how well it works. We enter these explanatory variables in a particular order so we can answer the basic question: *Do bobblehead promotions increase attendance, controlling for the date of the game (month and day of the week)?* Being data scientists, we employ a training-and-test regimen to provide an honest evaluation of the model's predictive performance.

For the Los Angeles Dodgers bobblehead promotion, the fitted model does a good job of predicting higher attendance at games when bobbleheads are distributed. Our computer programs can provide indices of goodness of fit, but, more importantly, they can provide predictions of attendance that we can display on scatter plots.

How does a training-and-test regimen play out for the model we have developed for the Dodgers? Figure 2.5 provides a picture of model performance that data scientists and business managers can understand. The model fit to the training set holds up when used with the test set.[3]

Running the code for the study on the complete set of home game data for the Los Angeles Dodgers in 2012 would yield a set of regression coefficients, estimates of the parameters in the linear model, as shown in table 2.2. A sequential analysis of variance shows a statistically significant effect for the bobblehead promotion, controlling for month and day of the week. A test of residuals from the model would identify any statistically significant outliers—there were none for this problem. Most importantly, the model

---

[3] In figure 2.5, TRAIN refers to the training set, the data on which we fit the model and TEST refers to the hold-out-data on which we test our model. Running the code for this example, we would see that, in the test set, more than 45 percent of the variance in attendance is accounted for by the linear model—this is the square of the correlation of observed and predicted attendance. To explain a model to management, however, it is better to show a performance graph than to talk about squared correlation coefficients, mean-squared errors of prediction, or other model summary statistics. This is one graph among many possible graphs that we could have produced for the Dodgers. It shows the results of one particular random splitting of the data into training and test.

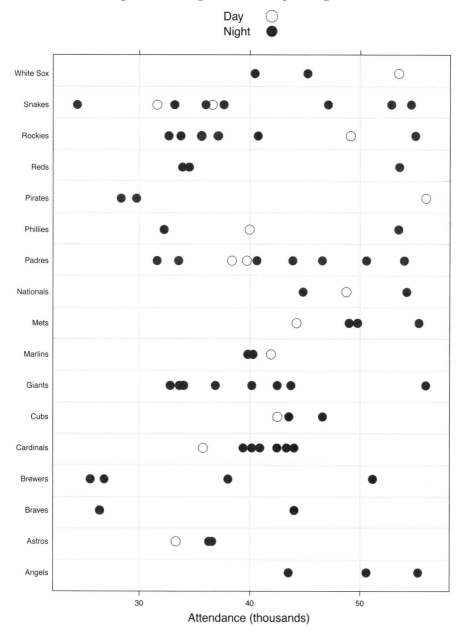

Figure 2.4. *Dodgers Attendance by Visiting Team*

Figure 2.5. *Regression Model Performance: Bobbleheads and Attendance*

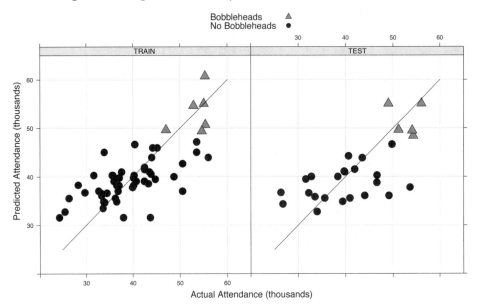

can provide an assessment of the effect of the bobblehead promotion. In particular, we can see that bobblehead promotions have the potential of increasing attendance by 10,715 fans per game, all other things being equal. This is the regression coefficient on the bobblehead indicator of the linear model.

The baseball promotions example, coming early in our discussion of predictive analytics, was chosen to be simple in structure, so that ordinary least squares regression could be employed. This is a cross-sectional study with the baseball game serving as the unit of analysis.

More complicated models are possible, and diagnostic plots for the model can provide additional information for the data scientist seeking to improve on the model we specified. Nonetheless, it is interesting to note how much information a linear regression model can provide. Predictive models like the one used in this small example, with results presented in graphical summaries, can help guide management decisions.

One of the things that distinguishes predictive analytics from statistics is its focus on business requirements. In evaluating the utility of a model, the

Table 2.2. *Regression of Attendance on Month, Day of Week, and Bobblehead Promotion*

Response: Attendance	
Month (May)	-2,385.625
Month (June)	7,163.234**
Month (July)	2,849.828
Month (August)	2,377.924
Month (September)	29.030
Month (October)	-662.668
Day of Week (Tuesday)	7,911.494***
Day of Week (Wednesday)	2,460.023
Day of Week (Thursday)	775.364
Day of Week (Friday)	4,883.818*
Day of Week (Saturday)	6,372.056**
Day of Week (Sunday)	6,724.003***
Bobblehead Promotion (YES)	10,714.900***
Constant	33,909.160***
Observations	81
R^2	0.544
Adjusted R^2	0.456
Residual Std. Error	$6,120.158(df = 67)$
F statistic	$6.158^{***}(df = 13; 67)$
Notes:	***Significant at the 1 percent level.
	**Significant at the 5 percent level.
	*Significant at the 10 percent level.

analyst or data scientist considers financial criteria as well as statistical criteria. And, in presenting predictions to management, she provides financial analysis as well as a description of the statistical model itself.

Using the fitted predictive model for the Dodgers bobblehead promotion, we can predict the attendance for each game in the forthcoming season, and we can predict this attendance with and without a bobblehead promotion. Using predicted attendance, we can compute the Dodgers' revenue with and without the promotion.

Knowing fixed and variable costs associated with a bobblehead promotion, as well as expected revenues from ticket sales and concessions, we can help the Los Angeles Dodgers assess the financial contribution of bobblehead promotions. Ticket prices for bobblehead games vary from $20 for a top deck seat to $120 for a VIP field box seat. A portion of ticket revenues also supports concessions and the additional staff needed to distribute the bobbleheads. We would obtain these cost estimates from Dodger management.

Considering costs for the forthcoming season in this example, the unit cost of a bobblehead doll is expected to be no more than $3 when ordered in quantities of at least 20,000. Bobbleheads are provided to the first 50,000 fans entering Dodger Stadium. To complete our work, then, we would use cost/volume/profit analysis[4] to assess the profit contribution of a bobblehead promotion for each game at Dodger Stadium. In this way, Dodger management could decide whether or not to use bobbleheads in the forthcoming season and which games most benefit from the use of bobbleheads.

Promotions like the bobblehead promotion do more than drive up attendance. They also reinforce the name of the brand in the minds of consumers. Advertising and promotion are the "promotion" part of the marketing mix or *the four Ps:* product, price, promotion, and place. Here "product" relates to product or service, and "price" is simply price. The word "place" refers to channels of distribution (face-to-face selling, wholesale, retail, brick-and-mortar, mail-order, online, or mobile). Advertising and promotion are thought of as distinct fields of study by marketing academics. Advertising refers to the message, the marketing communication, while promotion is what firms do in addition to the message.

---

[4] Cost/volume/profit analysis is a common technique in management accounting. It is sometimes called break even analysis or cost/benefit analysis.

As we have shown, traditional regression models are especially relevant to these areas of inquiry. Useful sources for regression modeling include Kutner, Nachtsheim, Neter, and Li (2004), Ryan (2008), and Chatterjee and Hadi (2012). For guidance in R programming, see Venables and Ripley (2002), Fox and Weisberg (2011), Matloff (2011), and Fox (2013). Moving beyond traditional linear models, we can consider modern, data-adaptive regression methods, as reviewed by Izenman (2008). Additional discussion of regression methods is provided in appendix A.

For an overview of advertising and promotion, marketing management textbooks may be consulted (Dickson 1997; Kotler and Keller 2012). Market response models attempt to predict sales and market shares across products within categories. These build upon econometric and time series methods. Hanssens, Parsons, and Schultz (2001) discuss market response modeling. Lilien and Rangaswamy (2003) suggest applications of market response modeling in sales force and channel management. For an overview of marketing models, see Lilien, Kotler, and Moorthy (1992) and Leeflang et al. (2000).

The program *Shaking Our Bobbleheads Yes and No* is shown in exhibit 2.1. The program draws upon R packages developed by Fox (2013) for regression modeling and Sarkar (2013) for lattice graphics.

Exhibit 2.1. *Shaking Our Bobbleheads Yes and No*

```
# Predictive Model for Los Angeles Dodgers Promotion and Attendance

library(car)  # special functions for linear regression
library(lattice)  # graphics package
# read in data and create a data frame called dodgers
dodgers <- read.csv("dodgers.csv")
print(str(dodgers))  # check the structure of the data frame
# define an ordered day-of-week variable
# for plots and data summaries
dodgers$ordered_day_of_week <- with(data=dodgers,
  ifelse ((day_of_week == "Monday"),1,
  ifelse ((day_of_week == "Tuesday"),2,
  ifelse ((day_of_week == "Wednesday"),3,
  ifelse ((day_of_week == "Thursday"),4,
  ifelse ((day_of_week == "Friday"),5,
  ifelse ((day_of_week == "Saturday"),6,7)))))))
dodgers$ordered_day_of_week <- factor(dodgers$ordered_day_of_week, levels=1:7,
labels=c("Mon", "Tue", "Wed", "Thur", "Fri", "Sat", "Sun"))

# exploratory data analysis with standard graphics: attendance by day of week
with(data=dodgers,plot(ordered_day_of_week, attend/1000,
xlab = "Day of Week", ylab = "Attendance (thousands)",
col = "violet", las = 1))

# when do the Dodgers use bobblehead promotions
with(dodgers, table(bobblehead,ordered_day_of_week)) # bobbleheads on Tuesday
# define an ordered month variable
# for plots and data summaries
dodgers$ordered_month <- with(data=dodgers,
  ifelse ((month == "APR"),4,
  ifelse ((month == "MAY"),5,
  ifelse ((month == "JUN"),6,
  ifelse ((month == "JUL"),7,
  ifelse ((month == "AUG"),8,
  ifelse ((month == "SEP"),9,10)))))))
dodgers$ordered_month <- factor(dodgers$ordered_month, levels=4:10,
labels = c("April", "May", "June", "July", "Aug", "Sept", "Oct"))

# exploratory data analysis with standard R graphics: attendance by month
with(data=dodgers,plot(ordered_month,attend/1000, xlab = "Month",
ylab = "Attendance (thousands)", col = "light blue", las = 1))

# exploratory data analysis displaying many variables
# looking at attendance and conditioning on day/night
# the skies and whether or not fireworks are displayed
library(lattice) # used for plotting
# let us prepare a graphical summary of the dodgers data
group.labels <- c("No Fireworks","Fireworks")
group.symbols <- c(21,24)
group.colors <- c("black","black")
group.fill <- c("black","red")
```

```
xyplot(attend/1000 ~ temp | skies + day_night,
    data = dodgers, groups = fireworks, pch = group.symbols,
    aspect = 1, cex = 1.5, col = group.colors, fill = group.fill,
    layout = c(2, 2), type = c("p","g"),
    strip=strip.custom(strip.levels=TRUE,strip.names=FALSE, style=1),
    xlab = "Temperature (Degrees Fahrenheit)",
    ylab = "Attendance (thousands)",
    key = list(space = "top",
        text = list(rev(group.labels),col = rev(group.colors)),
        points = list(pch = rev(group.symbols), col = rev(group.colors),
        fill = rev(group.fill))))
# attendance by opponent and day/night game
group.labels <- c("Day","Night")
group.symbols <- c(1,20)
group.symbols.size <- c(2,2.75)
bwplot(opponent ~ attend/1000, data = dodgers, groups = day_night,
    xlab = "Attendance (thousands)",
    panel = function(x, y, groups, subscripts, ...)
        {panel.grid(h = (length(levels(dodgers$opponent)) - 1), v = -1)
        panel.stripplot(x, y, groups = groups, subscripts = subscripts,
        cex = group.symbols.size, pch = group.symbols, col = "darkblue")
        },
    key = list(space = "top",
    text = list(group.labels,col = "black"),
    points = list(pch = group.symbols, cex = group.symbols.size,
    col = "darkblue")))
# specify a simple model with bobblehead entered last
my.model <- {attend ~ ordered_month + ordered_day_of_week + bobblehead}
# employ a training-and-test regimen
set.seed(1234) # set seed for repeatability of training-and-test split
training_test <- c(rep(1,length=trunc((2/3)*nrow(dodgers))),
rep(2,length=(nrow(dodgers) - trunc((2/3)*nrow(dodgers)))))
dodgers$training_test <- sample(training_test) # random permutation
dodgers$training_test <- factor(dodgers$training_test,
  levels=c(1,2), labels=c("TRAIN","TEST"))
dodgers.train <- subset(dodgers, training_test == "TRAIN")
print(str(dodgers.train)) # check training data frame
dodgers.test <- subset(dodgers, training_test == "TEST")
print(str(dodgers.test)) # check test data frame
# fit the model to the training set
train.model.fit <- lm(my.model, data = dodgers.train)
# obtain predictions from the training set
dodgers.train$predict_attend <- predict(train.model.fit)

# evaluate the fitted model on the test set
dodgers.test$predict_attend <- predict(train.model.fit,
  newdata = dodgers.test)

# compute the proportion of response variance
# accounted for when predicting out-of-sample
cat("\n","Proportion of Test Set Variance Accounted for: ",
round((with(dodgers.test,cor(attend,predict_attend)^2)),
  digits=3),"\n",sep="")
```

```
# merge the training and test sets for plotting
dodgers.plotting.frame <- rbind(dodgers.train,dodgers.test)

# generate predictive modeling visual for management
group.labels <- c("No Bobbleheads","Bobbleheads")
group.symbols <- c(21,24)
group.colors <- c("black","black")
group.fill <- c("black","red")
xyplot(predict_attend/1000 ~ attend/1000 | training_test,
       data = dodgers.plotting.frame, groups = bobblehead, cex = 2,
       pch = group.symbols, col = group.colors, fill = group.fill,
       layout = c(2, 1), xlim = c(20,65), ylim = c(20,65),
       aspect=1, type = c("p","g"),
       panel=function(x,y, ...)
            {panel.xyplot(x,y,...)
             panel.segments(25,25,60,60,col="black",cex=2)
             },
       strip=function(...) strip.default(..., style=1),
       xlab = "Actual Attendance (thousands)",
       ylab = "Predicted Attendance (thousands)",
       key = list(space = "top",
              text = list(rev(group.labels),col = rev(group.colors)),
              points = list(pch = rev(group.symbols),
              col = rev(group.colors),
              fill = rev(group.fill))))

# use the full data set to obtain an estimate of the increase in
# attendance due to bobbleheads, controlling for other factors
my.model.fit <- lm(my.model, data = dodgers)  # use all available data
print(summary(my.model.fit))
# tests statistical significance of the bobblehead promotion
# type I anova computes sums of squares for sequential tests
print(anova(my.model.fit))

cat("\n","Estimated Effect of Bobblehead Promotion on Attendance: ",
round(my.model.fit$coefficients[length(my.model.fit$coefficients)],
digits = 0),"\n",sep="")

# standard graphics provide diagnostic plots
plot(my.model.fit)

# additional model diagnostics drawn from the car package
library(car)
residualPlots(my.model.fit)
marginalModelPlots(my.model.fit)
print(outlierTest(my.model.fit))

# additional work for the student
# examine regression diagnositics
# examine other linear predictors... other explanatory variables
# will transformations of variables help?
```

3

Preference and Choice

"REFUND! Refund! Are you crazy? Refund!"

—PAUL DOOLEY AS RAY STOLLER IN *Breaking Away* (1979)

While working on this book, I moved from Madison, Wisconsin to Los Angeles, and I had a difficult decision to make about mobile communications. I had been a customer of U.S. Cellular for many years. I had one smartphone and two data modems (a 3G and a 4G) and was quite satisfied with U.S Cellular services. By May of 2013, the company had no retail presence in Los Angeles and no 4G service in California. As a data scientist who needed an example of preference measurement, I decided to assess my preferences for mobile phone and data services.

The attributes in this small study are the mobile provider or brand, startup and monthly costs, if the provider offers 4G services in the area, whether the provider has a retail location nearby, and whether the provider supports Apple, Samsung, or Nexus phones in addition to tablet computers. Product profiles, representing combinations of these attributes, are easily computer generated. My consideration set includes AT&T, T-Mobile, U.S. Cellular, and Verizon. I generate sixteen product profiles and present them to myself in a random order. Product profiles, their attributes, and my ranks, are shown in table 3.1.

Table 3.1. *Preference Data for Mobile Communication Services*

brand	startup	monthly	service	retail	apple	samsung	google	ranking
"AT&T"	"$100"	"$100"	"4G NO"	"Retail NO"	"Apple NO"	"Samsung NO"	"Nexus NO"	11
"Verizon"	"$300"	"$100"	"4G NO"	"Retail YES"	"Apple YES"	"Samsung YES"	"Nexus NO"	12
"US Cellular"	"$400"	"$200"	"4G NO"	"Retail NO"	"Apple NO"	"Samsung YES"	"Nexus NO"	9
"Verizon"	"$400"	"$400"	"4G YES"	"Retail YES"	"Apple NO"	"Samsung NO"	"Nexus NO"	2
"Verizon"	"$200"	"$300"	"4G NO"	"Retail NO"	"Apple NO"	"Samsung YES"	"Nexus YES"	8
"Verizon"	"$100"	"$200"	"4G YES"	"Retail NO"	"Apple YES"	"Samsung NO"	"Nexus YES"	13
"US Cellular"	"$300"	"$300"	"4G YES"	"Retail NO"	"Apple YES"	"Samsung NO"	"Nexus NO"	7
"AT&T"	"$400"	"$300"	"4G NO"	"Retail YES"	"Apple YES"	"Samsung NO"	"Nexus YES"	4
"AT&T"	"$200"	"$400"	"4G YES"	"Retail NO"	"Apple YES"	"Samsung YES"	"Nexus NO"	5
"T-Mobile"	"$400"	"$100"	"4G YES"	"Retail NO"	"Apple YES"	"Samsung YES"	"Nexus YES"	16
"US Cellular"	"$100"	"$400"	"4G NO"	"Retail YES"	"Apple YES"	"Samsung YES"	"Nexus YES"	3
"T-Mobile"	"$200"	"$200"	"4G NO"	"Retail YES"	"Apple YES"	"Samsung NO"	"Nexus NO"	6
"T-Mobile"	"$100"	"$300"	"4G YES"	"Retail YES"	"Apple NO"	"Samsung YES"	"Nexus NO"	10
"US Cellular"	"$200"	"$100"	"4G YES"	"Retail YES"	"Apple NO"	"Samsung NO"	"Nexus YES"	15
"T-Mobile"	"$300"	"$400"	"4G NO"	"Retail NO"	"Apple NO"	"Samsung NO"	"Nexus YES"	1
"AT&T"	"$300"	"$200"	"4G YES"	"Retail YES"	"Apple NO"	"Samsung YES"	"Nexus YES"	14

The linear model fit to the preference rankings is an example of what is known as *traditional conjoint analysis.* We utilize *sum contrasts,* so that the sum of the fitted regression coefficients across the levels of each attribute is zero. The fitted regression coefficients represent conjoint measures of utility called *part-worths.* Part-worths reflect the strength of individual consumer preferences for each level of each attribute in the study. Positive part-worths add to a product's value in the mind of the consumer. Negative part-worths subtract from that value. When we sum across the part-worths of a product, we obtain a measure of the utility or benefit to the consumer.

To display the results of the conjoint analysis, we use a special type of dot plot called the *spine chart,* shown in figure 3.1. In the spine chart, part-worths can be displayed on a common, standardized scale across attributes. The vertical line in the center, the spine, is anchored at zero. The part-worth of each level of each attribute is displayed as a dot with a connecting horizontal line, extending from the spine. Preferred product or service characteristics have positive part-worths and fall to the right of the spine. Less preferred product or service characteristics fall to the left of the spine.

The spine chart shows standardized part-worths and attribute importance values. The relative importance of attributes in a conjoint analysis is defined using the ranges of part-worths within attributes. These importance values are scaled so that the sum across all attributes is 100 percent. Conjoint analysis is a measurement technology. Part-worths and attribute importance values are conjoint measures.

Figure 3.1. *Spine Chart of Preferences for Mobile Communication Services*

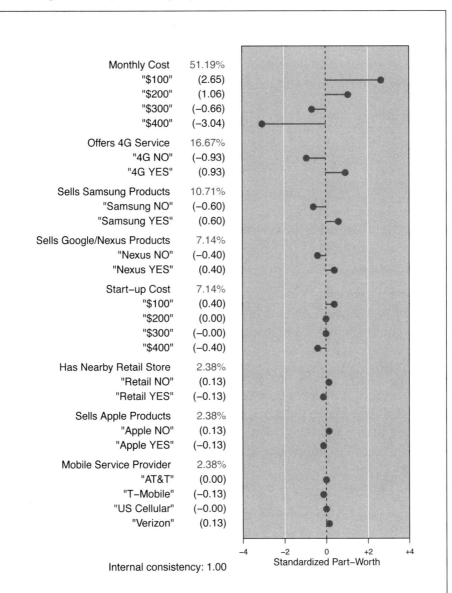

What does the spine chart say about this consumer's preferences? It shows that monthly cost is of considerable importance. Next in order of importance is 4G availability. Start-up cost, being a one-time cost, is much less important than monthly cost. This consumer ranks the four service providers about equally. And having a nearby retail store is not an advantage. This consumer is probably an Android user because we see higher importance for service providers that offer Samsung phones and tablets first and Nexus second, while the availability of Apple phones and tablets is of little importance.

This simple study reveals a lot about the consumer—it measures consumer preferences. Furthermore, the linear model fit to conjoint rankings can be used to predict what the consumer is likely to do about mobile communications in the future.

Traditional conjoint analysis represents a modeling technique in predictive analytics. Working with groups of consumers, we fit a linear model to each individual's ratings or rankings, thus measuring the utility or part-worth of each level of each attribute, as well as the relative importance of attributes.

The measures we obtain from conjoint studies can be analyzed to identify consumer segments. Conjoint measures can be used to predict each individual's choices in the marketplace. Furthermore, using conjoint measures, we can perform marketplace simulations, exploring alternative product designs and pricing policies.

Consumers reveal their preferences in responses to surveys and ultimately in choices they make in the marketplace. Marketing analytics, a specialization of predictive analytics, involves building models of consumer preference and using those models to make predictions about future marketplace behavior.

Conjoint analysis is really *conjoint measurement*. Marketing analysts present product profiles to consumers. Product profiles are defined by their attributes. By ranking, rating, or choosing products, consumers reveal their preferences for products and the corresponding attributes that define products. The computed attribute importance values and part-worths associated with levels of attributes represent measurements that are obtained as a group or jointly—thus the name conjoint measurement. The task—ranking, rating, or choosing—can take many forms.

The method of conjoint measurement was originally developed by Luce and Tukey (1964). A comprehensive review of conjoint methods, including traditional conjoint analysis, choice-based conjoint, best-worst scaling, and menu-based choice, is provided by Bryan Orme (2013).

We employ principles of experimental design in constructing conjoint tasks, and we use linear models in the analysis of the consumer responses. Methods for the design and analysis of conjoint studies have been discussed by Carroll and Green (1995), Marshall and Bradlow (2002), and authors in the edited volume by Gustafsson, Herrmann, and Huber (2000).

For the construction of conjoint and choice study product profiles in R, see Aizaki (2012, 2013). Murrell (2011) explains how to use standard R graphics functions to generate customized graphs.

Ask consumers what they want, and they may say, *the best of everything*. Ask them what they would like to spend, and they may say, *as little as possible*. There are limitations to assessing consumer willingness to pay and product preferences with direct-response rating scales, or what are sometimes called self-explicative scales. Simple rating scale items arranged as they often are, with separate questions about product attributes, brands, and prices, fail to capture tradeoffs that are fundamental to consumer choice. To learn more from consumer surveys, we provide a context for responding and gather as much information as we can. This is what conjoint and choice studies do, and many of them do it quite well. In the measurement appendix of this book we provide examples of preference and choice measures.

Exhibit 3.1 shows the program used to analyze ranking or rating data relating to consumer preferences. This is a program for performing traditional conjoint analysis. It generates a conjoint survey, analyzes conjoint rankings, and assesses consumer preferences. The code for the spine chart function in appendix exhibit C.1 shows how to construct a customized data visualization for conjoint studies. Using standard R graphics functions, the spine chart is built one point, line, and text string at a time. The precise placement of points, lines, and text is under control of the programmer.

Exhibit 3.1. *Measuring and Modeling Individual Preferences*

```
# Traditional Conjoint Analysis

#  user-defined function for spine chart
load(file="mtpa_spine_chart.Rdata")

# spine chart accommodates up to 45 part-worths on one page
# |part-worth| <= 40 can be plotted directly on the spine chart
# |part-worths| > 40 can be accommodated through standardization

print.digits <- 2  # set number of digits on print and spine chart

library(support.CEs)  # package for survey construction

# generate a balanced set of product profiles for survey
provider.survey <- Lma.design(attribute.names =
  list(brand = c("AT&T","T-Mobile","US Cellular","Verizon"),
  startup = c("$100","$200","$300","$400"),
  monthly = c("$100","$200","$300","$400"),
  service = c("4G NO","4G YES"),
  retail = c("Retail NO","Retail YES"),
  apple = c("Apple NO","Apple YES"),
  samsung = c("Samsung NO","Samsung YES"),
  google = c("Nexus NO","Nexus YES")), nalternatives = 1, nblocks=1, seed=9999)
print(questionnaire(provider.survey))  # print survey design for review

sink("questions_for_survey.txt")  # send survey to external text file
questionnaire(provider.survey)
sink() # send output back to the screen

# user-defined function for plotting descriptive attribute names
effect.name.map <- function(effect.name) {
  if(effect.name=="brand") return("Mobile Service Provider")
  if(effect.name=="startup") return("Start-up Cost")
  if(effect.name=="monthly") return("Monthly Cost")
  if(effect.name=="service") return("Offers 4G Service")
  if(effect.name=="retail") return("Has Nearby Retail Store")
  if(effect.name=="apple") return("Sells Apple Products")
  if(effect.name=="samsung") return("Sells Samsung Products")
  if(effect.name=="google") return("Sells Google/Nexus Products")
  }

# read in conjoint survey profiles with respondent ranks
conjoint.data.frame <- read.csv("mobile_services_ranking.csv")

# set up sum contrasts for effects coding as needed for conjoint analysis
options(contrasts=c("contr.sum","contr.poly"))

# fit linear regression model using main effects only (no interaction terms)
main.effects.model <- lm(ranking ~ brand + startup + monthly + service +
  retail + apple + samsung + google, data=conjoint.data.frame)
print(summary(main.effects.model))
```

```
# save key list elements of the fitted model as needed for conjoint measures
conjoint.results <-
  main.effects.model[c("contrasts","xlevels","coefficients")]
conjoint.results$attributes <- names(conjoint.results$contrasts)

# compute and store part-worths in the conjoint.results list structure
part.worths <- conjoint.results$xlevels  # list of same structure as xlevels
end.index.for.coefficient <- 1  # intitialize skipping the intercept
part.worth.vector <- NULL # used for accumulation of part worths
for(index.for.attribute in seq(along=conjoint.results$contrasts)) {
  nlevels <- length(unlist(conjoint.results$xlevels[index.for.attribute]))
  begin.index.for.coefficient <- end.index.for.coefficient + 1
  end.index.for.coefficient <- begin.index.for.coefficient + nlevels -2
  last.part.worth <- -sum(conjoint.results$coefficients[
    begin.index.for.coefficient:end.index.for.coefficient])
  part.worths[index.for.attribute] <-
    list(as.numeric(c(conjoint.results$coefficients[
      begin.index.for.coefficient:end.index.for.coefficient],
      last.part.worth)))
  part.worth.vector <-
    c(part.worth.vector,unlist(part.worths[index.for.attribute]))
  }
conjoint.results$part.worths <- part.worths

# compute standardized part-worths
standardize <- function(x) {(x - mean(x)) / sd(x)}
conjoint.results$standardized.part.worths <-
  lapply(conjoint.results$part.worths,standardize)

# compute and store part-worth ranges for each attribute
part.worth.ranges <- conjoint.results$contrasts
for(index.for.attribute in seq(along=conjoint.results$contrasts))
  part.worth.ranges[index.for.attribute] <-
  dist(range(conjoint.results$part.worths[index.for.attribute]))
conjoint.results$part.worth.ranges <- part.worth.ranges

sum.part.worth.ranges <- sum(as.numeric(conjoint.results$part.worth.ranges))

# compute and store importance values for each attribute
attribute.importance <- conjoint.results$contrasts
for(index.for.attribute in seq(along=conjoint.results$contrasts))
  attribute.importance[index.for.attribute] <-
  (dist(range(conjoint.results$part.worths[index.for.attribute]))/
  sum.part.worth.ranges) * 100
conjoint.results$attribute.importance <- attribute.importance

# data frame for ordering attribute names
attribute.name <- names(conjoint.results$contrasts)
attribute.importance <- as.numeric(attribute.importance)
temp.frame <- data.frame(attribute.name,attribute.importance)
conjoint.results$ordered.attributes <-
  as.character(temp.frame[sort.list(
  temp.frame$attribute.importance,decreasing = TRUE),"attribute.name"])
```

```
# respondent internal consistency added to list structure
conjoint.results$internal.consistency <- summary(main.effects.model)$r.squared

# user-defined function for printing conjoint measures
if (print.digits == 2)
  pretty.print <- function(x) {sprintf("%1.2f",round(x,digits = 2))}
if (print.digits == 3)
  pretty.print <- function(x) {sprintf("%1.3f",round(x,digits = 3))}

# report the conjoint measures to console
# use pretty.print to provide nicely formated output
for(k in seq(along=conjoint.results$ordered.attributes)) {
  cat("\n","\n")
  cat(conjoint.results$ordered.attributes[k],"Levels: ",
  unlist(conjoint.results$xlevels[conjoint.results$ordered.attributes[k]]))

  cat("\n"," Part-Worths:  ")
  cat(pretty.print(unlist(conjoint.results$part.worths
    [conjoint.results$ordered.attributes[k]])))

  cat("\n"," Standardized Part-Worths:  ")
  cat(pretty.print(unlist(conjoint.results$standardized.part.worths
    [conjoint.results$ordered.attributes[k]])))

  cat("\n"," Attribute Importance:  ")
  cat(pretty.print(unlist(conjoint.results$attribute.importance
    [conjoint.results$ordered.attributes[k]])))
  }

# plotting of spine chart begins here
# all graphical output is routed to external pdf file
pdf(file = "fig_preference_mobile_services_results.pdf", width=8.5, height=11)
spine.chart(conjoint.results)
dev.off()  # close the graphics output device


# additional work for the student
# note that the model fit to the data is a linear main-effects model
# what other models would be posssible?
# what about interactions between service provider attributes?
```

4

Market Basket Analysis

Bobby: "Okay, I'll make it as easy for you as I can. Give me an omelette, plain, and a chicken salad sandwich on wheat toast—no butter, no mayonnaise, no lettuce—and a cup of coffee."

Waitress: "One Number Two, and a chicken sal san—hold the butter, the mayo, the lettuce—and a cup of coffee . . . Anything else?"

Bobby: "Now all you have to do is hold the chicken, bring me the toast, charge me for the sandwich, and you haven't broken any rules."

Waitress: "You want me to hold the chicken."

Bobby: "Yeah. I want you to hold it between your knees."

—JACK NICHOLSON AS BOBBY (ROBERT EROICA DUPEA) AND
LORNA THAYER AS WAITRESS IN *Five Easy Pieces* (1970)

Shopping on the weekend is a half-hour walk to the grocery store. I am fairly predictable in what I buy—milk, juices, poultry items, granola, and bread...a jar of peanut butter and treats (strawberry fruit bars this week). The items for this shopping trip are shown in figure 4.1. These represent my market basket and would go into one row of the store's database along with thousands of shopping trips or market baskets from other customers. The individual market basket is the unit of analysis. Thousands of columns in the database correspond to the full set of products available at the store.

Figure 4.1. *Market Basket for One Shopping Trip*

GROCERY		
		4.99
BARS OATS N HONEY	5.49	
Card Savings	-0.50	
		2.49
OATS & HONEY CEREAL	4.49	
Card Savings	-2.00	
VEGGIE JCE		3.29
		2.00
OCEAN SPRAY	3.99	
Card Savings	-1.99	
		2.99
SKIPPY RF CRMY	4.79	
Card Savings	-1.80	
REFRIG/FROZEN		
		3.00
FLORIDAS NATURAL J	4.19	
Card Savings	-1.19	
		9.00
3 QTY DREYERS STRWBRY	13.47	
Card Savings	-2.97	
Mfr Cpn	-1.50	
5 QTY EATING RIGHT CHKN		10.00
PANTRY ESTNL MILK		3.19
BAKED GOODS		
PANTRY WHEAT BREAD		0.99
DELI		
DC TURKEY BREAST		3.43
BAL		45.37

Purchases of items would be part of the store's database, with system stocking units (SKUs), quantities, and prices duly noted. To prepare these data for market basket analysis, we would convert quantities to binary indicators. The purchase of granola bars would be represented by a one in the row of the input data for this shopping trip, as would the purchase of cereal and the nine other items in the market basket. The rest of the columns in this row of the input data would be set to zero. The resulting input data to market basket analysis would be a sparse binary matrix, thousands of rows and columns with ones and zeroes.[1]

Market baskets reveal consumer preferences and lifestyles in a way that no survey can fully capture. Market basket analysis (also called affinity or association analysis) asks, *What goes with what? What products are ordered or purchased together?* This is not association in the sense of correlation. It is contingency analysis on a large scale.

There are obvious examples of things that go together, such as hot dogs and hot dog buns, party favors and ice, peanut butter, jelly, and bread (or, in my case, just peanut butter and bread). There are reports, sometimes surprising, sometimes bogus, of less obvious things going together, like diapers and beer. The job of market basket analysis is to find what things go together, providing information to guide product placement in stores, cross-category and co-marketing promotions, and product bundling plans.

To provide an example of market basket analysis, we draw upon a grocery data set first analyzed by Hahsler, Hornik, and Reutterer (2006) and available in Hahsler et al. (2013a). The data set consists of $N = 9,835$ market baskets across $K = 169$ generically-labeled grocery items. The data set, which represents one month of real transaction data from a grocery outlet, is small enough to be processed on a laptop computer and large enough to demonstrate methods of market basket analysis.

A key challenge in market basket analysis and association rule modeling in general is the sheer number of rules that are generated. An *item set* is a collection of items selected from the set of items in the store. The size of an item set is the number of items in that set. Item sets may be composed of

---

[1] Note that we have simplified the market basket problem by using ones and zeroes in our data set or matrix. Three fruit bars in my market basket are represented by the number 1, not 3. Five frozen chicken dinners are represented by the number 1, not 5. The resulting binary matrix is easier to work with than a matrix with actual quantities in the cells.

two items, three items, and so on. The number of distinct item sets is very large, even for the grocery store data set.

An *association rule* is a division of each item set into two subsets with one subset, the *antecedent*, thought of as preceding the other subset, the *consequent*. There are more association rules than there are item sets.[2] The Apriori algorithm of Agraval et al. (1996) deals with the large-number-of-rules problem by using selection criteria that reflect the potential utility of association rules.

The first criterion relates to the *support* or prevalence of an item set. Each item set is evaluated to determine the proportion of times it occurs in the store data set. If this proportion exceeds a minimum support threshold or criterion, then it is passed along to the next phase of analysis. A support criterion of 0.01 implies that one in every one hundred market baskets must contain the item set. A support criterion of 0.001 implies that one in every one thousand market baskets must contain the item set.

The second criterion relates to the *confidence* or predictability of an association rule. This is computed as the support of the item set divided by the support of the subset of items in the antecedent. This is an estimate of the conditional probability of the consequent, given the antecedent. In the selection of association rules, we set the confidence criterion much higher than the support criterion.[3] Support and confidence criteria are arbitrarily set by the researcher. These vary from one market basket problem to another. For the groceries data set, we set the support criterion to 0.025 and make an initial plot showing item frequencies for individual items meeting this criterion. See figure 4.2.

---

[2] For the grocery store data set, with its $K = 169$ items and its corresponding binary data matrix, the number of distinct item sets will be

$$2^K = 2^{169} \approx 7.482888 \times 10^{50}$$

[3] With item subsets identified as A and B, there are two possible association rules: $(A \Rightarrow B)$ and $(B \Rightarrow A)$. We need to consider only one of these rules because we favor rules with higher confidence. Consider our confidence in the rule $(A \Rightarrow B)$. This is the conditional probability of B given A. Similarly, confidence in rule $(B \Rightarrow A)$ is the conditional probability of A given B:

$$P(B|A) = \frac{P(AB)}{P(A)} \qquad P(A|B) = \frac{P(AB)}{P(B)}$$

It follows that, if the item subset A has more support than the item subset B, then $P(A) > P(B)$ and $P(B|A) > P(A|B)$. Given our preference for rules of higher confidence, then, it is clear that the item subset with higher support will take the role of the antecedent.

Figure 4.2. *Market Basket Prevalence of Initial Grocery Items*

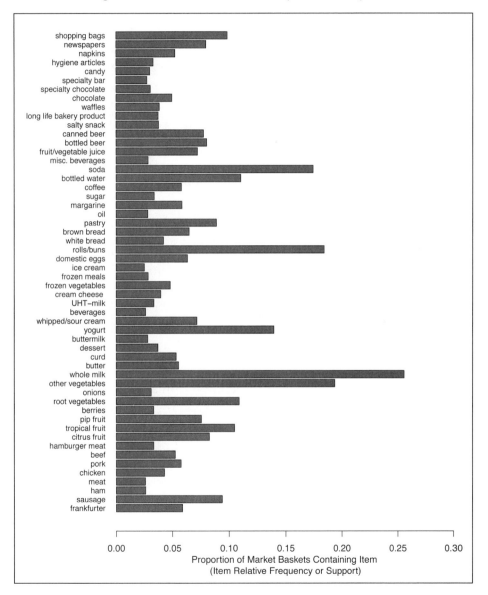

We see that there are groups of similar items: (1) candy and specialty bar, (2) specialty chocolate and chocolate, (3) canned beer and bottled beer, and so on. We can combine similar items into categories to provide a more meaningful analysis, obtaining the reduced set of fifty-five item categories in figure 4.3.

A set of 344 association rules may be obtained by setting thresholds for support and confidence of 0.025 and 0.05, respectively. Figure 4.4 provides a scatter plot of these rules with support on the horizontal axis and confidence on the vertical axis. Color-coding of the points relates to *lift*, a measure of relative predictive confidence.[4]

Figure 4.5 provides a clearer view of the identified association rules: a matrix bubble chart. An item in the antecedent subset or left-hand side (LHS) of an association rule provides the label at the top of the matrix, and an item in the consequent or right-hand side (RHS) of an association rule provides the label at the right of the matrix. Support relates to the size of the bubbles and lift is reflected in the color intensity of the bubble.

Suppose we are working for a local farmer, and we want to identify products that are commonly purchased along with vegetables. Selecting rules with consequent item subsets that include vegetables, we obtain forty-one rules from the set of 344. We rank these rules by lift and identify the top ten rules for display in table 4.1 and figure 4.6.

Reviewing the reported measures for association rules, support is prevalence. As a relative frequency or probability estimate it takes values from zero to one. Low values are tolerated, but values that are extremely low

---

[4] As with support and confidence, probability formulas define lift. Think of lift as the confidence we have in predicting the consequent B with the rule $(A \Rightarrow B)$, divided by the confidence we would have in predicting B without the rule. Without knowledge of A and the association rule $(A \Rightarrow B)$, our confidence in observing the item subset B is $P(B)$. With knowledge of A and the association rule $(A \Rightarrow B)$, our confidence in observing item subset B is $P(B|A)$, as we have defined earlier. The ratio of these quantities is lift:

$$\frac{P(B|A)}{P(B)} = \left(\frac{P(AB)}{P(A)}\right)\left(\frac{1}{P(B)}\right) = \frac{P(AB)}{P(A)P(B)}$$

Looking at the numerator and denominator of the ratio on the far right-hand side of this equation, we note that these are equivalent under an independence assumption. That is, if there is no relationship between item subsets A and B, then the joint probability of A and B is the product of their individual probabilities: $P(AB) = P(A)P(B)$. So lift is a measure of the degree to which item subsets in an association rule depart from independence.

Figure 4.3. *Market Basket Prevalence of Grocery Items by Category*

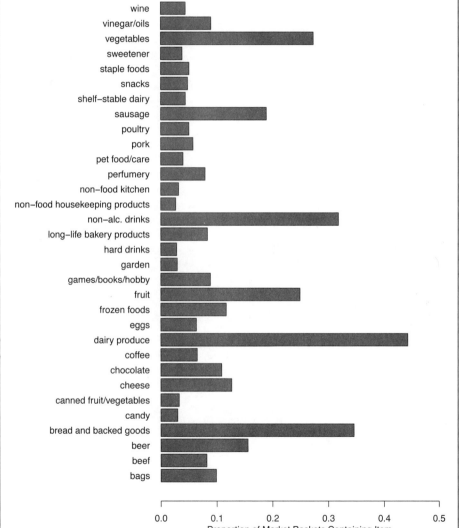

Figure 4.4. *Market Basket Association Rules: Scatter Plot*

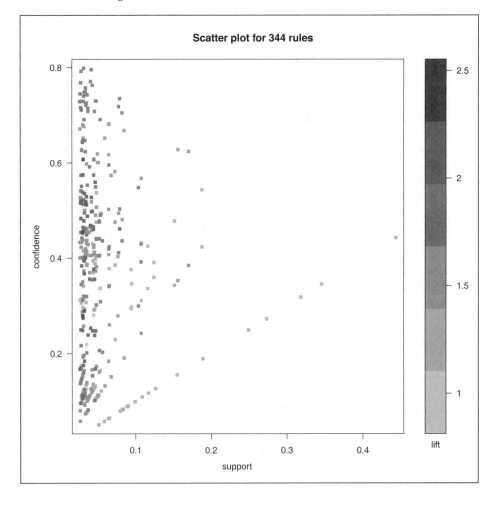

Figure 4.5. Market Basket Association Rules: Matrix Bubble Chart

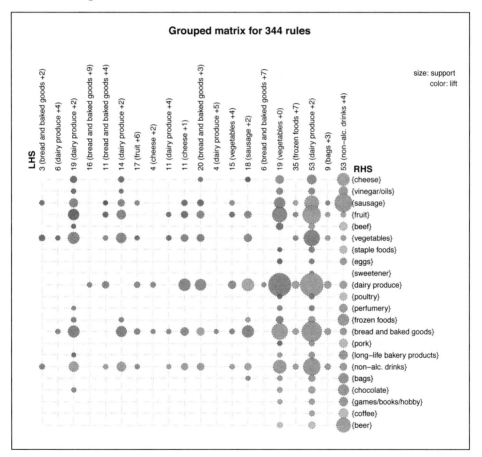

Table 4.1. *Association Rules for a Local Farmer*

Rule No.	Left-Hand Side (Antecedent)		Right-Hand Side (Consequent)	Support	Confidence	Lift
1	{beef, dairy produce}	=>	{vegetables}	0.030	0.607	2.225
2	{poultry}	=>	{vegetables}	0.029	0.575	2.105
3	{dairy produce, fruit, sausage}	=>	{vegetables}	0.027	0.574	2.103
4	{beef}	=>	{vegetables}	0.046	0.560	2.050
5	{dairy produce, vinegar/oils}	=>	{vegetables}	0.031	0.536	1.962
6	{fruit, sausage}	=>	{vegetables}	0.034	0.529	1.938
7	{bread and baked goods, dairy produce, fruit}	=>	{vegetables}	0.041	0.528	1.933
8	{pork}	=>	{vegetables}	0.030	0.522	1.912
9	{cheese, fruit}	=>	{vegetables}	0.027	0.520	1.904
10	{dairy produce, fruit, non-alc. drinks}	=>	{vegetables}	0.033	0.518	1.899

Figure 4.6. *Association Rules for a Local Farmer: A Network Diagram*

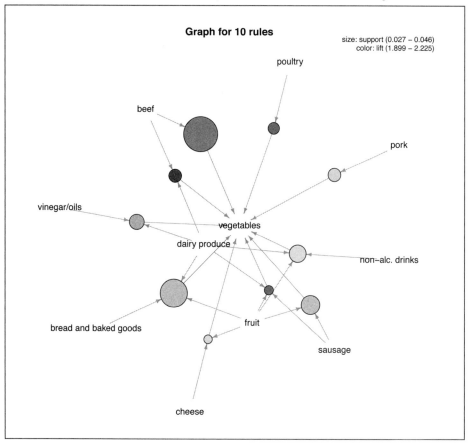

relative to other items in the store may indicate a lack of importance to shoppers.

Confidence relates to the predictability of the consequent, given the antecedent. As a conditional probability, confidence takes values from zero to one. Higher values are preferred. Lift, being a ratio of nonzero probabilities, takes positive values on the real number line. Lift needs to be above 1.00 to be of use to management. The higher the lift, the better.

Another way to serve the information needs of a producer is to employ transaction clustering. That is, we use cluster analysis prior to market basket analysis to identify groups of shoppers who are market-basket-similar. Groups that purchase the producer's products may be targeted for separate market basket analyses. In this way, we can develop cross-selling, co-marketing, or product bundling recommendations tailored to particular consumer segments.

Finding the proverbial "needle in the haystack" could be the easy part, given the efficient algorithms at our disposal. But have we learned anything of value in the process? Do we know where to look in the next haystack?

What we have done in the analysis of the grocery data set is descriptive rather than predictive. Identified association rules provide a description of shopping behavior or an analysis of the quantitative structure of shopping. Description of consumer shopping behavior is interesting and important. To see how description plays out in the marketplace, we go to the stores.

Marketers use association rules to make decisions about store layout, product bundling, or cross-selling. Store managers run field experiments, observing how shoppers respond to new store layouts and cross-selling promotions. The ultimate test of market basket predictive models is provided by marketing response or sales.

The vision of early workers in the field, such as Nielsen (1979), has been clearly realized with the prevalence of bar code scanners at checkout counters. Scanner data collection, category management methods, and market basket analysis are utilized by most large manufacturers and retailers.

Hastie, Tibshirani, and Friedman (2009) review the theory behind association rules, providing formal definitions for support, confidence (predictability), and lift (confidence divided by expected confidence), as well as a discussion of market basket applications and the Apriori algorithm of Agraval et al. (1996). Additional discussion may be found in the data mining literature (Tan, Steinbach, and Kumar 2005; Witten, Frank, and Hall 2011). Bruzzese and Davino (2008) review data visualization of association rules.

A data scientist may have to look through a lot of rules before finding one that is interesting. It is not surprising, then, that considerable attention has been paid to methods for selecting association rules (Hahsler, Buchta, and Hornik 2008), selecting variables in association rules modeling (Dippold and Hruschka 2013), and combining market segmentation and market basket analysis in the same analysis (Boztug and Reutterer 2008).

General models of buyer behavior help us understand trial purchase, repeat purchase, brand loyalty, and switching. Probability models are often used to represent regularities in aggregate buyer behavior over time, as is observed in the diffusion of new products. Examples of applied probability models for understanding buyer behavior may be found in the work of Fader and Hardie (1996, 2002).

Discussion of market basket analysis in R is provided by Hahsler, Grün, and Hornik (2005), Hahsler et al. (2011), and Hahsler et al. (2013a, 2013b), with data visualization support by Hahsler and Chelluboina (2013a, 2013b). Additional association rule algorithms are available through the R interface to Weka (Hornik 2013b, 2013a).

The program for the worked example in this chapter is provided in exhibit 4.1. It draws upon R packages developed by Hahsler et al. (2013a) and Hahsler and Chelluboina (2013a).

Exhibit 4.1. Market Basket Analysis of Grocery Store Data

```
# Association Rules for Market Basket Analysis

library(arules)  # association rules
library(arulesViz)  # data visualization of association rules
library(RColorBrewer)  # color palettes for plots

data(Groceries)  # grocery transcations object from arules package

# show the dimensions of the transactions object
print(dim(Groceries))

print(dim(Groceries)[1])  # 9835 market baskets for shopping trips
print(dim(Groceries)[2])  # 169 initial store items

# examine frequency for each item with support greater than 0.025
pdf(file="fig_market_basket_initial_item_support.pdf",
  width = 8.5, height = 11)
itemFrequencyPlot(Groceries, support = 0.025, cex.names=0.8, xlim = c(0,0.3),
  type = "relative", horiz = TRUE, col = "dark red", las = 1,
  xlab = paste("Proportion of Market Baskets Containing Item",
    "\n(Item Relative Frequency or Support)"))
dev.off()

# explore possibilities for combining similar items
print(head(itemInfo(Groceries)))
print(levels(itemInfo(Groceries)[["level1"]]))  # 10 levels... too few
print(levels(itemInfo(Groceries)[["level2"]]))  # 55 distinct levels

# aggregate items using the 55 level2 levels for food categories
# to create a more meaningful set of items
groceries <- aggregate(Groceries, itemInfo(Groceries)[["level2"]])

print(dim(groceries)[1])  # 9835 market baskets for shopping trips
print(dim(groceries)[2])  # 55 final store items (categories)

pdf(file="fig_market_basket_final_item_support.pdf", width = 8.5, height = 11)
itemFrequencyPlot(groceries, support = 0.025, cex.names=1.0, xlim = c(0,0.5),
  type = "relative", horiz = TRUE, col = "blue", las = 1,
  xlab = paste("Proportion of Market Baskets Containing Item",
    "\n(Item Relative Frequency or Support)"))
dev.off()

# obtain large set of association rules for items by category and all shoppers
# this is done by setting very low criteria for support and confidence
first.rules <- apriori(groceries,
  parameter = list(support = 0.001, confidence = 0.05))
print(summary(first.rules))  # yields 69,921 rules... too many
```

```
# select association rules using thresholds for support and confidence
second.rules <- apriori(groceries,
  parameter = list(support = 0.025, confidence = 0.05))
print(summary(second.rules))  # yields 344 rules

# data visualization of association rules in scatter plot
pdf(file="fig_market_basket_rules.pdf", width = 8.5, height = 8.5)
plot(second.rules,
  control=list(jitter=2, col = rev(brewer.pal(9, "Greens")[4:9])),
  shading = "lift")
dev.off()

# grouped matrix of rules
pdf(file="fig_market_basket_rules_matrix.pdf", width = 8.5, height = 8.5)
plot(second.rules, method="grouped",
  control=list(col = rev(brewer.pal(9, "Greens")[4:9])))
dev.off()

# select rules with vegetables in consequent (right-hand-side) item subsets
vegie.rules <- subset(second.rules, subset = rhs %pin% "vegetables")
inspect(vegie.rules)  # 41 rules

# sort by lift and identify the top 10 rules
top.vegie.rules <- head(sort(vegie.rules, decreasing = TRUE, by = "lift"), 10)
inspect(top.vegie.rules)

pdf(file="fig_market_basket_farmer_rules.pdf", width = 11, height = 8.5)
plot(top.vegie.rules, method="graph",
  control=list(type="items"),
  shading = "lift")
dev.off()

# suggestions for the student
# suppose your client is someone other than the local farmer,
# a meat producer/butcher, dairy, or brewer perhaps
# determine association rules relevant to your client's products
# guided by the market basket model, what recommendations
# would you make about future marketplace actions?
```

5

Economic Data Analysis

"Are you crazy? The fall will probably kill you."

—Paul Newman as Butch Cassidy in

Butch Cassidy and the Sundance Kid (1969)

I have seen *The Time Machine* and *Back to the Future*. I watched *Superman* turning time backwards by flying faster than the speed of light with suspense-killing precision. There was *The Curious Case of Benjamin Button*, a child/man who somehow managed to age backwards without fully knowing what was coming. Time and the future are a fascination for all. This is life. We know what is coming; we know the inevitable. But we lack the details.

Turning to economic data, we know that there will be ups and downs. But when will the economy turn up? When will it go down? Much economic research relies on gathering economic data to answer difficult up-and-down questions. Economic data are typically measures organized in time or time series.

In this chapter we draw upon United States economic data from the Federal Reserve Bank of St. Louis. We explore these data with statistical graphics and time series models. We show how to use time series data to make economic forecasts.

Suppose we work with four economic measures that are often thought of as leading indicators:

- National Civilian Unemployment Rate (percentage)
- Manufacturers' New Orders: Durable Goods (millions of dollars)
- University of Michigan Index of Consumer Sentiment (1Q 1966 = 100)
- New Homes Sold (millions)

For the last three of these measures higher values mean economic well-being. Let us compute the national employment rate as 100 minus the un-employment rate. And for convenience in graphing, we convert durable goods orders in millions of dollars to billions of dollars. We gather the four indices into a multiple time series object for plotting. The resulting plot, provided in figure 5.1, shows the Great Recession reflected in the four economic measures, labeled as IER, IDGO, ICS, and INHS.[1]

Parallel indexing can be especially useful in the analysis of multiple time series. The University of Michigan Index of Consumer Sentiment is an indexed series (1Q 1966 = 100). It is interesting to note that this measure hit its base index value of 100 in March 1997, a date at which we have observations for the other three series. Using March 1997 as our reference date for the 100 index value, we can compute like-indexed series for the employment rate, durable goods orders, and new home sales. That is, each economic measure can be scaled so that its value at the reference date March 1997 is exactly 100. So we will use March 1997 as our base month for converting the other three economic indicators to index values.[2] With each economic measure scaled so that its value on March 1997 is 100, we can plot the multiple time series again using a horizon plot.[3]

---

[1] According to the Business Cycle Dating Committee of the National Bureau of Economic Research (2010), the Great Recession extended from December 2007 through June 2009, the longest of any recession since World War II.

[2] The mathematics for parallel indexing is straightforward. Let x_t be the value of an economic measure at time t, and let x_0 be the value of the economic measure on the reference date. Then the indexed value of the economic measure y_t is given by $y_t = 100 \left(\frac{x_t}{x_0} \right)$.

[3] Introduced by Heer, Kong, and Agrawala (2009), the horizon plot represents a space-efficient data visualization for multiple time series. To make a visual like the one shown in figure 5.2, we first determine a center-value or origin, a reference point for standardization across the time series. Our choice here was to use the index value 100 as the origin. Then, instead of plotting each individual time series with its actual values, we plot both below-origin and above-origin values above the bottom line of each panel, with below-origin values in one color and above-origin values in another color. Intensities of color reflect the degree to which time series values are below- or above-origin.

Figure 5.1. *Multiple Time Series of Economic Data*

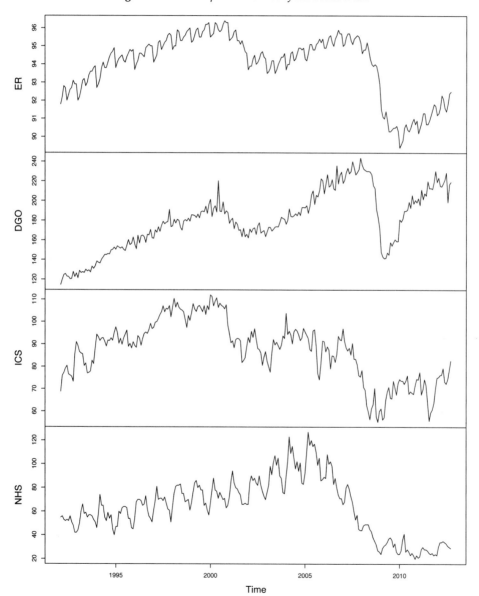

The horizon plot represents exploratory data analysis for economic research. It is common to use a two-color gradient, such as a red-to-white-to-blue gradient, to display distinct levels of below-origin to above-origin values. The origin we have selected for the four economic series is the value 100, the base for each indexed time series. The result is shown in figure 5.2.

The horizon plot reduces the amount of space needed to display multiple time series and, through the use of color, makes it easier to detect relationships across time series. Granger causality tests and dynamic regressions notwithstanding, we may detect a leading indicator in a horizon plot long before statistical indicators reveal its existence.

Looking at the horizon plot in figure 5.2, we can see that three of the four indices (IER, ICS, and INHS) move in consort. Red indicates below-average (below-index-100) values, and the deeper the red, the further below. Note that deep red in ICS is observed a couple months before deep red in IER, suggesting that the University of Michigan Index of Consumer Sentiment may be a leading indicator for the level employment. The index for New Homes Sold (INHS) also experiences deep declines prior to declines in the employment rate and remains at very low levels throughout the period of observation.

Having gathered the data and looked at the plots, we turn to forecasting the future. For these economic time series, we use autoregressive integrated moving average (ARIMA) models or what are often called Box-Jenkins models (Box, Jenkins, and Reinsel 2008).

Drawing upon software from Hyndman et al.(2013) and working with one economic measure at a time, our program searches across a large set of candidate models including autoregressive, moving-average, and seasonal components. It selects the very best model in terms of the Akaike Information Criterion (AIC). Then, having found the model that the algorithm determines as the best model for each measure, we use that model to forecast future values of the economic measure. In particular, we ask for forecasts for a time horizon of two years or twenty-four months. We obtain the forecast mean as well as a prediction interval around that mean for each month of the forecasting horizon. This is done for each of the four measures being investigated. In the figures 5.3 through 5.6, the original time series data are shown as well as the forecasts and prediction intervals.

Figure 5.2. *Horizon Plot of Indexed Economic Time Series*

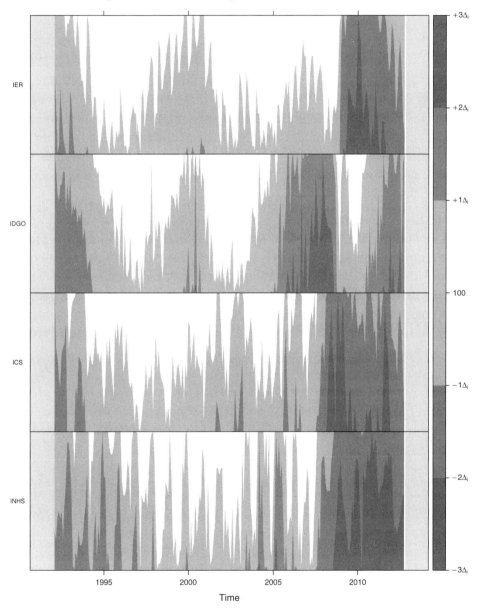

Economic measures indexed so that they have the value 100 at the reference date, March 1997.

Forecasting uncertainty is reflected in the grey area around the forecasted values. As we can see from these economic forecasts, there is much uncertainty about the future, and the further we look into the future, the greater our uncertainty. Notice the megaphone effect in the figures, with a wider prediction interval further into the future. The value of a model lies in the quality of its predictions. We have work to do with these forecasts.

As a next step in our work, we might fit a multivariate time series or vector autoregressive (VAR) model to the four time series. Alternatively, we could explore dynamic linear models, regressing one time series on another. We could utilize ARIMA transfer function models or state space models with regression components. The possibilities are many, as are the modeling issues to be addressed.[4]

Similar to other data with which we work, economic data are organized by observational unit, time, and space. The observational unit is typically an economic agent (individual or firm) or a group of such agents as in an aggregate analysis. It is common to use geographical areas as a basis for aggregation. Alternatively, space (longitude and latitude) can be used directly in spatial data analyses. Time considerations are especially important in macroeconomic analysis, which focuses upon nationwide economic measures.

---

[4] There is a subtle but important distinction to be made here. The term *time series regression* refers to regression analysis in which the organizing unit of analysis is time. We look at relationships among economic measures organized in time. Much economic analysis concerns time series regression. Special care must be taken to avoid what might be called spurious relationships, as many economic time series are correlated with one another because they depend upon underlying factors, such as population growth or seasonality. In time series regression, we use standard linear regression methods. We check the residuals from our regression to ensure that they are not correlated in time. If they are correlated in time (autocorrelated), then we use a method such as generalized least squares as an alternative to ordinary least squares. That is, we incorporate an error data model as part of our modeling process. Longitudinal data analysis or panel data analysis is an example of a mixed data method with a focus upon data organized by cross-sectional units and time. When we use the term *time series analysis*, however, we are not talking about time series regression. We are talking about methods that start by focusing upon one economic measure at a time and its pattern across time. We look for trends, seasonality, and cycles in that individual time series. Then, after working with that single time series, we look at possible relationships with other time series. If we are concerned with forecasting or predicting the future, as we often are in predictive analytics, then we use methods of time series analysis. Recently, there has been considerable interest in state space models for time series, which provide a convenient mechanism for incorporating regression components into dynamic time series models (Commandeur and Koopman 2007; Hyndman, Koehler, Ord, and Snyder 2008; Durbin and Koopman 2012).

Figure 5.3. *Forecast of National Civilian Employment Rate (percentage)*

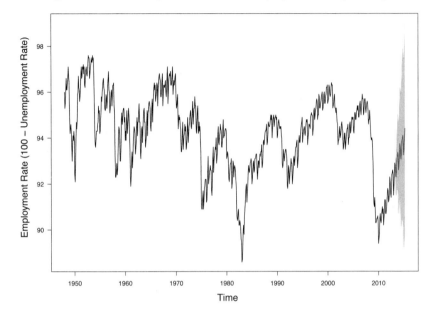

Figure 5.4. *Forecast of Manufacturers' New Orders: Durable Goods (billions of dollars)*

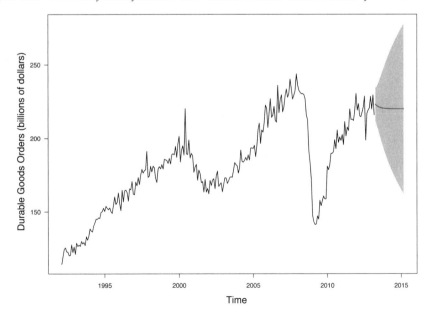

Figure 5.5. *Forecast of University of Michigan Index of Consumer Sentiment (1Q 1966 = 100)*

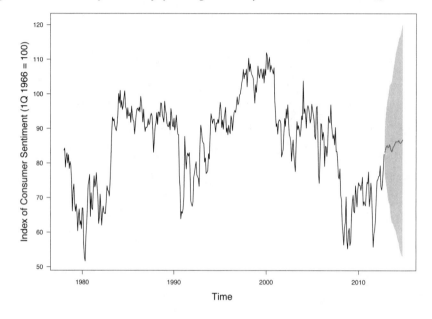

Figure 5.6. *Forecast of New Homes Sold (millions)*

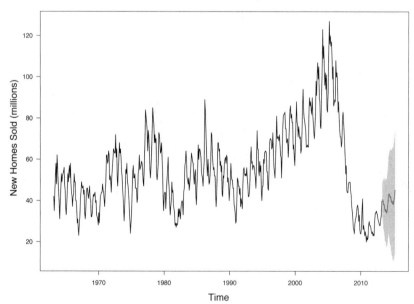

Baumohl (2008) provides a review of economic measures that are commonly thought of as leading indicators. Kennedy (2008) provides an introduction to the terminology of econometrics. Key references in the area of econometrics include Judge et al.(1985), Berndt (1991), Enders (2010), and Greene (2012). Reviews of time series modeling and forecasting methods are provided by Holden, Peel, and Thompson (1990) and in the edited volume by Armstrong (2001). More detailed discussion of time series methods is provided by Hamilton (1994), Makridakis, Wheelwright, and Hyndman (2005), Box, Jenkins, and Reinsel (2008), Hyndman et al. (2008), and Durbin and Koopman (2012). Time-series, panel (longitudinal) data, financial, and econometric modeling methods are especially relevant in demand and sales forecasting. Frees and Miller (2004) present a longitudinal sales forecasting method, reflecting the special structure of sales data in space and time. Hierarchical and grouped time series methods are discussed by Athanasopoulos, Ahmed, and Hyndman (2009) and Hyndman et al. (2011), with implementation in R by Hyndman, Ahmed, and Shang (2013).

For gathering economic data, we build on the foundation R code provided by Ryan (2013). Useful for programming with dates are R functions provided by Grolemund and Wickham (2011, 2013). Associated sources for econometric and time series programming are Kleiber and Zeileis (2008), Cowpertwait and Metcalfe (2009), Petris, Petrone, and Campagnoli (2009), Hothorn et al. (2013), and Tsay (2013). Most useful for time series forecasting is R code from Hyndman et al.(2013), Petris (2010), Petris and Gilks (2013), and Szymanski (2013).

The Granger test of causality, a test of temporal ordering, was introduced in the classic reference by Granger (1969). The interested reader should also check out a delightful article that answers the perennial question *Which came first, the chicken or the egg?* (Thurman and Fisher 1988).

Exhibit 5.1 shows the code used to obtain time series economic data, create plots and visualizations, and perform time series analyses using ARIMA methods. As well, the code shows how to search for leading indicators using the Granger test of causality. The code draws upon R packages developed by Ryan (2013), Grolemund and Wickham (2013), Sarkar and Andrews (2013), Hyndman et al. (2013), and Hothorn et al. (2013).

Exhibit 5.1. *Working with Economic Data*

```
# Analysis of Economic Time Series

library(quantmod) # use for gathering and charting economic data
library(lubridate) # date functions
library(latticeExtra) # package used for horizon plot
library(forecast) # functions for time series forecasting
library(lmtest) # for Granger test of causality

par(mfrow = c(2,2)) # four plots on one window/page

# Economic Data from Federal Reserve Bank of St. Louis (FRED system)
# National Civilian Unemployment Rate (monthly, percentage)
getSymbols("UNRATESA", src="FRED", return.class = "xts")
ER <- 100 - UNRATESA # convert to employment rate
dimnames(ER)[2] <- "ER"
chartSeries(ER,theme="white")
ER.data.frame <- as.data.frame(ER)
ER.data.frame$date <- ymd(rownames(ER.data.frame))
ER.time.series <- ts(ER.data.frame$ER,
  start = c(year(min(ER.data.frame$date)),month(min(ER.data.frame$date))),
  end = c(year(max(ER.data.frame$date)),month(max(ER.data.frame$date))),
  frequency=12)


# Manufacturers' New Orders: Durable Goods (millions of dollars)
getSymbols("DGORDER", src="FRED", return.class = "xts")
DGO <- DGORDER/1000 # convert to billions of dollars
dimnames(DGO)[2] <- "DGO" # use simple name for index
chartSeries(DGO, theme="white")
DGO.data.frame <- as.data.frame(DGO)
DGO.data.frame$DGO <- DGO.data.frame$DGO
DGO.data.frame$date <- ymd(rownames(DGO.data.frame))
DGO.time.series <- ts(DGO.data.frame$DGO,
  start = c(year(min(DGO.data.frame$date)),month(min(DGO.data.frame$date))),
  end = c(year(max(DGO.data.frame$date)),month(max(DGO.data.frame$date))),
  frequency=12)


# University of Michigan Index of Consumer Sentiment (1Q 1966 = 100)
getSymbols("UMCSENT", src="FRED", return.class = "xts")
ICS <- UMCSENT # use simple name for xts object
dimnames(ICS)[2] <- "ICS" # use simple name for index
chartSeries(ICS, theme="white")
ICS.data.frame <- as.data.frame(ICS)
ICS.data.frame$ICS <- ICS.data.frame$ICS
ICS.data.frame$date <- ymd(rownames(ICS.data.frame))
ICS.time.series <- ts(ICS.data.frame$ICS,
  start = c(year(min(ICS.data.frame$date)), month(min(ICS.data.frame$date))),
  end = c(year(max(ICS.data.frame$date)),month(max(ICS.data.frame$date))),
  frequency=12)
```

```
# New Homes Sold in the US, not seasonally adjusted (monthly, millions)
getSymbols("HSN1FNSA",src="FRED",return.class = "xts")
NHS <- HSN1FNSA
dimnames(NHS)[2] <- "NHS" # use simple name for index
chartSeries(NHS, theme="white")
NHS.data.frame <- as.data.frame(NHS)
NHS.data.frame$NHS <- NHS.data.frame$NHS
NHS.data.frame$date <- ymd(rownames(NHS.data.frame))
NHS.time.series <- ts(NHS.data.frame$NHS,
  start = c(year(min(NHS.data.frame$date)),month(min(NHS.data.frame$date))),
  end = c(year(max(NHS.data.frame$date)),month(max(NHS.data.frame$date))),
  frequency=12)

# define multiple time series object
economic.mts <- cbind(ER.time.series, DGO.time.series, ICS.time.series,
  NHS.time.series)
  dimnames(economic.mts)[[2]] <- c("ER","DGO","ICS","NHS") # keep simple names
modeling.mts <- na.omit(economic.mts) # keep overlapping time intervals only

# plot multiple time series
plot(modeling.mts,main="")

# create new indexed series IER using base date March 1997
ER0 <- mean(as.numeric(window(ER.time.series,start=c(1997,3),end=c(1997,3))))
IER.time.series <- (ER.time.series/ER0) * 100

# create new indexed series IDGO using base date March 1997
DGO0 <- mean(as.numeric(window(DGO.time.series,start=c(1997,3),end=c(1997,3))))
IDGO.time.series <- (DGO.time.series/DGO0) * 100

# create new indexed series INHS using base date March 1997
NHS0 <- mean(as.numeric(window(NHS.time.series,start=c(1997,3),end=c(1997,3))))
INHS.time.series <- (NHS.time.series/NHS0) * 100

# create a multiple time series object from the index series
economic.mts <- cbind(IER.time.series,
IDGO.time.series,
ICS.time.series,
INHS.time.series)
dimnames(economic.mts)[[2]] <- c("IER","IDGO","ICS","INHS")
working.economic.mts <- na.omit(economic.mts) # months complete for all series

# plot multiple economic time series as horizon plot
# using the index 100 as the reference point
# use ylab rather than strip.left, for readability
# also shade any times with missing data values.
print(horizonplot(working.economic.mts, colorkey = TRUE,
  layout = c(1,4), strip.left = FALSE, origin = 100,
  ylab = list(rev(colnames(working.economic.mts)), rot = 0, cex = 0.7)) +
  layer_(panel.fill(col = "gray90"), panel.xblocks(..., col = "white")))
```

```
# return to the individual economic time series prior to indexing

# ARIMA model fit to the employment rate data
ER.auto.arima.fit <- auto.arima(ER.time.series, d=NA, D=NA, max.p=3, max.q=3,
  max.P=2, max.Q=2, max.order=3, start.p=2, start.q=2,
  start.P=1, start.Q=1, stationary=FALSE, seasonal=TRUE,
  ic=c("aic"), stepwise=TRUE, trace=FALSE,
  approximation=FALSE, xreg=NULL,
  test=c("kpss","adf","pp"), seasonal.test=c("ocsb","ch"),
  allowdrift=FALSE, lambda=NULL, parallel=FALSE, num.cores=NULL)
print(summary(ER.auto.arima.fit))
# national employment rate two-year forecast (horizon h = 24 months)
ER.forecast <- forecast.Arima(ER.auto.arima.fit, h=24, level=c(90),
  fan=FALSE, xreg=NULL, bootstrap=FALSE)
# plot national employment rate time series with two-year forecast
plot(ER.forecast,main="", ylab="Employment Rate (100 - Unemployment Rate)",
  xlab = "Time", las = 1, lwd = 1.5)

# ARIMA model fit to the manufacturers durable goods orders
DGO.auto.arima.fit <- auto.arima(DGO.time.series, d=NA, D=NA, max.p=3, max.q=3,
  max.P=2, max.Q=2, max.order=3, start.p=2, start.q=2,
  start.P=1, start.Q=1, stationary=FALSE, seasonal=TRUE,
  ic=c("aic"), stepwise=TRUE, trace=FALSE,
  approximation=FALSE, xreg=NULL,
  test=c("kpss","adf","pp"), seasonal.test=c("ocsb","ch"),
  allowdrift=FALSE, lambda=NULL, parallel=FALSE, num.cores=NULL)
print(summary(DGO.auto.arima.fit))
# durable goods orders two-year forecast (horizon h = 24 months)
DGO.forecast <- forecast.Arima(DGO.auto.arima.fit, h=24, level=c(90),
  fan=FALSE, xreg=NULL, bootstrap=FALSE)
# plot durable goods time series with two-year forecast
plot(DGO.forecast,main="", ylab="Durable Goods Orders (billions of dollars)",
  xlab = "Time", las = 1, lwd = 1.5)

# ARIMA model fit to index of consumer sentiment
ICS.auto.arima.fit <- auto.arima(ICS.time.series, d=NA, D=NA, max.p=3, max.q=3,
  max.P=2, max.Q=2, max.order=3, start.p=2, start.q=2,
  start.P=1, start.Q=1, stationary=FALSE, seasonal=TRUE,
  ic=c("aic"), stepwise=TRUE, trace=FALSE,
  approximation=FALSE, xreg=NULL,
  test=c("kpss","adf","pp"), seasonal.test=c("ocsb","ch"),
  allowdrift=FALSE, lambda=NULL, parallel=FALSE, num.cores=NULL)
print(summary(ICS.auto.arima.fit))
# index of consumer sentiment two-year forecast (horizon h = 24 months)
ICS.forecast <- forecast.Arima(ICS.auto.arima.fit, h=24, level=c(90),
  fan=FALSE, xreg=NULL, bootstrap=FALSE)
# plot index of consumer sentiment time series with two-year forecast
plot(ICS.forecast,main="", ylab="Index of Consumer Sentiment (1Q 1966 = 100)",
  xlab = "Time", las = 1, lwd = 1.5)
```

```
# ARIMA model fit to new home sales
NHS.auto.arima.fit <- auto.arima(NHS.time.series, d=NA, D=NA, max.p=3, max.q=3,
  max.P=2, max.Q=2, max.order=3, start.p=2, start.q=2,
  start.P=1, start.Q=1, stationary=FALSE, seasonal=TRUE,
  ic=c("aic"), stepwise=TRUE, trace=FALSE,
  approximation=FALSE, xreg=NULL,
  test=c("kpss","adf","pp"), seasonal.test=c("ocsb","ch"),
  allowdrift=FALSE, lambda=NULL, parallel=FALSE, num.cores=NULL)
print(summary(NHS.auto.arima.fit))
# new home sales two-year forecast (horizon h = 24 months)
NHS.forecast <- forecast.Arima(NHS.auto.arima.fit, h=24, level=c(90),
  fan=FALSE, xreg=NULL, bootstrap=FALSE)
# plot new home sales time series with two-year forecast
plot(NHS.forecast,main="", ylab="New Homes Sold (millions)",
  xlab = "Time", las = 1, lwd = 1.5)


# Which regressors have potential as leading indicators?
# look for relationships across three of the time series
# using the period of overlap for those series
grangertest(ICS~ER, order = 3, data=modeling.mts)
grangertest(ICS~DGO, order = 3, data=modeling.mts)
grangertest(DGO~ER, order = 3, data=modeling.mts)
grangertest(DGO~ICS, order = 3, data=modeling.mts)
grangertest(ER~DGO, order = 3, data=modeling.mts)
grangertest(ER~ICS, order = 3, data=modeling.mts)


# suggestions for the student
# explore additional forecasting methods such as exponential smoothing
# explore dynamic linear models and state space approaches
# gather data on additional economic measures that might be regarded
# as leading indicators
# select an industry to study, examine relevant economic indicators and
# possible relationships to the financial performance of companies
# within that industry (stock prices or returns)
```

6

Operations Management

"Go ahead, make my day."

—CLINT EASTWOOD AS HARRY CALLAHAN IN *Sudden Impact* (1983)

I have something in common with Michael Feldman of the public radio show *Whad'Ya Know*. For a few years I worked with Union Cab Cooperative of Madison. Union Cab, an employee-owned and operated cooperative, has years of data showing when and where they pick up and drop off passengers. The precise path of travel of every ride is tracked by GPS sensors and logged with time-stamps every few seconds. With an active call center, a sixty-cab fleet, and an operation that never shuts down, Union Cab is a treasure trove of data. Working with these data gave me an appreciation for the importance of analytics in operations management.

Operations managers benefit by using the tools of operations research, including queueing theory, mathematical programming, and process simulation. We can touch on the first two of these areas using public domain data from the call center of "Anonymous Bank" in Israel.[1] We focus on data from February 1999. We begin, as we often do, with data visualization, looking at wait times for service. Then we use a queueing model to estimate workforce requirements and mathematical programming to define an optimal workforce schedule.

---

[1] Call center data from "Anonymous Bank" were provided by Avi Mandelbaum, with the help of Ilan Guedj. These data have been used in other published works, including Brown et al. (2005).

Exhibits 6.1 through 6.6 include wait-time ribbon plots for the days that the bank was open during the first week of February 1999. Each wait-time ribbon provides a visualization of twenty-four wait-time distributions, one for each hour of the day. The bottom of a ribbon represents the 50th percentile or median of wait times during any given hour. Fifty percent of calls fall below the bottom of the ribbon. The top of the ribbon represents the 90th percentile of wait times, so ten percent of calls fall above the top of the ribbon. Tabled values below the ribbons provide additional documentation for operations managers, displaying numbers of service operators, total calls per hour, calls served, and calls dropped (abandoned).

Call center performance is judged relative to management goals, which are portrayed as horizontal lines on each wait-time ribbon. Suppose that one of the bank's service goals is to realize wait times of thirty seconds or less, with wait times in excess of ninety seconds being considered intolerable. For each day's data, we can see that large segments of many ribbons fall above the ninety-second line. This means that many callers are waiting for more than ninety seconds before being served.

The wait-time ribbons suggest that the bank may want to schedule additional call center staff in order to meet its service performance goals. Workforce scheduling involves two modeling tasks: estimating workforce needs and scheduling workers to meet those needs. There can be wide variability in requirements from one hour to the next, with bank customers calling during their lunch hour or afternoon break times. To match call center traffic, the bank may benefit by having flexible shifts or shifts with various start times.

Given wide variability in traffic, estimating workforce requirements for a call center is a challenging analytic problem. Alternative methods include call-level forecasting models, queueing models, process simulation, or some combination of these. With data from the first week of February 1999, we can estimate arrival rates and service rates for any day of the week. We use data from Wednesdays in February to demonstrate the process. Call arrival and service rates for Wednesdays in February are shown in figure 6.7.

Figure 6.1. *Call Center Operations for Monday*

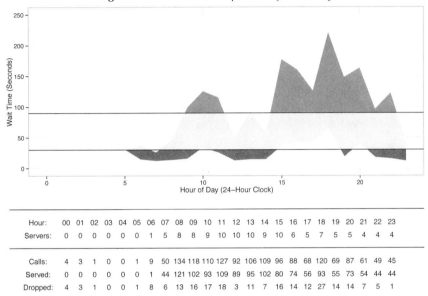

Hour:	00	01	02	03	04	05	06	07	08	09	10	11	12	13	14	15	16	17	18	19	20	21	22	23
Servers:	0	0	0	0	0	0	1	5	8	8	9	10	10	10	9	10	6	5	7	5	5	4	4	4
Calls:	4	3	1	0	0	1	9	50	134	118	110	127	92	106	109	96	88	68	120	69	87	61	49	45
Served:	0	0	0	0	0	0	1	44	121	102	93	109	89	95	102	80	74	56	93	55	73	54	44	44
Dropped:	4	3	1	0	0	1	8	6	13	16	17	18	3	11	7	16	14	12	27	14	14	7	5	1

Bottom of ribbon = 50th percentile of wait times   Top of ribbon = 90th percentile of wait times.

Figure 6.2. *Call Center Operations for Tuesday*

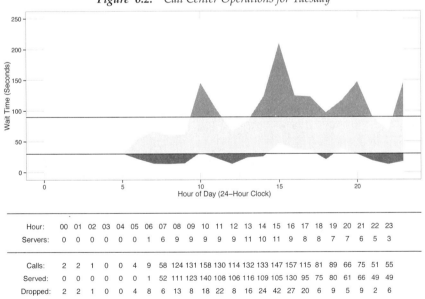

Hour:	00	01	02	03	04	05	06	07	08	09	10	11	12	13	14	15	16	17	18	19	20	21	22	23
Servers:	0	0	0	0	0	0	1	6	9	9	9	9	9	11	10	11	9	8	8	7	7	6	5	3
Calls:	2	2	1	0	0	4	9	58	124	131	158	130	114	132	133	147	157	115	81	89	66	75	51	55
Served:	0	0	0	0	0	0	1	52	111	123	140	108	106	116	109	105	130	95	75	80	61	66	49	49
Dropped:	2	2	1	0	0	4	8	6	13	8	18	22	8	16	24	42	27	20	6	9	5	9	2	6

Bottom of ribbon = 50th percentile of wait times   Top of ribbon = 90th percentile of wait times.

Figure 6.3. Call Center Operations for Wednesday

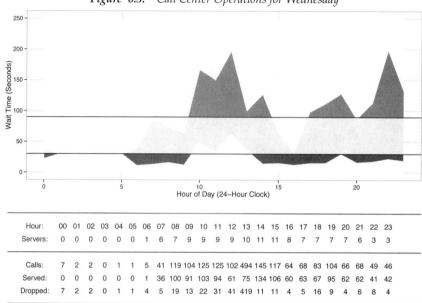

Hour:	00	01	02	03	04	05	06	07	08	09	10	11	12	13	14	15	16	17	18	19	20	21	22	23
Servers:	0	0	0	0	0	0	1	6	7	9	9	9	9	9	10	11	11	8	7	7	7	7	6	3	3
Calls:	7	2	2	0	1	1	5	41	119	104	125	125	102	494	145	117	64	68	83	104	66	68	49	46
Served:	0	0	0	0	0	0	1	36	100	91	103	94	61	75	134	106	60	63	67	95	62	62	41	42
Dropped:	7	2	2	0	1	1	4	5	19	13	22	31	41	419	11	11	4	5	16	9	4	6	8	4

Bottom of ribbon = 50th percentile of wait times   Top of ribbon = 90th percentile of wait times.

Figure 6.4. Call Center Operations for Thursday

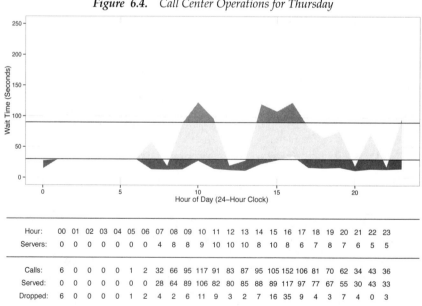

Hour:	00	01	02	03	04	05	06	07	08	09	10	11	12	13	14	15	16	17	18	19	20	21	22	23
Servers:	0	0	0	0	0	0	0	4	8	8	9	10	10	10	8	10	8	6	7	8	7	6	5	5
Calls:	6	0	0	0	0	1	2	32	66	95	117	91	83	87	95	105	152	106	81	70	62	34	43	36
Served:	0	0	0	0	0	0	0	28	64	89	106	82	80	85	88	89	117	97	77	67	55	30	43	33
Dropped:	6	0	0	0	0	1	2	4	2	6	11	9	3	2	7	16	35	9	4	3	7	4	0	3

Bottom of ribbon = 50th percentile of wait times   Top of ribbon = 90th percentile of wait times.

Figure 6.5. *Call Center Operations for Friday*

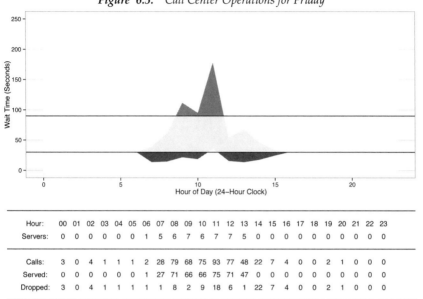

Hour:	00	01	02	03	04	05	06	07	08	09	10	11	12	13	14	15	16	17	18	19	20	21	22	23
Servers:	0	0	0	0	0	0	1	5	6	7	6	7	7	5	0	0	0	0	0	0	0	0	0	0
Calls:	3	0	4	1	1	1	2	28	79	68	75	93	77	48	22	7	4	0	0	2	1	0	0	0
Served:	0	0	0	0	0	0	1	27	71	66	66	75	71	47	0	0	0	0	0	0	0	0	0	0
Dropped:	3	0	4	1	1	1	1	1	8	2	9	18	6	1	22	7	4	0	0	2	1	0	0	0

Bottom of ribbon = 50th percentile of wait times   Top of ribbon = 90th percentile of wait times.

Figure 6.6. *Call Center Operations for Sunday*

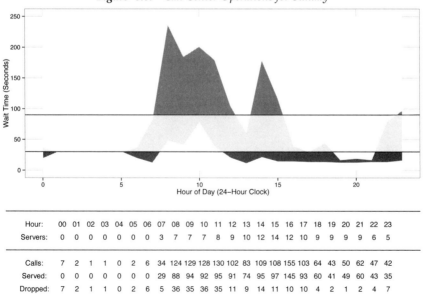

Hour:	00	01	02	03	04	05	06	07	08	09	10	11	12	13	14	15	16	17	18	19	20	21	22	23
Servers:	0	0	0	0	0	0	0	3	7	7	7	8	9	10	12	14	12	10	9	9	9	9	6	5
Calls:	7	2	1	1	0	2	6	34	124	129	128	130	102	83	109	108	155	103	64	43	50	62	47	42
Served:	0	0	0	0	0	0	0	29	88	94	92	95	91	74	95	97	145	93	60	41	49	60	43	35
Dropped:	7	2	1	1	0	2	6	5	36	35	36	35	11	9	14	11	10	10	4	2	1	2	4	7

Bottom of ribbon = 50th percentile of wait times   Top of ribbon = 90th percentile of wait times.

Figure 6.7. *Call Center Arrival and Service Rates on Wednesdays*

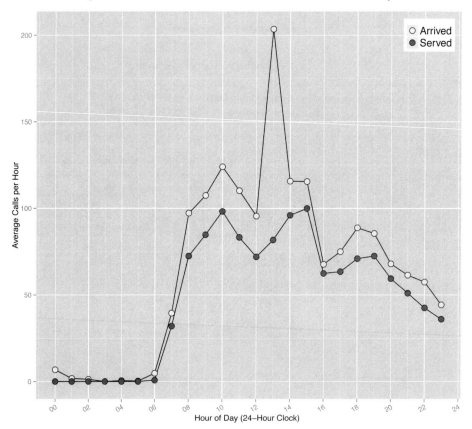

Table 6.1. *Call Center Shifts and Needs for Wednesdays*

Hour	StartTime	Shift1	Shift2	Shift3	Shift4	Shift5	Shift6	Shift7	Shift8	Need
"00"	Midnight	1	0	0	0	0	0	0	0	0
"01"	1am	1	0	0	0	0	0	0	0	0
"02"	2am	1	0	0	0	0	0	0	0	0
"03"	3am	1	0	0	0	0	0	0	0	0
"04"	4am	1	0	0	0	0	0	0	0	0
"05"	5am	1	0	0	0	0	0	0	0	0
"06"	6am	0	1	0	0	0	0	0	0	1
"07"	7am	0	1	0	0	0	0	0	0	4
"08"	8am	0	1	1	0	0	0	0	0	8
"09"	9am	0	1	1	0	0	0	0	0	9
"10"	10am	0	1	1	1	0	0	0	0	10
"11"	11am	0	1	1	1	0	0	0	0	9
"12"	Noon	0	0	1	1	1	0	0	0	8
"13"	1pm	0	0	1	1	1	0	0	0	16
"14"	2pm	0	0	0	1	1	1	0	0	10
"15"	3pm	0	0	0	1	1	1	0	0	10
"16"	4pm	0	0	0	0	1	1	1	0	6
"17"	5pm	0	0	0	0	1	1	1	0	7
"18"	6pm	0	0	0	0	0	1	1	1	8
"19"	7pm	0	0	0	0	0	1	1	1	8
"20"	8pm	0	0	0	0	0	0	1	1	6
"21"	9pm	0	0	0	0	0	0	1	1	6
"22"	10pm	0	0	0	0	0	0	0	1	5
"23"	11pm	0	0	0	0	0	0	0	1	4

For this example, we apply standard queueing models to estimate the work-force requirements for each hour of the day on Wednesdays. We suppose that the bank wants no more than 50 percent of callers to wait in queue before speaking with a service agent. The bank can benefit from having flexible shift start times. Let us assume that the bank's call center shifts are six hours in duration, beginning at specific even-numbered hours of the day and evening. In particular, suppose that there is a midnight-to-6 a.m. shift and shifts beginning every two hours from 6 a.m. through 6 p.m. Work-force shifts are shown in table 6.1, with one column for each shift. Binary indicators in cells for each shift column provide a representation of the shift for input to mathematical programming. The number 1 indicates that an hour is part of a shift, and the number 0 indicates that an hour is not part of a shift. Workforce hourly needs are also shown in the table. These were estimated from a queueing model.[2]

---

[2] We used a standard Erlang C model to estimate the number of service operators for each hour of the day on Wednesdays. "Anonymous Bank" case data suggest that workers can handle an average of fifteen calls an hour. Many organizations utilize the Erlang C model for workforce scheduling. The Erlang C model assumes that calls are random Poisson arrivals. The model does not take abandoned calls into account. Revisions of Erlang C have been proposed by statisticians and operations researchers (Brown et al. 2005; Janssen, Leeuwaarden, and Zwart 2011).

Table 6.2. *Call Center Problem and Solution*

Shift	Start Time	Duration (hours)	Hourly Cost	Shift Cost	Optimal Shift Schedule	Total Cost for Shift Schedule
1	0	6	42	252	0	0
2	6	6	48	288	4	1,152
3	8	6	30	180	8	1,440
4	10	6	30	180	4	720
5	12	6	30	180	4	720
6	2	6	48	288	2	576
7	4	6	48	288	1	288
8	6	6	48	288	5	1,440
			Total Minimum Daily Cost (ILS)			6,336

The business problem of workforce scheduling concerns scheduling workers in a way that satisfies resource needs while minimizing costs. This is a constrained optimization problem requiring an integer solution. We use integer programming, a type of mathematical programming, to obtain the optimal workforce schedule for the bank. Inputs to the program include results from the queueing model, information about workforce shifts, and salaries paid to workers in each shift. Table 6.2 and figure 6.8 show the optimal call center solution obtained through integer programming.[3]

---

[3] Mathematical programming methods for optimal shift scheduling date back to the work of Dantzig (1954). Let a_{ij} be 1 if shift type j includes hour i and be zero otherwise. Let c_j be the cost of shift type j. And let the decision variable x_j be the number of call center operators to be scheduled for shift type j. Hourly workloads are expressed in terms of the number of call center operators needed: b_j. We define a constrained optimization problem with an objective function to be minimized. For call center shift scheduling, we minimize total call operator costs subject to constraints defined by hourly needs:

$$\textbf{Minimize}\ \sum_{ij} c_i x_j\ \ \textbf{subject to}\ \ \sum_{ij} a_{ij} x_j \geq b_i$$

Hourly worker needs b_i and operators to be scheduled for shifts x_j are constrained to be whole numbers, making call center scheduling an integer programming problem. For our example, suppose this is a 24-hour call center with six-hour shifts for workers. In particular, there are eight shift types, defined by start times at midnight, 6 a.m., 8 a.m., 10 a.m., noon, 2 p.m., 4 p.m., and 6 p.m. Suppose workers starting shifts at 8 a.m., 10 a.m., and noon make 30 ILS per hour (180 ILS shift cost). Workers starting shifts at 6 a.m., 2 p.m., 4 p.m., and 6 p.m. make 48 ILS per hour (288 ILS shift cost). And workers who start shifts at midnight make 42 ILS per hour (252 ILS shift cost). These data define the elements of a cost vector c_j. To determine the best schedule of call center shifts, we set up the matrix elements a_{ij} and the operators-needed-vector elements b_i. Then we use computer algorithms to solve the integer programming problem. Our objective is to minimize costs, so the best or optimal call center schedule will be the cost-minimizing schedule. The solution to this integer programming problem will show the number of shifts of each type x_j, number of operators available each hour of the day, and the total operator cost. (The conversion rate from Israeli shekels to United States dollars was 1 ILS = 3.61 USD in June 2013.)

Figure 6.8. *Call Center Needs and Optimal Workforce Schedule*

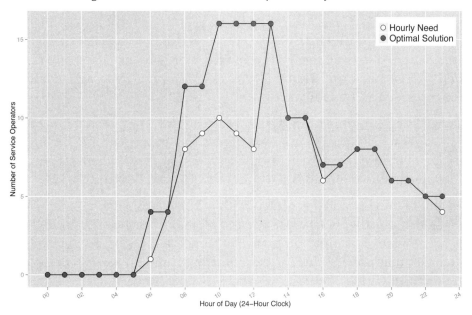

We could test what we are calling the optimal solution through *process simulation* or, more specifically, *discrete event simulation*. We imagine that callers arrive according to a random Poisson process and that service operators continue to provide services as they have in the past, serving approximately fifteen calls per minute. We run a computer program that behaves as callers and service operators have behaved in the past. The wait-time output from the program could the be displayed in wait-time ribbons for management review.

Another way to build confidence in a proposed solution and to explore alternative solutions is to vary inputs to the integer programming algorithm. That is, we test the utility or stability of the solution in the face of varying inputs for staffing needs. Within operations research and the mathematical programming literature, this is called *sensitivity testing.*

Discussion of workforce scheduling methods is provided by Ernst et al. (2004). Aksin, Armony, and Mehrotra (2007) review methods for call center management. For statistical approaches to workforce scheduling that move beyond the standard Erlang C model, see Brown et al. (2005). General discussion of queueing theory is provided by Kleinrock (2009) and Gross, Shortle, Thompson, and Harris (2008). Relevant programming methods in R are provided by Canadilla (2013).

Mathematical programming is a set of constrained optimization methods with applications across many areas of business and economics. For further reading in the area of mathematical programming, see Williams (1999) and R documentation in Braun and Murdoch (2007) and Berkelaar (2013).

Sensitivity testing can be executed within a statistical simulation environment, such as provided by Alfons, Templ, and Filzmoser (2010). Matloff (2011) provides a sample program for simulating a single-server queue, demonstrating possibilities for discrete event simulation with the R programming environment.

The R program in exhibit 6.1 shows how to read the data for "Anonymous Bank," as well as information for call center shifts. The program sets up an hours-by-shift matrix and uses a queueing theory model to estimate the operators-needed-vector for each hour of the day. To determine the optimal or cost-minimizing schedule, the program utilizes an integer programming algorithm. The solution, reported in tables and figures, shows the number of shifts of each type, the number of operators scheduled for each hour of the day, and the total operator cost for the day. The program draws upon R packages provided by Grolemund and Wickham (2013), Wickham and Chang (2013), Canadilla (2013), and Berkelaar (2013). For the plotting of wait-time ribbons, the program calls upon utility functions in appendix exhibits C.3 and C.4.

Exhibit 6.1. *Call Center Scheduling Problem and Solution*

```
# Workforce Scheduling for Anonymous Bank Call Center

library(lubridate)  # date functions
library(grid)  # graphics utilities needed for split-plotting
library(ggplot2)  # graphics package with ribbon plot
library(queueing)  # queueing functions, including Erlang C
library(lpSolve)  # linear programming package
load("mtpa_split_plotting_utilities.Rdata")  # utilities based on grid graphics
load("mtpa_wait_time_ribbon_utility.Rdata")  # wait-time ribbon plot

put.title.on.plots <- TRUE  # put title on wait-time ribbon plots

# The call center data from "Anonymous Bank" in Israel were provided
# by Avi Mandelbaum, with the help of Ilan Guedj.
# data source: http://ie.technion.ac.il/serveng/callcenterdata/index.html
# variable names and definitions from documentation
# VRU  Voice Response Unit automated service
# vru.line  6 digits Each entering phone-call is first routed through a VRU:
#           There are 6 VRUs labeled AA01 to AA06. Each VRU has several lines
#           labeled 1-16. There are a total of 65 lines. Each call is assigned
#           a VRU number and a line number.
# call.id  unique call identifier
# customer.id  unique identifier for existing customer, zero for non-customer
# priority  0 or 1 for inidentified or regular customers
#           2 for priority customers who receive advanced position in queue
# type  type of service
#       PS  regular activity (coded 'PS' for 'Peilut Shotefet')
#       PE  regular activity in English (coded 'PE' for 'Peilut English')
#       IN  internet consulting (coded 'IN' for 'Internet')
#       NE  stock exchange activity (coded 'NE' for 'Niarot Erech')
#       NW  potential customer getting information
#       TT  customers who left a message asking the bank to return their call
#           but, while the system returned their call, the calling-agent became
#           busy hence the customers were put on hold in the queue.
# date  year-month-day
# vru_entry  time that the phone-call enters the call-center or VRU
# vru_exit  time of exit from VRU directly to service or to queue
# vru_time  time in seconds spent in the VRU
#           (calculated by exit_time  entry_time)
# q_start  time of joining the queue (00:00:00 for customers who abandon VRU
#          or do not enter the queue)
# q_exit  time in seconds of exiting queue to receive service or abandonment
# q_time  time spent in queue (calculated by q_exit  q_start)
# outcome  AGENT = service
#          HANG = hang up
#          PHANTOM = a virtual call to be ignored
# ser_start  time of beginning of service by agent
# ser_exit  time of end of service by agent
# ser_time  service duration in seconds (calculated by ser_exit  ser_start)
# server  name of agent, NO_SERVER if no service provided
```

```
# focus upon February 1999
call.center.input.data <- read.table("data_anonymous_bank_february.txt",
  header = TRUE, colClasses = c("character","integer","numeric",
  "integer","character","character","character","character","integer",
  "character","character","integer","factor","character","character",
  "integer","character"))

# check data frame object and variable values
print(summary(call.center.input.data))

# delete PHANTOM calls
call.center.data <- subset(call.center.input.data, subset = (outcome != "PHANTOM"))

# negative VRU times make no sense... drop these rows from data frame
call.center.data <- subset(call.center.data, subset = (vru_time >= 0))

# calculate wait time as sum of vru_time and q_time
call.center.data$wait_time <-
  call.center.data$vru_time + call.center.data$q_time

# define date variable
call.center.data$date <- ymd(call.center.data$date)

# identify day of the week 1 = Sunday ... 7 = Saturday
call.center.data$day_of_week <- wday(call.center.data$date)
call.center.data$day_of_week <- factor(call.center.data$day_of_week,
  levels = c(1:7), labels = c("Sunday","Monday","Tuesday",
  "Wednesday","Thursday","Friday","Saturday"))

# check frequency of calls by day of week
print(table(call.center.data$day_of_week))

# decompose date into list structure and extract the hour
time.list <- strsplit(call.center.data$vru_entry,":")
call.hour <- numeric(nrow(call.center.data))
for (index.for.call in 1:nrow(call.center.data))
  call.hour[index.for.call] <- as.numeric(time.list[[index.for.call]][1])
call.center.data$call_hour <- call.hour

# check frequency of calls by hour and day of week
print(with(call.center.data, table(day_of_week, call_hour)))

# select first week of February 1999 for data visualization and analysis
# that week began on Monday, February 1 and ended on Sunday, February 7
selected.week <- subset(call.center.data, subset = (date < ymd("990208")))

# loop for day of week ignoring Saturdays in Israel
day.of.week.list <- c("Monday","Tuesday",
  "Wednesday","Thursday","Friday","Sunday")
```

```
# wait-time ribbon plots for the six selected days
# call upon utility function wait.time.ribbon
# the utility makes use of grid split-plotting
# place ribbon plot and text table/plot on each file
# each plot goes to its own external pdf file
for(index.day in seq(along=day.of.week.list)) {
  this.day.of.week <- day.of.week.list[index.day]
  pdf(file = paste("fig_operations_management_ribbon_",
  tolower(this.day.of.week),".pdf",sep=""), width = 11, height = 8.5)
  if(put.title.on.plots) {
    ribbon.plot.title <- paste(this.day.of.week,"Call Center Operations")
    }
    else {
    ribbon.plot.title <- ""
    }
  selected.day <- subset(selected.week,
    subset = (day_of_week == this.day.of.week),
    select = c("call_hour","wait_time","ser_time","server"))
  colnames(selected.day) <- c("hour","wait","service","server")
  wait.time.ribbon(wait.service.data = selected.day,
    title = ribbon.plot.title,
    use.text.tagging = TRUE, wait.time.goal = 30, wait.time.max = 90,
    plotting.min = 0, plotting.max = 250)
  dev.off()
  }

# select Wednesdays in February for the queueing model
wednesdays <- subset(call.center.data, subset = (day_of_week == "Wednesday"))

# compute arrival rate of calls as calls for hour
# we do not use table() here because some hours could have zero calls
calls.for.hour <- numeric(24)
for(index.for.hour in 1:24) {
# 24-hour clock has first hour coded as zero in input data file
  coded.index.for.hour <- index.for.hour - 1
  this.hour.calls <-
    subset(wednesdays, subset = (call_hour == coded.index.for.hour))
  if(nrow(this.hour.calls) > 0)
    calls.for.hour[index.for.hour] <- nrow(this.hour.calls)
  }

# compute arrival rate as average number of calls into VRU per hour
hourly.arrival.rate <- calls.for.hour/4  # four Wednesdays in February

# service times can vary hour-by-hour due to differences
# in service requests and individuals calling hour-by-hour
# begin by selecting calls that receive service
wednesdays.served <- subset(wednesdays, subset = (server != "NO_SERVER"))

hourly.mean.service.time <- numeric(24)
served.for.hour <- numeric(24)
```

```
for(index.for.hour in 1:24) {
# 24-hour clock has first hour coded as zero in input data file
  coded.index.for.hour <- index.for.hour - 1
  this.hour.calls <-
    subset(wednesdays.served, subset = (call_hour == coded.index.for.hour))
  if(nrow(this.hour.calls) > 0) {
    served.for.hour[index.for.hour] <- nrow(this.hour.calls)
    hourly.mean.service.time[index.for.hour] <- mean(this.hour.calls$ser_time)
    }
  }

# hourly service rate given the current numbers of service operators
hourly.served.rate <- served.for.hour/4  # four Wednesdays in February

# build data frame for plotting arrival and service rates
hour <- 1:24  # hour for horizontal axix of line chart
type <- rep("Arrived", length = 24)
value <- hourly.arrival.rate
arrival.data.frame <- data.frame(hour, value, type)
type <- rep("Served", length = 24)
value <- hourly.served.rate
service.data.frame <- data.frame(hour, value, type)
arrival.service.data.frame <- rbind(arrival.data.frame, service.data.frame)

pdf(file = "fig_operations_management_wednesdays_arrived_served.pdf",
  width = 11, height = 8.5)
plotting.object <- ggplot(data = arrival.service.data.frame,
  aes(x = hour, y = value, fill = type)) +
  geom_line() +
  geom_point(size = 4, shape = 21) +
  scale_x_continuous(breaks = c(1,3,5,7,9,11,13,15,17,19,21,23,25),
    labels =
      c("00","02","04","06","08","10","12","14","16","18","20","22","24")) +
  theme(axis.text.x = element_text(angle = 30, hjust = 1, vjust = 1)) +
  labs(x = "Hour of Day (24-Hour Clock)", y = "Average Calls per Hour") +
  scale_fill_manual(values = c("yellow","dark green"),
    guide = guide_legend(title = NULL))  +
  theme(legend.position = c(1,1), legend.justification = c(1,1)) +
  theme(legend.text = element_text(size=15)) +
  coord_fixed(ratio = 1/10)
print(plotting.object)
dev.off()

# examine service times per service operator
# for hours with no service time information use the mean as value
hourly.mean.service.time <-
  ifelse((hourly.mean.service.time == 0),
    mean(wednesdays.served$ser_time),
    hourly.mean.service.time)
# compute service rate noting that there are 3600 seconds in an hour
# adding 60 seconds to each mean service time for time between calls
# this 60 seconds is the wrap up time or time an service agent remains
# unavailable to answer a new call after a call has been completed
```

```
hourly.service.rate <- 3600/(hourly.mean.service.time + 60)

# we observe that mean service times do not vary that much hour-by-hour
# so we use the mean hourly service rate in queueing calculations
# mean(hourly.service.rate) is 14.86443
# so we use 15 calls per hour as the rate for one service operator
SERVICE.RATE <- 15

# C_erlang function from the queueing package
# inputs c = number of servers
#        r = ratio of rate of arrivals and rate of service
# returns the propability of waiting in queue because all servers are busy
# let us set a target for the probability of waiting in queue to be 0.50
# using while-loop iteration we determine the number of servers needed
# we do this for each hour of the day knowing the hourly arrival rate

PROBABILITY.GOAL <- 0.50
servers.needed <- integer(24)  # initialize to zero
for(index.for.hour in 1:24) {
  if (hourly.arrival.rate[index.for.hour] > 0) {
    erlang.probability <- 1.00  # intialization prior to entering while-loop
    while (erlang.probability > PROBABILITY.GOAL) {
      servers.needed[index.for.hour] <- servers.needed[index.for.hour] + 1
      erlang.probability <- C_erlang(c = servers.needed[index.for.hour],
          r = hourly.arrival.rate[index.for.hour]/SERVICE.RATE)
      }  # end while-loop for defining servers needed given probability goal
    }  # end if-block for hours with calls
  }  # end for-loop for the hour
# the result for servers.needed is obtained as
# 1  1  1  0  1  1  1  4  8  9 10  9  8 16 10 10  6  7  8  8  6  6  5  4
# we will assume the bank call center will be closed hours 00 through 05
# but use the other values as the bank's needed numbers of servers
servers.needed[1:6] <- 0
cat("\n","----- Hourly Operator Requirements -----","\n")
print(servers.needed)
# read in case data
bank.shifts.data.frame <- read.csv("data_anonymous_bank_shifts.csv")
# examine the structure of the case data frame
print(str(bank.shifts.data.frame))
constraint.matrix <- as.matrix(bank.shifts.data.frame[,3:10])
cat("\n","----- Call Center Shift Constraint Matrix -----","\n")
print(constraint.matrix)
# six-hour shift salaries in Israeli sheqels
# 1 ILS = 3.61 USD in June 2013
# these go into the objective function for integer programing
# with the objective of minimizing total costs
cost.vector <- c(252,288,180,180,180,288,288,288)
call.center.schedule <- lp(const.mat=constraint.matrix,
const.rhs = servers.needed,
const.dir = rep(">=",times=8),
int.vec = 1:8,
objective = cost.vector,
direction = "min")
```

```
# printed summary of the results for the call center problem
ShiftID <- 1:8
StartTime <- c(0,6,8,10,12,2,4,6)
# c("Midnight","6 AM","8 AM","10 AM","Noon","2 PM","4 PM","6 PM")
ShiftDuration <- rep(6,times=8)
HourlyShiftSalary <- c(42,48,30,30,30,48,48,48)
HourlyShiftCost <- call.center.schedule$objective # six x hourly shift salary
Solution <- call.center.schedule$solution
ShiftCost <- call.center.schedule$solution * call.center.schedule$objective
call.center.summary <-
  data.frame(ShiftID,StartTime,ShiftDuration,HourlySalary,
  HourlyShiftCost,Solution,ShiftCost)
cat{"\n\n","Call Center Summary","\n\n")
print(call.center.summary)
# the solution is obtained by print(call.center.schedule)
# or by summing across the hourly solution times the cost objective
 print(call.center.schedule)
cat("\n\n","Call Center Summary Minimum Cost Solution:",sum(ShiftCost),"\n\n")
# build data frame for plotting the solution compared with need
hour <- 1:24  # hour for horizontal axix of line chart
type <- rep("Hourly Need", length = 24)
value <- servers.needed
needs.data.frame <- data.frame(hour, value, type)
type <- rep("Optimal Solution", length = 24)
value <- schedule.fit.to.need
solution.data.frame <- data.frame(hour, value, type)
plotting.data.frame <- rbind(needs.data.frame, solution.data.frame)

# plot the solution... solution match to the workforce need
pdf(file = "fig_operations_management_solution.pdf", width = 11, height = 8.5)
plotting.object <- ggplot(data = plotting.data.frame,
  aes(x = hour, y = value, fill = type)) +
  geom_line() +
  geom_point(size = 4, shape = 21) +
  scale_x_continuous(breaks = c(1,3,5,7,9,11,13,15,17,19,21,23,25),
    labels =
      c("00","02","04","06","08","10","12","14","16","18","20","22","24")) +
  theme(axis.text.x = element_text(angle = 30, hjust = 1, vjust = 1)) +
  labs(x = "Hour of Day (24-Hour Clock)", y = "Number of Service Operators") +
  scale_fill_manual(values = c("white","blue"),
    guide = guide_legend(title = NULL)) +
  theme(legend.position = c(1,1), legend.justification = c(1,1)) +
  theme(legend.text = element_text(size=15)) +
  coord_fixed(ratio = 2/2.25)
print(plotting.object)
dev.off()

# suggestion for the student
# try running a sensitivity test, varying the workforce requirements
# and noting the effect upon the optimal schedule of workers to shifts
# this can be done in a loop
```

7

Text Analytics

Roger Rumack: "Can you fly this plane, and land it?"

Ted Striker: "Surely you can't be serious."

Roger Rumack: "I am serious... and don't call me Shirley."

—LESLIE NIELSEN AS ROGER RUMACK AND
ROBERT HAYS AS TED STRIKER IN *Airplane!* (1980)

Given the quotations that start each chapter, it should come as no surprise that I would choose movies to introduce text analytics. Context is important when working with text. We would not analyze medical records in the same way we analyze political discourse. Sports blog postings are different from song lyrics. As for movies—they are a world unto themselves.

Movies have changed considerably over the years. Films from the 1960s and '70s are my favorites. I can enjoy watching *Butch Cassidy and the Sundance Kid* (1969), *The Conversation* (1974), and *Chinatown* (1974) again and again. My favorite movie of all time is *The Last Picture Show* (1971). There are a few films from the '80s and '90s that I like: *The Year of Living Dangerously* (1982) and *Maverick* (1994), for example. I think *Young Adam* (2003) and the remake of *Alfie* (2004) were well done, and, despite its length, I like *The Curious Case of Benjamin Button* (2008). But many movies since 2000 fail to hold my interest. I watch once and move on. What is it about movies that makes them so different from one decade to the next?

Figure 7.1. *Movie Taglines from The Internet Movie Database (IMDb)*

"30 by 30: Kid Flicks" (2001)
    Zooming In on the Future of Film
    Movies by kids for kids and about kids.

"30 Dates to a Soul Mate" (2012)
    Finding a Soulmate can be tough...finding one in 30 days can be impossible!

"30 Days of Dice Living" (2011)
    Some games will change your life.

"30 for 30" (2009) {Once Brothers (#1.25)}
    Dreams brought them together. Reality tore them apart.

"30 Rock" (2006)
    Work can be such a production.
    Enjoy the ride. (Season 2)
    Comedy night done right
    Duck!! (Season 6)

"30" (2012)
    Only one rule. Never make a vampire under thirty

A good source for information about movies is *The Internet Movie Database* (IMDb). Data from this source are freely available on the Internet and may be downloaded in the form of text files for personal use. For our example, we choose one of the smaller text files from the IMDb, the taglines file.[1]

A movie tagline is composed of one or more comments, phrases, or sentences. The tagline is linked to the movie title and is used on movie posters and video covers. It is included in advertising copy, its sole purpose to encourage people to watch the movie. It is also a source of text describing what a movie is about. Tagline examples from the IMDb are shown in figure 7.1.

In our daily work, data do not come neatly packaged and ready for analysis. We need to gather, organize, and edit the data. This process is brought to

---

[1] About one hundred years of movie tagline information was obtained courtesy of The Internet Movie Database (http://www.imdb.com), used with permission.

the fore in text analysis because the base from which we learn is a body of unstructured text files. We must process text before we can understand what it says. We need to impose structure on text before it can be analyzed and modeled. And for many projects, we have to devise text measures that make sense, measures that are of interest and value to the organization.

Predictive analytics is a numbers game. Text analytics is also a numbers game, but with words rather than numbers as the raw input. The initial materials of text analytics lack the organization of a traditional database. Rather than being divided into discrete records and fields of numeric data, raw text is a string of characters separated by spaces and punctuation marks. There is no data dictionary or index to guide us to the relevant information. There is no organization for the data until we create one. The tools of text analytics help us move from raw text to something that can be searched for answers. We work with words, millions of words transcribed and stored in electronic files. Our job is to turn words into numbers for analysis. Context is important. The order of words and word combinations are important. The meaning of words is important.

The IMDb tagline file represents partially structured text because it follows a particular format. Each observation represents one movie and begins with a pound sign (#). Dates are enclosed in parentheses, and movie titles are in quotation marks. The tagline text itself is free-formatted and may include various forms of punctuation. Exclamation marks are common. There may be extraneous data or comments. These are identified by being enclosed in curly brackets. We make use of this formatting in parsing the tagline data for entry into a text database.

Because we want to look for trends in movies over the years, the date of a movie's release is important information to retain.[2] We define a simple structure for the parsed text. The document collection we create includes items for the movie title alone, the date alone, and the tagline text (as many lines of text as are provided). Also, each item or document is identified by a merged character string consisting of the movie title and date, thus

---

[2] The word *tag* in text analytics refers to information associated with a text document. It is not to be confused with the tagline in the problem we are working. For our data, the date of release is a tag. It provides information describing the document but is not part of the text document itself. As a group, tags are also referred to as document *metadata*.

Figure 7.2. *Movies by Year of Release*

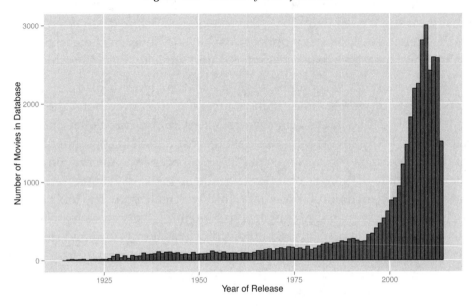

ensuring that *Invasion of the Body Snatchers* (1956), for example, is identified as a separate item from *Invasion of the Body Snatchers* (1978).

To determine the ranges of years to consider in our study, we look at the distribution of release dates in the movie taglines data. The histogram in figure 7.2 shows more than one hundred movies a year from the mid 1970s through 2013 and more than one thousand movies a year from 2003 to 2013. To ensure that we have sufficient numbers of documents for our study, we focus on the last forty years of taglines, going from 1974 to 2013.

In developing text measures for the movie document collection, we take what is affectionately called a *bag-of-words* approach to this analysis. We create one document for each of the forty years by combining the taglines from all movies of each year. A bag-of-words approach does not evaluate the meaning of taglines, the order of words, or word combinations. Rather, it considers each word as an individual item for analysis. A bag-of-words approach is distinct from a natural language processing (NLP) approach to text analytics. A bag-of-words approach makes sense for what we are doing here because we are aggregating taglines from hundreds to thousands of movies in the document for each year. These yearly documents are, in fact, bags of words.

The set of forty documents, one for each year from 1974 to 2013, constitutes the document collection or text *corpus* for analysis. Working with the corpus, we eliminate extra blank characters or whitespace from the documents and convert uppercase characters to lowercase. We remove numbers, punctuation marks, pronouns, and common verb forms like "is" and "has." We create a terms-by-documents matrix for the corpus and identify the most frequently occurring words in that matrix. The top 200 words in the corpus are shown in figure 7.3.

To see if there there is any possibility of detecting trends across the years, we compute the degree to which tagline documents differ from one year to the next. In particular, we compute a matrix of distances between all pairs of document years. Using these distances, we are able to create a picture of the corpus through time, as shown in figure 7.4.[3] We detect a time trend in these data. Oriented as they are in a two-dimensional space, we see documents from the 1970s at the top center, with dates increasing from the top center to the bottom left and bottom center. Then, moving toward the top right-hand side of the plot, we have documents from the most recent years. Documents closer in time are closer to one another in the space displayed in this figure. The pattern of distances among the years' documents suggests that there are time trends in these text data.[4]

How have movies (or, to be more specific, movie taglines) changed across the years? To answer this question, we return to the terms-by-documents matrix. We identify five common groups or clusters of words, defining text measures that we call LOVED, WORLDS, TRUTH, LIFE, and STORY. In figure 7.5 we display these text measures along with the forty years of documents.[5]

---

[3] The picture of documents through time is obtained using a multivariate method known as multidimensional scaling. A two-dimensional picture is sufficient for our purposes here. See Izenman (2008) for a review of multidimensional scaling.

[4] Note that the precise locations of points, axis scaling, and axis orientations in multidimensional scaling are entirely arbitrary. We can rotate, reflect, or rescale axes without distorting the solution. What is important to our interpretation is the relative positioning of the documents in space.

[5] The display showing text measures and documents in the same space is known as a principal components biplot (Gabriel 1971; Gower and Hand 1996).

Figure 7.3. *A Bag of 200 Words from Forty Years of Movie Taglines*

action	adventure	alive	america	american
americas	bad	battle	beautiful	begin
begins	beyond	biggest	black	blood
body	born	boy	boys	business
call	challenge	chance	city	classic
comedy	comes	coming	cop	cops
crazy	crime	dangerous	dark	day
days	dead	deadly	death	deep
desire	destroy	die	director	dream
dreams	earth	easy	enemy	evil
experience	eyes	family	fantasy	fast
father	fear	feel	fight	fighting
film	five	force	forever	forget
found	friend	friends	fun	funny
future	game	girl	girls	guys
hands	happen	happens	hard	head
heart	hell	help	hero	history
home	hope	horror	hot	house
human	journey	justice	kids	kill
killed	killer	killing	king	law
left	legend	life	lifetime	little
live	lives	living	look	looking
lost	lot	love	loved	loves
magic	mans	master	meet	million
mind	money	mother	movie	murder
music	mystery	name	night	nightmare
original	party	passion	past	people
perfect	picture	play	pleasure	power
powerful	race	ready	real	reality
remember	revenge	ride	rock	run
save	school	secret	secrets	seen
sex	sexual	shell	sometimes	son
space	special	stand	star	stars
stop	story	streets	summer	survival
survive	sweet	takes	tale	tell
terrifying	terror	thriller	time	tough
town	true	truth	ultimate	universe
video	war	watch	weapon	welcome
wife	wild	win	woman	women
world	worlds	worst	wrong	york

Figure 7.4. Picture of Text in Time: Forty Years of Movie Taglines

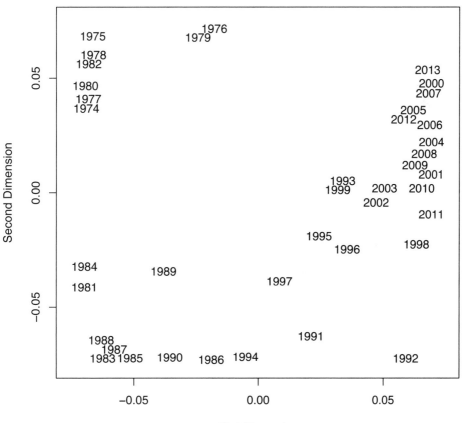

Figure 7.5. *Text Measures and Documents on a Single Graph*

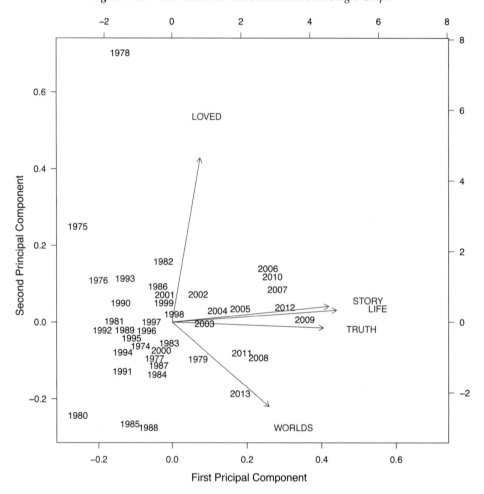

We can use a horizon plot to visualize text measures in time. This is similar to what we do for horizon plots of economic time series. Here we compute standard scores for each text measure and each document year and then plot the resulting multiple time series. The horizon plot for the standardized text measures is shown in figure 7.6.

What is it about movies that makes them so different from one decade to the next? Our analysis of movie taglines from The Internet Movies Database (IMDb) suggests that movies from the turn of the century onward are decidedly different from movies prior to the turn of the century. Text measures suggest a shift in the words used to describe movies. In particular, there seems to be a shift toward true-to-life stories. This could be a reality TV effect worthy of further study. [6]

Text analytics draws from a variety of disciplines, including linguistics, communication and language arts, experimental psychology, political discourse analysis, journalism, computer science, and statistics. And, given the amount of text being gathered and stored by organizations, text analytics is an important and growing area of predictive analytics.

To do text analytics we must find ways to structure text so that it can be understood by computers. The two primary ways to do this are the *bag of words* approach and *natural language processing*. As illustrated in figure 7.7, the original document collection or corpus is in the natural language. We have to parse the corpus, creating commonly formatted expressions, indices, keys, and matrices that are more easily analyzed by computer.

Natural language is what we speak and what we write every day. Natural language processing is more than a matter of collecting individual words. Natural language conveys meaning. Natural language documents contain

---

[6] To answer the original question about trends in movies over the years, we may have more work to do. What we call a reality TV effect could be due to sampling bias because recent entries in the database contain a higher proportion of television shows. Continuing along this line of research, it may make sense to return to the original taglines data and drop all videos associated with television programs. There is also work to be done with the text measures. We used words from the movie taglines corpus to describe the clusters and compute text measures for the words. We start with the words "loved," "worlds," "truth," "life," and "story." For this analysis, each text measure was computed as the percentage of words in a document that match any of the top three words in the cluster (that is, the word defining the cluster and the two words closest to that word). It would be preferable to have more words in the definition of each text measure. Traditional measurement theory tells us that scales with larger numbers of items are more reliable (Gulliksen 1950; Nunnally 1967; Lord and Novick 1968).

Figure 7.6. Horizon Plot of Text Measures across Forty Years of Movie Taglines

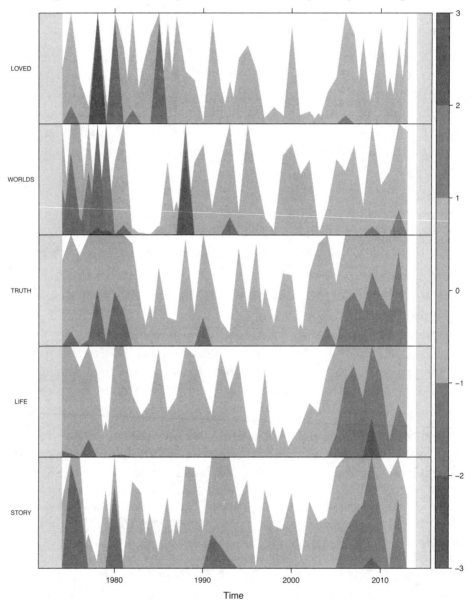

Figure 7.7. From Text Processing to Text Analytics

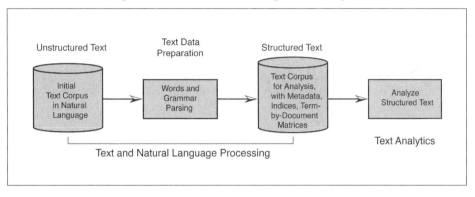

Source: Adapted from Miller (2005).

paragraphs, paragraphs contain sentences, and sentences words. Natural language follows grammatical rules, with many ways to convey the same idea, with exceptions to rules, and rules about exceptions. Words and the rules of grammar comprise the linguistic foundations of text analytics as shown in figure 7.8.

Linguists study natural language, the words and the rules that we use to form meaningful utterances. "Generative grammar" is a general term for the rules; "morphology," "syntax," and "semantics" are more specific terms. Computer programs for natural language processing use linguistic rules to mimic human communication and convert natural language into structured text for further analysis.

Natural language processing is a broad area of academic study itself, and an important area of computational linguistics. The location of words in sentences is a key to understanding text. Words follow a sequence, with earlier words often more important than later words, and with early sentences and paragraphs often more important than later sentences and paragraphs. Words in the title of a document are especially important to understanding the meaning of a document. Some words occur with high frequency and help to define the meaning of a document. Other words, such as the definite article "the" and the indefinite articles "a" and "an," as well as many prepositions and pronouns, occur with high frequency but have little to do

Figure 7.8. Linguistic Foundations of Text Analytics

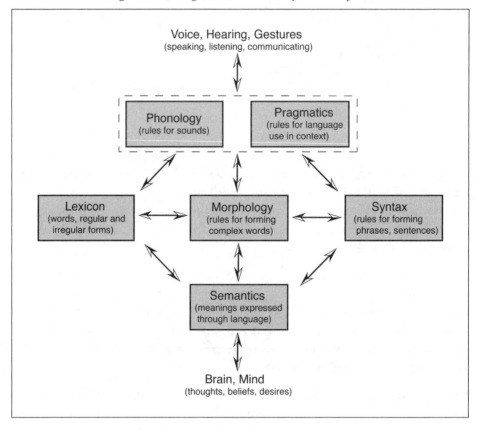

Source: Adapted from Pinker (1999).

with the meaning of a document. These *stop words* are dropped from the analysis.

The features or attributes of text are often associated with terms—collections of words that mean something special. There are collections of words relating to the same concept or word stem. The words "marketer," "marketeer," and "marketing" build on the common word stem "market." There are syntactic structures to consider, such as adjectives followed by nouns and nouns followed by nouns. Most important to text analytics are sequences of words that form terms. The words "New" and "York" have special meaning when combined to form the term "New York." The words "financial" and "analysis" have special meaning when combined to form the term "financial analysis." We often employ *stemming*, which is the identification of word stems, dropping suffixes (and sometimes prefixes) from words. More generally, we are parsing natural language text to arrive at structured text.

In English, it is customary to place the subject before the verb and the object after the verb. In English verb tense is important. The sentence "Daniel carries the Apple computer," can have the same meaning as the sentence "The Apple computer is carried by Daniel." "Apple computer," the object of the active verb "carry" is the subject of the passive verb "is carried." Understanding that the two sentences mean the same thing is an important part of building intelligent text applications.

As we have shown in our movie taglines example, a key step in text analysis is the creation of a terms-by-documents matrix (sometimes called a lexical table). The rows of this data matrix correspond to words or word stems from the document collection, and the columns correspond to documents in the collection. The entry in each cell of a terms-by-documents matrix could be a binary indicator for the presence or absence of a term in a document, a frequency count of the number of times a term is used in a document, or a weighted frequency indicating the importance of a term in a document.

Figure 7.9 illustrates the process of creating a terms-by-documents matrix. The first document comes from Steven Pinker's *Words and Rules* (1999, p. 4), the second from Richard K. Belew's *Finding Out About* (2000, p. 73). Terms correspond to words or word stems that appear in the documents. In this example, each matrix entry represents the number of times a term appears in a document. We treat nouns, verbs, and adjectives similarly in the defini-

Figure 7.9. *Creating a Terms-by-Documents Matrix*

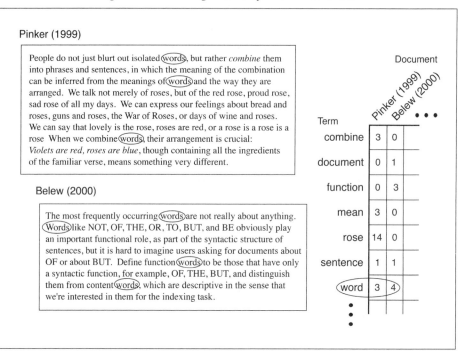

Source: Adapted from Miller (2005).

tion of stems. The stem "combine" represents both the verb "combine" and the noun "combination." Likewise, "function" represents the verb, noun, and adjective form "functional." An alternative system might distinguish among parts of speech, permitting more sophisticated syntactic searches across documents. After being created, the terms-by-documents matrix is like an index, a mapping of document identifiers to terms (keywords or stems) and vice versa. For information retrieval systems or search engines we might also retain information regarding the specific location of terms within documents.

Typical text analytics applications have many more terms than documents, resulting in sparse rectangular terms-by-documents matrices. To obtain meaningful results for text analytics applications, analysts examine the distribution of terms across the document collection. Very low frequency terms, those used in few documents, are dropped from the terms-by-documents matrix, reducing the number of rows in the matrix.

Unsupervised text analytics problems are those for which there is no response or class to be predicted. Rather, as we showed with the movie taglines, the task is to identify common patterns or trends in the data. As part of the task, we may define text measures describing the documents in the corpus.

For supervised text analytics problems there is a response or class of documents to be predicted. We build a model on a training set and test it on a test set. Text classification problems are common. Span filtering has long been a subject of interest as a classification problem, and many e-mail users have benefitted from the efficient algorithms that have evolved in this area. In the context of information retrieval, search engines classify documents as being relevant to the search or not. Useful modeling techniques for text classification include logistic regression, linear discriminant function analysis, classification trees, and support vector machines. Various ensemble or committee methods may be employed.

Automatic text summarization is an area of research and development that can help with information management. Imagine a text processing program with the ability to read each document in a collection and summarize it in a sentence or two, perhaps quoting from the document itself. Today's search engines are providing partial analysis of documents prior to their being displayed. They create automated summaries for fast information retrieval. They recognize common text strings associated with user requests. These applications of text analysis comprise tools of information search that we take for granted as part of our daily lives.

Programs with syntactic processing capabilities, such as IBM's Watson, provide a glimpse of what intelligent agents for text analytics are becoming. These programs perform grammatical parsing with an understanding of the roles of subject, verb, object, and modifier. They know parts of speech (nouns, verbs, adjective, adverbs). And, using identified entities representing people, places, things, and organizations, they perform relationship searches.

Those interested in learning more about text analytics can refer to Jurafsky and Martin (2009), Weiss, Indurkhya, and Zhang (2010) and the edited volume by Srivastava and Sahami (2009). Reviews may be found in Miller (2005), Trybula (1999), Witten, Moffat, and Bell (1999), Meadow, Boyce, and Kraft (2000), Sullivan (2001), Feldman (2002b), and Sebastiani (2002). Hausser (2001) gives an account of generative grammar and computational linguistics. Statistical language learning and natural language processing are discussed by Charniak (1993), Manning and Schütze (1999), and Indurkhya and Damerau (2010).

The writings of Steven Pinker (1994, 1997, 1999) provide insight into grammar and psycholinguistics. Maybury (1997) reviews data preparation for text analytics and the related tasks of source detection, translation and conversion, information extraction, and information exploitation. Detection relates to identifying relevant sources of information; conversion and translation involve converting from one medium or coding form to another.

Belew (2000), Meadow, Boyce, and Kraft (2000) and the edited volume by Baeza-Yates and Ribeiro-Neto (1999) provide reviews of computer technologies for information retrieval, which depend upon text classification, among other technologies and algorithms.

Authorship identification, a problem addressed a number of years ago in the statistical literature by Mosteller and Wallace (1984), continues to be an active area of research (Joula 2008). Merkl (2002) provides discussion of clustering techniques, which explore similarities between documents and group documents into classes. Dumais (2004) reviews latent semantic analysis and statistical approaches to extracting relationships among terms in a document collection.

Special topics from computational linguistics provide additional insights into working with text. Text tiling (Hearst 1997) involves the automatic division of text documents into blocks or units for further analysis. Adjacent blocks of text are more likely to have words in common with one another and thus be topically related. Text tiling can be used in text summarization and information retrieval, as well as stylistic analysis of literature and discourse (Youmans 1990; Youmans 1991).

Modeling techniques for unsupervised text analytics include multivariate methods such as multidimensional scaling and cluster analysis, which are based upon dissimilarity or distance measures, and principal components analysis, which works from covariance or correlation matrices. Dissimilarity and distance measures and cluster analysis are discussed by Meyer (2013a, 2013b) and Kaufman and Rousseeuw (1990) and Izenman (2008), with R code provided by Maechler (2013a). For multidimensional scaling, see Davison (1992), Cox and Cox (1994), Everitt and Rabe-Hesketh (1997), Izenman (2008) and Borg and Groenen (2010). Principal components are reviewed in various multivariate texts (Manly 1994; Sharma 1996; Gnanadesikan 1997; Johnson and Wichern 1998; Everitt and Dunn 2001; Seber 2000; Izenman 2008), with biplots discussed by Gabriel (1971) and Gower and Hand (1996).

For an overview of text analytics in R, refer to Feinerer, Hornik, and Meyer (2008), Feinerer and Hornik (2013a), and Feinerer (2013). Of special interest are books that deal with the overlap between linguistics and statistics with R (Baayen 2008; Johnson 2008; Gries 2013). The work of Gries (2009) is of special note as it shows how to work with document corpuses. Text analytics utilities are provided by Grothendieck (2013a, 2013b) and Wickham (2010, 2013b). Understanding regular expression coding in R can be of special value to anyone interested in doing text analytics (Friedl 2006; Wickham 2013b). Dictionary capabilities are provided through an interface to WordNet (Miller 1995; Fellbaum 1998; Feinerer 2012; Feinerer and Hornik 2013b). For fun, we have word clouds with utilities for plotting non-overlapping text in scatter plots (Fellows 2013b; Fellows 2013a). A word cloud for more than three thousand lines of R code from this book is shown in figure 7.10.

Exhibit 8.1 shows the R program for working with the movie taglines data. There is initial data preparation, parsing of the partially structured text data. These parsed data were used to define the corpus. Text measures are computed on the corpus. Results are presented using multivariate methods for data visualization. The program ends with the word cloud. The program draws upon R packages provided by Feinerer and Hornik (2013a), Wickham (2013b), Wickham and Chang (2013), Sarkar and Andrews (2013), Maechler (2013a), and Fellows (2013a).

Figure 7.10. An R Programmer's Word Cloud

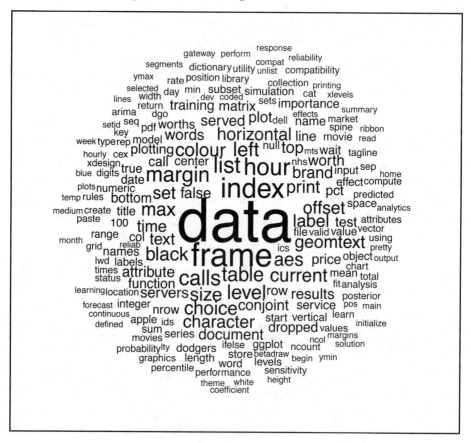

Exhibit 7.1. *Text Analytics of Movie Taglines*

```
# Text Analysis of Movie Tag Lines

library(tm)  # text mining and document management
library(stringr)  # character manipulation with regular expressions

library(grid)  # grid graphics utilities
library(ggplot2)  # graphics
library(latticeExtra)  # package used for text horizon plot

library(wordcloud)  # provides utility for plotting non-overlapping text
library(cluster)  # cluster analysis

# standardization needed for text measures
standardize <- function(x) {(x - mean(x)) / sd(x)}

# convert to bytecodes to avoid "invalid multibyte string" messages
bytecode.convert <- function(x) {iconv(enc2utf8(x), sub = "byte")}

# NLINES <- 21  # for development and test runs
# input.data.file.name <- "taglines_list_sample.txt"
#   scan("taglines_list_sample.txt", what = "character")  # development runs
# nlines_to_read <- 21  # for development and test runs

# there are 345317 records in the full taglines data file
# the number of lines in the input data file
# or maximum number of lines to read
NLINES <- 345317
input.data.file.name <- "taglines_copy_data.txt"  # production runs
# read the data in blocks of nlines_to_read at a time
nlines_to_read <- 10000  # size of block of lines to read
# debug print was used during the code development process
debub.print.mode <- FALSE
debug.print <- function(title,date,tagline,status) {
  cat("\n title =",title,"  date = ", date," tagline",
    tagline, " status = ",status,"\n")
  }

# this user-defined function shows how R can be used to parse text input
tagline.parser <- function(input.list) {
# where we start depends upon the status on entry
# tagline parser can only be in one status at a time
# begin
# indicator
# title (actually a title and date status)
# moretitle (another title and data status, but following a previous title)
# tagline
# comment
# data are not clean... if you get a new movie indicator "#" start a new movie
# we may lose a few movies this way... but that is better than editing a file
# with about 40 thousand movies..
```

```
# at this time all valid dates should look be six characters long
# four numbers surrounded by parentheses
# lets use The Birth of a Nation (1915) as the earliest possible valid date
# and the current year as the latest possible valid date
# obtained by as.numeric(format(Sys.time(), "%Y"))
valid.years <- 1915:as.numeric(format(Sys.time(), "%Y"))
valid.years.strings.four <- paste("(",as.character(valid.years),sep="")

    text <- input.list[[1]]
    status <- input.list[[2]]
    title <- input.list[[3]]
    date <- input.list[[4]]
    tagline <- input.list[[5]]
    nitems <- length(text)
    ncount <- 1  # initialize on entry
    tagline_data.store <- NULL

    while(ncount < nitems) {
# debug printing was used in the development and testing of parsing logic
        if (debub.print.mode) debug.print(title,date,tagline,status)
        if (status == "indicator" | status == "begin") {
          if (ncount <= nitems) {
            ncount <- ncount + 1
            status <- "initialtitle"
            title <- " "  # blank title to start
            date <- " "   # blank date to start
            tagline <- " "  # blank tagline to start
            }
          }

        if (status == "initialtitle") {
          if (ncount <= nitems) {
            title <- text[ncount]
            ncount <- ncount + 1
            if (ncount <= nitems) {
              test_date <- text[ncount]
              if (substring(test_date,1,5) %in% valid.years.strings.four) {
                date <- test_date
                ncount <- ncount + 1
                status <- "tagline"
                }
              if (!(substring(test_date,1,5) %in% valid.years.strings.four)) {
                if (test_date == "#") {
                  status <- "indicator"
                  }
                if (test_date != "#") {
                  title <- paste(title, test_date)
                  ncount <- ncount + 1
                  status <- "moretitle"
                  }
                }
              }
            }
          }
```

```
if (status == "moretitle") {
  if (ncount <= nitems) {
    ncount <- ncount + 1
    if (ncount <= nitems) {
      test_date <- text[ncount]
      if (substring(test_date,1,5) %in% valid.years.strings.four) {
        date <- test_date
        ncount <- ncount + 1
        status <- "tagline"
        }
      if (!(substring(test_date,1,5) %in% valid.years.strings.four)) {
        if (test_date == "#") {
            status <- "indicator"
            }
        if (test_date != "#") {
            title <- paste(title, test_date)
            ncount <- ncount + 1
            }
        }
      }
    }
  }

  if (status == "tagline") {
    if (ncount <= nitems) {
      new_text <- text[ncount]
      if (new_text == "#") {
        tagline_data.store <- rbind(tagline_data.store,
          data.frame(title, date, tagline, stringsAsFactors = FALSE))
          status <- "indicator"
        }
      if (new_text != "#") {
        if (substring(new_text,1,1) == "{") {
          ncount <- ncount + 1
          status <- "comment"
          }
        if (substring(new_text,1,1) != "{") {
          tagline <- paste(tagline, new_text)
          ncount <- ncount + 1
          }
        }
      }
    }

  if (status == "comment") {
    if (ncount <= nitems) {
      new_text <- text[ncount]
      if (substring(new_text,nchar(new_text),nchar(new_text)) == "}") {
        ncount <- ncount + 1
        status <- "tagline"
        }
```

```
           if (substring(new_text,nchar(new_text),nchar(new_text)) != "}") {
             ncount <- ncount + 1
             }
           }
         }
  } # end of primary while-loop
list(tagline_data.store, status, title, date, tagline) # return list
} # end of function

cat("\n\n","NUMBER OF LINES READ: ")

skip <- 0 # initialize the number of lines to skip
nlines_read_so_far <- 0 # intitialze number of lines read so far


status <- "begin" # initial status
title <- " "  # blank title to start
date <- " "   # blank date to start
tagline <- " "  # blank tagline to start

data.store <- NULL # initialize the data frame for storing text data

while(nlines_read_so_far < NLINES)  {

if ((NLINES - nlines_read_so_far) < nlines_to_read)
  nlines_to_read <- (NLINES - nlines_read_so_far)

text <- scan(file = input.data.file.name, what = "character",
    skip = nlines_read_so_far, nlines = nlines_to_read)

# convert individual text items to bytecodes
# to avoid to avoid "invalid multibyte string" error messages going forward
text <- bytecode.convert(text)

input.list <- list(text, status, title, date, tagline)

# parse this block of text with the tagline parser function
output.list <- tagline.parser(input.list)

  new_data_for_store <- output.list[[1]]
  status <- output.list[[2]]
  title <- output.list[[3]]
  date <- output.list[[4]]
  tagline <- output.list[[5]]

  data.store <- rbind(data.store, new_data_for_store)

  nlines_read_so_far <- nlines_read_so_far + nlines_to_read

  cat(" ","nlines_read_so_far:",nlines_read_so_far)
  }
# if there is full movie info in output list
# add this last movie to the end of the data.store
```

```
if ((!is.null(output.list[[3]])) &
   (!is.null(output.list[[4]])) &
   (!is.null(output.list[[5]]))) {
       title <- output.list[[3]]
       date <- output.list[[4]]
       tagline <- output.list[[5]]
     data.store <- rbind(data.store,
       data.frame(title, date, tagline, stringsAsFactors = FALSE))
  }

# data cleaning... check the date field...
# if it does not start with "(" or end with ")"
# strip any character other than numeric in the date field
# using regular experessions coding and the replace function from stringr
data.store$replace.date <- str_replace_all(data.store$date, "[^.(0-9)]", "")

# at this time all valid dates should look be six characters long
# four numbers surrounded by parentheses
# lets use The Birth of a Nation (1915) as the earliest possible valid date
# and the current year as the latest possible valid date
# obtained by as.numeric(format(Sys.time(), "%Y"))
valid.years <- 1915:as.numeric(format(Sys.time(), "%Y"))
valid.years.strings <- paste("(",as.character(valid.years),")",sep="")

# valid observations must have dates with valid.years.strings
data.store$valid <-
  ifelse((data.store$replace.date %in% valid.years.strings),"YES","NO")

# use the subset of movies with valid data
valid.data.store <- subset(data.store, subset = (valid == "YES"))
# add date field to title field to create unique identifier for each movie
valid.data.store$movie <- paste(valid.data.store$title, valid.data.store$date)

# strip parenteses from replace.date and create an integer variable for year
valid.data.store$replace.date <-
  str_replace(valid.data.store$replace.date,"[(]","")
valid.data.store$replace.date <-
  str_replace(valid.data.store$replace.date,"[)]","")
valid.data.store$year <- as.integer(valid.data.store$replace.date)
# merge title and tagline text into new movie text variable for text analysis
valid.data.store$text <-
  paste(valid.data.store$title, valid.data.store$tagline)
# drop replace.date and reorder variables for text analysis
# at this point we have one large data frame with text columns
movies <- valid.data.store[,c("movie","year","title","tagline","text")]

# plot frequency of movies by year
pdf(file = "fig_text_movies_by_year_histogram.pdf", width = 11, height = 8.5)
ggplot.object <- ggplot(data = movies, aes(x = year)) +
  geom_histogram(binwidth = 1, fill = "blue", colour = "black") +
    labs(x = "Year of Release",
         y = "Number of Movies in Database") +
         coord_fixed(ratio = 1/50)
```

```
ggplot.print.with.margins(ggplot.object.name = ggplot.object,
  left.margin.pct=10, right.margin.pct=10,
  top.margin.pct=10,bottom.margin.pct=10)
dev.off()

# let us work with movies from 1974 to 2013
# creating an aggregate tagline_text collection for each year of interest
years.list <- 1974:2013
document.collection <- NULL  # initialize
for (index.for.year in seq(along=years.list)) {

  working.year.data.frame =
    subset(movies, subset = (year == years.list[index.for.year]))

  tagline_text <- NULL
  for(index.for.movie in seq(along = working.year.data.frame$movie))
    tagline_text <-
      paste(tagline_text, working.year.data.frame$tagline[index.for.movie])

  document <- PlainTextDocument(x = tagline_text, author = "Tom",
    description = paste("movie taglines for ",
    as.character(years.list[index.for.year]),sep = ""),
    id = paste("movies_",as.character(years.list[index.for.year]),sep=""),
    heading = "taglines",
    origin = "IMDb", language = "en_US",
    localmetadata = list(year = years.list[index.for.year]))

# give each created document a unique name
  if (years.list[index.for.year] == 1974) Y1974 <- document
  if (years.list[index.for.year] == 1975) Y1975 <- document
  if (years.list[index.for.year] == 1976) Y1976 <- document
  if (years.list[index.for.year] == 1977) Y1977 <- document
  if (years.list[index.for.year] == 1978) Y1978 <- document
  if (years.list[index.for.year] == 1979) Y1979 <- document
  if (years.list[index.for.year] == 1980) Y1980 <- document
  if (years.list[index.for.year] == 1981) Y1981 <- document
  if (years.list[index.for.year] == 1982) Y1982 <- document
  if (years.list[index.for.year] == 1983) Y1983 <- document
  if (years.list[index.for.year] == 1984) Y1984 <- document
  if (years.list[index.for.year] == 1985) Y1985 <- document
  if (years.list[index.for.year] == 1986) Y1986 <- document
  if (years.list[index.for.year] == 1987) Y1987 <- document
  if (years.list[index.for.year] == 1988) Y1988 <- document
  if (years.list[index.for.year] == 1989) Y1989 <- document
  if (years.list[index.for.year] == 1990) Y1990 <- document
  if (years.list[index.for.year] == 1991) Y1991 <- document
  if (years.list[index.for.year] == 1992) Y1992 <- document
  if (years.list[index.for.year] == 1993) Y1993 <- document
  if (years.list[index.for.year] == 1994) Y1994 <- document
  if (years.list[index.for.year] == 1995) Y1995 <- document
  if (years.list[index.for.year] == 1996) Y1996 <- document
  if (years.list[index.for.year] == 1997) Y1997 <- document
```

```
    if (years.list[index.for.year] == 1998) Y1998 <- document
    if (years.list[index.for.year] == 1999) Y1999 <- document
    if (years.list[index.for.year] == 2000) Y2000 <- document
    if (years.list[index.for.year] == 2001) Y2001 <- document
    if (years.list[index.for.year] == 2002) Y2002 <- document
    if (years.list[index.for.year] == 2003) Y2003 <- document
    if (years.list[index.for.year] == 2004) Y2004 <- document
    if (years.list[index.for.year] == 2005) Y2005 <- document
    if (years.list[index.for.year] == 2006) Y2006 <- document
    if (years.list[index.for.year] == 2007) Y2007 <- document
    if (years.list[index.for.year] == 2008) Y2008 <- document
    if (years.list[index.for.year] == 2009) Y2009 <- document
    if (years.list[index.for.year] == 2010) Y2010 <- document
    if (years.list[index.for.year] == 2011) Y2011 <- document
    if (years.list[index.for.year] == 2012) Y2012 <- document
    if (years.list[index.for.year] == 2013) Y2013 <- document
    } # end of for-loop for selected years

document.collection <- c(Y1974,Y1975,Y1976,Y1977,Y1978,Y1979,
    Y1980,Y1981,Y1982,Y1983,Y1984,Y1985,Y1986,Y1987,Y1988,Y1989,
    Y1990,Y1991,Y1992,Y1993,Y1994,Y1995,Y1996,Y1997,Y1998,Y1999,
    Y2000,Y2001,Y2002,Y2003,Y2004,Y2005,Y2006,
    Y2007,Y2008,Y2009,Y2010,Y2011,Y2012,Y2013)

# strip whitspace from the documents in the collection
document.collection <- tm_map(document.collection, stripWhitespace)

# convert uppercase to lowercase in the document collection
document.collection <- tm_map(document.collection, tolower)

# remove numbers from the document collection
document.collection <- tm_map(document.collection, removeNumbers)

# remove punctuation from the document collection
document.collection <- tm_map(document.collection, removePunctuation)

# using a standard list, remove English stopwords from the document collection
document.collection <- tm_map(document.collection,
    removeWords, stopwords("english"))

# there is more we could do in terms of data preparation
# stemming... looking for contractions... pronoun possessives...

# we take what is clearly a "bag of words" approach here
# the workhorse technique will be TermDocumentMatrix()
# for creating a terms-by-documents matrix across the document collection
initial.movies.tdm <- TermDocumentMatrix(document.collection)

# remove sparse terms from the matrix and report the most common terms
# looking for additional stop words and stop word contractions to drop
examine.movies.tdm <- removeSparseTerms(initial.movies.tdm, sparse = 0.25)
top.words <- Terms(examine.movies.tdm)
print(top.words)
```

```
# an analysis of this initial list of top terms shows a number of word
# contractions which we might like to drop from further analysis,
# recognizing them as stop words to be dropped from the document collection
more.stop.words <- c("cant","didnt","doesnt","dont","goes","isnt","hes",
  "shes","thats","theres","theyre","wont","youll","youre","youve")
document.collection <- tm_map(document.collection,
  removeWords, more.stop.words)

# create terms-by-documents matrix across the final document collection
movies.tdm <- TermDocumentMatrix(document.collection)

# save movie documents and document collection (corpus)
save("movies","document.collection","movies.tdm",
  file = "000_movies_data.Rdata")
# remove sparse terms from the matrix and report the most common terms
examine.movies.tdm <- removeSparseTerms(movies.tdm, sparse = 0.25)
top.words <- Terms(examine.movies.tdm)
print(top.words)  # the result of this is a bag of 200 words
# now comes a test...
# does looking at taglines hold promise as a way of identifying movie trends?
# if it does, then years closest in time should be closest to one
# another in a text measurement space as reflected, say,
# by multidimensional scaling...
# create a dictionary of the top words from the corpus
top.words.dictionary <- Dictionary(c(top.words))

# create terms-by-documents matrix using the mtpa.Dictionary
top.words.movies.tdm <- TermDocumentMatrix(document.collection,
  list(dictionary = top.words.dictionary))

# dissimilarity measures and multidimensional scaling
# with wordlayout from the wordcloud package for non-overlapping labels
pdf(file = "fig_text_mds_1974_2013.pdf", width = 7, height = 7)
years.dissimilarity.matrix <-
  dissimilarity(x = top.words.movies.tdm, y = NULL, method = "cosine")
years.mds.solution <- cmdscale(years.dissimilarity.matrix, k = 2, eig = TRUE)
x <- years.mds.solution$points[,1]
y <- - years.mds.solution$points[,2]  # rotated to be consistent with biplot
w <- c("1974","1975","1976","1977","1978","1979",
  "1980","1981","1982","1983","1984","1985","1986",
  "1987","1988","1989","1990","1991","1992","1993",
  "1994","1995","1996","1997","1998","1999","2000",
  "2001","2002","2003","2004","2005","2006","2007",
  "2008","2009","2010","2011","2012","2013")
plot(x,y,type="n", xlim = c(-0.075,0.075), ylim = c(-0.075,0.075),
  xlab = "First Dimension", ylab = "Second Dimension")
lay <- wordlayout(x, y, w, xlim = c(-0.075,0.075), ylim = c(-0.075,0.075))
text(lay[,1]+.5*lay[,3],lay[,2]+.5*lay[,4],w)
dev.off()
# classification of words into groups for further analysis
# use transpose of the terms-by-document matrix and cluster analysis
words.distance.object <-
  dist(x = as.matrix(top.words.movies.tdm), method = "euclidean")
```

```
pdf(file = "fig_text_hcluster_top_words.pdf", width = 11, height = 8.5)
top.words.hierarchical.clustering <-
  agnes(words.distance.object,diss=TRUE,
    metric = "euclidean", stand = FALSE, method = "ward")
plot(top.words.hierarchical.clustering, cex.lab = 0.05)
dev.off()

# hierarchical solution suggests that four or five clusters may work
# examine possible clustering soltions with partitioning
number.of.clusters.test <- NULL
for(number.of.clusters in 2:20) {
  try.words.clustering <- pam(words.distance.object,diss=TRUE,
    metric = "euclidean", stand = FALSE, k = number.of.clusters)
  number.of.clusters.test <-
    rbind(number.of.clusters.test,
      data.frame(number.of.clusters,
        ave.sil.width = try.words.clustering$silinfo$avg.width))
    cat("\n\n","Number of clusters: ",number.of.clusters,
      " Average silhouette width: ",try.words.clustering$silinfo$avg.width,
      "\nKey identified concepts: ",try.words.clustering$medoids,
      "\nCluster average silhouette widths: ")
    print(try.words.clustering$silinfo$clus.avg.widths)
    } # end of for-loop for number-of-clusters test
print(number.of.clusters.test)

# results suggest that five clusters may work best here
# we examine these clusters and give them names corresponding to medoids
top.words.clustering <- pam(words.distance.object,diss=TRUE,
    metric = "euclidean", stand = FALSE, k = 5)

# review the clustering results
print(summary(top.words.clustering))
# the medoid identified through the clustering process
# is an object at the center of the cluster...
# it is used to define the cluster here we identify their names
cat("\nKey Words Identified by Cluster Analysis: \n")
key.word.set <- top.words.clustering$medoids
print(key.word.set)

# convert the distance object to an actual distance matrix
# for doing word searches directly on the matrix calculations
words.distance.matrix <- as.matrix(words.distance.object)

# for each medoid... identify the closest words from distance matrix
# let us choose the two closest words to have five lists of three words
# for further analysis... note that there is some overlap in word sets
for(index.for.key.word in seq(along=key.word.set)) {
  # identify the column for the key word
  key.word.column <-
    words.distance.matrix[,c(key.word.set[index.for.key.word])]
  # sort the key word column by distance
  sorted.key.word.column <- sort(key.word.column)
```

```
# the smallest distance will be the distance of the key word to itself
# so choose the second through tenth words in from the sorted column
print(sorted.key.word.column[1:5])
if (index.for.key.word == 1)
  loved.word.set <- names(sorted.key.word.column[1:3])
if (index.for.key.word == 2)
  worlds.word.set <- names(sorted.key.word.column[1:3])
if (index.for.key.word == 3)
  truth.word.set <- names(sorted.key.word.column[1:3])
if (index.for.key.word == 4)
  life.word.set <- names(sorted.key.word.column[1:3])
if (index.for.key.word == 5)
  story.word.set <- names(sorted.key.word.column[1:3])
}


# turn the word sets into dictionaries for analysis
loved.words.dictionary <- Dictionary(c(loved.word.set))
worlds.words.dictionary <- Dictionary(c(worlds.word.set))
truth.words.dictionary <- Dictionary(c(truth.word.set))
life.words.dictionary <- Dictionary(c(life.word.set))
story.words.dictionary <- Dictionary(c(story.word.set))
# do word counts across the dictionaries
year <- 1974:2013
total.words <- integer(length(year))
loved.words <- integer(length(year))
worlds.words <- integer(length(year))
truth.words <- integer(length(year))
life.words <- integer(length(year))
story.words <- integer(length(year))

for(index.for.document in seq(along=year)) {
  loved.words[index.for.document] <-
    sum(termFreq(document.collection[[index.for.document]],
    control = list(dictionary = loved.words.dictionary)))

  worlds.words[index.for.document] <-
    sum(termFreq(document.collection[[index.for.document]],
    control = list(dictionary = worlds.words.dictionary)))

  truth.words[index.for.document] <-
    sum(termFreq(document.collection[[index.for.document]],
    control = list(dictionary = truth.words.dictionary)))

  life.words[index.for.document] <-
    sum(termFreq(document.collection[[index.for.document]],
    control = list(dictionary = life.words.dictionary)))

  story.words[index.for.document] <-
    sum(termFreq(document.collection[[index.for.document]],
    control = list(dictionary = story.words.dictionary)))

  total.words[index.for.document] <-
    length(movies.tdm[,index.for.document][["i"]])
}
```

```
# gather the results up in a data frame
movie.analytics.data.frame <- data.frame(year, total.words,
  loved.words, worlds.words, truth.words, life.words, story.words)

# compute text measures as percentages of words in each set

movie.analytics.data.frame$LOVED <-
  100 * movie.analytics.data.frame$loved.words /
    movie.analytics.data.frame$total.words
LOVED <- standardize(movie.analytics.data.frame$LOVED)
LOVED.ts <- ts(LOVED, start = c(1974,1), end = c(2013,1), frequency = 1)

movie.analytics.data.frame$WORLDS <-
  100 * movie.analytics.data.frame$worlds.words /
    movie.analytics.data.frame$total.words
WORLDS <- standardize(movie.analytics.data.frame$WORLDS)
WORLDS.ts <- ts(WORLDS, start = c(1974,1), end = c(2013,1), frequency = 1)

movie.analytics.data.frame$TRUTH <-
  100 * movie.analytics.data.frame$truth.words /
    movie.analytics.data.frame$total.words
TRUTH <- standardize(movie.analytics.data.frame$TRUTH)
TRUTH.ts <- ts(TRUTH, start = c(1974,1), end = c(2013,1), frequency = 1)

movie.analytics.data.frame$LIFE <-
  100 * movie.analytics.data.frame$life.words /
    movie.analytics.data.frame$total.words
LIFE <- standardize(movie.analytics.data.frame$LIFE)
LIFE.ts <- ts(LIFE, start = c(1974,1), end = c(2013,1), frequency = 1)

movie.analytics.data.frame$STORY <-
  100 * movie.analytics.data.frame$story.words /
    movie.analytics.data.frame$total.words
STORY <- standardize(movie.analytics.data.frame$STORY)
STORY.ts <- ts(STORY, start = c(1974,1), end = c(2013,1), frequency = 1)

# data frame of standardized text measures
text.measures.data.frame <- data.frame(LOVED,WORLDS,TRUTH,LIFE,STORY)
rownames(text.measures.data.frame) <- 1974:2013

principal.components.solution <-
  princomp(text.measures.data.frame, cor = TRUE)
print(summary(principal.components.solution))
# biplot rendering of text measures and documents by year
pdf(file = "fig_text_text_measures_biplot.pdf", width = 8.5, height = 11)
biplot(principal.components.solution, xlab = "First Pricipal Component",
  ylab = "Second Principal Component")
dev.off()

# multiple time series object for text measures
text.measures.mts <- cbind(LOVED.ts, WORLDS.ts, TRUTH.ts, LIFE.ts, STORY.ts)
colnames(text.measures.mts) <- c("LOVED","WORLDS","TRUTH","LIFE","STORY")
```

```
# text horizons for forty years of movies
pdf(file = "fig_text_horizon_1974_2013.pdf", width = 8.5, height = 11)
print(horizonplot(text.measures.mts, colorkey = TRUE,
  layout = c(1,5), strip.left = FALSE, horizonscale = 1,
  origin = 0,
  ylab = list(rev(colnames(text.measures.mts)), rot = 0, cex = 0.7)) +
  layer_(panel.fill(col = "gray90"), panel.xblocks(..., col = "white")))
dev.off()

# wordcloud for all R program code up to this point in the book
R.code.text <- scan("MTPA_R_code.txt", what = "char", sep = "\n")
# replace uppercase with lowercase letters
R.code.text <- tolower(R.code.text)
# strip out all non-letters and return vector
R.code.text.preword.vector <- unlist(strsplit(R.code.text, "\\W"))
# drop all empty words
R.code.text.vector <-
  R.code.text.preword.vector[which(nchar(R.code.text.preword.vector) > 0)]
pdf(file = "fig_text_wordcloud_of_R_code.pdf", width = 11, height = 8.5)
set.seed(1234)
wordcloud(R.code.text.vector,   min.freq = 10,
  max.words = 300,
  random.order=FALSE,
  random.color=FALSE,
  rot.per=0.0,
  colors="black",
  ordered.colors=FALSE,
  use.r.layout=FALSE,
  fixed.asp=TRUE)
dev.off()

# suggestions for students
# try word stemming prior to the analysis with
# terms-by-documents matrices
# try longer lists of words for the identified clusters
# see if there are ways to utilize information from wordnet
# to guide further analyses
```

8

Sentiment Analysis

"Frankly, my dear, I don't give a damn."

—CLARK GABLE AS RHETT BUTLER IN *Gone with the Wind* (1940)

As all must know by now, I am not shy about sharing my opinions. So to start on the topic for this chapter, I have written a few movie reviews. Along with the reviews, shown in figures 8.1 and 8.2, I give each of the movies a rating from 1 to 10, with 1 being "horrible" and 10 being "fantastic." Such is sentiment.

Sentiment analysis is text analytics with a purpose. It is the use of text measures to learn about the past and make predictions about the future. Sometimes called opinion mining, sentiment analysis draws upon positive and negative word sets (lexicons, dictionaries) that convey human emotion or feeling. These word sets are specific to the language being spoken and the context of application.

To do sentiment analysis correctly, we need to design text measures that work. In this chapter we explore various methods for developing text measures of sentiment, including list-based measures, item-weighted measures, and models for text classification. We employ a training-and-test regimen in evaluating the predictive performance of text measures and models.

Figure 8.1. *A Few Movie Reviews According to Tom*

The Effect of Gamma Rays on Man-in-the-Moon Marigolds (1972)

Based on a Pulizer-Prize-winning play by Paul Zindel, with Paul Newman directing Joanne Woodward, this is one of the most uplifting movies you will ever see. It is a tribute to the human spirit, the will to look beyond the limitations of one's current circumstances and overcome adversity. Not a bad plug for education either. Watch it if you can find it.

My rating: 10

Blade Runner (1982)

Even better than Harrison Ford's *Raiders* movies. This one is a keeper. Replicants with feeling—that's a twist. The visual effects and fine photography draw you in. It's like you are really there in the metropolis of the future. Not a pretty picture of what's coming our way, but a great movie nonetheless.

My rating: 9

My Cousin Vinny (1992)

Joe Pesci and Marisa Tomei—now that's an odd couple. The movie builds on stereotypes of Brooklyn and Alabama, and it's hard to sympathize with the hapless cousin and his male friend. Nor is there much suspense because we know what's going to happen at the end. It has to work out. Tomei makes the hour or so go by just fine. Without the life she breathes into her fiancée role, this one would have been a waste.

My rating: 4

Mars Attacks (1996)

A mindless diversion to be sure. I have the DVD, and every six months or so I watch it for a laugh. Nicholson plays two roles: POTUS and a real estate developer. The exploding Martian heads are great. Not for country music fans, though.

My rating: 7

Figure 8.2. *A Few More Movie Reviews According to Tom*

To demonstrate list-based measures of sentiment, we draw upon a lexicon developed by Hu and Liu (2004). This lexicon includes lists of 2,006 positive and 4,783 negative opinion and sentiment words. We see how these lists match up with a movie reviews corpus from Mass et al. (2011).[1]

There are three data set types in the corpus provided by Mass et al. (2011). The first is a data set with review text but no ratings. We will use this first data set to identify word sets for sentiment text measures. The second data set contains movie reviews with known ratings. We use this as our training data for developing text measurement models. And the third data set, like the second, has known ratings. We use this for evaluating developed text measures. At the end of the process we will evaluate developed text measures and models on the ratings provided at the beginning of the chapter.

Figure 8.3 shows fifty words from the Hu and Liu (2004) lexicon that worked for the data set of movie reviews with no ratings. Review of the positive and negative word lists suggests that positive words may come from movie love stories and comedies, uplifting or "feel good" movies. Negative words, on the other hand, are more likely to be associated with horror, violence, and tragedy.[2]

Note that there is nothing inherently good about the positive words or inherently bad about the negative words. As with any words we might use in communication, it is context that gives them meaning. In fact, it would be easy for us to review a bad movie using words chosen from the positive list or a good movie using words chosen from the negative list.

Moving forward with these identified lists, suppose we count numbers of positive and negative words in each of the movie reviews, computing two list-based text measures. Let POSITIVE be the percentage of words in the review that match up with the list of twenty-five positive words, and let NEGATIVE be the percentage of words in the review that match up with

---

[1] The movie reviews data are available from the authors of Mass et al. (2011), Andrew L. Maas, Raymond E. Daly, Peter T. Pham, Dan Huang, Andrew Y. Ng, and Christopher Potts, who were kind enough to place these data in the public domain. The original source for these data was The Internet Movie Database (IMDb). The full unsupervised data set includes 50,000 movie reviews with no associated ratings. There are similarly sized training and test data sets. We are using a small sample from each of these data sets in this chapter. The movie reviews data may be downloaded from http://ai.stanford.edu/ amaas/data/sentiment/.

[2] Notice that we are not using word stemming in creating word sets, as we have both "enjoy" and "enjoyed," as well as "love" and "loved," in the positive word set, and "kill" and "killed" in the negative word set. Stemming may be used in future studies with these data.

Figure 8.3. *Fifty Words of Sentiment*

Positive Words

amazing	beautiful	classic	enjoy	enjoyed
entertaining	excellent	fans	favorite	fine
fun	humor	lead	liked	love
loved	modern	nice	perfect	pretty
recommend	strong	top	wonderful	worth

Negative Words

bad	boring	cheap	creepy	dark
dead	death	evil	hard	kill
killed	lack	lost	miss	murder
mystery	plot	poor	sad	scary
slow	terrible	waste	worst	wrong

Table 8.1. *List-Based Sentiment Measures from Tom's Reviews*

Movie	Total Words	Positive Words	Negative Words	Text Measures POSITIVE	NEGATIVE	Rating	Thumbs Up/Down
Marigolds	26	0	1	0.00	3.85	10	UP
Blade Runner	21	2	0	9.52	0.00	9	UP
Vinny	29	1	2	3.45	6.90	4	DOWN
Mars Attacks	20	1	0	5.00	0.00	7	UP
Fight Club	18	0	2	0.00	11.11	2	DOWN
Congeneality	10	0	1	0.00	10.00	1	DOWN
Find Me Guilty	18	0	2	0.00	11.11	7	UP
Moneyball	36	2	1	5.56	2.78	4	DOWN

the list of twenty-five negative words. Figure 8.4 shows four movie reviews and their associated POSITIVE and NEGATIVE scores.

The scatter plot in figure 8.5 shows how the two list-based measures play out across the set of 500 movie reviews. If POSITIVE and NEGATIVE were at opposite ends of a single underlying dimension, we would expect these text measures to correlate close to -1.0. In fact, when we compute the correlation between POSITIVE and NEGATIVE, we see that it is -0.095, negative but much closer to zero than -1.0.

How do POSITIVE and NEGATIVE scores play out as far as the eight movie reviews at the beginning of the chapter? Table 8.1 suggests that they may not be doing so well. The list-based measures are missing favorable ratings of *The Effect of Gamma Rays on Man-in-the-Moon Marigolds* and *Find Me Guilty*, as well as the unfavorable rating of *Moneyball*.

Perhaps POSITIVE and NEGATIVE can be combined in a way to yield effective predictions of movie ratings. Alternatively, we can go back to the list of fifty sentiment terms and use them in data-based models to predict movie ratings. To move forward with text measures and model development, let us look at the training set of movie reviews with known ratings.

We select 500 records from the training set of positive reviews (reviews with ratings between 7 and 10) and 500 records from the training set of negative reviews (reviews with ratings between 1 and 4). We combine these to form a training data set of 1,000 movie reviews. We employ the same procedure to creat a test set of 1,000 movie reviews.

Figure 8.4. *List-Based Text Measures for Four Movie Reviews*

Ginger Snaps 2: Unleashed (2004)

I liked it a lot, in fact even more than the first movie. I loved the character of Ghost and all the comic book shots and her third person lines. Good ending. One thing they could have done was make the identity of the werewolf clearer. Also when the sister appeared it was kind of forced.. it didn't seem like she was a delusion

(20 analysis words, 2 from positive list, 0 from negative list)
List-based text measures: POSITIVE = 10, NEGATIVE = 0

Johnny Lingo (1969)

Beyond the tremendous and true romantic love Johnny Lingo proves for his dear Mahana, he gives a tremendous object lesson in how to properly treat others, and bring out the very best in them. If all husbands would treat their wives the way Johnny treated Mahana, there could be no evil in the world.

(20 analysis words, 1 from positive list, 1 from negative list)
List-based text measures: POSITIVE = 5, NEGATIVE = 5

Tomorrow Is Forever (1946)

The greatest and most poignant anguish we conscious beings experience is our recognition of the irretrievability of the past. All else we endure could be easily borne. The background strains of music as Orson Welles first recognizes Claudette Colbert haunts me still. She experienced a fragmentary nuance of remembrance that did not reach the level of her conscious recall.

(25 analysis words, 0 from positive list, 0 from negative list)
List-based text measures: POSITIVE = 0, NEGATIVE = 0

Malas temporadas (2005)

There are some exciting scenes in this movie but in general it is second-rate. The shoots are overextended, the characters are not life-like and some actors don't perform well either. I also didn't like multiple nationalist statements which have nothing to do with the plot. I guess the director intended to make his characters mysterious but instead they came out to be unnatural. We are supposed to see how different people successfully struggle with hard times in their lives. But two stories, the one of Carlos and that of Mikel, end up with nothing and the third, the story of Ana, makes a turn without any reason. The movie is very depressive but without any message that derives from it.

(40 analysis words, 0 from positive list, 2 from negative list)
List-based text measures: POSITIVE = 0, NEGATIVE = 5

Figure 8.5. Scatter Plot of Text Measures of Positive and Negative Sentiment

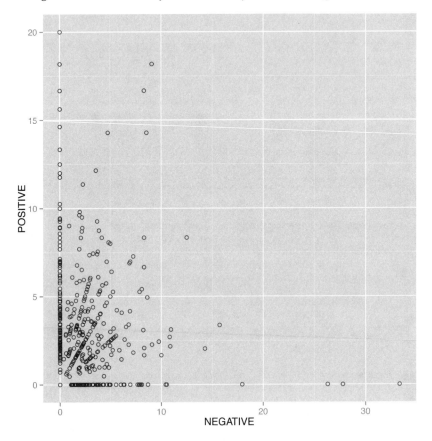

Working with alternative text measures and predictive modeling techniques, we employ a training-and-test regimen, developing measures and models on a training set and testing on a test set. Our goal is to predict whether a movie review is *thumbs-up* (a rating higher than 6) or *thumbs-down* (a rating less than 5). This is a text classification problem that may be addressed using various techniques. Here are six measures and modeling techniques we use for this example:

- Simple difference. We compute difference scores (POSITIVE minus NEGATIVE scores) and use a training-set-developed cutoff for predicting thumbs-up or thumbs-down.
- Regression difference. We use linear regression to determine weights to use for combining POSITIVE and NEGATIVE scores into a linear predictor of ratings. Here, too, we use a training-set-developed cutoff for predicting thumbs-up or thumbs-down.
- Word/item analysis. Working with the original set of fifty words, we use the training data to identify positive-leaning and negative-leaning words. We create a smaller set of words, with each word being weighted +1 for thumbs up or -1 for thumbs down. We define an item-based text measure as the sum of these item scores. Predicting thumbs-up or thumbs-down is then a matter of noting the sign (plus or minus) of the resulting text measure. This procedure is similar to traditional item analysis procedures in psychometrics. See Nunnally (1967) or Lord and Novick (1968).
- Logistic regression. Here we employ a traditional statistical modeling method for predicting a binary response. In particular, we use stepwise logistic regression to select useful predictors from the set of fifty sentiment words. Coefficients or weights in a linear predictor are determined by the method of maximum likelihood. Logistic regression is a common approach to binary classification problems. Discussion of logistic regression is provided in many sources (Ryan 2008; Fox and Weisberg 2011; Hosmer, Lemeshow, and Sturdivant 2013).
- Support vector machines. This machine learning algorithm has been shown to be an effective technique in text classification problems and, more generally, in problems with large numbers of explanatory variables, as we have here with the full set of fifty sentiment words. Most closely identified with Vladimir Vapnik (Boser, Guyon, and Vapnik

Table 8.2. *Accuracy of Text Classification for Movie Reviews (Thumbs-Up or Thumbs-Down)*

Text Measure/Model	Percentage of Reviews Correctly Classified	
	Training Set	Test Set
Simple difference	67.4	66.1
Regression difference	67.3	66.4
Word/item analysis	73.9	74.0
Logistic regression	75.2	72.6
Support vector machines	79.0	71.6
Random forests	82.2	74.0

1992; Vapnik 1998; Vapnik 2000), discussion of support vector machines may be found in Cristianini and Shawe-Taylor (2000), Izenman (2008), and Hastie, Tibshirani, and Friedman (2009). Tong and Koller (2001) discuss support vector machines for text classification.

- Random forests. This is a committee or ensemble method that uses thousands of tree-structured classifiers to arrive at a single prediction. The tree-structured classifiers themselves follow methods described in the work of Breiman et al. (1984). Review of tree-structured methods is provided by Izenman (2008) and Hastie, Tibshirani, and Friedman (2009). This is recursive partitioning on the training set to develop classification trees for predicting thumbs-up or thumbs-down. The set of explanatory variables is the full set of fifty sentiment words. Many such trees are constructed to form the random forest. Like support vector machines, this method has been shown to be very effective when working with large numbers of explanatory variables. It is based on bootstrap resampling techniques. Introduced by Breiman (2001a), useful introductions to this method may be found in Izenman (2008) and Hastie, Tibshirani, and Friedman (2009).

Testing various measurement and modeling techniques as we are doing here constitutes a first iteration of a *benchmark* experiment. How shall we evaluate the predictive accuracy in this study? For the movie reviews text classification problem, we use an index that is easy for managers to understand: the percentage of correct thumbs-up/thumbs-down predictions in the test set of movie reviews. In table 8.2 we report this statistic along with the percentage of correct predictions in the training set.

Table 8.3.   *Random Forest Text Measurement Model Applied to Tom's Movie Reviews*

Movie	Rating	Actual Thumbs Up/Down	Predicted Thumbs Up/Down
Marigolds	10	UP	DOWN
Blade Runner	9	UP	UP
Vinny	4	DOWN	DOWN
Mars Attacks	7	UP	UP
Fight Club	2	DOWN	DOWN
Congeneality	1	DOWN	DOWN
Find Me Guilty	7	UP	DOWN
Moneyball	4	DOWN	UP

Word/item analysis following traditional psychometric methods and random forests do equally well in text classification in the test set, with random forests doing the best on the training data. Random forests have the added advantage of providing measures of explanatory variable importance (word importance in text classification), as shown in as a dot chart in figure 8.6.

To complete the work with the movie reviews, we select the best performing measurement model from the benchmark study, random forests, and use it to classify the movie reviews presented at the beginning of the chapter. Table 8.3 shows the results. Five of the eight reviews (62.5 percent) are correctly classified. Like the list-based measures NEGATIVE and POSITIVE, that we had reviewed earlier, the random forest method fails in its classification of the thumbs-up movies *The Effect of Gamma Rays on Man-in-the-Moon Marigolds* and *Find Me Guilty* and in its classification of the thumbs-down movie *Moneyball*.

If we were to build a simple tree classifier for the movie ratings data, it would look like the one in figure 8.7. The simple tree tells us that if we are to classify on the basis of one word and one word alone, that word would be "worst." People who use the word "worst" tend to give a movie thumbs-down, with "bad" and "waste" following closely as thumbs-down predictors. If a review has none of those three words, but instead has the word "amazing," the simple tree classifier would predict thumbs-up. Beyond that, we have to look at additional words, such as "plot," "favorite," "terrible," and "death." A simple tree may not be the best predictor, but

Figure 8.6. *Word Importance in Classifying Movie Reviews as Thumbs-Up or Thumbs-Down*

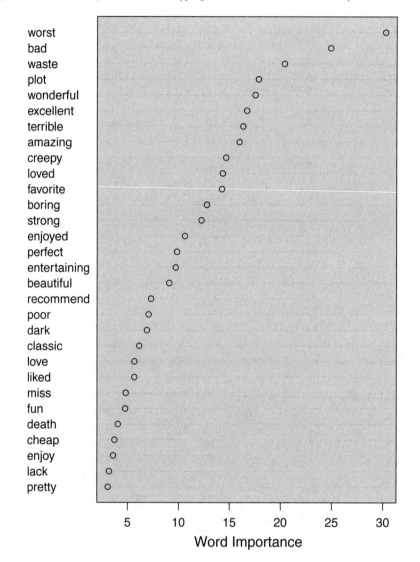

Figure 8.7. *A Simple Tree Classifier for Thumbs-Up or Thumbs-Down*

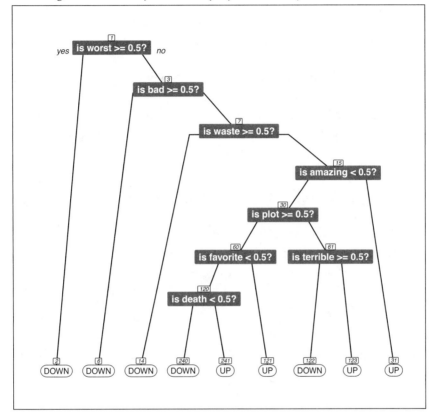

it can help explain the way models work. The random forest, the best text classifier we found in this study is composed of hundreds of trees, each one a little different from the next.

The value of a model lies in the quality of its predictions. How well does the simple tree classifier do in predicting thumbs-up or down for the eight movie reviews at the beginning of the chapter? Not very well. It makes the same mistakes as the list and random forest classifiers and one additional mistake—it classifies *Fight Club* as thumbs-up, when it should be thumbs-down. To see why it does this, we have only to trace the path taken down the tree. The review of *Fight Club* contains none of the words in the tree, so we end in the second terminal node from the right, a thumbs-up node.

The term *text measures*, introduced by Miller (2005), is at the heart of sentiment analysis, a bourgeoning area of research. Text measures are scores on attributes that describe text. Measurement, in its most basic sense, is the assignment of numbers to attributes according to rules. Text measures can be used to assess personality, consumer preferences, and political opinions, just as survey instruments can. The difference between text measures and survey instruments is that text measures begin with unstructured text as their input data, rather than questionnaire responses. The sentiment data are drawn from a variety of sources, including any accessible public communication medium, including, of course, social networks.

Precursors of sentiment analysis may be found in content analysis, thematic, semantic, and network text analysis (Roberts 1997; Popping 2000; West 2001; Leetaru 2011; Krippendorff 2012). These methods have seen a wide range of applications within the social sciences, including the analysis of political discourse. An early computer implementation of content analysis is found in the General Inquirer program (Stone et al. 1966; Stone 1997). Buvač and Stone (2001) describe a version of the program that provides text measures based upon word counts across numerous semantic categories.

Text measures flow from a measurement model (algorithms for scoring) and a dictionary, both defined by the researcher or analyst. A dictionary in this context is not a traditional dictionary; it is not an alphabetized list of words and their definitions. Rather, the dictionary used to construct text measures is a repository of word lists, such as synonyms and antonyms, positive and negative words, strong and weak sounding words, bipolar adjectives, parts of speech, and so on. The lists come from expert judgments about the meaning of words. A text measure assigns numbers to documents according to rules, with the rules being defined by the word lists, scoring algorithms, and modeling techniques in predictive analytics.

Among the more popular measurement schemes from the psychometric literature is Charles Osgood's semantic differential (Osgood, Suci, and Tannenbaum 1957; Osgood 1962). Exemplary bipolar dimensions include the positive–negative, strong–weak, and active–passive dimensions.

An example of text measures may be found in Roderick P. Hart's (2000a, 2000b, 2001) work with political discourse across thirteen U.S. presidential campaigns from 1948 to 1996. Hart developed general text measures summarizing the tone of documents along dimensions called certainty, optimism, activity, realism, and commonality (shared values). Each measure involved counting words from selected word lists. Some words received positive weights, others negative weights. The optimism measure, for example, assigned positive weights to words relating to praise, satisfaction, and inspiration, while recording negative weights for words relating to blame, hardship, and denial. The realism measure drew upon the concept of familiarity. A text measure in its own right, familiarity was computed with reference to a dictionary of forty-four words that are regarded as the most common words in the English language. Reviewing the voices of the three main groups (politicians, press, and public), Hart observed increasing complexity (lower familiarity scores) over time. Across the entire period of the study, the voice of the press was decidedly negative in tone (low in optimism), compared to politicians and the public. Normalcy in speech, if not in policy, is rewarded in American politics. Among political candidates, centrist speakers, those who spoke in common parlance, were more successful than non-centrist candidates.

Text measurement holds promise as a technology for understanding consumer opinion and markets. Just as political researchers can learn from the words of the public, press, and politicians, business researchers can learn from the words of customers and competitors. There are customer service logs, telephone transcripts, and sales call reports, along with user group, listserv, and blog postings. And we have ubiquitous social media from which to build document collections for text and sentiment analysis.

The measurement story behind opinion and sentiment analysis is an important story that needs to be told. Sentiment analysis, like all measurement, is the assignment of numbers to attributes according to rules. But what do the numbers mean? To what extent are text measures reliable or valid? To demonstrate content or face validity, we show that the content of the text measure relates to the attribute being measured. We examine word sets, and we try to gain agreement (among subject matter experts, perhaps) that they measure a particular attribute or trait. Sentiment research also involves the testing of word sets within specific contexts and, when possible, testing against external criteria. To demonstrate predictive validity, we show that a text measure can be used for prediction, as we have with text measures in predicting movie review thumbs-up or thumbs-down.

For the evaluation text measures, we employ a training-and-test regimen. We can use a simple index of predictive accuracy: the proportion of correct predictions. Or we can use other measures of predictive accuracy. See appendix A and exhibit A.1 for additional discussion of classification and the evaluation of binary classifiers.

Regarding Twitter-based text measures, there have been various attempts to predict the success of movies prior to their being distributed to theaters nationwide (Sharda and Delen 2006; Delen, Sharda, and Kumar 2007). Most telling is work completed at HP Labs that utilized chat on Twitter as a predictor of movie revenues (Asur and Huberman 2010). Bollen, Mao, and Zeng (2011) utilize Twitter sentiment analysis in predicting stock market movements. Taddy's (2013b, 2013c) sentiment analysis work builds on the inverse regression methods of Cook (1998, 2007). Taddy (2013a) uses Twitter data to examine political sentiment.

We expect sentiment analysis to be an active area of research for many years. Some have voiced concerns about unidimensional measures of sentiment. There have been attempts to develop more extensive sentiment word sets, as well as multidimensional measures (Turney 2002; Asur and Huberman 2010). Recent developments in machine learning and quantitative linguistics point to sentiment measurement methods that employ natural language processing rather than relying on positive and negative word sets (Socher et al. 2011).

Exhibit 8.1 lists the R program for the movie reviews example. It shows the development of text measures of sentiment and models for predicting thumbs-up versus thumbs-down movie reviews based upon the text from those reviews. Traditional methods and machine learning techniques are employed. The program draws on R packages provide by Feinerer (2013), Wickham (2013b), Wickham and Chang (2013), Sarkar and Andrews (2013), Kuhn (2013), Liaw and Wiener (2013), Therneau, Atkinson, and Ripley (2013), Milborrow (2013), and Meyer et al. (2013).

Exhibit 8.1. *Sentiment Analysis and Classification of Movie Ratings*

```
# Sentiment Analysis Using the Movie Ratings Data

library(tm)  # text mining and document management
library(stringr)  # character manipulation with regular expressions
library(grid)  # grid graphics utilities
library(ggplot2)  # graphics
library(latticeExtra) # package used for text horizon plot
library(caret)  # for confusion matrix function
library(rpart)  # tree-structured modeling
library(e1071)  # support vector machines
library(randomForest)  # random forests
library(rpart.plot)  # plot tree-structured model information

# load user-defined plotting utilities
load("mtpa_split_plotting_utilities.Rdata")

# standardization needed for text measures
standardize <- function(x) {(x - mean(x)) / sd(x)}

# convert to bytecodes to avoid "invalid multibyte string" messages
bytecode.convert <- function(x) {iconv(enc2utf8(x), sub = "byte")}

# read in positive and negative word lists from Hu and Liu (2004)
positive.data.frame <- read.table(file = "Hu_Liu_positive_word_list.txt",
  header = FALSE, colClasses = c("character"), row.names = NULL,
  col.names = "positive.words")
positive.data.frame$positive.words <-
  bytecode.convert(positive.data.frame$positive.words)

negative.data.frame <- read.table(file = "Hu_Liu_negative_word_list.txt",
  header = FALSE, colClasses = c("character"), row.names = NULL,
  col.names = "negative.words")
negative.data.frame$negative.words <-
  bytecode.convert(negative.data.frame$negative.words)

# we use movie ratings data from Mass et al. (2011)
# available at http://ai.stanford.edu/~amaas/data/sentiment/
# we set up a directory under our working directory structure
# /reviews/train/unsup/ for the unsupervised reviews

directory.location <-
  paste("~/Desktop/000_Demo_Sentiment_Analysis/tryreviews/train/unsup/",
  sep = "")
unsup.corpus <- Corpus(DirSource(directory.location, encoding = "UTF-8"),
  readerControl = list(language = "en_US"))
print(summary(unsup.corpus))

document.collection <- unsup.corpus

# strip whitspace from the documents in the collection
document.collection <- tm_map(document.collection, stripWhitespace)
```

```
# convert uppercase to lowercase in the document collection
document.collection <- tm_map(document.collection, tolower)

# remove numbers from the document collection
document.collection <- tm_map(document.collection, removeNumbers)

# remove punctuation from the document collection
document.collection <- tm_map(document.collection, removePunctuation)

# using a standard list, remove English stopwords from the document collection
document.collection <- tm_map(document.collection,
  removeWords, stopwords("english"))

# there is more we could do in terms of data preparation
# stemming... looking for contractions... possessives...
# previous analysis of a list of top terms showed a number of word
# contractions which we might like to drop from further analysis,
# recognizing them as stop words to be dropped from the document collection
initial.tdm <- TermDocumentMatrix(document.collection)
examine.tdm <- removeSparseTerms(initial.tdm, sparse = 0.96)
top.words <- Terms(examine.tdm)
print(top.words)

more.stop.words <- c("cant","didnt","doesnt","dont","goes","isnt","hes",
  "shes","thats","theres","theyre","wont","youll","youre","youve")
document.collection <- tm_map(document.collection,
  removeWords, more.stop.words)
some.proper.nouns.to.remove <-
  c("dick","ginger","hollywood","jack","jill","john","karloff",
    "kudrow","orson","peter","tcm","tom","toni","welles","william","wolheim")
document.collection <- tm_map(document.collection,
  removeWords, some.proper.nouns.to.remove)

# there is still more we could do in terms of data preparation
# but we will work with the bag of words we have for now
# the workhorse technique will be TermDocumentMatrix()
# for creating a terms-by-documents matrix across the document collection
# in previous text analytics with the taglines data we let the data
# guide us to the text measures... with sentiment analysis we have
# positive and negative dictionaries (to a large extent) defined in
# advance of looking at the data...
# positive.words and negative.words lists were read in earlier
# these come from the work of Hu and Liu (2004)
# positive.words = list of  positive words
# negative.words = list of  negative words
# we will start with these lists to build dictionaries
# that seem to make sense for movie reviews analysis
Hu.Liu.positive.dictionary <- Dictionary(positive.data.frame$positive.words)
reviews.tdm.Hu.Liu.positive <- TermDocumentMatrix(document.collection,
  list(dictionary = Hu.Liu.positive.dictionary))
examine.tdm <- removeSparseTerms(reviews.tdm.Hu.Liu.positive, 0.95)
top.words <- Terms(examine.tdm)
print(top.words)
```

```
Hu.Liu.frequent.positive <- findFreqTerms(reviews.tdm.Hu.Liu.positive, 25)
# this provides a list positive words occurring at least 25 times
# across the document collection... as it turns out this is 25 words
# a review of this list suggests that all make sense (have content validity)
test.positive.dictionary <- Dictionary(Hu.Liu.frequent.positive)


# .... now for the negative words
Hu.Liu.negative.dictionary <- Dictionary(negative.data.frame$negative.words)
reviews.tdm.Hu.Liu.negative <- TermDocumentMatrix(document.collection,
  list(dictionary = Hu.Liu.negative.dictionary))
examine.tdm <- removeSparseTerms(reviews.tdm.Hu.Liu.negative, 0.97)
top.words <- Terms(examine.tdm)
print(top.words)
Hu.Liu.frequent.negative <- findFreqTerms(reviews.tdm.Hu.Liu.negative, 16)
# this provides a short list negative words occurring at least 15 times
# across the document collection... one of these words seems out of place
# as they could be thought of as positive: "funny"
test.negative <- setdiff(Hu.Liu.frequent.negative,c("funny"))
test.negative.dictionary <- Dictionary(test.negative) # set of 32 words


# we need to evaluate the text measures we have defined
# for each of the documents count the total words
# and the number of words that match the positive and negative dictionaries
total.words <- integer(length(names(document.collection)))
positive.words <- integer(length(names(document.collection)))
negative.words <- integer(length(names(document.collection)))
other.words <- integer(length(names(document.collection)))

reviews.tdm <- TermDocumentMatrix(document.collection)

for(index.for.document in seq(along=names(document.collection))) {
  positive.words[index.for.document] <-
    sum(termFreq(document.collection[[index.for.document]],
    control = list(dictionary = test.positive.dictionary)))
  negative.words[index.for.document] <-
    sum(termFreq(document.collection[[index.for.document]],
    control = list(dictionary = test.negative.dictionary)))
  total.words[index.for.document] <-
    length(reviews.tdm[,index.for.document][["i"]])
  other.words[index.for.document] <- total.words[index.for.document] -
    positive.words[index.for.document] - negative.words[index.for.document]
  }

document <- names(document.collection)
text.measures.data.frame <- data.frame(document,total.words,
  positive.words, negative.words, other.words, stringsAsFactors = FALSE)
rownames(text.measures.data.frame) <- paste("D",as.character(0:499),sep="")

# compute text measures as percentages of words in each set
text.measures.data.frame$POSITIVE <-
  100 * text.measures.data.frame$positive.words /
  text.measures.data.frame$total.words
```

```
text.measures.data.frame$NEGATIVE <-
  100 * text.measures.data.frame$negative.words /
    text.measures.data.frame$total.words

# let us look at the resulting text measures we call POSITIVE and NEGATIVE
# to see if negative and positive dimensions appear to be on a common scale
# that is... is this a single dimension in the document space
# we use principal component biplots to explore text measures
# here we can use the technique to check on POSITIVE and NEGATIVE

principal.components.solution <-
  princomp(text.measures.data.frame[,c("POSITIVE","NEGATIVE")], cor = TRUE)
print(summary(principal.components.solution))
# biplot rendering of text measures and documents by year
pdf(file = "fig_sentiment_text_measures_biplot.pdf", width = 8.5, height = 11)
biplot(principal.components.solution, xlab = "First Pricipal Component",
  xlabs = rep("o", times = length(names(document.collection))),
  ylab = "Second Principal Component", expand = 0.7)
dev.off()

# results... the eigenvalues suggest that there are two underlying dimensions
# POSITIVE and NEGATIVE vectors rather than pointing in opposite directions
# they appear to be othogonal to one another... separate dimensions

# here we see the scatter plot for the two measures...
# if they were on the same dimension, they would be negatively correlated
# in fact they are correlated negatively but the correlation is very small
with(text.measures.data.frame, print(cor(POSITIVE, NEGATIVE)))  # -0.09464118

pdf(file = "fig_sentiment_text_measures_scatter_plot.pdf",
  width = 8.5, height = 8.5)
ggplot.object <- ggplot(data = text.measures.data.frame,
  aes(x = NEGATIVE, y = POSITIVE)) +
    geom_point(colour = "darkblue", shape = 1)
ggplot.print.with.margins(ggplot.object.name = ggplot.object,
  left.margin.pct=10, right.margin.pct=10,
  top.margin.pct=10,bottom.margin.pct=10)
dev.off()

# Perhaps POSITIVE and NEGATIVE can be combined in a way to yield effective
# predictions of movie ratings. Let us move to a set of movie reviews for
# supervised learning.  We select the 500 records from a set of positive
# reviews (ratings between 7 and 10) and 500 records from a set of negative
# reviews (ratings between 1 and 4).
# a set of 500 positive reviews... part of the training set
directory.location <-
  paste("~/Desktop/000_Demo_Sentiment_Analysis/tryreviews/train/pos/",
  sep = "")
pos.train.corpus <- Corpus(DirSource(directory.location, encoding = "UTF-8"),
  readerControl = list(language = "en_US"))
print(summary(pos.train.corpus))
```

```
# a set of 500 negative reviews... part of the training set
directory.location <-
  paste("~/Desktop/000_Demo_Sentiment_Analysis/tryreviews/train/neg/",
  sep = "")
neg.train.corpus <- Corpus(DirSource(directory.location, encoding = "UTF-8"),
  readerControl = list(language = "en_US"))
print(summary(neg.train.corpus))


# combine the positive and negative training sets
train.corpus <- c(pos.train.corpus, neg.train.corpus)
# strip whitspace from the documents in the collection
train.corpus <- tm_map(train.corpus, stripWhitespace)
# convert uppercase to lowercase in the document collection
train.corpus <- tm_map(train.corpus, tolower)
# remove numbers from the document collection
train.corpus <- tm_map(train.corpus, removeNumbers)
# remove punctuation from the document collection
train.corpus <- tm_map(train.corpus, removePunctuation)


# using a standard list, remove English stopwords from the document collection
train.corpus <- tm_map(train.corpus,
  removeWords, stopwords("english"))


# there is more we could do in terms of data preparation
# stemming... looking for contractions... possessives...
# previous analysis of a list of top terms showed a number of word
# contractions which we might like to drop from further analysis,
# recognizing them as stop words to be dropped from the document collection
initial.tdm <- TermDocumentMatrix(train.corpus)
examine.tdm <- removeSparseTerms(initial.tdm, sparse = 0.96)
top.words <- Terms(examine.tdm)
print(top.words)


more.stop.words <- c("cant","didnt","doesnt","dont","goes","isnt","hes",
  "shes","thats","theres","theyre","wont","youll","youre","youve")
train.corpus <- tm_map(train.corpus,
  removeWords, more.stop.words)
some.proper.nouns.to.remove <-
  c("dick","ginger","hollywood","jack","jill","john","karloff",
    "kudrow","orson","peter","tcm","tom","toni","welles","william","wolheim")
train.corpus <- tm_map(train.corpus,
  removeWords, some.proper.nouns.to.remove)


# compute list-based text measures for the training corpus
# for each of the documents count the total words
# and the number of words that match the positive and negative dictionaries
total.words <- integer(length(names(train.corpus)))
positive.words <- integer(length(names(train.corpus)))
negative.words <- integer(length(names(train.corpus)))
other.words <- integer(length(names(train.corpus)))


reviews.tdm <- TermDocumentMatrix(train.corpus)
```

```
for(index.for.document in seq(along=names(train.corpus))) {
  positive.words[index.for.document] <-
    sum(termFreq(train.corpus[[index.for.document]],
    control = list(dictionary = test.positive.dictionary)))
  negative.words[index.for.document] <-
    sum(termFreq(train.corpus[[index.for.document]],
    control = list(dictionary = test.negative.dictionary)))
  total.words[index.for.document] <-
    length(reviews.tdm[,index.for.document][["i"]])
  other.words[index.for.document] <- total.words[index.for.document] -
    positive.words[index.for.document] - negative.words[index.for.document]
  }

document <- names(train.corpus)
train.data.frame <- data.frame(document,total.words,
  positive.words, negative.words, other.words, stringsAsFactors = FALSE)
rownames(train.data.frame) <- paste("D",as.character(0:999),sep="")
# compute text measures as percentages of words in each set
train.data.frame$POSITIVE <-
  100 * train.data.frame$positive.words /
  train.data.frame$total.words

train.data.frame$NEGATIVE <-
  100 * train.data.frame$negative.words /
    train.data.frame$total.words

# rating is embedded in the document name... extract with regular expressions
for(index.for.document in seq(along = train.data.frame$document)) {
  first_split <- strsplit(train.data.frame$document[index.for.document],
    split = "[_]")
  second_split <- strsplit(first_split[[1]][2], split = "[.]")
  train.data.frame$rating[index.for.document] <- as.numeric(second_split[[1]][1])
  } # end of for-loop for defining ratings and thumbsupdown

train.data.frame$thumbsupdown <- ifelse((train.data.frame$rating > 5), 2, 1)
train.data.frame$thumbsupdown <-
  factor(train.data.frame$thumbsupdown, levels = c(1,2),
    labels = c("DOWN","UP"))

# a set of 500 positive reviews... part of the test set
directory.location <-
  paste("~/Desktop/000_Demo_Sentiment_Analysis/tryreviews/test/pos/",
  sep = "")
pos.test.corpus <- Corpus(DirSource(directory.location, encoding = "UTF-8"),
  readerControl = list(language = "en_US"))
print(summary(pos.test.corpus))
# a set of 500 negative reviews... part of the test set
directory.location <-
  paste("~/Desktop/000_Demo_Sentiment_Analysis/tryreviews/test/neg/",
  sep = "")
neg.test.corpus <- Corpus(DirSource(directory.location, encoding = "UTF-8"),
  readerControl = list(language = "en_US"))
print(summary(neg.test.corpus))
```

```
# combine the positive and negative testing sets
test.corpus <- c(pos.test.corpus, neg.test.corpus)
# strip whitspace from the documents in the collection
test.corpus <- tm_map(test.corpus, stripWhitespace)
# convert uppercase to lowercase in the document collection
test.corpus <- tm_map(test.corpus, tolower)
# remove numbers from the document collection
test.corpus <- tm_map(test.corpus, removeNumbers)
# remove punctuation from the document collection
test.corpus <- tm_map(test.corpus, removePunctuation)
# using a standard list, remove English stopwords from the document collection
test.corpus <- tm_map(test.corpus,
  removeWords, stopwords("english"))

# there is more we could do in terms of data preparation
# stemming... looking for contractions... possessives...
# previous analysis of a list of top terms showed a number of word
# contractions which we might like to drop from further analysis,
# recognizing them as stop words to be dropped from the document collection
initial.tdm <- TermDocumentMatrix(test.corpus)
examine.tdm <- removeSparseTerms(initial.tdm, sparse = 0.96)
top.words <- Terms(examine.tdm)
print(top.words)
more.stop.words <- c("cant","didnt","doesnt","dont","goes","isnt","hes",
  "shes","thats","theres","theyre","wont","youll","youre","youve")
test.corpus <- tm_map(test.corpus,
  removeWords, more.stop.words)
some.proper.nouns.to.remove <-
  c("dick","ginger","hollywood","jack","jill","john","karloff",
    "kudrow","orson","peter","tcm","tom","toni","welles","william","wolheim")
test.corpus <- tm_map(test.corpus,
  removeWords, some.proper.nouns.to.remove)
# compute list-based text measures for the testing corpus
# for each of the documents count the total words
# and the number of words that match the positive and negative dictionaries
total.words <- integer(length(names(test.corpus)))
positive.words <- integer(length(names(test.corpus)))
negative.words <- integer(length(names(test.corpus)))
other.words <- integer(length(names(test.corpus)))

reviews.tdm <- TermDocumentMatrix(test.corpus)

for(index.for.document in seq(along=names(test.corpus))) {
  positive.words[index.for.document] <-
    sum(termFreq(test.corpus[[index.for.document]],
    control = list(dictionary = test.positive.dictionary)))
  negative.words[index.for.document] <-
    sum(termFreq(test.corpus[[index.for.document]],
    control = list(dictionary = test.negative.dictionary)))
  total.words[index.for.document] <-
    length(reviews.tdm[,index.for.document][["i"]])
  other.words[index.for.document] <- total.words[index.for.document] -
    positive.words[index.for.document] - negative.words[index.for.document]
  }
```

```
document <- names(test.corpus)
test.data.frame <- data.frame(document,total.words,
  positive.words, negative.words, other.words, stringsAsFactors = FALSE)
rownames(test.data.frame) <- paste("D",as.character(0:999),sep="")
# compute text measures as percentages of words in each set
test.data.frame$POSITIVE <-
  100 * test.data.frame$positive.words /
  test.data.frame$total.words
 test.data.frame$NEGATIVE <-
  100 * test.data.frame$negative.words /
    test.data.frame$total.words

# rating is embedded in the document name... extract with regular expressions
for(index.for.document in seq(along = test.data.frame$document)) {
  first_split <- strsplit(test.data.frame$document[index.for.document],
    split = "[_]")
  second_split <- strsplit(first_split[[1]][2], split = "[.]")
  test.data.frame$rating[index.for.document] <- as.numeric(second_split[[1]][1])
  } # end of for-loop for defining
test.data.frame$thumbsupdown <- ifelse((test.data.frame$rating > 5), 2, 1)
test.data.frame$thumbsupdown <-
  factor(test.data.frame$thumbsupdown, levels = c(1,2),
    labels = c("DOWN","UP"))
# a set of 4 positive and 4 negative reviews... testing set of Tom's reviews
directory.location <-
  paste("~/Desktop/000_Demo_Sentiment_Analysis/tryreviews/test/tom/",
  sep = "")
tom.corpus <- Corpus(DirSource(directory.location, encoding = "UTF-8"),
  readerControl = list(language = "en_US"))
print(summary(tom.corpus))

# strip whitspace from the documents in the collection
tom.corpus <- tm_map(tom.corpus, stripWhitespace)
# convert uppercase to lowercase in the document collection
tom.corpus <- tm_map(tom.corpus, tolower)
# remove numbers from the document collection
tom.corpus <- tm_map(tom.corpus, removeNumbers)
# remove punctuation from the document collection
tom.corpus <- tm_map(tom.corpus, removePunctuation)
# using a standard list, remove English stopwords from the document collection
tom.corpus <- tm_map(tom.corpus,
  removeWords, stopwords("english"))

# there is more we could do in terms of data preparation
# stemming... looking for contractions... possessives...
# previous analysis of a list of top terms showed a number of word
# contractions which we might like to drop from further analysis,
# recognizing them as stop words to be dropped from the document collection
initial.tdm <- TermDocumentMatrix(tom.corpus)
examine.tdm <- removeSparseTerms(initial.tdm, sparse = 0.96)
top.words <- Terms(examine.tdm)
print(top.words)
```

```
more.stop.words <- c("cant","didnt","doesnt","dont","goes","isnt","hes",
  "shes","thats","theres","theyre","wont","youll","youre","youve")
tom.corpus <- tm_map(tom.corpus,
  removeWords, more.stop.words)

some.proper.nouns.to.remove <-
  c("dick","ginger","hollywood","jack","jill","john","karloff",
    "kudrow","orson","peter","tcm","tom","toni","welles","william","wolheim")
tom.corpus <- tm_map(tom.corpus,
  removeWords, some.proper.nouns.to.remove)

# compute list-based text measures for the test corpus
# for each of the documents count the total words
# and the number of words that match the positive and negative dictionaries
total.words <- integer(length(names(tom.corpus)))
positive.words <- integer(length(names(tom.corpus)))
negative.words <- integer(length(names(tom.corpus)))
other.words <- integer(length(names(tom.corpus)))

reviews.tdm <- TermDocumentMatrix(tom.corpus)

for(index.for.document in seq(along=names(tom.corpus))) {
  positive.words[index.for.document] <-
    sum(termFreq(tom.corpus[[index.for.document]],
    control = list(dictionary = test.positive.dictionary)))
  negative.words[index.for.document] <-
    sum(termFreq(tom.corpus[[index.for.document]],
    control = list(dictionary = test.negative.dictionary)))
  total.words[index.for.document] <-
    length(reviews.tdm[,index.for.document][["i"]])
  other.words[index.for.document] <- total.words[index.for.document] -
    positive.words[index.for.document] - negative.words[index.for.document]
  }

document <- names(tom.corpus)
tom.data.frame <- data.frame(document,total.words,
  positive.words, negative.words, other.words, stringsAsFactors = FALSE)
rownames(tom.data.frame) <- paste("D",as.character(0:7),sep="")

# compute text measures as percentages of words in each set
tom.data.frame$POSITIVE <-
  100 * tom.data.frame$positive.words /
  tom.data.frame$total.words
tom.data.frame$NEGATIVE <-
  100 * tom.data.frame$negative.words /
    tom.data.frame$total.words
# rating is embedded in the document name... extract with regular expressions
for(index.for.document in seq(along = tom.data.frame$document)) {
  first_split <- strsplit(tom.data.frame$document[index.for.document],
    split = "[_]")
  second_split <- strsplit(first_split[[1]][2], split = "[.]")
  tom.data.frame$rating[index.for.document] <- as.numeric(second_split[[1]][1])
  } # end of for-loop for defining initial tom.data.frame components
```

```
tom.data.frame$thumbsupdown <- ifelse((tom.data.frame$rating > 5), 2, 1)
tom.data.frame$thumbsupdown <-
  factor(tom.data.frame$thumbsupdown, levels = c(1,2),
    labels = c("DOWN","UP"))

tom.movies <- data.frame(movies =
  c("The Effect of Gamma Rays on Man-in-the-Moon Marigolds",
    "Blade Runner","My Cousin Vinny","Mars Attacks",
    "Fight Club","Miss Congeneality 2","Find Me Guilty","Moneyball"))
# check out the measures on Tom's ratings
tom.data.frame.review <-
  cbind(tom.movies,tom.data.frame[,names(tom.data.frame)[2:9]])
print(tom.data.frame.review)

# develop predictive models using the training data
# -------------------------------------
# Simple difference method
# -------------------------------------
train.data.frame$simple <-
    train.data.frame$POSITIVE - train.data.frame$NEGATIVE

# check out simple difference method... is there a correlation with ratings?
with(train.data.frame, print(cor(simple, rating)))  # positive r = 0.4252565

# we use the training data to define an optimal cutoff...
# trees can help with finding the optimal split point for simple.difference
try.tree <- rpart(thumbsupdown ~ simple, data = train.data.frame)
print(try.tree)  # note that the first split is at -0.7969266
# create a user-defined function for the simple difference method
predict.simple <- function(x) {
  if (x >= -0.7969266) return("UP")
  if (x < -0.7969266) return("DOWN")
  }
# evaluate predictive accuracy in the training data
train.data.frame$pred.simple <- character(nrow(train.data.frame))
for (index.for.review in seq(along = train.data.frame$pred.simple)) {
  train.data.frame$pred.simple[index.for.review] <-
    predict.simple(train.data.frame$simple[index.for.review])
  }
train.data.frame$pred.simple <-
  factor(train.data.frame$pred.simple)
train.pred.simple.performance <-
  confusionMatrix(data = train.data.frame$pred.simple,
  reference = train.data.frame$thumbsupdown, positive = "UP")
# report full set of statistics relating to predictive accuracy
print(train.pred.simple.performance)
cat("\n\nTraining set percentage correctly predicted by",
  "simple difference method = ",
  sprintf("%1.1f",train.pred.simple.performance$overall[1]*100)," Percent",sep="")

# evaluate predictive accuracy in the test data
test.data.frame$simple <-
    test.data.frame$POSITIVE - train.data.frame$NEGATIVE
```

```
test.data.frame$pred.simple <- character(nrow(test.data.frame))
for (index.for.review in seq(along = test.data.frame$pred.simple)) {
  test.data.frame$pred.simple[index.for.review] <-
    predict.simple(test.data.frame$simple[index.for.review])
  }
test.data.frame$pred.simple <-
  factor(test.data.frame$pred.simple)

test.pred.simple.performance <-
  confusionMatrix(data = test.data.frame$pred.simple,
  reference = test.data.frame$thumbsupdown, positive = "UP")

# report full set of statistics relating to predictive accuracy
print(test.pred.simple.performance)

cat("\n\nTest set percentage correctly predicted = ",
  sprintf("%1.1f",test.pred.simple.performance$overall[1]*100),"
    Percent",sep="")

# --------------------------------------
# Regression difference method
# --------------------------------------
# regression method for determining weights on POSITIVE AND NEGATIVE
# fit a regression model to the training data
regression.model <- lm(rating ~ POSITIVE + NEGATIVE, data = train.data.frame)
print(regression.model)  # provides 5.5386 + 0.2962(POSITIVE) -0.3089(NEGATIVE)

train.data.frame$regression <-
  predict(regression.model, newdata = train.data.frame)

# determine the cutoff for regression.difference
  try.tree <- rpart(thumbsupdown ~ regression, data = train.data.frame)
print(try.tree)  # note that the first split is at 5.264625
# create a user-defined function for the simple difference method
predict.regression <- function(x) {
  if (x >= 5.264625) return("UP")
  if (x < 5.264625) return("DOWN")
  }
train.data.frame$pred.regression <-  character(nrow(train.data.frame))
for (index.for.review in seq(along = train.data.frame$pred.simple)) {
  train.data.frame$pred.regression[index.for.review] <-
    predict.regression(train.data.frame$regression[index.for.review])
  }
train.data.frame$pred.regression <-
  factor(train.data.frame$pred.regression)
train.pred.regression.performance <-
  confusionMatrix(data = train.data.frame$pred.regression,
  reference = train.data.frame$thumbsupdown, positive = "UP")

# report full set of statistics relating to predictive accuracy
print(train.pred.regression.performance)  # result 67.3 Percent
```

```
cat("\n\nTraining set percentage correctly predicted by regression = ",
  sprintf("%1.1f",train.pred.regression.performance$overall[1]*100),
    " Percent",sep="")

# regression method for determining weights on POSITIVE AND NEGATIVE
# for the test set we use the model developed on the training set

test.data.frame$regression <-
  predict(regression.model, newdata = test.data.frame)

test.data.frame$pred.regression <-  character(nrow(test.data.frame))
for (index.for.review in seq(along = test.data.frame$pred.simple)) {
  test.data.frame$pred.regression[index.for.review] <-
    predict.regression(test.data.frame$regression[index.for.review])
  }
test.data.frame$pred.regression <-
  factor(test.data.frame$pred.regression)
test.pred.regression.performance <-
  confusionMatrix(data = test.data.frame$pred.regression,
  reference = test.data.frame$thumbsupdown, positive = "UP")
# report full set of statistics relating to predictive accuracy
print(test.pred.regression.performance)  # result 67.3 Percent
cat("\n\nTest set percentage correctly predicted = ",
  sprintf("%1.1f",test.pred.regression.performance$overall[1]*100),
    " Percent",sep="")


# --------------------------------------------
# Word/item analysis method for train.corpus
# --------------------------------------------
# return to the training corpus to develop simple counts
# for each of the words in the sentiment list
# these new variables will be given the names of the words
# to keep things simple.... there are 50 such variables/words
working.corpus <- train.corpus
# run common code from utilities for scoring the working corpus
source("prog_sentiment_score_working_corpus.R")
add.data.frame <- data.frame(amazing,beautiful,classic,enjoy,
  enjoyed,entertaining,excellent,fans,favorite,fine,fun,humor,
  lead,liked,love,loved,modern,nice,perfect,pretty,
  recommend,strong,top,wonderful,worth,bad,boring,cheap,creepy,dark,dead,
  death,evil,hard,kill,killed,lack,lost,miss,murder,mystery,plot,poor,
  sad,scary,slow,terrible,waste,worst,wrong)
train.data.frame <- cbind(train.data.frame,add.data.frame)


# --------------------------------------------
# Word/item analysis method for test.corpus
# --------------------------------------------
# return to the testing corpus to develop simple counts
# for each of the words in the sentiment list
# these new variables will be given the names of the words
# to keep things simple.... there are 50 such variables/words

working.corpus <- test.corpus
```

```
# run common code from utilities for scoring the working corpus
source("prog_sentiment_score_working_corpus.R")
add.data.frame <- data.frame(amazing,beautiful,classic,enjoy,
  enjoyed,entertaining,excellent,fans,favorite,fine,fun,humor,
  lead,liked,love,loved,modern,nice,perfect,pretty,
  recommend,strong,top,wonderful,worth,bad,boring,cheap,creepy,dark,dead,
  death,evil,hard,kill,killed,lack,lost,miss,murder,mystery,plot,poor,
  sad,scary,slow,terrible,waste,worst,wrong)
test.data.frame <- cbind(test.data.frame,add.data.frame)

# -------------------------------------------
# Word/item analysis method for tom.corpus
# -------------------------------------------
# return to the toming corpus to develop simple counts
# for each of the words in the sentiment list
# these new variables will be given the names of the words
# to keep things simple.... there are 50 such variables/words
working.corpus <- tom.corpus
# run common code from utilities for scoring the working corpus
source("prog_sentiment_score_working_corpus.R")

add.data.frame <- data.frame(amazing,beautiful,classic,enjoy,
  enjoyed,entertaining,excellent,fans,favorite,fine,fun,humor,
  lead,liked,love,loved,modern,nice,perfect,pretty,
  recommend,strong,top,wonderful,worth,bad,boring,cheap,creepy,dark,dead,
  death,evil,hard,kill,killed,lack,lost,miss,murder,mystery,plot,poor,
  sad,scary,slow,terrible,waste,worst,wrong)

tom.data.frame <- cbind(tom.data.frame,add.data.frame)

# use phi coefficient... correlation with rating as index of item value
phi <- numeric(50)
item <- c(test.positive.dictionary,test.negative.dictionary)
item.analysis.data.frame <- data.frame(item,phi)
item.place <- 14:63
for (index.for.column in 1:50) {
  item.analysis.data.frame$phi[index.for.column] <-
    cor(train.data.frame[, item.place[index.for.column]],train.data.frame[,8])
  }
# sort by absolute value of the phi coefficient with the rating
item.analysis.data.frame$absphi <- abs(item.analysis.data.frame$phi)
item.analysis.data.frame <-
  item.analysis.data.frame[sort.list(item.analysis.data.frame$absphi,
    decreasing = TRUE),]

# subset of words with phi coefficients greater than 0.05 in absolute value
selected.items.data.frame <-
  subset(item.analysis.data.frame, subset = (absphi > 0.05))

# use the sign of the phi coefficient as the item weight
selected.positive.data.frame <-
  subset(selected.items.data.frame, subset = (phi > 0.0))
selected.positive.words <- as.character(selected.positive.data.frame$item)
```

```
selected.negative.data.frame <-
  subset(selected.items.data.frame, subset = (phi < 0.0))
selected.negative.words <- as.character(selected.negative.data.frame$item)

# these lists define new dictionaries for scoring

reviews.tdm <- TermDocumentMatrix(train.corpus)

temp.positive.score <- integer(length(names(train.corpus)))
temp.negative.score <- integer(length(names(train.corpus)))
for(index.for.document in seq(along=names(train.corpus))) {
  temp.positive.score[index.for.document] <-
    sum(termFreq(train.corpus[[index.for.document]],
    control = list(dictionary = selected.positive.words)))
  temp.negative.score[index.for.document] <-
    sum(termFreq(train.corpus[[index.for.document]],
    control = list(dictionary = selected.negative.words)))
  }

train.data.frame$item.analysis.score <-
  temp.positive.score - temp.negative.score

# use the training set and tree-structured modeling to determine the cutoff
  try.tree<-rpart(thumbsupdown ~ item.analysis.score, data = train.data.frame)
print(try.tree)  # note that the first split is at -0.5
# create a user-defined function for the simple difference method
predict.item.analysis <- function(x) {
  if (x >= -0.5) return("UP")
  if (x < -0.5) return("DOWN")
  }

train.data.frame$pred.item.analysis <-  character(nrow(train.data.frame))
for (index.for.review in seq(along = train.data.frame$pred.simple)) {
  train.data.frame$pred.item.analysis[index.for.review] <-
  predict.item.analysis(train.data.frame$item.analysis.score[index.for.review])
  }
train.data.frame$pred.item.analysis <-
  factor(train.data.frame$pred.item.analysis)

train.pred.item.analysis.performance <-
  confusionMatrix(data = train.data.frame$pred.item.analysis,
  reference = train.data.frame$thumbsupdown, positive = "UP")

# report full set of statistics relating to predictive accuracy
print(train.pred.item.analysis.performance)  # result 73.9 Percent

cat("\n\nTraining set percentage correctly predicted by item analysis = ",
  sprintf("%1.1f",train.pred.item.analysis.performance$overall[1]*100),
    " Percent",sep="")

# use item analysis method of scoring with the test set

reviews.tdm <- TermDocumentMatrix(test.corpus)
```

```
temp.positive.score <- integer(length(names(test.corpus)))
temp.negative.score <- integer(length(names(test.corpus)))
for(index.for.document in seq(along=names(test.corpus))) {
  temp.positive.score[index.for.document] <-
    sum(termFreq(test.corpus[[index.for.document]],
    control = list(dictionary = selected.positive.words)))
  temp.negative.score[index.for.document] <-
    sum(termFreq(test.corpus[[index.for.document]],
    control = list(dictionary = selected.negative.words)))
  }
test.data.frame$item.analysis.score <-
  temp.positive.score - temp.negative.score
test.data.frame$pred.item.analysis <-  character(nrow(test.data.frame))
for (index.for.review in seq(along = test.data.frame$pred.simple)) {
  test.data.frame$pred.item.analysis[index.for.review] <-
  predict.item.analysis(test.data.frame$item.analysis.score[index.for.review])
  }
test.data.frame$pred.item.analysis <-
  factor(test.data.frame$pred.item.analysis)
test.pred.item.analysis.performance <-
  confusionMatrix(data = test.data.frame$pred.item.analysis,
  reference = test.data.frame$thumbsupdown, positive = "UP")
# report full set of statistics relating to predictive accuracy
print(test.pred.item.analysis.performance)  # result 74 Percent

cat("\n\nTest set percentage correctly predicted by item analysis = ",
  sprintf("%1.1f",test.pred.item.analysis.performance$overall[1]*100),
    " Percent",sep="")


# -------------------------------------
# Logistic regression method
# -------------------------------------
text.classification.model <- {thumbsupdown ~ amazing + beautiful +
  classic + enjoy + enjoyed +
  entertaining + excellent +
  fans + favorite + fine + fun + humor + lead + liked +
  love + loved + modern + nice + perfect + pretty +
  recommend + strong + top + wonderful + worth +
  bad + boring + cheap + creepy + dark + dead +
  death + evil + hard + kill +
  killed + lack + lost + miss + murder + mystery +
  plot + poor + sad + scary +
  slow + terrible + waste + worst + wrong}

# full logistic regression model
logistic.regression.fit <- glm(text.classification.model,
  family=binomial(link=logit), data = train.data.frame)
print(summary(logistic.regression.fit))

# obtain predicted probability values for training set
logistic.regression.pred.prob <-
  as.numeric(predict(logistic.regression.fit, newdata = train.data.frame,
  type="response"))
```

```
train.data.frame$pred.logistic.regression <-
  ifelse((logistic.regression.pred.prob > 0.5),2,1)
train.data.frame$pred.logistic.regression <-
  factor(train.data.frame$pred.logistic.regression, levels = c(1,2),
    labels = c("DOWN","UP"))
train.pred.logistic.regression.performance <-
  confusionMatrix(data = train.data.frame$pred.logistic.regression,
  reference = train.data.frame$thumbsupdown, positive = "UP")
# report full set of statistics relating to predictive accuracy
print(train.pred.logistic.regression.performance)  # result 75.2 Percent
cat("\n\nTraining set percentage correct by logistic regression = ",
  sprintf("%1.1f",train.pred.logistic.regression.performance$overall[1]*100),
    " Percent",sep="")
# now we use the model developed on the training set with the test set
# obtain predicted probability values for test set
logistic.regression.pred.prob <-
  as.numeric(predict(logistic.regression.fit, newdata = test.data.frame,
  type="response"))

test.data.frame$pred.logistic.regression <-
  ifelse((logistic.regression.pred.prob > 0.5),2,1)

test.data.frame$pred.logistic.regression <-
  factor(test.data.frame$pred.logistic.regression, levels = c(1,2),
    labels = c("DOWN","UP"))
test.pred.logistic.regression.performance <-
  confusionMatrix(data = test.data.frame$pred.logistic.regression,
  reference = test.data.frame$thumbsupdown, positive = "UP")
# report full set of statistics relating to predictive accuracy
print(test.pred.logistic.regression.performance)  # result 72.6 Percent
cat("\n\nTest set percentage correctly predicted by logistic regression = ",
  sprintf("%1.1f",test.pred.logistic.regression.performance$overall[1]*100),
    " Percent",sep="")

# ----------------------------------------
# Support vector machines
# ----------------------------------------
# determine tuning parameters prior to fitting model
train.tune <- tune(svm, text.classification.model, data = train.data.frame,
                ranges = list(gamma = 2^(-8:1), cost = 2^(0:4)),
                tunecontrol = tune.control(sampling = "fix"))
# display the tuning results (in text format)
print(train.tune)
# fit the support vector machine to the training data using tuning parameters
train.data.frame.svm <- svm(text.classification.model, data = train.data.frame,
  cost=4, gamma=0.00390625, probability = TRUE)
train.data.frame$pred.svm <- predict(train.data.frame.svm, type="class",
 newdata=train.data.frame)
train.pred.svm.performance <-
  confusionMatrix(data = train.data.frame$pred.svm,
  reference = train.data.frame$thumbsupdown, positive = "UP")
# report full set of statistics relating to predictive accuracy
print(train.pred.svm.performance)  # result 79.0 Percent
```

```
cat("\n\nTraining set percentage correctly predicted by SVM = ",
  sprintf("%1.1f",train.pred.svm.performance$overall[1]*100),
    " Percent",sep="")

# use the support vector machine model identified in the training set
# to do text classification on the test set
test.data.frame$pred.svm <- predict(train.data.frame.svm, type="class",
 newdata=test.data.frame)
test.pred.svm.performance <-
  confusionMatrix(data = test.data.frame$pred.svm,
  reference = test.data.frame$thumbsupdown, positive = "UP")
# report full set of statistics relating to predictive accuracy
print(test.pred.svm.performance)  # result 71.6 Percent
cat("\n\nTest set percentage correctly predicted by SVM = ",
  sprintf("%1.1f",test.pred.svm.performance$overall[1]*100),
    " Percent",sep="")


# ----------------------------------------
# Random forests
# ----------------------------------------
# fit random forest model to the training data
set.seed (9999)  # for reproducibility
train.data.frame.rf <- randomForest(text.classification.model,
  data=train.data.frame, mtry=3, importance=TRUE, na.action=na.omit)
# review the random forest solution
print(train.data.frame.rf)
# check importance of the individual explanatory variables
pdf(file = "fig_sentiment_random_forest_importance.pdf",
width = 11, height = 8.5)
varImpPlot(train.data.frame.rf, main = "")
dev.off()
train.data.frame$pred.rf <- predict(train.data.frame.rf, type="class",
  newdata = train.data.frame)
train.pred.rf.performance <-
  confusionMatrix(data = train.data.frame$pred.rf,
  reference = train.data.frame$thumbsupdown, positive = "UP")
# report full set of statistics relating to predictive accuracy
print(train.pred.rf.performance)  # result 82.2 Percent
cat("\n\nTraining set percentage correctly predicted by random forests = ",
  sprintf("%1.1f",train.pred.rf.performance$overall[1]*100),
    " Percent",sep="")

# use the model fit to the training data to predict the the test data
test.data.frame$pred.rf <- predict(train.data.frame.rf, type="class",
  newdata = test.data.frame)
test.pred.rf.performance <-
  confusionMatrix(data = test.data.frame$pred.rf,
  reference = test.data.frame$thumbsupdown, positive = "UP")
# report full set of statistics relating to predictive accuracy
print(test.pred.rf.performance)  # result 74.0 Percent
cat("\n\nTest set percentage correctly predicted by random forests = ",
  sprintf("%1.1f",test.pred.rf.performance$overall[1]*100),
    " Percent",sep="")
```

```
# measurement model performance summary
methods <- c("Simple difference","Regression difference",
  "Word/item analysis","Logistic regression",
  "Support vector machines","Random forests")

methods.performance.data.frame <- data.frame(methods)

methods.performance.data.frame$training <-
  c(train.pred.simple.performance$overall[1]*100,
    train.pred.regression.performance$overall[1]*100,
    train.pred.item.analysis.performance$overall[1]*100,
    train.pred.logistic.regression.performance$overall[1]*100,
    train.pred.svm.performance$overall[1]*100,
    train.pred.rf.performance$overall[1]*100)

methods.performance.data.frame$test <-
  c(test.pred.simple.performance$overall[1]*100,
    test.pred.regression.performance$overall[1]*100,
    test.pred.item.analysis.performance$overall[1]*100,
    test.pred.logistic.regression.performance$overall[1]*100,
    test.pred.svm.performance$overall[1]*100,
    test.pred.rf.performance$overall[1]*100)

# random forest predictions for Tom's movie reviews
tom.data.frame$pred.rf <- predict(train.data.frame.rf, type="class",
  newdata = tom.data.frame)

print(tom.data.frame[,c("thumbsupdown","pred.rf")])

tom.pred.rf.performance <-
  confusionMatrix(data = tom.data.frame$pred.rf,
  reference = tom.data.frame$thumbsupdown, positive = "UP")

# report full set of statistics relating to predictive accuracy
print(tom.pred.rf.performance)  # result 74.0 Percent

cat("\n\nTraining set percentage correctly predicted by random forests = ",
  sprintf("%1.1f",tom.pred.rf.performance$overall[1]*100),
    " Percent",sep="")

# building a simple tree to classify reviews
simple.tree <- rpart(text.classification.model,
  data=train.data.frame,)

# plot the regression tree result from rpart
pdf(file = "fig_sentiment_simple_tree_classifier.pdf", width = 8.5, height = 8.5)
prp(simple.tree, main="",
  digits = 3,  # digits to display in terminal nodes
  nn = TRUE,  # display the node numbers
  fallen.leaves = TRUE,  # put the leaves on the bottom of the page
  branch = 0.5,  # change angle of branch lines
  branch.lwd = 2,  # width of branch lines
  faclen = 0,  # do not abbreviate factor levels
```

```
  trace = 1,  # print the automatically calculated cex
  shadow.col = 0,  # no shadows under the leaves
  branch.lty = 1,  # draw branches using dotted lines
  split.cex = 1.2,  # make the split text larger than the node text
  split.prefix = "is ",  # put "is" before split text
  split.suffix = "?",  # put "?" after split text
  split.box.col = "blue",  # lightgray split boxes (default is white)
  split.col = "white",  # color of text in split box
  split.border.col = "blue",  # darkgray border on split boxes
  split.round = .25)  # round the split box corners a tad
dev.off()

# simple tree predictions for Tom's movie reviews
tom.data.frame$pred.simple.tree <- predict(simple.tree, type="class",
  newdata = tom.data.frame)

print(tom.data.frame[,c("thumbsupdown","pred.rf","pred.simple.tree")])

# suggestions for the student
# employ stemming prior to the creation of terms-by-document matrices
# try alternative positive and negative word sets
# try word sets that relate to a wider variety of emotional or opinion states
# better still... move beyond a simple bag-of-words approach to sentiment
# run a true benchmark within a loop using hundreds or thousands of iterations
# try other indices of classifier performance such as area under the ROC curve
```

9

Sports Analytics

"Sometimes you win, sometimes you lose, sometimes it rains."

—TIM ROBBINS AS EBBY CALVIN LaLOOSH IN *Bull Durham* (1988)

The Great Recession had a profound effect upon my consulting practice, which, at the time, was largely focused upon new product research and retail site selection. As a result, I had time to pursue a personal interest in sports analytics and enough time to write the book *Without a Tout: How to Pick a Winning Team* (Miller 2008b).

Although most data scientists and statisticians would argue that sports betting is a waste of time and money, there are statistically inspired touts like Bob Stoll (best known as *Dr. Bob*) who, using predictive models and published data about competing teams and players, realized a winning percentage (against point spreads) in seven of eight years of his sports information service. Dr. Bob's winning streak, as documented in an article in *The Wall Street Journal* in 2007, inspired my book.

Drawing on public domain data from Major League Baseball, *Without a Tout* presents a generic, data-driven, approach to picking a winning team. This approach is illustrated in figure 9.1.

Figure 9.1. Predictive Modeling Framework for Picking a Winning Team

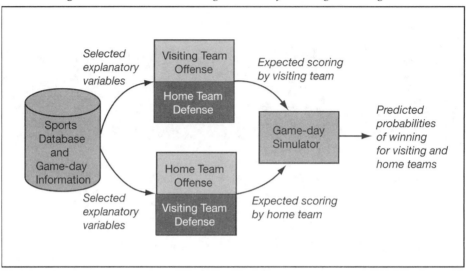

The modeling framework of *Without a Tout* follows the principles of predictive modeling outlined in this book. Explanatory variables relate to past player and team performance. These are used to predict runs or points scored by opposing teams. We note where and when games are played and any other conditions that may affect game outcomes. As always, a training-and-test regimen is employed in the evaluation of models. An important part of this modeling is game-day simulation, which we illustrate in this chapter with an example from Major League Baseball in 2007.

The framework allows distinct sets of explanatory variables to be used for visiting and home teams. The drivers of success for the Yankees may be different from the drivers of success for the Red Sox, the drivers for the Red Sox different from the Angels, the Angels different from the Indians, and so on. For each team, the things that matter when playing at home may be different from the things that matter when playing away. Various measures of win/loss strength and offensive and defensive performance may be used as explanatory variables. Runs-scored models can be traditional or data-adaptive, or a combination of the two.

Winning and losing in baseball depend upon the number of runs scored by opposing teams. If we can predict runs scored, then we can estimate the probability that one team will beat another. Winning/losing and the number of runs scored are response variables, much as we would have in any other predictive model.

Runs scored data may be organized by games, teams, and time (or schedule). In 2007, there were thirty teams—sixteen in the National League and fourteen in the American League. We can use simulation to pick winning teams. Taking 2007 inter-league games as an example, we note that games were scheduled between the Mets and Yankees for Friday, Saturday, and Sunday, June 15, 16, and 17. On Thursday, June 14, we could have asked questions like these: *How many runs can the Mets be expected to score against the Yankees when playing at Yankee Stadium? How many runs can the Yankees be expected to score? And, consequently, which team is expected to win these games?*

To predict straight-up runs scored in the future, we start with runs scored in the past. We select Mets' and Yankees' data for the current season, ignoring team statistics from previous seasons and the 2007 preseason. June 15 was the first meeting of the Mets and Yankees in the regular 2007 season, so we need to use runs scored against other teams. For the Mets, we can select all Mets' regular season away games between opening day in St. Louis with the Cardinals on May 1 to an away game on June 13 with the Los Angeles Dodgers. And for the Yankees, we can select all Yankees home games prior to June 15, which begin with the home opener with the Devil Rays on April 2 to a home game with the Diamondbacks on June 14.

Table 9.1 provides a complete list of Mets' games and scores between April 1 and June 15, and table 9.2 provides a complete list of Yankees' games and scores for the same period.[1] Looking over the data from the Mets' and Yankees' tables, we can see that the Mets have been scoring more runs than their opponents in away games, but fewer in home games. The Yankees, on the other hand, have been scoring more runs than their opponents both at home and away.

Overall, Yankees' games appear to have more scoring than Mets' games. This is understandable because American League games have a designated hitter. All but three Yankees' games were played in American League parks.

---

[1] The date ranges for games used in the simulation do not need to be over the same period of time, but we will use the same period for this simulation example.

The three games that the Yankees played in a National League park prior to June 15, 2007 happened to be at Shea Stadium against the Mets:

May 18	Yankees 2	Mets 3
May 19	Yankees 7	Mets 10
May 20	Yankees 6	Mets 2

One might be tempted to use the results of these three games to predict the outcome of the games on June 15, 16, and 17. But three games do not provide sufficient data from which to draw trustworthy inferences. Furthermore, the upcoming Yankees-Mets games will be played at Yankee Stadium with the designated hitter rule in force, a fact that we would like to accommodate (at least in part) through our simulation.

Game-day simulation uses data from real games in the past to generate data about hypothetical games, past and future. Many sports fans are familiar with simulation from fantasy sports. A fantasy baseball game can have Babe Ruth hitting against Bob Gibson or Honus Wagner hitting against Sandy Koufax. Simulations are executed by computer. They utilize baseball statistics from the history of the game and its players. Randomness is introduced by random number generators, so that playing the same game again and again provides a distinct outcome each time.

Taking the lead from fantasy sports, we can create fantasy games with an objective to estimate the probability that one team will beat another. For example, suppose we use a simple game-day simulation to pick the winning team in the June Mets-Yankees' series. Drawing from the away runs-scored distribution of the Mets and the home runs-scored distribution of the Yankees on each playing of our fantasy game (each iteration of the simulation), we observe the runs scored by the Mets and the runs scored by the Yankees. If tied, we discard the observation. If the Mets' score is higher than the Yankees' score, we count a win for the Mets. If the Yankees' score is higher than the Mets' score, we count a win for the Yankees. Dividing the number of times the Mets win by the number of times we play the game without a tie provides an estimate of the probability of the Mets winning. Dividing the number of times the Yankees win by the number of times we play the game without a tie gives an estimate of the the probability of the Yankees winning, which is one minus the probability of the Mets winning.

Table 9.1. *New York Mets' Early Season Games in 2007*

	Away Games ($n = 31$)				Home Games ($n = 33$)		
		Runs Scored				**Runs Scored**	
Date	**Home Team**	**Mets**	**Home Team**	**Date**	**Away Team**	**Away Team**	**Mets**
4/1/07	STL	6	1	4/9/07	PHI	5	11
4/3/07	STL	4	1	4/11/07	PHI	5	2
4/4/07	STL	10	0	4/12/07	PHI	3	5
4/6/07	ATL	11	1	4/13/07	WSH	2	3
4/7/07	ATL	3	5	4/14/07	WSH	6	2
4/8/07	ATL	2	3	4/20/07	ATL	7	3
4/17/07	PHI	8	1	4/21/07	ATL	2	7
4/18/07	FLA	9	2	4/22/07	ATL	9	6
4/19/07	FLA	11	3	4/23/07	COL	1	6
4/27/07	WSH	3	4	4/24/07	COL	1	2
4/28/07	WSH	6	2	4/25/07	COL	11	5
4/29/07	WSH	1	0	4/30/07	FLA	9	6
5/3/07	ARI	9	4	5/1/07	FLA	5	2
5/4/07	ARI	5	3	5/2/07	FLA	3	6
5/5/07	ARI	6	2	5/11/07	MIL	4	5
5/6/07	ARI	1	3	5/12/07	MIL	12	3
5/7/07	SF	4	9	5/13/07	MIL	1	9
5/8/07	SF	4	1	5/14/07	CHC	4	5
5/9/07	SF	5	3	5/15/07	CHC	10	1
5/22/07	ATL	1	8	5/16/07	CHC	1	8
5/23/07	ATL	3	0	5/17/07	CHC	5	6
5/24/07	ATL	1	2	5/18/07	NYY	2	3
5/25/07	FLA	6	2	5/19/07	NYY	7	10
5/26/07	FLA	7	2	5/20/07	NYY	6	2
5/27/07	FLA	6	4	5/29/07	SF	4	5
6/8/07	DET	3	0	5/30/07	SF	3	0
6/9/07	DET	7	8	5/31/07	SF	2	4
6/10/07	DET	7	15	6/1/07	ARI	5	1
6/11/07	LAD	3	5	6/2/07	ARI	1	7
6/12/07	LAD	1	4	6/3/07	ARI	4	1
6/13/07	LAD	1	9	6/5/07	PHI	4	2
				6/6/07	PHI	4	2
				6/7/07	PHI	6	3
Average Runs		4.97	3.45	**Average Runs**		4.67	4.33

Table 9.2. *New York Yankees' Early Season Games in 2007*

Away Games ($n = 31$)				Home Games ($n = 33$)			
		Runs Scored				Runs Scored	
Date	Home Team	Yankees	Home Team	Date	Away Team	Away Team	Yankees
4/9/07	MIN	8	2	4/2/07	TB	5	9
4/10/07	MIN	10	1	4/5/07	TB	7	6
4/11/07	MIN	1	5	4/6/07	BAL	6	4
4/13/07	OAK	4	5	4/7/07	BAL	7	10
4/14/07	OAK	4	3	4/8/07	BAL	6	4
4/15/07	OAK	4	5	4/17/07	CLE	3	10
4/20/07	BOS	6	7	4/18/07	CLE	2	9
4/21/07	BOS	5	7	4/19/07	CLE	6	8
4/22/07	BOS	6	7	4/26/07	TOR	6	0
4/23/07	TB	8	10	4/27/07	BOS	11	4
4/24/07	TB	4	6	4/28/07	BOS	1	3
5/1/07	TEX	10	1	4/29/07	BOS	7	4
5/3/07	TEX	4	3	5/4/07	SEA	15	11
5/3/07	TEX	5	2	5/5/07	SEA	1	8
5/11/07	SEA	0	3	5/6/07	SEA	0	5
5/12/07	SEA	7	2	5/7/07	SEA	3	2
5/13/07	SEA	1	2	5/8/07	TEX	2	8
5/16/07	CWS	3	5	5/9/07	TEX	2	6
5/16/07	CWS	8	1	5/10/07	TEX	14	2
5/17/07	CWS	1	4	5/21/07	BOS	2	6
5/18/07	NYM	2	3	5/22/07	BOS	7	3
5/19/07	NYM	7	10	5/23/07	BOS	3	8
5/20/07	NYM	6	2	5/25/07	LAA	10	6
5/28/07	TOR	2	7	5/26/07	LAA	3	1
5/29/07	TOR	2	3	5/27/07	LAA	4	3
5/30/07	TOR	10	5	6/8/07	PIT	4	5
6/1/07	BOS	9	5	6/9/07	PIT	3	9
6/2/07	BOS	6	11	6/10/07	PIT	6	13
6/3/07	BOS	6	5	6/12/07	ARI	1	4
6/4/07	CWS	4	6	6/13/07	ARI	2	7
6/5/07	CWS	7	3	6/14/07	ARI	1	7
6/6/07	CWS	5	1				
6/7/07	CWS	10	3				
Average Runs		5.30	4.39	**Average Runs**		4.84	5.97

The game-day simulation we are describing is an empirical simulation because it is based upon empirical distributions of runs scored by the two teams. The simulation uses only past runs scored and an identification of the Mets and Yankees as the teams. Figure 9.2 illustrates the results of such a simulation.

We see that one way to pick a winning team is to simulate play between teams. We should not expect too much from this simple game-day simulation. Knowing visiting and home teams, where the game is played, and past team scores is only the beginning. Our simulation ignores the fact that the Mets play most of their games in National League parks without a designated hitter and the Yankees play most of their games in American League parks with a designated hitter. Furthermore, this first simulation is focused solely upon offense, considering runs scored by each team with no recognition of runs allowed. It gives a picture of offense without defense. Based only on runs scored, the Yankees look like they could beat the Mets.

To get a picture of how the Mets and Yankees stack up against each other, we juxtapose the teams' offensive and defensive performance data. For games played at Yankee Stadium, the Mets' away offense is pitted against the Yankees' home defense and the Yankees' home offense is pitted against the Mets away defense. See figure 9.3.

A balanced simulation would consider both offense and defense, as shown in figure 9.4, with offense being runs scored and defense being runs allowed (runs scored by the other team). Here we take random drawings from the empirical distributions of runs scored and allowed by opposing teams to estimate expected runs scored by each team. Our approach in this example is to average opposing team offensive and defensive numbers. Taking both offense and defense into consideration, the Mets and Yankees appear to be more evenly matched, with the Mets' probability of winning 0.52 and the Yankees' probability of winning 0.48.[2]

When working with a count like the number of runs scored, it is convenient to employ probability distributions such as the Poisson distribution and the negative binomial distribution. Using a Poisson distribution to represent

---

[2] What actually happened in these three interleague games? On Friday evening, June 15, 2007 the Mets beat the Yankees 2 to 0. The following day the Yankees beat the Mets 11 to 8. And on Sunday, June 17, the Yankees won again, beating the Mets 8 to 2.

Figure 9.2. *Game-day Simulation (offense only)*

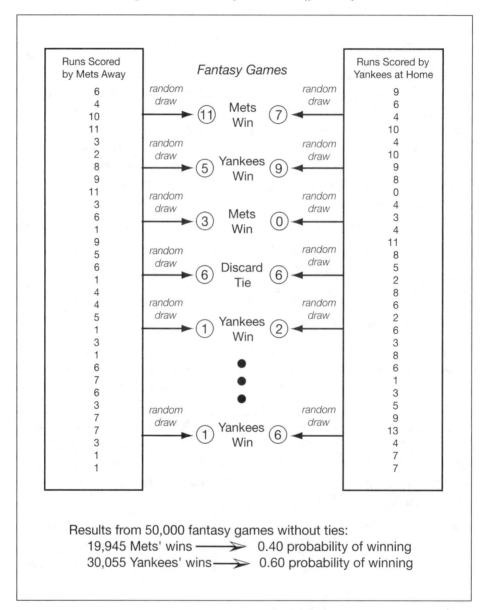

Figure 9.3. *Mets' Away and Yankees' Home Data (offense and defense)*

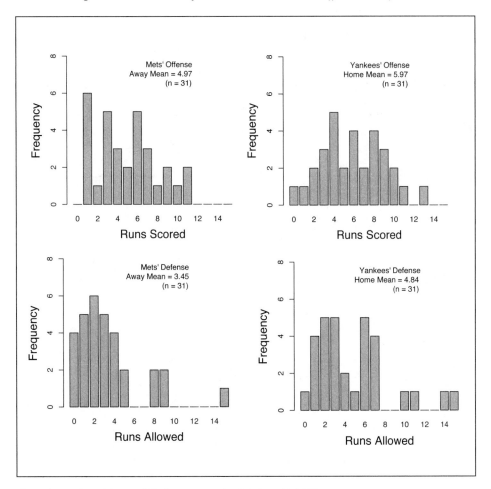

Data drawn from Mets and Yankees games April 1–June 14, 2007.

Figure 9.4. *Balanced Game-day Simulation (offense and defense)*

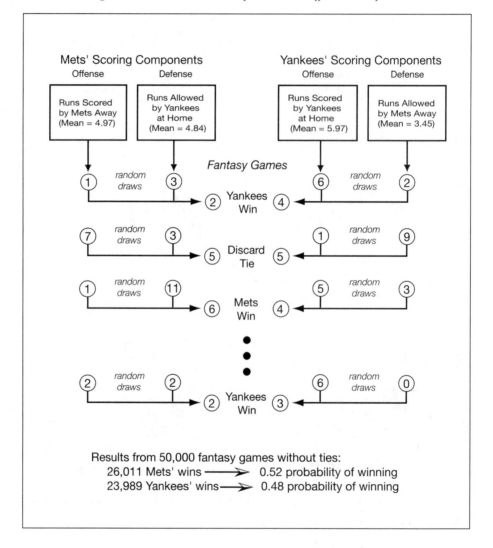

runs scored, shutouts (zero runs scored) are viewed as rare events, especially for teams scoring an average of three or more runs per game. Scores of more than twenty runs are also seen as rare events for teams scoring fewer than seven runs a game on average.[3]

For the 2007 baseball season, taking runs scored across all teams and all games between April 1 and July 8 (prior to the All Star Game), we obtain 2,598 observations and an average or mean runs scored of 4.68. The frequency distribution of these runs-scored observations is shown in the upper left-hand panel of figure 9.5. This figure also shows the relative frequency distribution and theoretical probabilities for a Poisson distribution with mean 4.68 and for a negative binomial distribution with mean 4.68 and shape parameter 4.00. Notice that for these runs-scored data the negative binomial appears to provide a better fit or match. This is especially apparent at the low end of the distribution.

Mean runs-scored and shape $(k = 4)$ are the defining parameters of a negative binomial probability distribution.[4] Using a negative binomial distribution to represent runs scored, shutouts are not so rare as with the Poisson

---

[3] The word *Poisson*, pronounced "poy san," refers to Siméon D. Poisson (1781–1840), who published the first derivation of the distribution in 1837. Statisticians tell us that the Poisson probability distribution is given by the formula:

$$P(x) = \frac{e^{-\lambda}\lambda^x}{x!}$$

where e is the exponential constant and λ (Greek letter lambda) is its one parameter, representing both the mean (average) and variance of the distribution. Calculations may be carried out on a hand calculator by starting with no runs scored, for which the probability is $P(0) = e^{-\lambda}$. For one run scored we have $P(1) = P(0)\lambda$. And, generalizing, for x runs scored we have $P(x) = P(x-1)\frac{\lambda}{x}$. Fortunately, as with other modeling work, we let the computer do the calculations for us. Those interested in the mathematics behind probability distributions as well as other topics in probability theory, may refer to Feller (1968). Keller (1994) showed that the Poisson probability distribution can be used as a model for baseball scores. The Poisson model works best when the rate or probability of run scoring does not vary substantially from game to game, which might make sense when working with a single team with a stable lineup from day to day.

[4] The negative binomial distribution may be thought of as the reverse or flip-side of the binomial. While the binomial distribution gives the number of successes in n trials, the negative binomial gives the number of trials x until we observe some number of success. The negative binomial may be derived as a mixture of Poisson distributions and is sometimes called the compound Poisson distribution. It is defined by two parameters, the mean μ and the shape parameter k. The probability of observing x runs in a game is given by the formula

$$p(x) = \left(1 + \frac{\mu}{k}\right)^{-k} \frac{(k+x-1)!}{x!(k-1)!} \left(\frac{\mu}{u+k}\right)^x$$

For zero runs scored, we obtain a much simpler expression:

$$p(0) = \left(1 + \frac{\mu}{k}\right)^{-k}$$

Figure 9.5. *Actual and Theoretical Runs-scored Distributions*

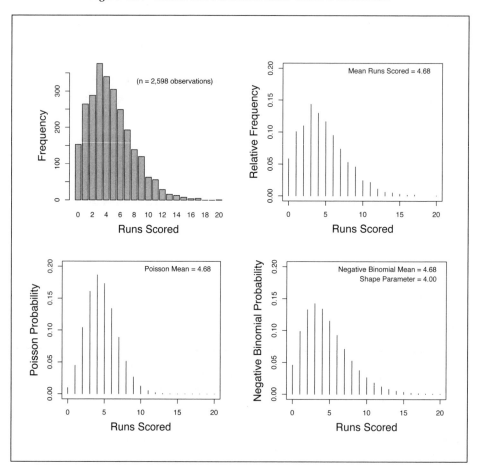

distribution. Higher scores are also more common with the negative binomial than with the Poisson. As a theoretical representation of runs scored,
then, we would seem to be well served by the negative binomial.

Another way to execute a simulation is to use theoretical probability distributions. For example, we could simulate Mets-Yankees' games as paired
random drawings from theoretical probability distributions, with the stip-
ulation that drawings with ties be discarded. That is, we can draw random
pairs of observations from the Mets' away and Yankees' home distributions,
executing a balanced simulation of offensive and defensive performance
with Poisson or negative binomial models for runs scored.

We show a Poisson model for how the Mets and Yankees stack up against
each other in figure 9.6. The corresponding negative binomial model is
shown in figure 9.7. With the Poisson model, executing the Mets-Yankees
simulation for 50,000 games without ties, we observe the Mets beating the
Yankees in 26,863 games, obtaining an estimated probability of 0.54.

Moving away from the Poisson model and using a negative binomial model
with shape parameter k set to 4, we observe the Mets beating the Yankees in
26,202 of 50,000 games without ties, obtaining an estimated probability of
0.52. The Poisson estimate is close to the estimate from the balanced empirical runs-scored simulation, and the negative binomial estimate, rounded to
two significant digits, is the same as the estimate from the empirical simulation. Both simulations predict the Yankees winning about two out of three
games.

When we use game-day simulator to estimate a team's probability of winning, we are employing a model-dependent approach to predictive modeling. We generate data from a model and note how well they conform

---

The negative binomial distribution is especially useful for working with counts for which the variance
is larger than the mean, a situation that statisticians call overdispersion. The shape or dispersion parameter k may be estimated by comparing the mean and variance of the observed counts. Our research
with baseball runs scored suggests that a shape parameter k between 3 and 5 works well for the number
of runs scored by a group of major league baseball teams. For the examples in this chapter we set k to
4, which was determined to be a good fit to actual runs-scored data according to a statistical procedure
called maximum likelihood estimation. The negative binomial distribution represents a good model
for runs-scored distributions when the rate or probability of scoring varies from one game to the next,
as it would for a group of teams or a team that shows considerable variability in its performance across
time. The negative binomial distribution has been shown to be useful for modeling scores in various
sports (Reep, Pollard, and Benjamin 1971; Pollard 1973). Again, we refer to Feller (1968) for probability
theory and use the computer to do the work.

Figure 9.6. *Poisson Model for Mets vs. Yankees at Yankee Stadium*

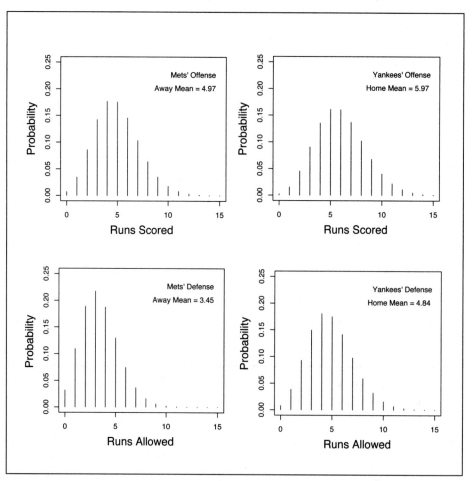

Poisson means estimated from Mets and Yankees games April 1–June 14, 2007.

Figure 9.7. *Negative Binomial Model for Mets vs. Yankees at Yankee Stadium*

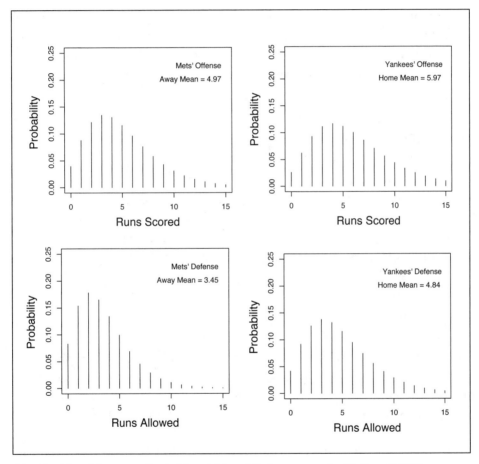

Negative binomial means estimated from Mets and Yankees games April 1–June 14, 2007.

The negative binomial shape parameter *k* set to 4.

to real or empirical data. The Poisson and negative binomial distributions conform well, so we use them to build models. We can use them to estimate the probability that one team will beat another and to pick a winning team. The simulator is model-dependent, but the inputs to the simulator come from predictive models fit to observed data.

Figure 9.8 shows results from a probability simulator for home and away teams scoring between one and nine runs each, again using a negative binomial probability model with shape parameter k set to 4. This probability heat map is the result of running $\frac{(9 \times 8)}{2}$ or 36 game-day simulations, with each simulation consisting of 100,000 games.

Precise mathematical calculations and well designed simulations are the easy part of predictive inference in sports. We have algorithms and computer programs to do the work. What is not so easy is obtaining the runs-scored estimates for input to the programs.

Do not underestimate the difficulty of predicting which team will win the next game. As we have said numerous times, predictive analytics is a precarious enterprise. It is a process of extrapolating and forecasting. In sports, it takes a very good model to do a better job than the bookmakers, to win against the spread and cover betting fees in the process. Accurate models for predicting the outcome of sporting events may be elusive. Nonetheless, it is comforting to know that we have a plan for finding accurate models if indeed they do exist.

Applications of predictive modeling in sports extend beyond the world of sports betting of course, as any owner or manager is interested in predicting game outcomes. By changing the composition of a team, an owner can influence a team's scoring, the opponent team's scoring, and the outcome of a game. The input to the model and the simulator consists of data for a newly constructed or hypothetical team. We begin by fitting a reasonable model for predicting runs or points scored. Then we use the simulator to estimate probabilities of winning for the new team, which in turn serve as input to attendance and revenue models. Fans like winners, and they are more likely go to ballparks, courts, and stadia to see winners.

Extensive data about sports are in the public domain, readily available in newspapers and online sources. These data offer opportunities for predictive modeling and research.

Figure 9.8. *Probability of Home Team Winning (Negative Binomial Model)*

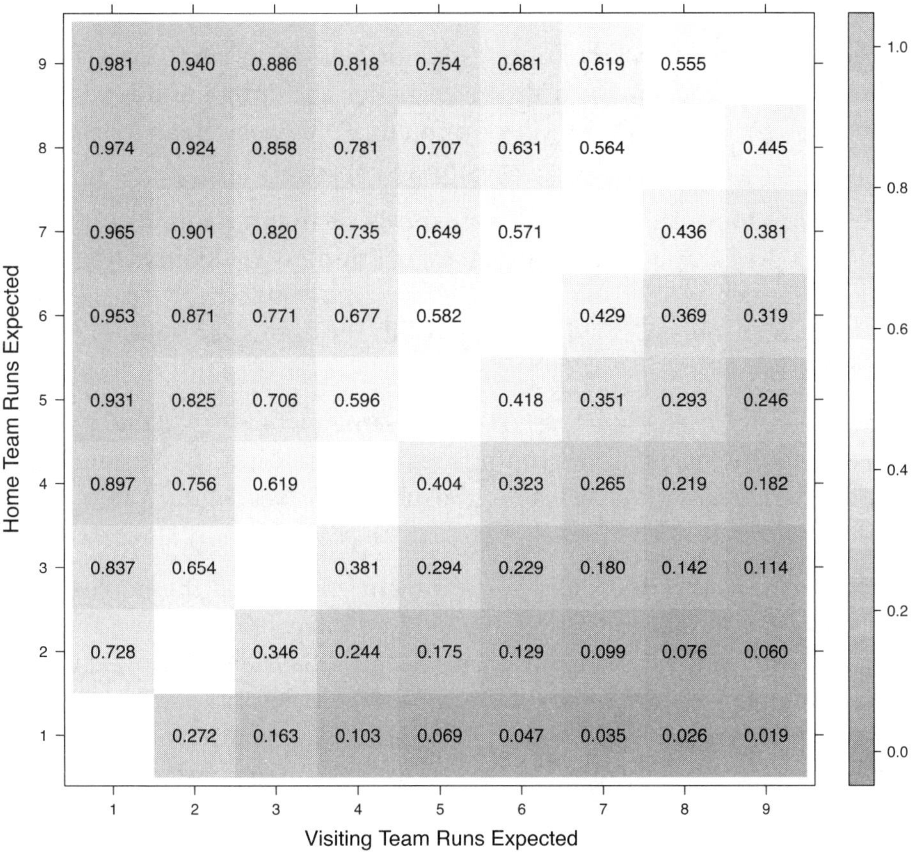

The negative binomial shape parameter k set to 4.

Sports wagering markets have been studied extensively by economists because they provide public information about price, volume, and rates of return. Furthermore, sports betting opportunities have fixed beginning and ending times and published odds or point spreads, making them easier to study than many financial investment opportunities. As a result, sports wagering markets have become a virtual field laboratory for the study of market efficiency. Sauer (1998) provides a comprehensive review of the economics of wagering markets.

Sports also represents a laboratory for labor market research. Sports is one of the few industries in which job performance and compensation are public knowledge. Economic studies examine player performance measures and value of individual players to teams (Kahn 2000).

There are also special applications in sports analytics relating to players, teams, and the competitive environment of sports. We identify five special problems, which we call the *Baseball Prospectus* problem, *Moneyball* problem, coaching problem, Bowl Championship Series problem, and Billy Walters problem.

We begin with the *Baseball Prospectus* problem. Nate Silver gained notoriety as one of the contributors in this area with the PECOTA system.[5] The question that *Baseball Prospectus* prognosticators ask each year? *How can we predict the performance of teams before the season begins?*

A second problem is the *Moneyball* problem. *Moneyball* the book (Lewis 2003) and *Moneyball* the movie have generated interest in applying analytics to sports, with noted cases cited in books and articles about predictive analytics (Goldman 2005; Hakes and Sauer 2006; Davenport and Harris 2007; Miller 2008b; Silver 2012). *What is the value of a current player to his team?* This is a question that is often answered by designing summary measures of individual player performance and seeing how those measures relate to team runs or points scored.

Next, we have the coaching question: *How shall we utilize player resources?* Pre-game and in-game decisions can be informed by play-by-play game

---

[5] PECOTA originally stood for *Pitcher Empirical Comparison and Optimization Test Algorithm*. Silver adapted the system to hitters, noting that the name PECOTA may be thought of as referring to Bill Pecota, a .249 hitter overall with the Kansas City Royals, who managed to hit .303 against the Detroit Tigers (Silver 2012).

data from the past. While business data scientists are focused on the challenges of big data, sports analysts are going micro, perusing the details of the game, the play-by-play, the location of each pitch and the position of every player. Let the analysis proceed.[6]

A fourth problem in sports analytics is the Bowl Championship Series (BCS) problem: *How do we judge the relative strength of teams that have never played each other?* Despite having adopted a limited playoff system for NCAA Division I football, BCS administrators continue to face this problem.

The BCS problem relates to strength-of-schedule differences across teams from various college football conferences. Mathematical models and mathematical programming algorithms (Winston 2009) are utilized in this domain, as evidenced by the popularity of Sagarin ratings in *USA Today*. The ranking of sports teams and models for predicting the outcome of sporting events have garnered considerable attention in the academic literature. Langville and Meyer (2012) provide a comprehensive review of rating and ranking algorithms and methods. Paired comparison psychometrics and preference scaling methods, similar to those used in consumer research, may be used in the rating and ranking of teams (Miller 2008b). Special interest has been shown in games of the National Football League (Thompson 1975; Stern 1991; Glickman and Stern 1998). And there has been much written about rating and ranking strategies for picking winning brackets in the men's Division I NCAA basketball tournament, commonly referred to as *March Madness* (Schwertman, McCready, and Howard 1991; Schwertman, Schenk, and Holbrook 1996; Carlin 1996; Kaplan and Garstka 2001; West 2006).

---

[6] The baseball manager determines the starting line-up, when to pull the starting pitcher, when to pinch hit, when to bunt or hit away, and of course when to argue a call. There are those hidden rules of baseball (Thorn and Palmer 1985; Keri 2006; Tango, Lichtman, and Dolphin 2007), football (Carrol et al. 1998), and basketball (Oliver 2004) that are understood by the best managers and coaches in sports. The mantra of Sabermetrics is to use objective evidence from baseball to evaluate past player performance and inform in-game decisions, and baseball has long been fascinated with data (Schwarz 2004; James 2010). Contributors to the *Journal of Quantitative Analysis in Sports*, an electronic journal introduced in 2005, have been most influential in developing predictive models to address game-day strategy and play calling (Alamar 2013). Key in basketball is the decision about which five players to put in the game at any given time, player match-ups in guarding opposing players, and the type of defense to employ. In football, we have offensive and defensive formations, whether to run or pass, and whether to punt or go for it on fourth and one (or two, or more). Data and predictive models often contradict conventional approaches to coaching, such as punting on fourth down (Romer 2006; Berri and Schmidt 2010; Moskowitz and Wertheim 2011).

Last but not least in our list of special problems in sports analytics is the problem we used to begin the chapter. We call this the Billy Walters problem. A high-stakes sports gambler and millionaire Las Vegas resident, with additional homes in numerous locations, Billy Walters claims to have had thirty winning years of betting on football and basketball. The question here: *How do we pick the winning team in the next game?*[7]

For those with a penchant for sports wagering, predictive modeling defines a new smart money approach. Data lead to predictions about points scored and points allowed. Predictions about points lead to estimated probabilities of winning. And probabilities of winning are used to evaluate betting opportunities. In sum, a model can tell us when it makes sense to bet.

The old smart-money approach from the 1990s was expert or rule-driven. There was hope that human intuition, or more precisely, human expertise could be captured in computer software.[8] The game plan was to find experts and model their thinking. Predictive analytics represents a new smart money approach, one that relies upon expertise in data analysis and modeling, not sports or sports betting per se. The emergence of the "quants"

---

[7] Some argue that an expectation of winning 55 percent of the time (or even 53 percent of the time) is reason enough to live the gambler's life (Yao 2007). Many others would disagree. The participant in a sports wagering market takes a financial position on the outcome of a sporting event, knowing that, lacking insider information, the expected return on his investment is negative. In a study of thirteen sports writers (supposed expert observers of the sporting scene) who had made point-spread predictions during the period from 1983 to 1994, Avery and Chevalier (1999) found that only one would have made a profit from his predictions. Regarding the likelihood of winning and of making money in the process, we have classic works in probability to serve as a guide (Dubins and Savage 1965; Feller 1968; Feller 1971). Most statisticians would agree with my former statistics advisor, Don Berry (1996), in arguing that sports betting is a waste of time and money.

[8] In the 1990s, the talk was about artificial intelligence and expert systems. There were people seeking specialized training in what was called knowledge engineering. A knowledge engineer would interview experts, learn the relevant heuristics and rules of thumb, and then implement to those rules in code. Lisp and Prolog were the languages of choice for these domain-specific imitator savants. Konig's (2006) description of what smart money players were doing circa 1997–2001 suggests the application of rules-based expert systems: *If we tell the program the rules, and keep adding rules, and throwing out the ones that don't apply, and continue adding data, and refining rules—you know, testing them in simulations—and we can compare them with a historical record (I assume you have all that) and then test your hypotheses (and, again, I assume you have plenty of assumptions, since you've been doing this for many, many years, right?), it's rather easy to get a couple of computers working against each other to assign values to every aspect of the data we feed them. In other words, if you can tell me what to tell the machine, I can tell you what it thinks about what you know."* (275) Much of the hype around artificial intelligence and knowledge engineering has subsided. The search for heuristics has been replaced by the search for relationships and computer programs that can learn a la Blondie24 (Fogel 2001). Machine learning and data science have replaced domain experts and knowledge engineers. This thinking was the rationale for the book title *Without a Tout* (Miller 2008b), recognizing that sports experts and handicappers are called touts.

(quantitative analysts and modelers) as a new class of sports betters and analysts validates this approach (Eden 2013).

Game-day simulations and modeling methods in predictive analytics have an advantage in that they may be employed by sports experts and non-experts alike. These methods are data-driven rather than expert- or rule-driven. And, being data-driven, we can test their accuracy before we use them to make decisions in the marketplace or bets at the sports books.

How do we test the accuracy of a predictive model? We employ a training-and-test regimen. As in economic and financial research, we see how well we can predict the past before we attempt to predict the future. That is, we use more distant past observations to predict less distant past observations. If we are working with a sixteen-week football season, for example, we use the first ten weeks' data to predict what will happen in the eleventh week. Then we use the first eleven weeks' data to predict what will happen in the twelfth week, and so on. Measures of uncertainty in predicting the past based upon hold-out test sets show us how uncertain we should be about predicting the future.

Sports is big business and an important part of the entertainment industry. In sports business management, predictive analytics serves a variety of purposes much as it does in other industries. There are questions of advertising and promotion, as we showed in our earlier example with the Los Angeles Dodgers. There are questions of branding, pricing, scheduling, and product design. Marketing and financial analytics, as well as operations management and research, are relevant to sports businesses.

Sports analytics is a fast growing area of application in predictive analytics, with applications to player selection and team composition, ratings of team competitive strength, game day strategies, and play calling. Sports data may be used to illustrate concepts in probability, statistics, and predictive modeling (Albert 2003; Albert and Bennett 2003). There are chapters of the Society for American Baseball Research scattered across the country. MIT hosts an annual sports analytics conference in Cambridge, Massachusetts. The American Statistical Association has a special interest section devoted to the subject of statistics in sports. The *Journal of Quantitative Analysis in Sports* and many other academic journals publish articles relating to statistics and sports.

To learn more about sports statistics, see Mosteller (1997) and the edited volume by Albert, Bennett, and Cochran (2005). Sports statistics offer many modeling challenges. The hot hand in basketball and hitting streaks and slumps in baseball, for example, have generated considerable interest in the statistical community (Bar-Eli, Avugos, and Raab 2006). For further review of modeling methods in sports analytics and how they may be employed within a rational sports betting framework, see Miller (2008b).

For reading in probability, refer to the Mosteller, Rourke, and Thomas (1970), the classic references of Feller (1968, 1971), and (for fun) a book of problems by Mosteller (1965). A Bayesian perspective is presented by Robert (2007), Albert (2009), and Hoff (2009).

Ross (2006) provides an introduction to probability modeling. Generating probability distributions and simulation programming in R are discussed by Robert and Casella (2009), Suess and Trumbo (2010), and Chihara and Hesterberg (2011).

The R program for the baseball probability simulator that we developed for this chapter is shown in exhibit 9.1. The program draws upon the lattice graphics package developed by Sarkar (2013).

Exhibit 9.1. *Winning Probabilities by Simulation (Negative Binomial Model)*

```
# Game-day Simulator for Baseball
library(lattice)  # graphics package used to create probability matrix visual
simulator <- function(away.mean,home.mean,niterations) {
# input is runs scored means output is probability of winning for away team
away.game.score <- numeric(niterations)
home.game.score <- numeric(niterations)
away.win <- numeric(niterations)
i <- 1
while (i < niterations + 1) {
  away.game.score[i] <- rnbinom(1,mu=away.mean, size = 4)
  home.game.score[i] <- rnbinom(1,mu=home.mean, size = 4)
  if(away.game.score[i]>home.game.score[i]) away.win[i] <- 1
  if(away.game.score[i]>home.game.score[i] ||
  away.game.score[i]<home.game.score[i]) i <- i + 1
  }
n.away.win <- sum(away.win)
n.away.win/niterations  # return probability of away team winning
}
set.seed(1234)  # set to obtain reproducible results
niterations <- 100000  # set to smaller number for testing
# probability matrix for results... home team is rows, away team is columns
probmat <- matrix(data = NA, nrow = 9, ncol = 9,
  dimnames = list(c(as.character(1:9), c(as.character(1:9)))))
for (index.home in 1:9)
for (index.away in 1:9)
if (index.home > index.away) {
  probmat[index.home,index.away] <-
    simulator(index.away, index.home, niterations)
  probmat[index.away,index.home] <- 1 - probmat[index.home, index.away]
  }
# create probability matrix visual
x <- rep(1:nrow(probmat),times=ncol(probmat))
y <- NULL
for (i in 1:ncol(probmat)) y <- c(y,rep(i,times=nrow(probmat)))
probtext <- sprintf("%0.3f", as.numeric(probmat))  # fixed format 0.XXX
text.data.frame <- data.frame(x, y, probtext)
text.data.frame$probtext <- as.character(text.data.frame$probtext)
text.data.frame$probtext <- ifelse((text.data.frame$probtext == "NA"),
   NA,text.data.frame$probtext)  # define diagonal cells as missing
text.data.frame <- na.omit(text.data.frame)  # diagonal cells
levelplot(probmat, cuts = 25, tick.number = 9,
  col.regions=colorRampPalette(c("violet", "white", "light blue")),
  xlab = "Visiting Team Runs Expected",
  ylab = "Home Team Runs Expected",
  panel = function(...) {
    panel.levelplot(...)
    panel.text(text.data.frame$x, text.data.frame$y,
    labels = text.data.frame$probtext)
    })
# suggestion for students: develop similar tables for football and basketball
```

## 10

Brand and Price

"What do ya want to hear? That I'd love to pay three hundred and fifty a month...is that what you want to hear? Tell me how much you want me to pay, and I'll tell you how much I'll pay, but don't do a hustle on me...I don't like that. How much do I want to pay? I'd like to pay nothing!"

—RICHARD DREYFUSS AS BILL BABOWSKY IN *Tin Men* (1987)

As a consumer, I am like two people. With almost everything—where I live and shop, how I travel, the clothes I buy, and the things I do for fun—I am extremely price-conscious. I walk rather than drive whenever I can, and I look for things on sale. As long as I am buying for myself, I rarely seek out particular brands. This is my economical side. I look for value.

There is another side to me, however. When it comes to computers and software, I am a person who buys only the best, highest quality, and most reliable products. Money is no object (until it runs out, of course). I read about fast computers and high-resolution displays, thinking, *Maybe that's what I should get next*. This most uneconomical side of me also applies to books. It is as though I have no control over my spending, no budget. When I see a book I like, I buy, and sometimes I pay for next-day delivery. I would be a good candidate for a "bibliophiles anoyomous" if there were one.

The example for this chapter takes us back to 1998. Microsoft introduced a new operating system, and computer manufacturers were interested in making predictions about the personal computer marketplace.[1] The study we consider, which we call the computer choice study, involved eight computer brands, price, and four other attributes of interest: compatibility, performance, reliability, and learning time. Table 10.1 provides a description of attribute levels used in the study.

The computer choice study was a nationwide study. We identified people who expressed an interest in buying a new personal computer within the next year. Consumers volunteering for the study were sent questionnaire booklets, answer sheets, and postage-paid return-mail envelopes. Each respondent received $25 for participating in the study. The survey consisted of sixteen pages, with each page showing a choice set of four product profiles. For each choice set, survey participants were asked first to select the computer they most preferred, and second, to indicate whether or not they would actually buy that computer. For our analysis we focus on the initial choice or most preferred computer in each set. Figure 10.1 shows the first page of the survey.

Each profile, defined in terms of its attributes, is associated with the consumer's binary response (0 = not chosen, 1 = chosen). Being diligent data scientists, we define an appropriate training-and-test regimen. In this context, we build predictive models on twelve choice sets and test on four.[2] The data for one individual are shown in table 10.2. To obtain useful conjoint measures for individuals, we employ hierarchical Bayes (HB) methods with constraints upon the signs of attribute coefficients other than brand.[3]

---

[1] This is a retrospective study, as a few of the companies involved have changed their roles in the computer industry or have left the industry entirely. Using a study more than ten years old has its advantages. None of the companies in question will care what our analysis shows. Like most of the examples in the book, these are real data, and at one time they had real meaning.

[2] When the prediction problem is to predict individual choice, the survey itself is divided into training and test. For this study, we split across the survey items or choice sets, arbitrarily selecting sets 3, 7, 11, and 15 as our hold-out choice sets. Items 1, 2, 4, 5, 6, 8, 9, 10, 12, 13, 14, and 16 serve as training data. With sixteen choice sets of four, we have 64 product profiles for each individual in the study. As a result of this training-and-test split, the training data include 48 rows of product profiles for each individual, and the test data include 16 rows of product profiles for each individual.

[3] We like to specify the signs of attribute coefficients when the order of preference for levels within attributes is obvious . For the computer choice study, we can specify the signs of coefficients for all attributes other than brand prior to fitting a model to the data. In particular, compatibility, performance, and reliability should have positive coefficients, whereas learning time and price should have negative coefficients.

Table 10.1. *Computer Choice Study: Product Attributes*

Attribute	Level Code	Level Description
Brand	Apple	Manufacturer: Apple
	Compaq	Manufacturer: Compaq
	Dell	Manufacturer: Dell
	Gateway	Manufacturer: Gateway
	HP	Manufacturer: HP
	IBM	Manufacturer: IBM
	Sony	Manufacturer: Sony
	Sun	Manufacturer: Sun Microsystems
Compatibility	1	65% Compatible
	2	70% Compatible
	3	75% Compatible
	4	80% Compatible
	5	85% Compatible
	6	90% Compatible
	7	95% Compatible
	8	100% Compatible
Performance	1	Just as fast
	2	Twice as fast
	3	Three times as fast
	4	Four times as fast
Reliability	1	As likely to fail
	2	Less likely to fail
Learn	1	4 hours to learn
	2	8 hours to learn
	3	12 hours to learn
	4	16 hours to learn
	5	20 hours to learn
	6	24 hours to learn
	7	28 hours to learn
	8	32 hours to learn
Price	1	$1,000
	2	$1,250
	3	$1,500
	4	$1,750
	5	$2,000
	6	$2,250
	7	$2,500
	8	$2,750

Figure 10.1. *Computer Choice Study: One Choice Set*

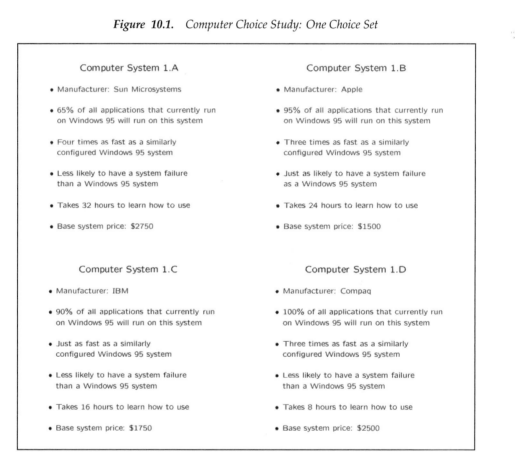

Table 10.2. *Computer Choice Study: Data for One Individual*

id	profile	setid	position	brand	compat	perform	reliab	learn	price	choice	buy
1	1	1	Top-Left	Sun	1	4	2	8	8	0	0
1	2	1	Top-Right	Apple	7	3	1	6	3	0	0
1	3	1	Bottom-Left	IBM	6	1	2	4	4	1	0
1	4	1	Bottom-Right	Compaq	8	3	2	2	7	0	0
1	5	2	Top-Left	Gateway	4	2	2	2	2	0	0
1	6	2	Top-Right	Sony	8	4	1	5	8	0	0
1	7	2	Bottom-Left	Sun	1	1	2	7	3	0	0
1	8	2	Bottom-Right	Dell	5	3	1	4	5	1	0
1	9	3	Top-Left	Dell	4	4	1	6	7	1	0
1	10	3	Top-Right	Sony	7	2	2	2	6	0	0
1	11	3	Bottom-Left	Apple	3	3	2	8	2	0	0
1	12	3	Bottom-Right	HP	8	1	1	2	5	0	0
1	13	4	Top-Left	Compaq	6	2	1	6	5	0	0
1	14	4	Top-Right	IBM	5	4	1	2	3	1	1
1	15	4	Bottom-Left	HP	7	3	2	7	1	0	0
1	16	4	Bottom-Right	Apple	2	1	1	4	7	0	0
1	17	5	Top-Left	Sony	6	1	1	8	3	0	0
1	18	5	Top-Right	Compaq	5	4	2	3	1	1	1
1	19	5	Bottom-Left	Dell	1	3	2	2	8	0	0
1	20	5	Bottom-Right	Gateway	8	2	1	1	1	0	0
1	21	6	Top-Left	IBM	1	4	2	4	2	1	1
1	22	6	Top-Right	Dell	8	4	2	8	6	0	0
1	23	6	Bottom-Left	Sun	4	2	1	3	4	0	0
1	24	6	Bottom-Right	Gateway	6	3	1	1	8	0	0
1	25	7	Top-Left	HP	2	4	2	1	3	1	1
1	26	7	Top-Right	Compaq	7	2	1	2	5	0	0
1	27	7	Bottom-Left	Sony	1	3	1	3	6	0	0
1	28	7	Bottom-Right	IBM	6	2	2	7	7	0	0
1	29	8	Top-Left	Dell	6	1	2	5	1	0	0
1	30	8	Top-Right	HP	5	2	2	6	6	0	0
1	31	8	Bottom-Left	Gateway	2	3	2	3	5	1	0
1	32	8	Bottom-Right	Compaq	1	4	1	1	4	0	0
1	33	9	Top-Left	Apple	1	2	2	5	5	0	0
1	34	9	Top-Right	Gateway	3	4	1	7	6	1	0
1	35	9	Bottom-Left	IBM	7	1	1	3	8	0	0
1	36	9	Bottom-Right	Sony	5	3	2	1	7	0	0
1	37	10	Top-Left	HP	4	1	2	4	8	0	0
1	38	10	Top-Right	Dell	8	3	2	1	2	1	1
1	39	10	Bottom-Left	IBM	2	2	1	5	6	0	0
1	40	10	Bottom-Right	Sun	7	4	1	8	5	0	0
1	41	11	Top-Left	Compaq	4	3	2	5	3	0	0
1	42	11	Top-Right	Sun	3	4	2	6	8	0	0
1	43	11	Bottom-Left	Gateway	5	1	2	8	4	0	0
1	44	11	Bottom-Right	HP	6	4	1	3	2	1	1
1	45	12	Top-Left	IBM	8	3	2	6	4	1	1
1	46	12	Top-Right	Gateway	7	4	2	5	7	0	0
1	47	12	Bottom-Left	Sony	3	2	1	2	1	0	0
1	48	12	Bottom-Right	Apple	4	1	1	1	6	0	0
1	49	13	Top-Left	Sun	5	1	1	5	2	0	0
1	50	13	Top-Right	Apple	6	4	2	2	4	0	0
1	51	13	Bottom-Left	Dell	3	2	2	3	3	0	0
1	52	13	Bottom-Right	IBM	4	3	1	8	1	1	1
1	53	14	Top-Left	Sony	4	4	2	7	5	0	0
1	54	14	Top-Right	HP	3	3	1	5	4	1	0
1	55	14	Bottom-Left	Compaq	2	2	2	8	8	0	0
1	56	14	Bottom-Right	Gateway	1	1	1	6	1	0	0
1	57	15	Top-Left	Apple	5	2	1	7	8	0	0
1	58	15	Top-Right	Sun	6	3	2	4	6	1	0
1	59	15	Bottom-Left	HP	1	2	1	8	7	0	0
1	60	15	Bottom-Right	Sony	2	1	2	6	2	0	0
1	61	16	Top-Left	Gateway	8	2	1	4	3	0	0
1	62	16	Top-Right	IBM	3	1	2	1	5	0	0
1	63	16	Bottom-Left	Compaq	5	4	2	3	1	1	1
1	64	16	Bottom-Right	Dell	2	1	1	7	4	0	0

Training: SET1, SET2, SET4, SET5, SET6, SET8, SET9, SET10, SET12, SET13, SET14, SET16
Test: SET3, SET7, SET11, SET15

The value of a model lies in the quality of its predictions. Here we are concerned with predictions for each individual respondent. We use the training set of twelve choice items to fit an HB model, estimating individual-level conjoint measures. Then we use the test set of four choice items to evaluate the fitted model. As a criterion of evaluation, we use the percentage of choices correctly predicted, noting that by chance alone we would expect to predict 25 percent of the choices correctly (because each choice item contains four product alternatives). The percentage of choices correctly predicted is the sensitivity or true positive rate in a binary classification problem (see figure A.1 in appendix A.).

How well does the HB model work? An HB model fit to the computer choice data provides training set sensitivity of 93.7 percent and test set sensitivity of 52.6 percent. As modeling techniques in predictive analytics, Bayesian methods hold considerable promise. (Exhibit 10.1 at the end of the chapter provides the programming documentation for this analysis.)

Returning to the original survey with sixteen choice sets, we estimate conjoint measures at the individual level with an HB model and place consumers into groups based upon their revealed preferences for computer products. Table 10.3 provides the cross-tabulation of top-ranked brands versus most valued attributes, where the top-ranked brands are determined within individuals and the most valued attributes are determined relative to all consumers in the study.[4] These data are rendered as a mosaic plot in figure 10.2.[5]

Brand and price are important. They help define how we behave in the marketplace—whether we buy, what we buy, when and how we buy. Product features are also important. Considered together, brand, price, and product features are key inputs to models of consumer preference and market response. Marketing managers benefit by having data and models presented in a clear and consistent manner. The model illustrated in figure

---

[4] The top-ranked brand is the brand with the highest estimated part-worth for the individual. Most favored attributes are determined relative to the entire study group. That is, we compute the value of an attribute to an individual as a standard score versus the entire study group. We do this because conventional attribute importance calculations are dependent upon relative ranges of sets of attribute levels utilized in surveys.

[5] Mosaic plots provide a convenient visualization of cross-tabulations (contingency tables). The relative heights of rows correspond to the relative row frequencies. The relative width of columns corresponds to the cell frequencies within rows. Mosaic plots are discussed in Hartigan and Kleiner (1984) and Friendly (2000), with R implementations reviewed in Meyer et al. (2006, 2013a).

Figure **10.2.** *Computer Choice Study: A Mosaic of Top Brands and Most Valued Attributes*

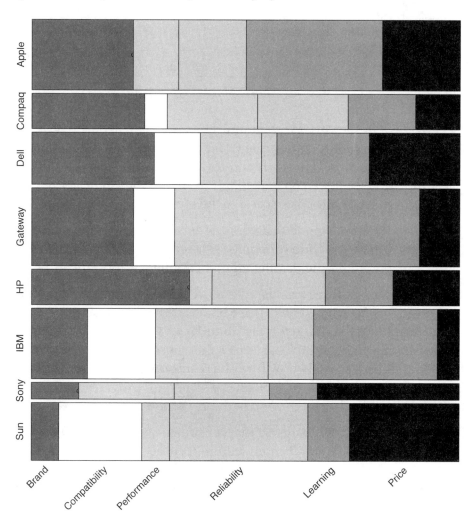

Table 10.3. Contingency Table of Top-ranked Brands and Most Valued Attributes

Top-Ranked Brand	Most Valued Attribute Relative to Other Consumers						Total
	Brand	Compatibility	Performance	Reliability	Learning	Price	
Apple	9	0	4	6	12	7	38
Compaq	5	1	4	4	3	2	19
Dell	8	3	4	1	6	6	28
Gateway	10	4	10	5	9	4	42
HP	7	0	1	5	3	3	19
IBM	5	6	10	4	11	2	38
Sony	1	0	2	2	1	3	9
Sun	2	6	2	10	3	8	31
Total	47	20	37	37	48	35	224

10.3, provides a framework for communicating with management. The plot in figure 10.4, referred to as a ternary plot or triplot, provides a visual of consumer preference and choice. Brand-loyal consumers fall to the bottom-left vertex, price-sensitive consumers fall to the bottom-right vertex, and feature-focused consumers are closest to the top vertex.

From the distribution of points across the ternary plot for the computer choice study, we can see wide variability or heterogeneity in consumer preferences. What does this mean for computer suppliers?

Suppose we focus on three brands, Apple, Dell, and HP, and select the subset of consumers for whom one of these brands is the top-ranked brand. We use density plots to examine the distributions of values for brand loyalty, price sensitivity, and feature focus across this subset of consumers. A density plot provides a smoothed picture of a distribution of measures. Showing densities for consumer groups on the same plot provides a picture of the degree to which there is overlap in these distributions.

The densities in figure 10.5 suggest that consumers rating Dell highest tend to be less price-sensitive and more feature-focused than consumers who rate Apple and HP highest. We can see, as well, that consumers rating HP highest have higher brand-loyalty than consumers rating Dell or Apple highest. A general finding that emerges from a review of these densities is that, in terms of the three measures from our ternary model, there is considerable overlap across consumers rating Apple, Dell, and HP highest.

A concern of marketers in many product categories is the extent to which consumers are open to switching from one brand to another. Parallel co-

Figure 10.3. *Framework for Describing Consumer Preference and Choice*

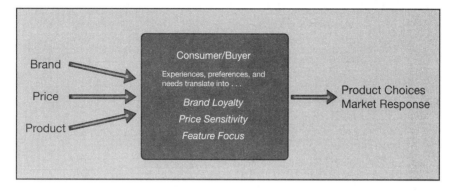

Figure 10.4. *Ternary Plot of Consumer Preference and Choice*

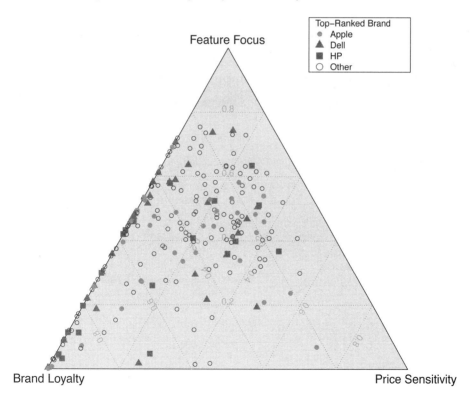

Figure 10.5. *Comparing Consumers with Differing Brand Preferences*

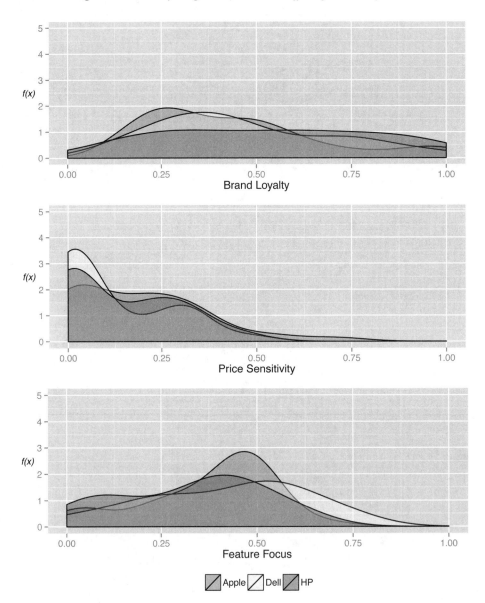

ordinate plots may be used to explore the potential for brand switching.[6] Parallel coordinates in figure 10.6 display thirty-eight lines for consumers rating Apple as the top brand, twenty-eight rating Dell as top, and nineteen rating HP as top. We can see that there is considerable variability in these individuals' part-worth profiles.

In figure 10.7 we show the mean part-worths for brands on parallel coordinates. Lines further to the right show stronger preference for a brand and stronger likelihood of switching to that brand. The figure shows that Apple consumers are most likely to switch to Sony or Sun, Dell consumers are most likely to switch to Gateway or Sun, and HP consumers are most likely to switch to Compaq, Gateway, or IBM.

While it is most interesting to describe consumer preferences and the extent to which consumers are brand-loyal, price-sensitive, or feature-focused, the most important contribution of choice models comes from their ability to predict consumer behavior in the marketplace.

We use models of consumer preference and choice to develop market simulations, exploring a variety of marketplace conditions and evaluating alternative management decisions. Market simulations are sometimes called *what-if analyses*.

To demonstrate market simulation with the computer choice study, suppose we are working for the Apple computer company, and we want to know what price to charge for our computer, given three other competitors in the market: Dell, Gateway, and HP. In addition, suppose that we have an objective of commanding a 25 percent share in the market. This is a hypothetical example but one that demonstrates market simulation as a modeling technique.

We describe the competitive products in terms of attributes, creating simulated choice sets for input to the market simulation. Let us imagine that the Dell system is a high-end system, 100 percent compatible with earlier systems, four times as fast, and less likely to fail. It takes sixteen hours to learn and costs $1,750. The Gateway offering is 90 percent compatible,

---

[6] A parallel coordinates plot shows relationships among many variables. It is like a univariate scatter plot of all displayed variables standardized and stacked parallel to one another (Inselberg 1985; Inselberg 1985; Wegman 1990; Moustafa and Wegman 2006). Parallel coordinates show common movements across variables with a line for each observational unit (individual consumer in the computer choice study).

Figure 10.6. *Potential for Brand Switching: Parallel Coordinates for Individual Consumers*

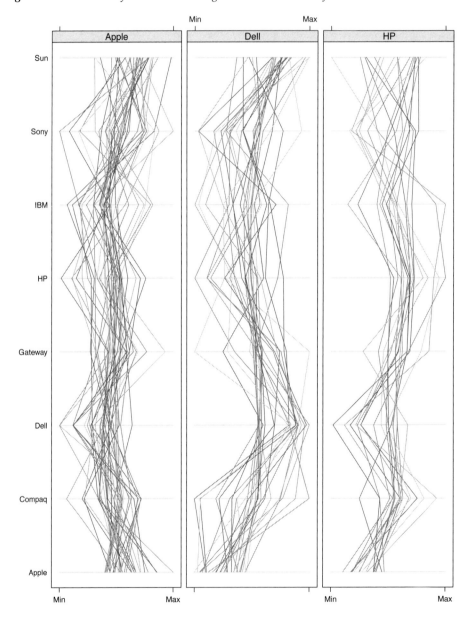

Figure 10.7. Potential for Brand Switching: Parallel Coordinates for Consumer Groups

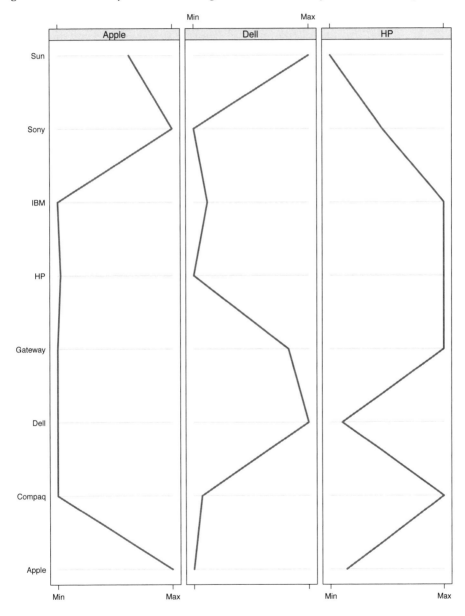

twice as fast, and just as likely to fail as earlier systems. The Gateway takes eight hours to learn and costs only $1,250. Finally, among the marketplace competitors, we have an HP system, 90 percent compatible, three times as fast, and less likely to fail. It takes eight hours to learn and costs $1,500. Suppose that Apple is entering this market with a system that, like the Dell system, is four times as fast as earlier systems and less likely to fail. The Apple system is only 50 percent compatible with prior systems and takes eight hours to learn. We allow Apple prices to vary across the full range of prices from the computer choice study, defining eight choice sets for the market simulation.

Choice sets for the market simulation are displayed in table 10.4 with coding of profile cells as required for use with the HB-estimated individual-level part-worths. Looking across the simulation choice sets, we can see that they are identical except for the one factor that is being studied—the price of the Apple computer. The variation in Apple prices is represented by the highlighted prices for Apple in the far right-hand-side column of the table.

Data visualization of market simulation results is provided by painting a mosaic of preference shares,[7] as shown in figure 10.8. The length/width of tiles in each row of the mosaic reflects brand market share. There is a row for each Apple price or simulation choice set. Obeying the law of demand, higher prices translate into lower market shares for Apple. The precise results of the simulation, shown in table 10.5, suggest that Apple would need to set its price below $1,750 to capture a 25 percent share.

We can take market simulations further, considering the actions and reactions of competitive firms in the marketplace. Suppose the battle lines had been drawn and the world of laptop computers had come down to two manufacturers: Apple and HP. The Apple system is selling for $2,000 and the HP for $1,750. Suppose further that both Apple and HP have the option of lowering their prices by $100, which each firm might do in order to increase its market share.

---

[7] The term *market share* is used with caution in this context. Many conjoint researchers, including Orme (2013), prefer to use the term *preference share*, highlighting the fact that estimates are based on choice-based surveys or revealed preferences rather than on actual behavior or choices in the marketplace. Of course, managers want estimates of market share, regardless of what we call it.

Table 10.4. *Market Simulation: Choice Set Input*

profile	setid	brand	compat	perform	reliab	learn	price
1	1	Dell	8	4	2	4	4
2	1	Gateway	6	2	1	2	2
3	1	HP	6	3	2	2	3
4	1	Apple	5	4	2	1	1
5	2	Dell	8	4	2	4	4
6	2	Gateway	6	2	1	2	2
7	2	HP	6	3	2	2	3
8	2	Apple	5	4	2	1	2
9	3	Dell	8	4	2	4	4
10	3	Gateway	6	2	1	2	2
11	3	HP	6	3	2	2	3
12	3	Apple	5	4	2	1	3
13	4	Dell	8	4	2	4	4
14	4	Gateway	6	2	1	2	2
15	4	HP	6	3	2	2	3
16	4	Apple	5	4	2	1	4
17	5	Dell	8	4	2	4	4
18	5	Gateway	6	2	1	2	2
19	5	HP	6	3	2	2	3
20	5	Apple	5	4	2	1	5
21	6	Dell	8	4	2	4	4
22	6	Gateway	6	2	1	2	2
23	6	HP	6	3	2	2	3
24	6	Apple	5	4	2	1	6
25	7	Dell	8	4	2	4	4
26	7	Gateway	6	2	1	2	2
27	7	HP	6	3	2	2	3
28	7	Apple	5	4	2	1	7
29	8	Dell	8	4	2	4	4
30	8	Gateway	6	2	1	2	2
31	8	HP	6	3	2	2	3
32	8	Apple	5	4	2	1	8

Figure 10.8. *Market Simulation: A Mosaic of Preference Shares*

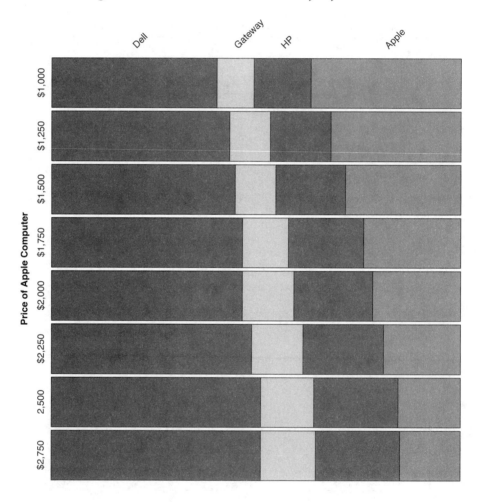

Table 10.5. *Market Simulation: Preference Shares in a Hypothetical Four-brand Market*

	Brand Preference Share (percentage)			
Apple Price	Apple	Dell	Gateway	HP
$1,000	36.6	40.6	8.9	13.8
1,250	31.7	43.8	9.8	14.7
1,500	28.1	45.1	9.8	17.0
1,750	23.7	46.9	11.2	18.3
2,000	21.4	46.9	12.5	19.2
2,250	18.8	49.1	12.5	19.6
2,500	15.2	51.3	12.9	20.5
2,750	14.7	51.3	13.4	20.5

Those with training in economics may recognize this Apple-HP scenario as a two-player competitive game. We could run market simulations with Apple and HP in the simulation choice sets, obtaining what we think of as market shares under each of four outcomes defined by no-price-change and price-change strategies. Knowing unit costs, we would have everything needed to make entries in the game outcome or payoff table.

Business managers look for profit-improving strategies, and modeling techniques in predictive analytics may be used to evaluate alternative strategies and how they play out in the marketplace. Consumer preferences translate into choices. Choices turn into sales, sales into market shares.

Recognize that all models have limitations. In a choice simulation we attempt to predict what consumers will do when faced with sets of potential (not actual) products with hypothetical (not actual) prices within a marketplace of possible (not actual) competitors. We would be most surprised if all such predictions were correct. Our uncertainty about prediction is something that we readily admit and estimate within the context of Bayesian analysis. Error bands can be provided around all conjoint measures, drawing on posterior distributions obtained from an HB estimation procedure.

To understand customers is to predict what they might do when the firm introduces a new product or changes the price of a current product. A good model, when paired with a market simulation, provides predictions to guide management action.

The term *brand equity* is used to describe the special value that a brand name has for products. Brand equity is built over time. Hollis (2005) talks about brand *presence*, which is awareness of what a brand stands for, *relevance* to the consumer, *performance* and *advantage* within the category of products being considered, and *bonding*, which is associated with a consumer's loyalty to or relationship with a brand. Brand equity and loyalty translate into long-term customer value and product profitability.

Choice-based conjoint studies with product profiles defined in terms of brand and price provide a way of measuring what a brand is worth relative to other brands. In fact, with HB-estimated part-worths, brand equity can be assessed for each individual in a conjoint study.[8]

An introduction to pricing theory and the economics of demand may be found in books about microeconomics (Stigler 1987; Varian 2005; Pindyck and Rubinfeld 2012) and econometrics (Greene 2012). For pricing research methods, see Lyon (2000, 2002), and Feldman (2002a). Marder (1997) reviews pricing research with monadic methods (each consumer seeing one and only one price). Nagle and Hogan (2005) and Krishnamurthi (2001) review pricing strategy and price planning for business managers.

Special considerations in the construction of choice studies have been discussed by Kuhfeld, Tobias, and Garratt (1994), Huber and Zwerina (1996), Zwerina (1997), Louviere, Hensher, and Swait (2000), and Hensher, Rose, and Greene (2005). Reviews of discrete choice methods may be found in the work of Ben-Akiva and Lerman (1985), McFadden (2001), Train (1985, 2003), and Greene (2012). Many discrete choice models fall within the general class of generalized linear models. (See "Regression" in appendix A.)

---

[8] To compute brand equity for an individual, we begin by observing the range in part-worths for price. Suppose that the price part-worths for an individual extend from -0.55 to 0.55. Then one unit of part-worth would be equivalent to $1,501, as shown in the following calculation:

$$\frac{|\$2,750 - \$1,000|}{|0.55 - (-0.55)|} = \frac{\$1,750}{1.10} = \$1,501$$

This is because the range of prices displayed to consumers in the computer choice study extends from $1,000 to $2,750. The computed conversion factor $1,501 is called a *dollar-metric* and can be applied to part-worth differences across any attribute in the study, including brand. Suppose this individual's part-worth for Sony is 0.44 and part-worth for Gateway is 0.36. Then we would say that Sony has a brand equity of $120 over Gateway for this individual. That is, a difference of 0.08 in part-worth units is worth $120:

$$(0.44 - 0.36) \times \$1,501 = 0.08 \times \$1,501 = \$120.$$

Orme (2013) provides a review of conjoint and choice methods for product design and pricing research, including discussion of brand equity estimation and market simulations. Louviere, Hensher, and Swait (2000) provide extensive discussion of choice study research design and analysis. In addition, specialized methods are available for market share estimation (Cooper and Nakanishi 1988; Cooper 1999).

Multinomial logit and conditional logit modeling methods implemented in R are especially useful in the analysis of choice study data (Elff 2013; Croissant 2013; Therneau 2013; Train and Croissant 2013). R programming for Bayesian analysis of choice studies is reviewed by Rossi, Allenby, and McCulloch (2005) and Rossi (2013).

Exhibit 10.1 shows the program to obtain hierarchical Bayes estimates for the computer choice study. This code shows how to implement training and test choice sets from the conjoint survey. Market simulation utilities are provided in exhibit C.2. This program and the next call upon an R packages developed by Sarkar (2013), Meyer, Zeileis, Hornik, and Friendly (2013a), Wickham and Chang (2013), Sermas (2013), and Kuhn (2013).

Exhibit 10.2 shows how to use individual-level part-worths in the modeling of consumer preferences. The program provides an analysis of the complete data from consumer choice study, following the logic of the ternary model introduced in this chapter. The program shows how to generate mosaic, ternary, and density visualizations. The program code also shows how to conduct a market simulation using individual-level part worths.

Exhibit 10.1. *Computer Choice Study: Training and Testing with Hierarchical Bayes*

```
# Hierarchical Bayes Part-Worth Estimation: Training and Test

# load market simulation utilities
load(file="mspa_market_simulation_utilities.RData")

library(ChoiceModelR)  # for Hierarchical Bayes Estimation

library(caret)  # for confusion matrix function

# read in the data from a case study in computer choice.
complete.data.frame <- read.csv("computer_choice_study.csv")

print.digits <- 2
# user-defined function for printing conjoint measures
if (print.digits == 2)
  pretty.print <- function(x) {sprintf("%1.2f",round(x,digits = 2))}
if (print.digits == 3)
  pretty.print <- function(x) {sprintf("%1.3f",round(x,digits = 3))}

# set up sum contrasts for effects coding
options(contrasts=c("contr.sum","contr.poly"))

# employ a training-and-test regimen across survey sets/items
test.set.ids <- c("3","7","11","15")  # select four sets/items
training.set.ids <- setdiff(unique(complete.data.frame$setid),test.set.ids)
training.data.frame <-
  subset(complete.data.frame,subset=(setid %in% training.set.ids))
test.data.frame <-
  subset(complete.data.frame,subset=(setid %in% test.set.ids))

UniqueID <- unique(training.data.frame$id)
# set up zero priors
cc.priors <- matrix(0,nrow=length(UniqueID),ncol=13)

# we could use coefficients from aggregate model as starting values
# here we comment out the code needed to do that
# aggregate.cc.betas <- c(as.numeric(conjoint.results$coefficients)[2:7],
#  -sum(as.numeric(conjoint.results$coefficients)[2:7]),
#  as.numeric(conjoint.results$coefficients)[8:13])
# clone aggregate part-worths across the individuals in the study
# set up Bayesian priors
# cc.priors <- matrix(0,nrow=length(UniqueID),ncol=length(aggregate.cc.betas))
# for(index.for.ID in seq(along=UniqueID))
# cc.priors[index.for.ID,] <- aggregate.cc.betas

colnames(cc.priors) <- c("A1B1","A1B2","A1B3","A1B4","A1B5","A1B6","A1B7",
  "A1B8","A2B1","A3B1","A4B1","A5B1","A6B1")
# note that the actual names are as follows:
AB.names <- c("Apple","Compaq","Dell","Gateway","HP","IBM","Sony","Sun",
  "Compatibility","Performance","Reliability","Learning","Price")
```

```
# set up run parameters for the MCMC
# using aggregate beta estimates to get started
truebetas <- cc.priors
cc.xcoding <- c(0,1,1,1,1,1)  # first variable categorical others continuous
cc.attlevels <- c(8,8,4,2,8,8) # test run with brand price and performance
# no constraint for order on brand so 8x8 matrix of zeroes
c1 <- matrix(0,ncol=8,nrow=8)
# compatibility is ordered higher numbers are better
# continuous attributes have 1x1 matrix representation
c2 <- matrix(1, ncol = 1, nrow = 1, byrow = TRUE)
# performance is ordered higher numbers are better
# continuous attributes have 1x1 matrix representation
c3 <- matrix(1, ncol = 1, nrow = 1, byrow = TRUE)
# reliability is ordered higher numbers are better
# continuous attributes have 1x1 matrix representation
c4 <- matrix(1, ncol = 1, nrow = 1, byrow = TRUE)
# learning has expected order... higher prices less valued
# continuous attributes have 1x1 matrix representation
c5 <- matrix(-1, ncol = 1, nrow = 1, byrow = TRUE)
# price has expected order... higher prices less valued
# continuous attributes have 1x1 matrix representation
c6 <- matrix(-1, ncol = 1, nrow = 1, byrow = TRUE)
cc.constraints <- list(c1,c2,c3,c4,c5,c6)
# controls for length of run and sampling from end of run
# cc.mcmc <- list(R = 10, use = 10) # fast trial run
# set run parameters 10000 total iterations with estimates based on last 2000
cc.mcmc <- list(R = 10000, use = 2000) # run parameters
# run options
cc.options <- list(none=FALSE, save=TRUE, keep=1)


# set up the data frame for analysis
# redefine set ids so they are a complete set 1-12 as needed for HB functions
training.data.frame$newsetid <- training.data.frame$setid
training.data.frame$newsetid <- ifelse((training.data.frame$newsetid == 16),
  3,training.data.frame$newsetid)
training.data.frame$newsetid <- ifelse((training.data.frame$newsetid == 14),
  7,training.data.frame$newsetid)
training.data.frame$newsetid <- ifelse((training.data.frame$newsetid == 13),
  11,training.data.frame$newsetid)

UnitID <- training.data.frame$id
Set <- as.integer(training.data.frame$newsetid)
Alt <- as.integer(training.data.frame$position)
X_1 <- as.integer(training.data.frame$brand) # categories by brand
X_2 <- as.integer(training.data.frame$compat)  # integer values 1 to 8
X_3 <- as.integer(training.data.frame$perform)  # integer values 1 to 4
X_4 <- as.integer(training.data.frame$reliab)  # integer values 1 to 2
X_5 <- as.integer(training.data.frame$learn)  # integer values 1 to 8
X_6 <- as.integer(training.data.frame$price)  # integer values 1 to 8
y <- as.numeric(training.data.frame$choice)  # using special response coding

cc.data <- data.frame(UnitID,Set,Alt,X_1,X_2,X_3,X_4,X_5,X_6,y)
```

```
# now for the estimation... be patient
set.seed(9999)  # for reproducible results
out <- choicemodelr(data=cc.data, xcoding = cc.xcoding,
  mcmc = cc.mcmc, options = cc.options, constraints = cc.constraints)

# out provides a list for the posterior parameter estimates
# for the runs sampled (use = 2000)

# the MCMC beta parameter estimates are traced on the screen as it runs

# individual part-worth estimates are provided in the output file RBetas.csv
# the final estimates are printed to RBetas.csv with columns labeled as
#  A1B1 = first attribute first level
#  A1B2 = first attribute second level
#  ....
#  A2B1 = second attribute first level
#  ....
# gather data from HB posterior parameter distributions
# we imposed constraints on all continuous parameters so we use betadraw.c
posterior.mean <- matrix(0, nrow = dim(out$betadraw.c)[1],
  ncol = dim(out$betadraw.c)[2])
posterior.sd <- matrix(0, nrow = dim(out$betadraw.c)[1],
  ncol = dim(out$betadraw.c)[2])
for(index.row in 1:dim(out$betadraw.c)[1])
for(index.col in 1:dim(out$betadraw.c)[2]) {
  posterior.mean[index.row,index.col] <-
    mean(out$betadraw.c[index.row,index.col,])
  posterior.sd[index.row,index.col] <-
    sd(out$betadraw.c[index.row,index.col,])
  }
# HB program uses effects coding for categorical variables and
# mean-centers continuous variables across the levels appearing in the data
# working with data for one respondent at a time we compute predicted choices
# for both the training and test choice sets
create.design.matrix <- function(input.data.frame.row) {
  xdesign.row <- numeric(12)
  if (input.data.frame.row$brand == "Apple")
    xdesign.row[1:7] <- c(1,0,0,0,0,0,0)
  if (input.data.frame.row$brand == "Compaq")
    xdesign.row[1:7] <- c(0,1,0,0,0,0,0)
  if (input.data.frame.row$brand == "Dell")
    xdesign.row[1:7] <- c(0,0,1,0,0,0,0)
  if (input.data.frame.row$brand == "Gateway")
    xdesign.row[1:7] <- c(0,0,0,1,0,0,0)
  if (input.data.frame.row$brand == "HP")
    xdesign.row[1:7] <- c(0,0,0,0,1,0,0)
  if (input.data.frame.row$brand == "IBM")
    xdesign.row[1:7] <- c(0,0,0,0,0,1,0)
  if (input.data.frame.row$brand == "Sony")
    xdesign.row[1:7] <- c(0,0,0,0,0,0,1)
  if (input.data.frame.row$brand == "Sun")
    xdesign.row[1:7] <- c(-1,-1,-1,-1,-1,-1,-1)
```

```
  xdesign.row[8] <- input.data.frame.row$compat -4.5
  xdesign.row[9] <- input.data.frame.row$perform -2.5
  xdesign.row[10] <- input.data.frame.row$reliab -1.5
  xdesign.row[11] <- input.data.frame.row$learn -4.5
  xdesign.row[12] <- input.data.frame.row$price -4.5
  t(as.matrix(xdesign.row))  # return row of design matrix
  }


# evaluate performance in the training set
training.choice.utility <- NULL  # initialize utility vector
# work with one row of respondent training data frame at a time
# create choice prediction using the individual part-worths
list.of.ids <- unique(training.data.frame$id)
for (index.for.id in seq(along=list.of.ids)) {
  this.id.part.worths <- posterior.mean[index.for.id,]
  this.id.data.frame <- subset(training.data.frame,
    subset=(id == list.of.ids[index.for.id]))
  for (index.for.profile in 1:nrow(this.id.data.frame)) {
    training.choice.utility <- c(training.choice.utility,
      create.design.matrix(this.id.data.frame[index.for.profile,]) %*%
      this.id.part.worths)
    }
  }

training.predicted.choice <-
  choice.set.predictor(training.choice.utility)
training.actual.choice <- factor(training.data.frame$choice, levels = c(0,1),
  labels = c("NO","YES"))
# look for sensitivity > 0.25 for four-profile choice sets
training.set.performance <- confusionMatrix(data = training.predicted.choice,
  reference = training.actual.choice, positive = "YES")
# report choice prediction sensitivity for training data
cat("\n\nTraining choice set sensitivity = ",
  sprintf("%1.1f",training.set.performance$byClass[1]*100)," Percent",sep="")


# evaluate performance in the test set
test.choice.utility <- NULL  # initialize utility vector
# work with one row of respondent test data frame at a time
# create choice prediction using the individual part-worths
list.of.ids <- unique(test.data.frame$id)
for (index.for.id in seq(along=list.of.ids)) {
  this.id.part.worths <- posterior.mean[index.for.id,]
  this.id.data.frame <- subset(test.data.frame,
    subset=(id == list.of.ids[index.for.id]))
  for (index.for.profile in 1:nrow(this.id.data.frame)) {
    test.choice.utility <- c(test.choice.utility,
      create.design.matrix(this.id.data.frame[index.for.profile,]) %*%
      this.id.part.worths)
    }
  }
```

```
test.predicted.choice <-
  choice.set.predictor(test.choice.utility)
test.actual.choice <- factor(test.data.frame$choice, levels = c(0,1),
  labels = c("NO","YES"))
# look for sensitivity > 0.25 for four-profile choice sets
test.set.performance <- confusionMatrix(data = test.predicted.choice,
  reference = test.actual.choice, positive = "YES")
# report choice prediction sensitivity for test data
cat("\n\nTest choice set sensitivity = ",
  sprintf("%1.1f",test.set.performance$byClass[1]*100)," Percent",sep="")

# suggestions for students
# having demonstrated the predictive power of the HB model...
# return to the complete set of 16 choice sets to obtain
# part-worths for individuals based upon the complete survey
# (the next program will provide guidance on how to do this)
# after estimating part-worths for individuals, average across
# individuals to obtain an aggregate profile of conjoint measures
# standardize the aggregate part-worths and display them
# on a spine chart using the spine chart plotting utility
# provided in the appendix of code and utilities
# interpret the spine chart, compare attribute importance values
# compare the brands, compute brand equity for each brand
# relative to each of the other brands in the study
```

Exhibit 10.2. *Preference, Choice, and Market Simulation*

```
# Analyzing Consumer Preferences and Building a Market Simulation

# having demonstrated the predictive power of the HB model...
# we now return to the complete set of 16 choice sets to obtain
# individual-level part-worths for further analysis
# analysis guided by ternary model of consumer preference and market response
# brand loyalty... price sensitivity... and feature focus... are key aspects
# to consider in determining pricing policy

library(lattice)  # package for lattice graphics
library(vcd)  # graphics package with mosaic plots for mosaic and ternary plots
library(ggplot2)  # package ggplot implements Grammar of Graphics approach
library(ChoiceModelR)  # for Hierarchical Bayes Estimation
library(caret)  # for confusion matrix... evaluation of choice set predictions

# load split-plotting utilities for work with ggplot
load("mtpa_split_plotting_utilities.Rdata")
# load market simulation utilities
load(file="mspa_market_simulation_utilities.RData")

# read in the data from a case study in computer choice.
complete.data.frame <- read.csv("computer_choice_study.csv")
# we employed a training-and-test regimen in previous research work
# here we will be using the complete data from the computer choice study
working.data.frame <- complete.data.frame

# user-defined function for plotting descriptive attribute names
effect.name.map <- function(effect.name) {
  if(effect.name=="brand") return("Manufacturer/Brand")
  if(effect.name=="compat") return("Compatibility with Windows 95")
  if(effect.name=="perform") return("Performance")
  if(effect.name=="reliab") return("Reliability")
  if(effect.name=="learn") return("Learning Time (4 to 32 hours)")
  if(effect.name=="price") return("Price ($1,000 to $2,750)")
  }
print.digits <- 2
# user-defined function for printing conjoint measures
if (print.digits == 2)
  pretty.print <- function(x) {sprintf("%1.2f",round(x,digits = 2))}
if (print.digits == 3)
  pretty.print <- function(x) {sprintf("%1.3f",round(x,digits = 3))}

# set up sum contrasts for effects coding
options(contrasts=c("contr.sum","contr.poly"))

UniqueID <- unique(working.data.frame$id)
# set up zero priors
cc.priors <- matrix(0,nrow=length(UniqueID),ncol=13)
colnames(cc.priors) <- c("A1B1","A1B2","A1B3","A1B4","A1B5","A1B6","A1B7",
  "A1B8","A2B1","A3B1","A4B1","A5B1","A6B1")
```

```
# note that the actual names are as follows:
AB.names <- c("Apple","Compaq","Dell","Gateway","HP","IBM","Sony","Sun",
  "Compatibility","Performance","Reliability","Learning","Price")

# set up run parameters for the MCMC
# using aggregate beta estimates to get started
truebetas <- cc.priors
cc.xcoding <- c(0,1,1,1,1,1)  # first variable categorical others continuous
cc.attlevels <- c(8,8,4,2,8,8) # test run with brand price and performance
# no constraint for order on brand so 8x8 matrix of zeroes
c1 <- matrix(0,ncol=8,nrow=8)
# compatibility is ordered higher numbers are better
# continuous attributes have 1x1 matrix representation
c2 <- matrix(1, ncol = 1, nrow = 1, byrow = TRUE)
# performance is ordered higher numbers are better
# continuous attributes have 1x1 matrix representation
c3 <- matrix(1, ncol = 1, nrow = 1, byrow = TRUE)
# reliability is ordered higher numbers are better
# continuous attributes have 1x1 matrix representation
c4 <- matrix(1, ncol = 1, nrow = 1, byrow = TRUE)
# learning has expected order... higher prices less valued
# continuous attributes have 1x1 matrix representation
c5 <- matrix(-1, ncol = 1, nrow = 1, byrow = TRUE)
# price has expected order... higher prices less valued
# continuous attributes have 1x1 matrix representation
c6 <- matrix(-1, ncol = 1, nrow = 1, byrow = TRUE)
cc.constraints <- list(c1,c2,c3,c4,c5,c6)
# controls for length of run and sampling from end of run
# cc.mcmc <- list(R = 10, use = 10) # fast trial run
# set run parameters 10000 total iterations with estimates based on last 2000
cc.mcmc <- list(R = 10000, use = 2000) # run parameters
# run options
cc.options <- list(none=FALSE, save=TRUE, keep=1)

# set up the data frame for analysis
UnitID <- working.data.frame$id
Set <- as.integer(working.data.frame$setid)
Alt <- as.integer(working.data.frame$position)
X_1 <- as.integer(working.data.frame$brand) # categories by brand
X_2 <- as.integer(working.data.frame$compat)  # integer values 1 to 8
X_3 <- as.integer(working.data.frame$perform) # integer values 1 to 4
X_4 <- as.integer(working.data.frame$reliab)  # integer values 1 to 2
X_5 <- as.integer(working.data.frame$learn)   # integer values 1 to 8
X_6 <- as.integer(working.data.frame$price)   # integer values 1 to 8
y <- as.numeric(working.data.frame$choice)  # using special response coding

cc.data <- data.frame(UnitID,Set,Alt,X_1,X_2,X_3,X_4,X_5,X_6,y)

# the estimation begins here... be patient
set.seed(9999)  # for reproducible results
out <- choicemodelr(data=cc.data, xcoding = cc.xcoding,
  mcmc = cc.mcmc, options = cc.options, constraints = cc.constraints)
```

```
# out provides a list for the posterior parameter estimates
# for the runs sampled (use = 2000)
# the MCMC beta parameter estimates are traced on the screen as it runs
# individual part-worth estimates are provided in the output file RBetas.csv
# the final estimates are printed to RBetas.csv with columns labeled as
#   A1B1 = first attribute first level
#   A1B2 = first attribute second level
#   ....
#   A2B1 = second attribute first level
#   ....
# gather data from HB posterior parameter distributions
# we imposed constraints on all continuous parameters so we use betadraw.c
posterior.mean <- matrix(0, nrow = dim(out$betadraw.c)[1],
  ncol = dim(out$betadraw.c)[2])
posterior.sd <- matrix(0, nrow = dim(out$betadraw.c)[1],
  ncol = dim(out$betadraw.c)[2])
for(index.row in 1:dim(out$betadraw.c)[1])
for(index.col in 1:dim(out$betadraw.c)[2]) {
  posterior.mean[index.row,index.col] <-
    mean(out$betadraw.c[index.row,index.col,])
  posterior.sd[index.row,index.col] <-
    sd(out$betadraw.c[index.row,index.col,])
  }
# HB program uses effects coding for categorical variables and
# mean-centers continuous variables across the levels appearing in the data
# working with data for one respondent at a time we compute predicted choices
# for the full set of consumer responses
create.design.matrix <- function(input.data.frame.row) {
  xdesign.row <- numeric(12)
  if (input.data.frame.row$brand == "Apple")
    xdesign.row[1:7] <- c(1,0,0,0,0,0,0)
  if (input.data.frame.row$brand == "Compaq")
    xdesign.row[1:7] <- c(0,1,0,0,0,0,0)
  if (input.data.frame.row$brand == "Dell")
    xdesign.row[1:7] <- c(0,0,1,0,0,0,0)
  if (input.data.frame.row$brand == "Gateway")
    xdesign.row[1:7] <- c(0,0,0,1,0,0,0)
  if (input.data.frame.row$brand == "HP")
    xdesign.row[1:7] <- c(0,0,0,0,1,0,0)
  if (input.data.frame.row$brand == "IBM")
    xdesign.row[1:7] <- c(0,0,0,0,0,1,0)
  if (input.data.frame.row$brand == "Sony")
    xdesign.row[1:7] <- c(0,0,0,0,0,0,1)
  if (input.data.frame.row$brand == "Sun")
    xdesign.row[1:7] <- c(-1,-1,-1,-1,-1,-1,-1)
  xdesign.row[8] <- input.data.frame.row$compat -4.5
  xdesign.row[9] <- input.data.frame.row$perform -2.5
  xdesign.row[10] <- input.data.frame.row$reliab -1.5
  xdesign.row[11] <- input.data.frame.row$learn -4.5
  xdesign.row[12] <- input.data.frame.row$price -4.5
  t(as.matrix(xdesign.row))  # return row of design matrix
  }
```

```
# evaluate performance in the full set of consumer responses
working.choice.utility <- NULL  # initialize utility vector
# work with one row of respondent training data frame at a time
# create choice prediction using the individual part-worths
list.of.ids <- unique(working.data.frame$id)
for (index.for.id in seq(along=list.of.ids)) {
  this.id.part.worths <- posterior.mean[index.for.id,]
  this.id.data.frame <- subset(working.data.frame,
    subset=(id == list.of.ids[index.for.id]))
  for (index.for.profile in 1:nrow(this.id.data.frame)) {
    working.choice.utility <- c(working.choice.utility,
      create.design.matrix(this.id.data.frame[index.for.profile,]) %*%
      this.id.part.worths)
    }
  }

working.predicted.choice <-
  choice.set.predictor(working.choice.utility)
working.actual.choice <- factor(working.data.frame$choice, levels = c(0,1),
  labels = c("NO","YES"))
# look for sensitivity > 0.25 for four-profile choice sets
working.set.performance <- confusionMatrix(data = working.predicted.choice,
  reference = working.actual.choice, positive = "YES")
# report choice prediction sensitivity for the full data
cat("\n\nFull data set choice set sensitivity = ",
  sprintf("%1.1f",working.set.performance$byClass[1]*100)," Percent",sep="")
#
# results: Full data set choice set sensitivity = 89.1 Percent
#

# to continue with our analysis of consumer preferences...
# we build a data frame for the consumers with the full set of eight brands
ID <- unique(working.data.frame$id)
Apple <- posterior.mean[,1]
Compaq <- posterior.mean[,2]
Dell <- posterior.mean[,3]
Gateway <- posterior.mean[,4]
HP <- posterior.mean[,5]
IBM <- posterior.mean[,6]
Sony <- posterior.mean[,7]
Sun <- -1 * (Apple + Compaq + Dell + Gateway + HP + IBM + Sony)
Compatibility <- posterior.mean[,8]
Performance <- posterior.mean[,9]
Reliability <- posterior.mean[,10]
Learning <- posterior.mean[,11]
Price <- posterior.mean[,12]

# creation of data frame for analysis of consumer preferences and choice
# starting with individual-level part-worths... more to be added shortly
id.data <- data.frame(ID,Apple,Compaq,Dell,Gateway,HP,IBM,Sony,Sun,
  Compatibility,Performance,Reliability,Learning,Price)
```

```
# compute attribute importance values for each attribute
id.data$brand.range <- numeric(nrow(id.data))
id.data$compatibility.range <- numeric(nrow(id.data))
id.data$performance.range <- numeric(nrow(id.data))
id.data$reliability.range <- numeric(nrow(id.data))
id.data$learning.range <- numeric(nrow(id.data))
id.data$price.range <- numeric(nrow(id.data))
id.data$sum.range <- numeric(nrow(id.data))
id.data$brand.importance <- numeric(nrow(id.data))
id.data$compatibility.importance <- numeric(nrow(id.data))
id.data$performance.importance <- numeric(nrow(id.data))
id.data$reliability.importance <- numeric(nrow(id.data))
id.data$learning.importance <- numeric(nrow(id.data))
id.data$price.importance <- numeric(nrow(id.data))

for(id in seq(along=id.data$ID)) {
  id.data$brand.range[id] <- max(id.data$Apple[id],
    id.data$Compaq[id],id.data$Dell[id],
    id.data$Gateway[id],id.data$HP[id],
    id.data$IBM[id],id.data$Sony[id],
    id.data$Sun[id]) -
    min(id.data$Apple[id],
    id.data$Compaq[id],id.data$Dell[id],
    id.data$Gateway[id],id.data$HP[id],
    id.data$IBM[id],id.data$Sony[id],
    id.data$Sun[id])

  id.data$compatibility.range[id] <- abs(8*id.data$Compatibility[id])
  id.data$performance.range[id] <- abs(4*id.data$Performance[id])
  id.data$reliability.range[id] <- abs(2*id.data$Reliability[id])
  id.data$learning.range[id] <- abs(8*id.data$Learning[id])
  id.data$price.range[id] <-  abs(8*id.data$Price[id])

  id.data$sum.range[id] <- id.data$brand.range[id] +
    id.data$compatibility.range[id] +
    id.data$performance.range[id] +
    id.data$reliability.range[id] +
    id.data$learning.range[id] +
    id.data$price.range[id]

  id.data$brand.importance[id] <-
    id.data$brand.range[id]/id.data$sum.range[id]
  id.data$compatibility.importance[id] <-
    id.data$compatibility.range[id]/id.data$sum.range[id]
  id.data$performance.importance[id] <-
    id.data$performance.range[id]/id.data$sum.range[id]
  id.data$reliability.importance[id] <-
    id.data$reliability.range[id]/id.data$sum.range[id]
  id.data$learning.importance[id] <-
    id.data$learning.range[id]/id.data$sum.range[id]
  id.data$price.importance[id] <-
    id.data$price.range[id]/id.data$sum.range[id]
```

```
# feature importance relates to the most important product feature
# considering product features as not brand and not price
  id.data$feature.importance[id] <- max(id.data$compatibility.importance[id],
    id.data$performance.importance[id],
    id.data$reliability.importance[id],
    id.data$learning.importance[id])
  }

# identify each individual's top brand defining top.brand factor variable
id.data$top.brand <- integer(nrow(id.data))
for(id in seq(along=id.data$ID)) {
  brand.index <- 1:8
  brand.part.worth <- c(id.data$Apple[id],id.data$Compaq[id],
    id.data$Dell[id],id.data$Gateway[id],id.data$HP[id],id.data$IBM[id],
    id.data$Sony[id],id.data$Sun[id])
  temp.data <- data.frame(brand.index,brand.part.worth)
  temp.data <- temp.data[sort.list(temp.data$brand.part.worth, decreasing = TRUE),]
  id.data$top.brand[id] <- temp.data$brand.index[1]
  }
id.data$top.brand <- factor(id.data$top.brand, levels = 1:8,
  labels = c("Apple","Compaq","Dell","Gateway",
  "HP","IBM","Sony","Sun"))

# note that the standard importance measures from conjoint methods are
# ipsative... their sum is always 1 for proportions or 100 for percentages
# this has advantages for triplots (ternary plots) but because importance
# is so dependent upon the levels of attributes, it has significant
# disadvantages as well... so we consider a relative-value-based measure
# lets us define an alternative to importance called "attribute value"

# compute "attribute value" relative to the consumer group
# it is a standardized measure... let "attribute value" be mean 50 sd 10
# here are user-defined functions to use to obtain "value"

standardize <- function(x) {
# standardize x so it has mean zero and standard deviation 1
  (x - mean(x))/sd(x)
  }
compute.value <- function(x) {
# rescale x so it has the same mean and standard deviation as y
  standardize(x) * 10 + 50
  }

id.data$brand.value <- compute.value(id.data$brand.range)
id.data$compatibility.value <- compute.value(id.data$compatibility.range)
id.data$performance.value <- compute.value(id.data$performance.range)
id.data$reliability.value <- compute.value(id.data$reliability.range)
id.data$learning.value <- compute.value(id.data$learning.range)
id.data$price.value <- compute.value(id.data$price.range)
```

```
# identify each individual's top value using computed relative attribute values
id.data$top.attribute <- integer(nrow(id.data))
for(id in seq(along=id.data$ID)) {
  attribute.index <- 1:6
  attribute.value <- c(id.data$brand.value[id],id.data$compatibility.value[id],
    id.data$performance.value[id],id.data$reliability.value[id],
    id.data$learning.value[id],id.data$price.value[id])
  temp.data <- data.frame(attribute.index,attribute.value)
  temp.data <-
    temp.data[sort.list(temp.data$attribute.value, decreasing = TRUE),]
  id.data$top.attribute[id] <- temp.data$attribute.index[1]
  }
id.data$top.attribute <- factor(id.data$top.attribute, levels = 1:6,
  labels = c("Brand","Compatibility","Performance","Reliability",
  "Learning","Price"))


# mosaic plot of joint frequencies top ranked brand by top value
pdf(file="fig_price_top_top_mosaic_plot.pdf", width = 8.5, height = 11)
  mosaic( ~ top.brand + top.attribute, data = id.data,
  highlighting = "top.attribute",
  highlighting_fill =
    c("blue", "white", "green","lightgray","magenta","black"),
  labeling_args =
  list(set_varnames = c(top.brand = "", top.attribute = ""),
  rot_labels = c(left = 90, top = 45),
  pos_labels = c("center","center"),
  just_labels = c("left","center"),
  offset_labels = c(0.0,0.0)))
dev.off()


# an alternative representation that is often quite useful in pricing studies
# is a triplot/ternary plot with three features identified for each consumer
# using the idea from importance caluclations we now use price, brand, and
# feature importance measures to obtain data for three-way plots
# as the basis for three relative measures, which we call brand.loyalty,
# price.sensitivity, and feature_focus...


id.data$brand.loyalty <- numeric(nrow(id.data))
id.data$price.sensitivity <- numeric(nrow(id.data))
id.data$feature.focus <- numeric(nrow(id.data))
for(id in seq(along=id.data$ID)) {
  sum.importances <- id.data$brand.importance[id] +
  id.data$price.importance[id] +
  id.data$feature.importance[id]  # less than 1.00 feature is an average
  id.data$brand.loyalty[id] <- id.data$brand.importance[id]/sum.importances
  id.data$price.sensitivity[id] <- id.data$price.importance[id]/sum.importances
  id.data$feature.focus[id] <- id.data$feature.importance[id]/sum.importances
  }
```

```
# ternary model of consumer response... the plot
pdf("fig_price_ternary_three_brands.pdf", width = 11, height = 8.5)
ternaryplot(id.data[,c("brand.loyalty","price.sensitivity","feature.focus")],
dimnames = c("Brand Loyalty","Price Sensitivity","Feature Focus"),
prop_size = ifelse((id.data$top.brand == "Apple"), 0.8,
            ifelse((id.data$top.brand == "Dell"),0.7,
            ifelse((id.data$top.brand == "HP"),0.7,0.5))),
pch = ifelse((id.data$top.brand == "Apple"), 20,
      ifelse((id.data$top.brand == "Dell"),17,
      ifelse((id.data$top.brand == "HP"),15,1))),
col = ifelse((id.data$top.brand == "Apple"), "red",
      ifelse((id.data$top.brand == "Dell"),"mediumorchid4",
      ifelse((id.data$top.brand == "HP"),"blue","darkblue"))),
grid_color = "#626262",
bg = "#E6E6E6",
dimnames_position = "corner", main = ""
)
grid_legend(0.725, 0.8, pch = c(20, 17, 15, 1),
col = c("red", "mediumorchid4", "blue", "darkblue"),
c("Apple", "Dell", "HP", "Other"), title = "Top-Ranked Brand")
dev.off()
# another way of looking at these data is to employ comparative densities
# for the three selected brands: Apple, Dell, and HP
# using those individual how selected these as the top brand
selected.brands <- c("Apple","Dell","HP")
selected.data <- subset(id.data, subset = (top.brand %in% selected.brands))
# plotting objects for brand.loyalty, price.sensitivity, and feature.focus
# create these three objects and then plot them together on one page
pdf("fig_price_density_three_brands.pdf", width = 8.5, height = 11)
first.object <- ggplot(selected.data,
  aes(x = brand.loyalty, fill = top.brand)) +
  labs(x = "Brand Loyalty",
      y = "f(x)") +
  theme(axis.title.y = element_text(angle = 0, face = "italic", size = 10)) +
  geom_density(alpha = 0.4) +
  coord_fixed(ratio = 1/15) +
  theme(legend.position = "none") +
  scale_fill_manual(values = c("red","white","blue"),
    guide = guide_legend(title = NULL)) +
  scale_x_continuous(limits = c(0,1)) +
  scale_y_continuous(limits = c(0,5))
second.object <- ggplot(selected.data,
  aes(x = price.sensitivity, fill = top.brand)) +
  labs(x = "Price Sensitivity",
      y = "f(x)") +
  theme(axis.title.y = element_text(angle = 0, face = "italic", size = 10)) +
  geom_density(alpha = 0.4) +
  coord_fixed(ratio = 1/15) +
  theme(legend.position = "none") +
  scale_fill_manual(values = c("red","white","blue"),
    guide = guide_legend(title = NULL)) +
  scale_x_continuous(limits = c(0,1)) +
  scale_y_continuous(limits = c(0,5))
```

```
third.object <- ggplot(selected.data,
  aes(x = feature.focus, fill = top.brand))  +
  labs(x = "Feature Focus",
       y = "f(x)") +
  theme(axis.title.y = element_text(angle = 0, face = "italic", size = 10)) +
  geom_density(alpha = 0.4) +
  coord_fixed(ratio = 1/15) +
  theme(legend.position = "bottom") +
  scale_fill_manual(values = c("red","white","blue"),
    guide = guide_legend(title = NULL)) +
  scale_x_continuous(limits = c(0,1)) +
  scale_y_continuous(limits = c(0,5))

three.part.ggplot.print.with.margins(ggfirstplot.object.name = first.object,
  ggsecondplot.object.name = second.object,
  ggthirdplot.object.name = third.object,
  left.margin.pct=5,right.margin.pct=5,
  top.margin.pct=10,bottom.margin.pct=9,
  first.plot.pct=25,second.plot.pct=25,
  third.plot.pct=31)
dev.off()

# to what extent are consumers open to switching from one brand to another
# can see this trough parallel coordinates plots for the brand part-worths
pdf(file = "fig_price_parallel_coordinates_individuals.pdf",
  width = 8.5, height = 11)
parallelplot(~selected.data[,c("Apple","Compaq","Dell","Gateway",
  "HP","IBM","Sony","Sun")] | top.brand, selected.data, layout = c (3,1))
dev.off()

# these get a little messy or cluttered...
# more easily interpreted are parallel coordinate plots of mean part-worths
# for brand part-worth columns and aggreate by top brand (Apple, Dell, or HP)
brands.data <- aggregate(x = selected.data[,2:9],
  by = selected.data[29], mean)

pdf(file = "fig_price_parallel_coordinates_groups.pdf",
  width = 8.5, height = 11)
parallelplot(~brands.data[,c("Apple","Compaq","Dell","Gateway",
  "HP","IBM","Sony","Sun")] | top.brand, brands.data, layout = c (3,1),
    lwd = 3, col = "mediumorchid4")
dev.off()

# market simulation for hypothetical set of products in the marketplace
# suppose we work for Apple and we focus upon a market with three
# competitors: Dell, Gateway, and HP.... we define the products in the
# market using values from the computer choice study just as we did
# in fitting the HB model... we create the simulation input data frame
# and use the previously designed function create.design.matrix
# along with simulation utility functions
```

```
# first product in market is Dell Computer defined as follows:
brand <- "Dell"
compat <- 8  # 100 percent compatibility
perform <- 4 # four times as fast as earlier generation system
reliab <- 2  # Less likely to fail
learn <- 4  # 16 hours to learn
price <- 4  # $1750
dell.competitor <- data.frame(brand,compat,perform,reliab,learn,price)

# second product in market is Gateway defined as follows:
brand <- "Gateway"
compat <- 6  # 90 percent compatibility
perform <- 2 # twice as fast as earlier generation system
reliab <- 1  # just as likely to fail
learn <- 2  # 8 hours to learn
price <- 2  # $1250
gateway.competitor <- data.frame(brand,compat,perform,reliab,learn,price)

# third product in market is HP defined as follows:
brand <- "HP"
compat <- 6  # 90 percent compatibility
perform <- 3 # three times as fast as earlier generation system
reliab <- 2  # less likely to fail
learn <- 2  # 8 hours to learn
price <- 3  # $1500
hp.competitor <- data.frame(brand,compat,perform,reliab,learn,price)

# Apple product has price varying across many choice sets:
brand <- "Apple"
compat <- 5  # 50 percent compatibility
perform <- 4 # four times as fast as earlier generation system
reliab <- 2  # less likely to fail
learn <- 1  # 4 hours to learn
price <- 1  # $1000 Apple price in first choice set
apple1000 <- data.frame(brand,compat,perform,reliab,learn,price)
price <- 2  # $1250 Apple price in second choice set
apple1250 <- data.frame(brand,compat,perform,reliab,learn,price)
price <- 3  # $1500 Apple price in third choice set
apple1500 <- data.frame(brand,compat,perform,reliab,learn,price)
price <- 4  # $1750 Apple price in fourth choice set
apple1750 <- data.frame(brand,compat,perform,reliab,learn,price)
price <- 5  # $2000 Apple price in fifth choice set
apple2000 <- data.frame(brand,compat,perform,reliab,learn,price)
price <- 6  # $2250 Apple price in sixth choice set
apple2250 <- data.frame(brand,compat,perform,reliab,learn,price)
price <- 7  # $2500 Apple price in seventh choice set
apple2500 <- data.frame(brand,compat,perform,reliab,learn,price)
price <- 8  # $2750 Apple price in eighth choice set
apple2750 <- data.frame(brand,compat,perform,reliab,learn,price)

# the competitive products are fixed from one choice set to the next
competition <- rbind(dell.competitor,gateway.competitor,hp.competitor)
```

```
# build the simulation choice sets with Apple varying across choice sets
simulation.choice.sets <-
  rbind(competition, apple1000, competition, apple1250,
  competition, apple1500, competition, apple1750, competition, apple2000,
  competition, apple2250, competition, apple2500, competition, apple2750)

# add set id to the simuation.choice sets for ease of analysis
setid <- NULL
for(index.for.set in 1:8) setid <- c(setid,rep(index.for.set, times = 4))
simulation.choice.sets <- cbind(setid,simulation.choice.sets)

# list the simulation data frame to check it out
print(simulation.choice.sets)

# create the simulation data frame for all individuals in the study
# by cloning the simulation choice sets for each individual
simulation.data.frame <- NULL  # initialize
list.of.ids <- unique(working.data.frame$id)  # ids from original study
for (index.for.id in seq(along=list.of.ids)) {
  id <- rep(list.of.ids[index.for.id], times = nrow(simulation.choice.sets))
  this.id.data <- cbind(data.frame(id),simulation.choice.sets)
  simulation.data.frame <- rbind(simulation.data.frame, this.id.data)
  }

# check structure of simulation data frame
print(str(simulation.data.frame))
print(head(simulation.data.frame))
print(tail(simulation.data.frame))

# using create.design.matrix function we evalutate the utility
# of each product profile in each choice set for each individual
# in the study... HP part-worths are used for individuals
# this code is similar to that used previously for original data
# from the computer choice study... except now we have simulation data
simulation.choice.utility <- NULL  # initialize utility vector
# work with one row of respondent training data frame at a time
# create choice prediction using the individual part-worths
list.of.ids <- unique(simulation.data.frame$id)
simulation.choice.utility <- NULL  # intitialize
for (index.for.id in seq(along=list.of.ids)) {
  this.id.part.worths <- posterior.mean[index.for.id,]
  this.id.data.frame <- subset(simulation.data.frame,
    subset=(id == list.of.ids[index.for.id]))
  for (index.for.profile in 1:nrow(this.id.data.frame)) {
    simulation.choice.utility <- c(simulation.choice.utility,
      create.design.matrix(this.id.data.frame[index.for.profile,]) %*%
      this.id.part.worths)
    }
  }
# use choice.set.predictor function to predict choices in market simulation
simulation.predicted.choice <-
  choice.set.predictor(simulation.choice.utility)
```

```
# add simulation predictions to simulation data frame for analysis
# of the results from the market simulation
simulation.analysis.data.frame <-
  cbind(simulation.data.frame,simulation.predicted.choice)

# contingency table shows results of market simulation
with(simulation.analysis.data.frame,
  table(setid,brand,simulation.predicted.choice))

# summary table of preference shares
YES.data.frame <- subset(simulation.analysis.data.frame,
  subset = (simulation.predicted.choice == "YES"), select = c("setid","brand"))

# check YES.data.frame to see that it reproduces the information
# from the contingency table
print(with(YES.data.frame,table(setid,brand)))

# create market share estimates by dividing by number of individuals
# no need for a spreadsheet program to work with tables
table.work <- with(YES.data.frame,as.matrix(table(setid,brand)))
table.work <- table.work[,c("Apple","Dell","Gateway","HP")] # order columns
table.work <- round(100 *table.work/length(list.of.ids), digits = 1)  # percent
Apple.Price <- c(1000,1250,1500,1750,2000,2250,2500,2750)  # new column
table.work <- cbind(Apple.Price,table.work) # add price column to table
print(table.work)  # print the market/preference share table

# data visualization of market/preference share estimates from the simulation
mosaic.data.frame <- YES.data.frame
mosaic.data.frame$setid <- factor(mosaic.data.frame$setid, levels = 1:8,
  labels = c("$1,000","$1,250","$1,500","$1,750",
  "$2,000","$2,250","2,500","$2,750"))
# mosaic plot of joint frequencies from the market simulation
# length/width of the tiles in each row reflects market share
# rows relate to Apple prices... simulation choice sets
pdf(file="fig_price_market_simulation_results.pdf", width = 8.5, height = 11)
  mosaic( ~ setid + brand, data = mosaic.data.frame,
  highlighting = "brand",
  highlighting_fill =
    c("mediumorchid4", "green", "blue","red"),
  labeling_args =
  list(set_varnames = c(brand = "", setid = "Price of Apple Computer"),
  rot_labels = c(left = 90, top = 45),
  pos_labels = c("center","center"),
  just_labels = c("left","center"),
  offset_labels = c(0.0,0.0)))
dev.off()

# suggestion for students
# try setting up your own market simulation study with a hypothetical client
# and competitive products... vary prices on your client's product
# and see what happens to preference shares
```

## 11

Spatial Data Analysis

"Of all the gin joints in all the towns in all the world, she walks into mine."

—HUMPHREY BOGART AS RICK BLAINE IN *Casablanca* (1942)

At 2 a.m. in Madison, Wisconsin in the middle of January, the temperature is well below freezing. The bars close and hundreds of partially to fully inebriated students stream onto State Street. Walking more than a few blocks in the cold weather is difficult, even for those who have not been drinking. It makes no sense to call a cab—the wait time is too long. But, if students walk a block or two from State Street, they might find a cab or two.

For the cabbie, this is the best of all worlds—many potential passengers with limited interest in walking. The cabbie can drive around until someone hails for his cab. Driving around looking for passengers is known as trolling. Or the cabbie can park in a cab post, a parking place the city has reserved for cabs. This is called posting.

The problem for the cabbie or the office worker dispatching cabs to downtown Madison is to identify the location of highest demand (foot traffic in this case). One additional consideration is the fact that State Street, the main pedestrian thoroughfare in Madison, is unavailable for trolling. On State Street, cabs can drop off or pick up passengers who have called for a cab, but cabs cannot drive along State Street looking for passengers.

The problem of positioning cabs in the right place at one point in time is a spatial data problem. Cab positioning is also a demand estimation problem, with demand generated by the exodus of students from bars. If we were to consider the positioning of cabs across downtown Madison at all points in time, then we would have a spatio-temporal problem.

"Location, location, location," long the mantra of retail business, has relevance today, despite our becoming a networked nation. Many products and services are location-dependent. Grocery and convenience stores, restaurants, laundromats, and health and fitness clubs know that it is good to be close to where people live and work. And, with consumers being so tied to their mobile devices, companies are learning that they can use information about where people are at every moment of the day. Direct marketing is turning into mobile marketing, with spatial location an important component of data and models.

As an example of spatial data modeling we draw upon public-domain data about California housing values. We use a variety of regression modeling techniques, showing how additional information about location (longitude and latitude) can contribute to the analysis. The data comprise observations of housing values, economic covariates, and longitude and latitude.[1] We follow Pace and Barry (1997) in defining response and explanatory variables for a linear regression model. Original database and computed variables are shown in table 11.1.

We select a subset of 1,206 block groups, focusing on the region around San Diego, further dividing the data into 803 training observations, and 403 test observations. Relationships between pairs of variables in this problem are shown in the correlation heat map in figure 11.1, which orders explanatory variables by their correlation with the response variable used in the Pace and Barry (1997) model, the log median housing value of homes in the block groups (in hundreds of thousands of dollars). From the correlation heat map we can see the importance of income in explaining housing values.

---

[1] The complete data set represents 20,640 California block groups from the 1990 U.S. Census. The original data were provided by R. Kelly Pace and Ronald Barry (1997) and are available from the StatLib archive as data file "houses.zip" at http://lib.stat.cmu.edu/datasets/.

Table 11.1. *California Housing Data: Original and Computed Variables*

California Housing Data (Unit of Analysis = Census Block Group)

Database Variables	Description
value	Median house value ($100,000)
* income	Median income ($10,000)
age	Housing median age (years)
rooms	Total rooms
bedrooms	Total bedrooms
pop	Population
hh	Households
latitude	Latitude
longitude	Longitude

Computed Variables	
log_value	Log of median housing value ($100,000)
* income_squared	Square of median income ($10,000)
* income_cubed	Cube of median income ($10,000)
* log_age	Log of median age
* log_pc_rooms	Log per capita rooms: log(total rooms / population)
* log_pc_bedrooms	Log per capita bedrooms: log(bedrooms / population)
* log_pop_hh	Log population per household
* log_hh	Log households

* Explanatory variables in regression model by Pace and Barry (1997).
  Response variable is log_value.

A review of the correlation heat map in figure 11.1 also reveals strong correlations among predictors. Correlations among predictors is called *multicollinearity* and is a special concern of modelers working in regression contexts (Belsley, Kuh, and Welsch 1980). Additional issues are raised by a review of the scatter plot matrix in figure 11.2. Note the apparent censoring for the log median value and age of houses.

The standard linear regression for the training data using the Pace and Barry (1997) model is shown in table 11.2. This model, which will serve as a baseline for comparing other regression models in this problem, explains 64.8 percent of response variance in the training set and 56.2 percent in the test set. The response in this problem is the natural logarithm of median home value in the block group. We note that multicollinearity is introduced into this problem by Pace and Barry's (1997) use of income, squared income, and cubed income in the linear predictor. We note as well that, in tests of hypotheses about regression coefficients, the model assumes independent observations. This is a questionable assumption given that observations are expected to be spatially autocorrelated.

These data provide an opportunity to examine various regression models. We begin with tree-structured regression using the original set of variables, ignoring the added variables from Pace and Barry (1997). This model fits the training data well, explaining 60.1 percent of response variance, but it does a poor job in predicting within the test set, explaining only 40.4 percent of response variance. If we include the full set of variables as input to tree-structured regression, we do better, with the model explaining 67.8 percent of response variance in the training set, and 57.4 percent in the test set. This model is shown in figure 11.3.

A random forest fit to these data, using the original explanatory variables only, performs very well on the training set, explaining 94.5 percent of response variance, but it falls short of desirable performance in the test set, explaining only 56.7 percent of response variance. Expanding the input variable list for random forests makes a big difference in test set performance, as the resulting model predicts 65.1 percent of response variance in the test set. The importance of individual explanatory variables is shown in figure 11.4.

Figure 11.1. California Housing Data: Correlation Heat Map for the Training Data

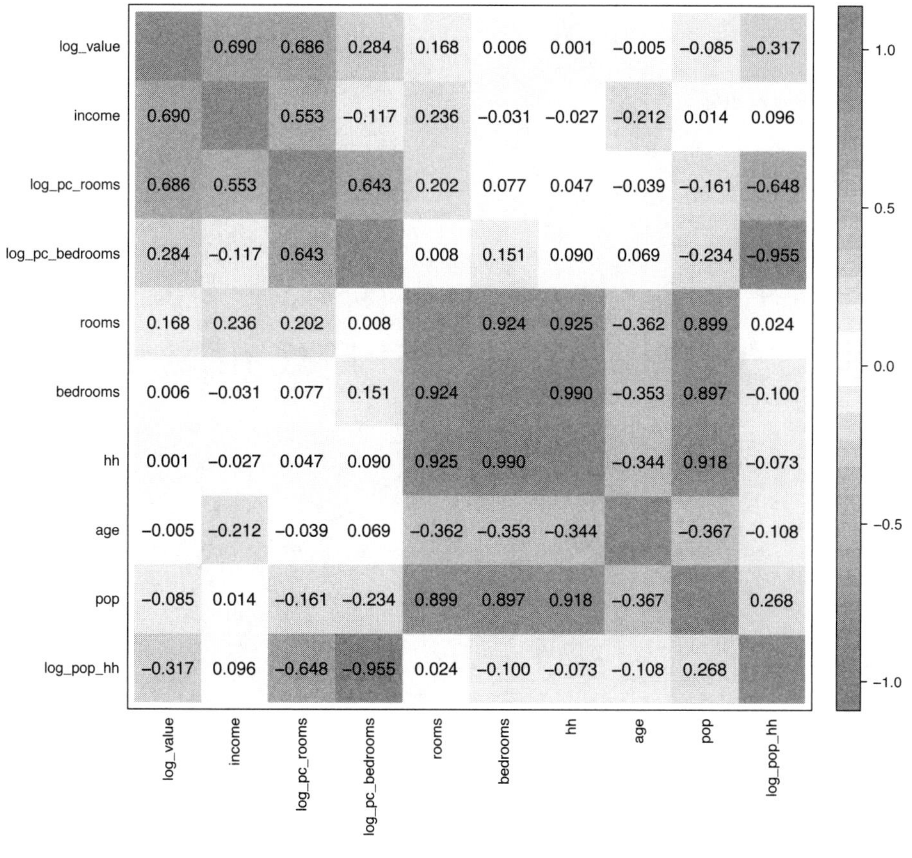

Figure 11.2. *California Housing Data: Scatter Plot Matrix of Selected Variables*

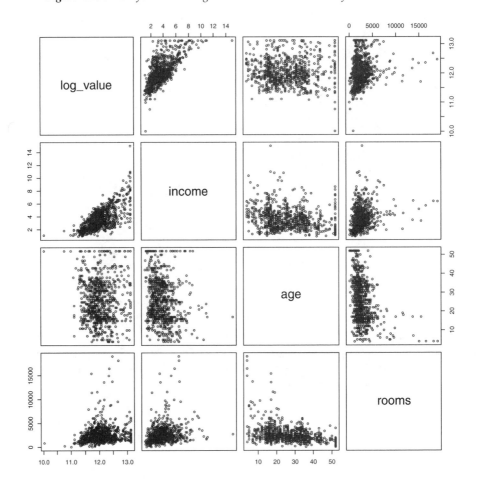

Table 11.2. *Linear Regression Fit to Selected California Block Groups*

Response: Log Median Housing Value ($100,000)	
Income	0.109**
	(0.047)
Income Squared	0.017**
	(0.008)
Income Cubed	-0.001***
	(0.000)
Log Age	0.105***
	(0.021)
Log Per Capita Rooms	0.141*
	(0.078)
Log Per Capita Bedrooms	-0.028
	(0.122)
Log Population per Household	-0.546***
	(0.126)
Log Households	0.039**
	(0.017)
Constant	11.329***
	(0.171)
Observations	803
R^2	0.648
Adjusted R^2	0.644
Residual Std. Error	$0.262 (df = 794)$
F statistic	$182.412^{***} (df = 8; 794)$

Notes:	***Significant at the 1 percent level.
	**Significant at the 5 percent level.
	*Significant at the 10 percent level.

Figure 11.3. Tree-Structured Regression for Predicting California Housing Values

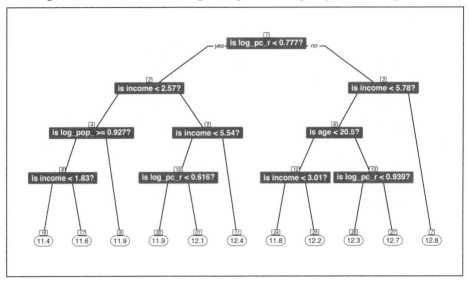

Predictive models with spatial data may be improved by adding a spatial component. All other things being equal, we expect that observations close together in space will be more similar to one another than observations separated by greater distances. In other words, there will be spatial auto-correlation. We expect that this will be true for housing values as well as for variables being used to explain housing values. Spatial data models use information about observations' location in space (longitude and latitude). Geographically weighted regression is especially useful for working with problems like the Californian housing study. When we fit a geographically weighted regression model to the data for the California housing study, we are able to explain 71.6 percent of response variability in the training set and 62.7 percent in the test set.

To improve further on the accuracy of predictive models for this problem, we use the two best performing models in the test set (random forests and geographically weighted regression) to create a hybrid model. In particular, we compute the average of the predictions from the random forests and geographically weighted regressions. The resulting hybrid model outperforms all other models tested on the test set, explaining 66.4 percent of response variance. A summary of the findings is shown in table 11.3.

Figure **11.4.** *Random Forests Regression for Predicting California Housing Values*

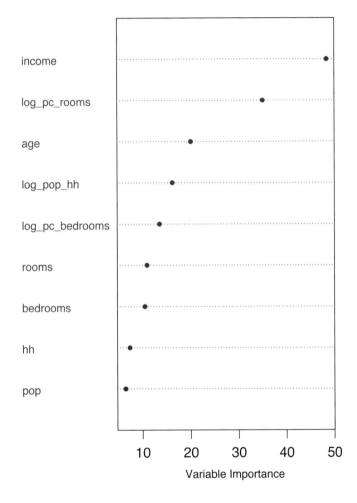

Table 11.3. *Comparison of Regressions on Spatially Referenced Data*

Method	Percentage of Response Variance Accounted for in . . .	
	Training Set	Test Set
Linear regression Pace and Barry (1997)	64.8	56.2
Tree-structured regression (simple model)	60.1	40.4
Tree-structured regression (full model)	67.8	57.4
Random forests (simple model)	94.5	56.7
Random forests (full model)	94.9	65.1
Geographically weighted regression (GWR)	71.6	62.7
Hybrid Random Forests and GWR	86.4	66.4

The value of a model lies in the quality of its predictions. Regression and spatial data models are important in predicting housing values. They are also important in location-based demand estimation, sales forecasting, and site selection research. Traditional theory-based, data-adaptive, and hybrid methods may be employed, as we have seen in working with the California housing study.

Working with block groups in the California housing study, we implicitly take location into account because response and explanatory variables are linked to the observational unit—the block group location. We can do more with spatially-referenced data such as these. Because we have information about longitude and latitude, we can use distances between observational units to build nearest-neighbor predictors, and we can use distance-referenced explanatory variables in predictive models.

We use the proportion of response variance accounted for as a criterion for evaluating regression performance in the California housing study. This criterion is also known as the coefficient of determination or R-squared. It varies from zero to one with higher numbers indicating higher goodness of fit and better models. We compute its value in the test set by squaring the correlation of observed and predicted response values. Proportion of response variance is an easy concept for managers to understand, and this index of goodness of fit takes values from zero to one in all studies. See appendix A for additional discussion of regression methods and the evaluation of regression model performance.

Alfons (2013a) provides cross-validation tools, which are useful in conducting benchmark studies as illustrated in this chapter. Benchmark studies, also known as statistical simulations, may be conducted within special packages designed for this type of research (Alfons 2013b; Alfons, Templ, and Filzmoser 2013).

Cressie (1993) and Lloyd (2010) provide an overview of methods in spatial data analysis. Spatially weighted regression can be especially useful in this domain of application (Fotheringham, Brunsdon, and Charlton 2002). Bivand, Pebesma, and Gómez-Rubio (2008), Bivand (2013), and Bivand and Yu (2013) review relevant software for spatial data modeling and geographically weighted regression.

Cressie and Wikle (2011) introduce the emerging area of spatio-temporal modeling. Spatio-temporal models are used in weather forecasting and in the study of global climate trends. They are used for research in spatial epidemiology, criminology, transportation, and logistics. We expect that spatio-temporal models will be utilized much more extensively in marketing analytics and predictive analytics in general as mobile data about consumers become more widely available. Cressie and Wikle (2011) describe spatio-temporal modeling as the next modeling frontier. Spatio-temporal models are, by definition, hierarchical models, typically Bayesian hierarchical models. Software for spatio-temporal modeling is available for the R programming environment (Pebesma 2013).

Exhibit 11.1 shows the R program for working with the California housing data. We show statistical graphics for the correlation heat map and for presenting model results with trees and random forests. This program presents the complete code for the regression comparisons used in this chapter. It draws upon R software packages provided by Becker et al. (2013), McIlroy et al. (2013), Bivand and Yu (2013), Therneau, Atkinson, and Ripley (2013), Liaw and Wiener (2013), Milborrow (2013), Sarkar (2013), and Alfons (2013a).

Utilities for computing distances between points defined by longitude and latitude are useful in defining nearest-neighbor predictors and distance-referenced explanatory variables. These utilities are provided in exhibit C.6 on page 296.

Exhibit 11.1. *California Housing Values: Regression and Spatial Regression Models*

```
# Regression Modeling with California Housing Values

library(maps)  # making making
library(mapproj)  # projections for map making
library(spgwr)  # spatially-weighted regression
library(rpart)  # tree-structured modeling
library(randomForest)  # random forests
library(rpart.plot)  # plot tree-structured model information
library(lattice)  # statistical graphics
library(cvTools)  # cross-validation tools including rmspe

# read in the housing data
houses <-  read.table("houses_data.txt", header = FALSE, sep = "",
   dec = ".", row.names = NULL,
   col.names = c("value", "income", "age", "rooms", "bedrooms",
   "pop", "hh", "latitude", "longitude"))

# computed variables for linear model used by Pace and Barry (1997)
houses$log_value <- log(houses$value)
houses$income_squared <- houses$income^2
houses$income_cubed <- houses$income^3
houses$log_age <- log(houses$age)
houses$log_pc_rooms <- log(houses$rooms / houses$pop)
houses$log_pc_bedrooms <- log(houses$bedrooms / houses$pop)
houses$log_pop_hh <- log(houses$pop / houses$hh)
houses$log_hh <- log(houses$hh)

# structure of the Pace and Barry (1997) model for baseline for comparisons
pace.barry.model <- {log_value ~ income + income_squared +
   income_cubed + log_age + log_pc_rooms + log_pc_bedrooms +
   log_pop_hh + log_hh}

# for comparison lets look at a simple model with the original variables
simple.model <-  {log_value ~ income + age + rooms + bedrooms +
   pop + hh}

# original variables plus variables that add value for trees
# that is... variables that are not simple monotonic transformations
# of the original explanatory variables
full.model <- {log_value ~ income + age + rooms + bedrooms +
   pop + hh + log_pc_rooms + log_pc_bedrooms + log_pop_hh}

# define variable for selecting a geographically defined
# subset of the data... San Diego area
# we use nested ifelse statements to do this
houses$select <- ifelse(((houses$latitude < 33)),
ifelse((houses$longitude < -116.75),1,2),2)
houses$select <- factor(houses$select, levels = c(1,2),
   labels = c("Selected","Not Selected"))
houses.selected <- subset(houses, subset = (select == "Selected"))
houses.notselected <- subset(houses, subset = (select == "Not Selected"))
```

```
# plot the locations of block groups red in the selected area, blue otherwise
pdf(file = "fig_spatial_map_selected_region.pdf", width = 8.5, height = 8.5)
pointsize <- 0.5
map("state", region = c("california"), project="albers",par=c(39,45))
  points(mapproject(houses.selected$longitude, houses.selected$latitude,
  projection=""),pch=20,cex=pointsize,col="red")
  points(mapproject(houses.notselected$longitude, houses.notselected$latitude,
  projection=""),pch=20,cex=pointsize,col="darkblue")
legend("right", legend = c("Selected Region","Not Selected"),
  col = c("red","darkblue"), pch = 20)
map.scale()
dev.off()

# define training and test sets for the selected houses
set.seed(4444)
partition <- sample(nrow(houses.selected)) # permuted list of row index numbers
houses.selected$Group <-
  ifelse((partition < nrow(houses.selected)/(3/2)),1,2)
houses.selected$Group <-
  factor(houses.selected$Group,levels=c(1,2),labels=c("TRAIN","TEST"))
print(table(houses.selected$Group))  # review the split into training and test
print(head(houses.selected))  # review the selected data

houses.train <-
  subset(houses.selected, subset = (Group == "TRAIN"))
houses.test <-
  subset(houses.selected, subset = (Group == "TEST"))

# let's examine the correlations across the variables before we begin modeling
houses.train.df.vars <- houses.train[,c("log_value","income","age",
  "rooms","bedrooms","pop","hh","log_pc_rooms",
  "log_pc_bedrooms","log_pop_hh")]

houses.train.cormat <- cor(as.matrix(houses.train.df.vars))
houses.train.cormat.line <- houses.train.cormat["log_value",]
# explanatory variables ordered by correlation with the response variable
ordered.houses.train.cormat <-
  houses.train.cormat[names(sort(houses.train.cormat.line,decreasing=TRUE)),
  names(sort(houses.train.cormat.line,decreasing=FALSE))]

# code to obtain default colors from ggplot2...
number.of.default.colors <- 2  # two end-points for our scale
end.point.colors <- hcl(h=seq(15, 375-360/number.of.default.colors,
  length=number.of.default.colors)%%360, c=100, l=65)
# end.point.colors[1] and [2] used to define the three-point color scale

pdf(file = "fig_spatial_correlation_heat_map.pdf", width = 11,
  height = 8.5)
x <- rep(1:nrow(ordered.houses.train.cormat),
  times=ncol(ordered.houses.train.cormat))
y <- NULL
for (i in 1:ncol(ordered.houses.train.cormat))
  y <- c(y,rep(i,times=nrow(ordered.houses.train.cormat)))
```

```
# use fixed format O.XXX in cells of correlation matrix
cortext <- sprintf("%0.3f", as.numeric(ordered.houses.train.cormat))
text.data.frame <- data.frame(x, y, cortext)
text.data.frame$cortext <- as.character(text.data.frame$cortext)
text.data.frame$cortext <- ifelse((text.data.frame$cortext == "1.000"),
   NA,text.data.frame$cortext)  # define diagonal cells as missing
text.data.frame <- na.omit(text.data.frame)  # diagonal cells have no text

levelplot(ordered.houses.train.cormat, cuts = 25, tick.number = 9,
  col.regions =
    colorRampPalette(c(end.point.colors[1], "white", end.point.colors[2])),
  scales=list(tck=0, x=list(rot=90)),
  xlab = "",
  ylab = "",
  panel = function(...) {
    panel.levelplot(...)
    panel.text(text.data.frame$x, text.data.frame$y,
    labels = text.data.frame$cortext)
    })
dev.off()


# scatter plot matrix (splom) demonstration
houses.train.splom.vars <-
  houses.train[,c("log_value","income","age","rooms")]
pdf(file = "fig_spatial_sample_splom.pdf", width = 8.5,
  height = 8.5)
pairs(houses.train.splom.vars, cex = 0.65, col = "darkblue")
dev.off()


# define spatial objects as needed for spatial modeling work
# explanation of spatial objects may be found in chapter 2 of
# Bivand, R. S., Pebesma, E. J., and Gomez-Rubio, V. (2008)
# Applied Spatial Data Analysis, New York: Springer.
# this involves adding coordinate objects to data frame objects
# training set coordinates to add
houses.coord <- cbind(houses.train$longitude,houses.train$latitude)
# define spatial points data frame object
houses.train <- SpatialPointsDataFrame(houses.coord,houses.train,bbox = NULL)

# test set coordinates to add
houses.coord <- cbind(houses.test$longitude,houses.test$latitude)
# define spatial points data frame object
houses.test <- SpatialPointsDataFrame(houses.coord,houses.test,bbox = NULL)

# examine the struction of the spatial points data frame
print(str(houses.train))

# -------------------------------------------------
# Linear regression a la Pace and Barry (1997)
# -------------------------------------------------
pace.barry.train.fit <- lm(pace.barry.model, data = houses.train)
print(pace.barry.train.fit)
print(summary(pace.barry.train.fit))
```

```
# direct calculation of root-mean-squared prediction error
# obtained directly on the training data
print(rmspe(houses.train$log_value, predict(pace.barry.train.fit)))
# report R-squared on training data
print(cor(houses.train$log_value,predict(pace.barry.train.fit))^2)

cat("\n\nTraining set proportion of variance accounted",
  " for by linear regression = ",
  sprintf("%1.3f",cor(houses.train$log_value,
  predict(pace.barry.train.fit))^2),sep=" ")

# test model fit to training set on the test set
print(rmspe(houses.test$log_value, predict(pace.barry.train.fit,
  newdata = houses.test)))
print(cor(houses.test$log_value,
  predict(pace.barry.train.fit, newdata = houses.test))^2)

cat("\n\nTest set proportion of variance accounted",
  " for by linear regression = ",
  sprintf("%1.3f",cor(houses.test$log_value,
  predict(pace.barry.train.fit, newdata = houses.test))^2),sep=" ")

# demonstrate cross-validation within the training set
# specify ten-fold cross-validation within the training set
# K = folds   R = replications of K-fold cross-validation
set.seed(1234)  # for reproducibility
folds <- cvFolds(nrow(houses.train), K = 10, R = 50)
cv.pace.barry.train.fit <- cvLm(pace.barry.train.fit, cost = rtmspe,
  folds = folds, trim = 0.1)
# root-mean-squared prediction error estimated by cross-validation
print(cv.pace.barry.train.fit)

# -------------------------------------
# Tree-structured regression (simple)
# -------------------------------------
# try tree-structured regression on the original explantory variables
# note that one of the advatates of trees is no need for transformations
# of the explanatory variables

rpart.train.fit <- rpart(simple.model, data = houses.train)
print(summary(rpart.train.fit))  # tree summary statistics and split detail
houses.train$rpart.train.fit.pred <- predict(rpart.train.fit,
  data = houses.train)

# root-mean-squared prediction error for trees on training set
print(rmspe(houses.train$log_value, houses.train$rpart.train.fit.pred))
# report R-squared on training data
print(cor(houses.train$log_value,houses.train$rpart.train.fit.pred)^2)

cat("\n\nTraining set proportion of variance accounted",
  " for by tree-structured regression = ",
  sprintf("%1.3f",cor(houses.train$log_value,
  houses.train$rpart.train.fit.pred)^2),sep=" ")
```

```
# root-mean-squared prediction error for trees on test set
houses.test$rpart.train.fit.pred <- predict(rpart.train.fit, newdata = houses.test)
print(rmspe(houses.test$log_value, houses.test$rpart.train.fit.pred))
# report R-squared on training data
print(cor(houses.test$log_value,houses.test$rpart.train.fit.pred)^2)

cat("\n\nTest set proportion of variance accounted",
  " for by tree-structured regression = ",
  sprintf("%1.3f",
  cor(houses.test$log_value,houses.test$rpart.train.fit.pred)^2),sep=" ")

# plot the regression tree result from rpart
pdf(file = "fig_spatial_rpart_model.pdf", width = 8.5, height = 8.5)
prp(rpart.train.fit, main="",
  digits = 3,  # digits to display in terminal nodes
  nn = TRUE,  # display the node numbers
  fallen.leaves = TRUE,  # put the leaves on the bottom of the page
  branch = 0.5,  # change angle of branch lines
  branch.lwd = 2,  # width of branch lines
  faclen = 0,  # do not abbreviate factor levels
  trace = 1,  # print the automatically calculated cex
  shadow.col = 0,  # no shadows under the leaves
  branch.lty = 1,  # draw branches using dotted lines
  split.cex = 1.2,  # make the split text larger than the node text
  split.prefix = "is ",  # put "is " before split text
  split.suffix = "?",  # put "?" after split text
  split.box.col = "blue",  # lightgray split boxes (default is white)
  split.col = "white",  # color of text in split box
  split.border.col = "blue",  # darkgray border on split boxes
  split.round = .25)  # round the split box corners a tad
dev.off()

# ----------------------------------------
# Tree-structured regression (full)
# ----------------------------------------
# try tree-structured regression on the original explantory variables
# note that one of the advantages of trees is no need for transformations
# of the explanatory variables

rpart.train.fit.full <- rpart(full.model, data = houses.train)
print(summary(rpart.train.fit.full))  # tree summary statistics and split detail
houses.train$rpart.train.fit.full.pred <-
  predict(rpart.train.fit.full, data = houses.train)

# root-mean-squared prediction error for trees on training set
print(rmspe(houses.train$log_value, houses.train$rpart.train.fit.full.pred))
# report R-squared on training data
print(cor(houses.train$log_value,houses.train$rpart.train.fit.full.pred)^2)

cat("\n\nTraining set proportion of variance accounted",
  " for by tree-structured regression (full model) = ",
  sprintf("%1.3f",cor(houses.train$log_value,
  houses.train$rpart.train.fit.full.pred)^2),sep=" ")
```

```
# root-mean-squared prediction error for trees on test set
houses.test$rpart.train.fit.full.pred <- predict(rpart.train.fit.full,
  newdata = houses.test)
print(rmspe(houses.test$log_value, houses.test$rpart.train.fit.full.pred))
# report R-squared on training data
print(cor(houses.test$log_value,houses.test$rpart.train.fit.full.pred)^2)

cat("\n\nTest set proportion of variance accounted",
    " for by tree-structured regression (full model) = ",
  sprintf("%1.3f",cor(houses.test$log_value,
  houses.test$rpart.train.fit.full.pred)^2),sep=" ")

# plot the regression tree result from rpart
pdf(file = "fig_spatial_rpart_model_full.pdf", width = 8.5, height = 8.5)
prp(rpart.train.fit.full, main="",
  digits = 3,  # digits to display in terminal nodes
  nn = TRUE,  # display the node numbers
  fallen.leaves = TRUE,  # put the leaves on the bottom of the page
  branch = 0.5,  # change angle of branch lines
  branch.lwd = 2,  # width of branch lines
  faclen = 0,  # do not abbreviate factor levels
  trace = 1,  # print the automatically calculated cex
  shadow.col = 0,  # no shadows under the leaves
  branch.lty = 1,  # draw branches using dotted lines
  split.cex = 1.2,  # make the split text larger than the node text
  split.prefix = "is ",  # put "is" before split text
  split.suffix = "?",  # put "?" after split text
  split.box.col = "blue",  # lightgray split boxes (default is white)
  split.col = "white",  # color of text in split box
  split.border.col = "blue",  # darkgray border on split boxes
  split.round = .25)  # round the split box corners a tad
dev.off()


# -------------------------------------
# Random forests (simple)
# -------------------------------------
set.seed (9999)  # for reproducibility
rf.train.fit <- randomForest(simple.model,
  data=houses.train, mtry=3, importance=TRUE, na.action=na.omit)
# review the random forest solution
print(rf.train.fit)
# check importance of the individual explanatory variables
pdf(file = "fig_spatial_random_forest_simple_importance.pdf",
width = 11, height = 8.5)
varImpPlot(rf.train.fit, main = "", pch = 20, col = "darkblue")
dev.off()
# random forest predictions for the trainings set
houses.train$rf.train.fit.pred <- predict(rf.train.fit, type="class",
  newdata = houses.train)
# root-mean-squared prediction error for random forest on training set
print(rmspe(houses.train$log_value, houses.train$rf.train.fit.pred))
# report R-squared on training data
print(cor(houses.train$log_value,houses.train$rf.train.fit.pred)^2)
```

```
cat("\n\nTraining set proportion of variance accounted",
    "for by random forests (simple model) = ",
  sprintf("%1.3f",
  cor(houses.train$log_value,houses.train$rf.train.fit.pred)^2),sep=" ")

# random forest predictions for the test set using model from training set
houses.test$rf.train.fit.pred <- predict(rf.train.fit,
  type="class", newdata = houses.test)

# root-mean-squared prediction error for random forest on training set
print(rmspe(houses.test$log_value, houses.test$rf.train.fit.pred))
# report R-squared on training data
print(cor(houses.test$log_value,houses.test$rf.train.fit.pred)^2)

cat("\n\nTest set proportion of variance accounted",
    " for by random forests (simple model) = ",
  sprintf("%1.3f",
  cor(houses.test$log_value,houses.test$rf.train.fit.pred)^2),sep=" ")

# -------------------------------------
# Random forests (full)
# -------------------------------------
set.seed (9999)  # for reproducibility
rf.train.fit.full <- randomForest(full.model,
  data=houses.train, mtry=3, importance=TRUE, na.action=na.omit)
# review the random forest solution
print(rf.train.fit.full)

# check importance of the individual explanatory variables
pdf(file = "fig_spatial_random_forest_full_importance.pdf",
width = 11, height = 8.5)
varImpPlot(rf.train.fit.full, main = "", pch = 20,
  cex = 1.25, col = "darkblue", lcolor = "black")
dev.off()

# random forest predictions for the trainings set
houses.train$rf.train.fit.full.pred <- predict(rf.train.fit.full, type="class",
  newdata = houses.train)



# root-mean-squared prediction error for random forest on training set
print(rmspe(houses.train$log_value, houses.train$rf.train.fit.full.pred))
# report R-squared on training data
print(cor(houses.train$log_value,houses.train$rf.train.fit.full.pred)^2)

cat("\n\nTraining set proportion of variance accounted",
    " for by random forests (full model) = ",
  sprintf("%1.3f",cor(houses.train$log_value,
    houses.train$rf.train.fit.full.pred)^2),sep=" ")

# random forest predictions for the test set using model from training set
houses.test$rf.train.fit.full.pred <- predict(rf.train.fit.full, type="class",
  newdata = houses.test)
```

```
# root-mean-squared prediction error for random forest on training set
print(rmspe(houses.test$log_value, houses.test$rf.train.fit.full.pred))
# report R-squared on training data
print(cor(houses.test$log_value,houses.test$rf.train.fit.full.pred)^2)

cat("\n\nTest set proportion of variance accounted",
    " for by random forests (full model) = ",
  sprintf("%1.3f",cor(houses.test$log_value,
    houses.test$rf.train.fit.full.pred)^2),sep=" ")


# --------------------------------------
# Geographically weighted regression
# --------------------------------------
# bandwidth calculation may take a while
set.bandwidth <- gwr.sel(pace.barry.model,
  data=houses.train, verbose = FALSE, show.error.messages = FALSE)

# fit the geographically-weighted regression with bandwidth value set.bandwidth
gwr.train.fit <- gwr(pace.barry.model, bandwidth = set.bandwidth,
  predictions = TRUE, data=houses.train, fit.points = houses.train)
# extract training set predictions
houses.train$grw.train.fit.pred <- gwr.train.fit$SDF$pred

# root-mean-squared prediction error for grw on training set
print(rmspe(houses.train$log_value, houses.train$grw.train.fit.pred))
# report R-squared on training data
print(cor(houses.train$log_value,houses.train$grw.train.fit.pred)^2)

cat("\n\nTraining set proportion of variance accounted",
    " for by geographically-weighted regression = ",
    sprintf("%1.3f",cor(houses.train$log_value,
    houses.train$grw.train.fit.pred)^2),sep=" ")

# fit the geographically-weighted regression with bandwidth value set.bandwidth
# fit to training data and specify test data
gwr.train.fit <- gwr(pace.barry.model, bandwidth = set.bandwidth,
  predictions = TRUE, data=houses.train, fit.points = houses.test)
# extract test set predictions
houses.test$grw.train.fit.pred <- gwr.train.fit$SDF$pred

# root-mean-squared prediction error for grw on test set
print(rmspe(houses.test$log_value, houses.test$grw.train.fit.pred))
# report R-squared on training data
print(cor(houses.test$log_value,houses.test$grw.train.fit.pred)^2)

cat("\n\nTest set proportion of variance accounted",
    " for by geographically-weighted regression = ",
    sprintf("%1.3f",cor(houses.test$log_value,
    houses.test$grw.train.fit.pred)^2),sep=" ")


# --------------------------------------
# Construct a hybrid prediction
# --------------------------------------
```

```
houses.train$hybrid.pred <- (houses.train$rf.train.fit.full.pred +
  houses.train$grw.train.fit.pred) / 2  # average of two best predictors
houses.test$hybrid.pred <- (houses.test$rf.train.fit.full.pred +
  houses.test$grw.train.fit.pred) / 2  # average of two best predictors
cat("\n\nTraining set proportion of variance accounted",
    " for by hybrid model = ",
  sprintf("%1.3f",cor(houses.train$log_value,houses.train$hybrid.pred)^2),sep=" ")
cat("\n\nTest set proportion of variance accounted",
  " for by hybrid model = ",
  sprintf("%1.3f",cor(houses.test$log_value,
  houses.test$hybrid.pred)^2),sep=" ")
# -------------------------------------
# Gather results into a single report
# -------------------------------------
# measurement model performance summary
methods <- c("Linear regression Pace and Barry (1997)",
  "Tree-structured regression (simple model)",
  "Tree-structured regression (full model)",
  "Random forests (simple model)",
  "Random forests (full model)",
  "Geographically weighted regression (GWR)",
  "Hybrid Random Forests and GWR")
methods.performance.data.frame <- data.frame(methods)
methods.performance.data.frame$training <-
  c(round(cor(houses.train$log_value,predict(pace.barry.train.fit))^2
    ,digits=3),
    round(cor(houses.train$log_value,
    houses.train$rpart.train.fit.pred)^2,digits=3),
    round(cor(houses.train$log_value,
    houses.train$rpart.train.fit.full.pred)^2,digits=3),
    round(cor(houses.train$log_value,
    houses.train$rf.train.fit.pred)^2,digits=3),
     round(cor(houses.train$log_value,
     houses.train$rf.train.fit.full.pred)^2,digits=3),
    round(cor(houses.train$log_value,
    houses.train$grw.train.fit.pred)^2,digits=3),
    round(cor(houses.train$log_value,
    houses.train$hybrid.pred)^2,digits=3))
 methods.performance.data.frame$test <-
  c(round(cor(houses.test$log_value,
  predict(pace.barry.train.fit, newdata = houses.test))^2,digits=3),
    round(cor(houses.test$log_value,
    houses.test$rpart.train.fit.pred)^2,digits=3),
    round(cor(houses.test$log_value,
    houses.test$rpart.train.fit.full.pred)^2,digits=3),
    round(cor(houses.test$log_value,
    houses.test$rf.train.fit.pred)^2,digits=3),
    round(cor(houses.test$log_value,
    houses.test$rf.train.fit.full.pred)^2,digits=3),
    round(cor(houses.test$log_value,
    houses.test$grw.train.fit.pred)^2,digits=3),
    round(cor(houses.test$log_value,houses.test$hybrid.pred)^2,digits=3))
print(methods.performance.data.frame)
```

```
# suggestions for students

# try alternative formulations for the linear predictor
# try subset selection and all possible regression approaches
# try additional transformations of predictors
# deal with the issues of censoring and multicollinearity

# evaluate possible interaction effects such as between
# median household age and occupancy (log population per household)

# try additional regression methods, including neural networks
# and robust regression methods

# try alternative spatial data models...
# spatial grid or lattice structures are possible

# explore the data further using data visualization... maps

# run a full benchmark study by evaluating models within a loop
# run a few hundred iterations within the benchmark study

# work on another metropolitan area in California by specifying
# different area selection values for longitude and latitude
# determine the degree to which models built on one region
# generalize to other regions
```

12

The Big Little Data Game

"You're gonna need a bigger boat."

—ROY SCHEIDER AS MARTIN BRODY IN *Jaws* (1975)

Among my fondest childhood memories is reading in the attic of my parents' home. Getting to my reading place was an adventure. I would tug at light cords and squeeze between overstuffed storage containers to find my way to a special box of books my father collected over the years. These were the Big Little Books®, a creation of the Whitman Publishing Company of Racine, Wisconsin. A contradiction unto themselves, the books were big because they were thick. They were also little. My favorites had images on the top right-hand corner of each page. Flipping quickly though the pages would be like watching a motion picture. I could see Tarzan fighting a tiger or Flash Gordon subduing a monster on the Planet Mongo.

Data are the lifeblood of business. To store, retrieve, manipulate, parse, process, and deliver data to users—these are essential activities and a prerequisite to analytics. Lately, there has been much talk about "big data" from suppliers of information systems and consulting services. While it is true that we live in a data-driven, data-intensive world, I believe that the best approach to understanding the world is to play what I call *the big little data game.* Cutting big data down to size, we analyze and make sense out of them. Using models, we hold data in our hands and make them come alive, like the Big Little Books® of yesteryear.

Figure 12.1. *From Data to Explanation*

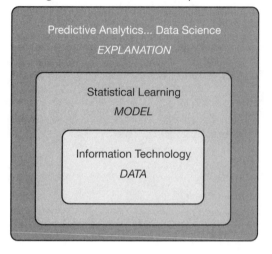

Information technology professionals deliver data as data. Statisticians and machine learning experts focus on models. Data scientists, building on a foundation of data and models, paint a picture that others can understand. Working in the area of predictive analytics, we are concerned with explaining and interpreting, and if the data warrant, recommending. The job of the data scientist is to derive meaning from data and models, to provide information so managers can make decisions and act. See figure 12.1.

Today's data come from many sources. They are often unstructured text data. They are sometimes pixels from sensors and cameras. These data are being gathered with increasing speed. This is what is meant by "big data." But in reality big data are just data, and big data technologies represent a set of data structures and algorithms that are conveniently scalable.

It is easy to understand why flexible, distributed systems are promoted as a way of dealing with today's data requirements. Traditional database systems require tables and fields be defined in advance of any storage. They have a predefined relational structure or scheme. They may rely on a centralized system too small or too expensive to accommodate the masses of data to be stored. Firms are moving away from internally owned and supported computing systems and toward external cloud-based services.

As data scientists, we gather data from the full range of database systems, relational and not-only-relational, commercial and open-source. We employ database query and analysis tools, gathering information across distributed systems, collating information, creating contingency tables, and computing indices of relationship across variables of interest. We use information technology and database systems as far as they can take us, and then we do more, applying what we know about statistical inference and the modeling techniques of predictive analytics.[1]

There have always been more data than we can use. What is new today is the ease of collecting data and the low cost of storing data. Aided by technology, we sample less by necessity and more by choice, but information selection endures. A penchant for selective attention is something we share. What distinguishes us from one another in both our approach to life and our approach to science is the nature of that attention.

More important than having large quantities of data is knowing what to look for in data and how to look for it. We do not have to analyze every piece of data coming our way. Often a small study can tell us what we need to know. So we focus on measures that make sense and sample as much data as are needed for predictive inference. Data are much less forbidding and overwhelming when we know what to do with them.

How do we deal with large data problems? We use methods designed for large-scale inference. Empirical Bayesian, machine learning, and statistical learning approaches are available for analyzing data sets with millions of rows and columns (Hastie, Tibshirani, and Friedman 2009; Efron 2012).

We can organize data from many sources, defining a hierarchical structure for those data. We gather precincts into wards, gather wards into legislative districts, districts into counties or states, and so on. The big data of the nation are merely a collection of little data communities. We know how to analyze data using hierarchical or multilevel models (Gelman and Hill 2007; Pinheiro and Bates 2009).

---

[1] Within the R programming community, there have been extensive efforts to extend R's data processing capabilities, improving performance and reducing memory requirements. R packages can interface with Hadoop and distributed cloud-based systems. R packages can utilize parallel processing and distribute workloads across networks of computers (Hoffmann 2013). McCallum and Weston (2012) introduce memory management and parallel processing packages and provide an overview of the performance benefits of working with Hadoop and MapReduce. Dean and Ghemawat (2004) discuss MapReduce. To keep up with the fast pace of developments in this area, see Eddelbuettel (2013b).

There are ways of generalizing from the findings of many small studies, gathering the results of others to arrive at conclusions of our own. We observe how treatment affects response across experiments that differ from one another. We see the big picture by combining many small views. These are the methods of meta-analysis (Borenstein, Hedges, Higgins, and Rothstein 2009).

We can learn about populations—big populations—populations we imagine to be infinite in size. How do we conquer this biggest of all data problems? We sample, and we do what statisticians have been doing for years—draw inferences from samples to populations. We study the theory of inference, classical and Bayesian, and apply probabilistic thinking to the problems at hand. There are many fine works from which to learn as we continue on this journey (Snedecor and Cochran 1989; Hinkley, Reid, and Snell 1991; Geisser 1993; Geisser and Johnson 2006; Robert 2007; Stuart, Ord, and Arnold 2010; O'Hagan 2010; Wasserman 2010).

A story I often tell students when introducing the topic of measurement is the three umpire story:

> After a long day of disputed calls at the ballpark, three umpires are asked to justify their methods. The first umpire, an empiricist by persuasion, says, *I call them as I see them*. The second, with the faith of a philosophical realist, replies, *I call them as they are*. Not to be outdone, the third umpire, with the self-proclaimed authority of an operationist or logical empiricist, says, *The way I call them—that's the way they are*.

We work with people, and people can be erratic. We work with imprecise measures of values, attitudes, and behavior, with controversial surveys of political opinion, with guesses (at best) of what short strings of text may say about public sentiment. We rely upon economic indicators of dubious value, not knowing which is leading and which lagging.

As data scientists, we sort through thousands of potential explanatory variables, most of them with ridiculously weak relationships to the response. We predict, extrapolate, forecast, and test...and test...and test again. We employ our best judgement, trying to build models we can trust.

We do amazing things with modeling techniques in predictive analytics. Many of our attempts at prognostication turn out quite well. But let us not deny our uncertainty about the future. The direction of the economy, the sales forecast, the go/no-go recommendation for a new product, the estimate of market share, the identification of a future buyer, high-return stock, or winning sports team—we would love to have complete confidence in these predictions. But, like the umpires in the story, we are left to our own devices when it comes to justifying calls.

The data we have are real. We understand them as well as we can through the measurements we make and the models we build. The data to come will be real as well and, yes, plentiful. To predict these data to come, providing honest advice to management, we use our models and our wits. Let the prediction and, by necessity, the modeling continue. As Vin Scully, Charley Steiner, or Rick Monday would say at the start of a Dodgers game,

It's a beautiful night for baseball.

A

There's a Pack' for That

Neo: "Can you fly that thing?"

Trinity: "Not yet." (cell phone call)

Tank: "Operator."

Trinity: "Tank, I need a pilot program for a B212 helicopter."
(fast learning download) "Alright, let's go."

—KEANU REEVES AS NEO, CARRIE-ANNE MOSS AS TRINITY,
AND MARCUS CHONG AS TANK IN *The Matrix* (1999)

Achieving competitive advantage through analytics is facilitated by implementing flexible, scalable, and extensible systems. Facilitated by the emergence of R (a well developed, fully functional, object-oriented programming environment designed for data analysis, visualization, and modeling), the power of predictive analytics is one download away.

Whatever the modeling problem or application interface (API), there is likely an R package that someone has written or is thinking about writing. Analysts familiar with the R programming environment know well the open-source programming game. They look for task views posted with the Comprehensive R Archive Network (CRAN). They download code and documentation from RForge and GitHub. They read R package vignettes and papers in *The R Journal* and the *Journal of Statistical Software*. They find worked examples and explanations of algorithms and methods.

A.1 Regression

There are two major types of predictive models: *classification* and *regression*. Classification involves prediction of a class or category. Regression is prediction of a response of meaningful magnitude. The most common form of regression is *least-squares regression*, also called ordinary least-squares regression, linear regression, or multiple regression. Coefficients that are fit to the linear predictor in least-squares regression minimize the sum of the squared residuals, where residuals are differences between the observed and predicted response values. In least-squares regression, the response may take any value along the real number line.

The method of *logistic regression,* although called "regression," is actually a classification method. It involves the prediction of a binary response. See Christensen (1997) and Hosmer, Lemeshow, and Sturdivant (2013) for discussion of logistic regression.

Poisson regression is useful for counts. The response has meaningful magnitude but takes discrete (whole number) values with a minimum value of zero. If a response of meaningful value is censored, then we use *survival analysis* (Le 1997; Therneau and Grambsch 2000; Therneau 2013; Therneau and Crowson 2013).

Most traditional modeling techniques involve *linear models* or linear equations. The response or transformed response is on the left-hand side of the linear model. The *linear predictor* is on the right-hand side. The linear predictor involves explanatory variables and is linear in its parameters. That is, it involves the addition of coefficients or the multiplication of coefficients by the explanatory variables. The coefficients we fit to linear models represent estimates of population parameters.

For regression examples in this book, we use R-squared or the coefficient of determination as an index of goodness of fit. This is a quantity that is easy to explain to management as the proportion of response variance accounted for by the model. An alternative index that many statisticians prefer is the *root mean-squared error of prediction* (RMSE), which is an index of badness or lack of fit. Other indices of badness of fit, such as the percentage error in prediction, are sometimes preferred by managers. Indices of regression performance may be utilized within a training-and-test regimen, in cross-validation and simulation environments.

Within the set of *generalized linear models* we have least-squares regression, Poisson regression, logistic regression, and survival models. Linear and generalized linear models are at the core of traditional statistical inference, both classical and Bayesian. An understanding of regression modeling terms and techniques is important to data science.[1]

Useful references for linear regression include Draper and Smith (1998), Harrell (2001), Chatterjee and Hadi (2012), and Fox and Weisberg (2011). Data-adaptive regression methods and machine learning algorithms are reviewed in Berk (2008), Izenman (2008), and Hastie, Tibshirani, and Friedman (2009). For traditional nonlinear models, see Bates and Watts (2007).

Regression diagnostics are data visualizations and indices we use to check on the adequacy of regression models. Discussion may be found in Belsley, Kuh, and Welsch (1980) and Cook (1998). The base R system provides many diagnostics, and Fox and Weisberg (2011) provide additional diagnostics. Diagnostics may suggest that transformations of the response or explanatory variables are needed in order to meet model assumptions or improve predictive performance. A theory of power transformations is provided in Box and Cox (1964) and reviewed by Fox and Weisberg (2011).

Graybill (1961, 2000) provides a review of linear models. Generalized linear models are discussed in McCullagh and Nelder (1989) and Firth (1991). Kutner, Nachtsheim, Neter, and Li (2004) provide a comprehensive review of linear and generalized linear models, including discussion of their application in experimental design. R methods for the estimation of linear and generalized linear models are reviewed in Chambers and Hastie (1992) and Venables and Ripley (2002).

Robust regression methods are useful for situations in which there are influential outliers or extreme observations. Robust methods represent an active area of research using R-based simulation tools (Fox 2002; Koller and Stahel 2011; Maronna, Martin, and Yohai 2006; Maechler 2013b; Koller 2013).

---

[1] Understanding of regression terminology is complicated by the use of the term *generalized least-squares* in econometrics, which refers to models that make special assumptions about error structure. For example, a generalized least-squares model may assume that errors are autocorrelated as in a time series regression (contrasted with ordinary least-squares regression, which assumes uncorrelated or independent errors). See Kennedy (2008).

A.2 Classification

Based on the four-fold table known as the *confusion matrix*, figure A.1 provides an overview of various indices available for evaluating binary classifiers. Summary statistics such as Kappa (Cohen 1960) and the area under the receiver operating characteristic (ROC) curve are sometimes used to evaluate classifiers. Kappa depends upon the probability cut-off used in classification. The ROC curve is a plot of the true positive rate against the false positive rate. It shows the tradeoff between sensitivity and specificity and measures how well the model separates positive from negative cases. The area under the curve provides an index of predictive accuracy independent of the probability cut-off that is being used to classify cases. Perfect prediction corresponds to an area of 1.0 (curve that touches the top-left corner). An area of 0.5 depicts random (null-model) predictive accuracy, with the curve being the diagonal line from bottom left to top right and with the area associated with lower triangle. See Fawcett (2003) and Sing et al. (2005) for further discussion of the ROC curve. Discussion of alternative methods for evaluating classifiers is provided in Hand (1997) and Kuhn and Johnson (2013).

The benchmark study of text classification in the chapter on sentiment analysis employed logistic regression, support vector machines, and random forests, as as well as providing a sample classification tree. Other techniques include are Naïve Bayes classifiers, linear discriminant analysis, and neural networks. Useful references in this area include Duda, Hart, and Stork (2001), Izenman (2008), Hastie, Tibshirani, and Friedman (2009), and Kuhn and Johnson (2013). Weka machine learning methods (Witten, Frank, and Hall 2011) are available in R (Hornik 2013b, 2013a). For tree-structured methods, see Hothorn, Hornik, and Zeileis (2013), Milborrow (2013), and Therneau, Atkinson, and Ripley (2013). For support vector machines, see Meyer (2013c, Meyer, Dimitriadou, Hornik, Weingessel, and Leisch (2013). See Hothorn et al. (2005) for principles of benchmark study design and Schauerhuber et al. (2008) for an example a benchmark study of classification methods. Alfons (2013a) provides cross-validation tools for benchmark studies. Benchmark studies, also known as statistical simulations or statistical experiments, may be conducted with special packages designed for this type of research (Alfons 2013b; Alfons, Templ, and Filzmoser 2013).

Figure A.1. *Evaluating Predictive Accuracy for a Binary Classifier*

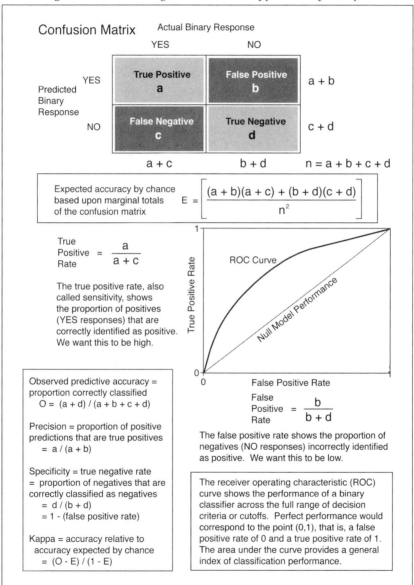

A.3 Recommender Systems

"I'll have what she's having."

—ESTELLE REINER AS CUSTOMER IN *When Harry Met Sally...*
(1989)

Being a frequent customer of Amazon.com, I receive many suggestions for book purchases. In May 2013, Amazon sent me an e-mail list of ten recommended books, and a book I was writing at the time, this book, was at the top of the list. My publisher, being a good publisher, made the book available for pre-order as early as March 2013. Amazon put Ratner (2011), which had been used in a predictive modeling course at Northwestern University, third on the list. Kuhn and Johnson (2013), a book I had reviewed prior to its publication, was seventh on the list. Ninth on the list was Matloff (2011), a book I recommend to students who want to learn R. In fact, all of the titles Amazon.com was recommending were right on target.

How is it that Amazon.com knows me so well? The company has information about past purchases, many books with "predictive analytics" and "modeling" in their titles. A few days before receiving the recommended list, for example, I had purchased Eric Siegel's (2013) *Predictive Analytics: The Power to Predict Who Will Click, Buy, Lie, or Die*. We see common terms across Amazon-recommended titles: "analytics," "statistical," "modeling," "techniques," and "R." Purchasing history and search terms may begin to explain the list of recommended titles. But there is more to the story of recommender systems—much more.

Businesses use recommender systems to make product recommendations to an existing customer using information about that customer as well as information from other customers. In addition to Amazon.com for books, well known examples include systems employed by Netflix for movies and Pandora for music.

The best known recommender system problem is the Netflix $1 million prize competition (May 29, 2006 though September 21, 2009). This famous modeling challenge presented Netflix data for 17,770 movies and 480,189 customers, but only around 100 million ratings, resulting in a movies-by-users matrix that was about 99 percent sparse. The Netflix competition demonstrates a common problem in recommender systems—sparsity.

Recommender systems build on products-by-users matrices. These sparse matrices are not unlike the terms-by-documents matrices of text analytics and the consumers-by-items matrices of market basket analysis. Special algorithms are needed for working with sparse matrices (Bates and Maechler 2013).

One class of recommender systems is *content-based* recommender systems. These draw on customer personal characteristics, past orders, and revealed preferences. Content-based systems may also rely on the characteristics of products. Another class of recommender systems is *collaborative filtering* (also called social or group filtering), which builds on the premise that customers with similar ratings for one set of products will have similar ratings for other sets of products. This suggests that one path to providing product recommendations is to find nearest neighbor customers. Suppose a customer named Brit has chosen ten movies and the movie service provider wants to suggest a new movie. One way to find the movie to recommend is to find other customers who have chosen the same ten movies as Brit or many of the same movies as Brit. Then searching across the lists of those nearest neighbor customers, the service provider identifies movies that those customers have in common with one another. Movies most in common across customers provide a basis for recommendations to Brit.

Interestingly, one of the problems chosen to test recommendation systems concerns R packages. A competition offered by kaggle asked analysts to develop a recommendation engine for users of R packages.[2] Conway and White (2012) use these data to demonstrate a recommendation system based on a nearest neighbor algorithm. Data for the kaggle R competition could be supplemented with information from the R programming environment, including R package source code and data for the "depends" and "reverse depends" (package-to-package) structure of R.

Reviews of recommender systems are provided in the edited volumes of Ricci et al. (2011) and Dehuri et al. (2012). Software for the evaluation of recommender systems is provided by Hahsler (2013b, 2013c).

---

[2] The competition, entitled *R Package Recommendation Engine*, presented 99,640 records of data for 52 R users. The description and data for this competition are available at http://www.kaggle.com/c/R.

A.4 Product Positioning

"Nobody puts Baby in a corner."

—Patrick Swayze as Johnny Castle in *Dirty Dancing* (1987)

Whether concerned with new or current products and services, product positioning is an important part of business and marketing strategy. There are basic questions to address: *What constitutes the category of products? How do products within the category compare with one another? What is the nature of the product space? Which products serve as close substitutes for one another? What can a firm do to distinguish its products and services from those offered by other firms?*

To study product positioning, data are collected for numerous products within a category, making sure that the primary competitive products are included. Data can relate to actual product specifications. Data can represent consumer ratings of product attributes. Multivariate procedures such as principal component analysis and factor analysis may be used in a search for dimensions that summarize the product attribute space.

Another approach to the study of product positioning is to use attribute data to obtain distance or dissimilarity scores for all pairs of products being considered. Alternatively, we can ask consumers to make similarity judgments for all pairs of products. Similarity judgments are especially useful in product categories for which attributes are difficult to identify or describe, such as categories defined by style, look, odor, or flavor. The resulting distance or dissimilarity matrix serves as input to cluster analysis for identifying groups of products and to multidimensional scaling for creating a map of the product space.

Product maps, sometimes called perceptual maps, are especially useful in product planning and competitive analysis. Products close to one another in space may be though of as substitute products or close competitors. Open areas in the product space may represent opportunities for new, differentiated products.

These same technologies may be applied to brands to obtain information about brand positioning and to guide branding strategy. Product or brand positioning may be studied in concert with product and brand preferences, yielding a joint perception/preference mapping of products or brands in space. Critical to strategic product positioning are areas of the product space most desirable to consumers. Product managers like to find areas of the product space where there are many potential customers and few competitive brands or products. Tybout and Sternthal (2001) and Reis and Trout (2001) discuss relevant management issues in product positioning.

Typical objects in consumer research represent alternative products or services, features of products, or names of products and brands. Assuming that consumer preferences for objects follow a normal distribution, mean proportions from the columns of a paired-comparisons preference matrix are converted to scale scores using standard normal quantiles. This is traditional unidimensional scaling. It results in scale scores that can be easily understood—products or product features positioned along a real number line.

Preference scaling has a long history, dating back to early work in psychometrics by Thurstone (1927), Guilford (1954, first published in 1936), and Torgerson (1958). Traditional univariate methods, building as they do upon a paired comparison preference matrix, may be used for data arising from actual paired comparisons, rank orders, and multiple rank orders, as well as from best-worst scaling items, choice studies, pick lists, and elimination pick lists.

Multivariate methods are reviewed by Seber (2000), Manly (1994), Sharma (1996), Gnanadesikan (1997), Johnson and Wichern (1998), and Izenman (2008). Principal component biplots represent an alternative to multidimensional scaling plots (Gabriel 1971; Gower and Hand 1996) for product positioning. Biplots allow us to plot consumers and products/brands in the same space.

There are many useful references for multidimensional scaling (Davison 1992; Cox and Cox 1994; Carroll and Green 1997; Borg and Groenen 2010). Lilien and Rangaswamy (2003) review joint perception/preference mappings. As we have seen in numerous examples in the book, conjoint and choice studies help us to assess consumer preferences across many products and attributes (Orme 2013), providing conjoint measures for product positioning.

A.5   Segmentation and Target Marketing

"Round up the usual suspects."

—Claude Rains as Capt. Louis Renault in *Casablanca* (1942)

A market segment is a group of consumers with distinct needs or behaviors, a group of people who are more similar to one another than to people outside their segment. Segments can be defined by geographic, demographic, psychographic, or behavioral characteristics. Most useful for target marketing are characteristics that are identifiable and easily measured. Market segmentation involves finding these groups of people.

Segmentation, when executed properly, contributes to marketing strategy and tactics. What consumers like, what they buy, where they buy, and how much they buy may differ across segments. Products, marketing messages, advertising, and promotions may be tailored to specific segments.

Marketing managers sometimes identify segmentation variables before doing research. Knowing the nature of their products, they feel confident describing potential buyers or groups of consumers. Identifying segments or segmentation variables before doing any research or data analysis is called *a priori* segmentation.

Market segmentation is usually guided by data. Variables that go into the segmentation should be easily available or accessible. We try to avoid variables that are difficult to measure, and we prefer publicly available data to survey data. Common segmentation variables reflect geographical location, age, income, and life style.

Using existing customer information for segmentation, we exclude buyer status and other sales response variables from the input variable set. This is because potential new customers have no buying sales history with the firm, and we want the segmentation model to be useful in finding new customers. Note, however, that we may utilize buyer status and sales response variables in the input variable selection process itself. For example, we may choose demographic variables that are related to sales response.

Traditional methods of cluster analysis are widely used in market segmentation. They represent multivariate techniques for grouping consumers based on their similarity to one another. Distance metrics or measures of agreement between consumers guide the segmentation process.

As with most methods in predictive analytics, statistical criteria are complemented by management criteria. When doing market segmentation research, we look for segments that are easy to describe to management. We also look for segments that large enough to be useful in target marketing.

Mass marketing treats all consumers as one group. One-to-one marketing focuses on one consumer at a time (Peppers and Rogers 1993). Target marketing to selected groups of consumers lies between mass marketing and one-to-one marketing and is often guided by market segmentation. Target marketing involves directing marketing activities to those consumers who are most likely to buy.

Market segmentation has been a controversial topic. There are people in the field of marketing who do not believe in doing segmentation and are philosophically opposed to using segments for targeting. Instead of targeting to market segments, these researchers promote a one-to-one marketing approach that targets each individual as an individual.

One-to-one target marketing has been bolstered by the emergence of hierarchical Bayesian methods. Bayesians use the phrase "consumer heterogeneity" to refer to individual differences across customers. The thinking is that describing consumers in terms of their positions along underlying attribute parameters is more informative than describing them as being members of segments.

The goal of target marketing is to reduce costs by directing marketing activities to those consumers who are most likely to buy. Target marketing involves classification of customers into likely-to-buy or not-likely-to-buy groups. The classification may utilize information about market segments or may be based on more complete information about customer individual differences when such information is available.

The benefits of market segmentation are described in marketing management references, such as Dickson (1997) and Kotler and Keller (2012). Sternthal and Tybout (2001) and Cespedes, Dougherty, and Skinner (2013) review management issues in segmentation and targeting. Neal (2000) and Wedel and Kamakura (2000) discuss methodologies for market segmentation.

Everitt, Landau, Leese, and Stahl (2011), Kaufman and Rousseeuw (1990) and Izenman (2008) review traditional clustering methods. Cluster analysis methods developed by Kaufman and Rousseeuw (1990) have been implemented in R by Maechler (2013a), including silhouette modeling and visualization techniques for determining the number of clusters.[3]

Within the machine learning literature, cluster analysis is often referred to as *unsupervised learning* to distinguish it from classification and regression, which are *supervised learning* (guided by a response variable). Duda, Hart, and Stork (2001) introduce clustering from a machine learning perspective. Additional discussion is provided by Hastie, Tibshirani, and Friedman (2009). A comprehensive review of clustering methods, including traditional clustering, self-organizing maps, fuzzy clustering, model-based clustering, and biclustering (block clustering) is provided by Izenman (2008).[4] Leisch and Gruen (2013) describe R packages for each of these clustering methods.

Bayesian methods in marketing, reviewed by Rossi, Allenby, and McCulloch (2005), have been implemented in R packages by Rossi (2013) and Sermas (2013).

---

[3] Silhouettes were introduced by Rousseeuw (1987), with additional documentation and examples provided in Kaufman and Rousseeuw (1990). Izenman (2008) provides an overview of the methods. For any clustering solution with two or or more clusters, each observation has a silhouette value that takes possible values between minus one and plus one. Higher positive values indicate better clustering solutions. The individual silhouette values relate to the distance of an observation from all other observations in the same cluster relative to the distance of that observation from observations in all other clusters. A silhouette plot shows the silhouette values for all observations in the data set. The average of the silhouette values for all observations in the data set is often used to select the clustering solution. This is a way to determine the number of clusters. We compare the average silhouette value for a two-cluster solution with the average silhouette value for a three-cluster solution. Then we compare a three-cluster solution with a four-cluster solution, and so on, looking for the solution that has the largest average silhouette width. The average of the silhouette values for all observations within a cluster is the average silhouette width for that cluster. We look for large positive values, and we like to see cluster averages of about the same size. In the silhouette plot, cluster averages that are about the same size translate into cluster silhouettes that have about the same width (distance from left to right). Also, if there are silhouettes that have observations to the left of the zero line (composed of observations with negative silhouette values) that is a signal of a poor clustering solution.

[4] Biclustering in market segmentation—the joint clustering of consumers and products—holds promise as a modeling technique for recommender systems.

A.6   Finance and Risk Analytics

"Greed, for lack of a better word, is good."

—MICHAEL DOUGLAS AS GORDON GEKKO IN *Wall Street* (1987)

Much financial data analysis utilizes methods developed in economics, including linear econometric models and time series analysis. Special issues of volatility must be addressed, and there are well developed research traditions in areas such as capital asset pricing theory, option pricing, investment analysis, and portfolio analysis. The objective is often to predict future prices or returns for financial securities.

Gathering financial data on publicly-traded securities is a straightforward process of using application program interfaces to sources of financial data such as Yahoo! or Google. We build on the foundation R code provided by Ryan (2013). R is utilized extensively in financial engineering, programmed trading, and empirical finance. See Eddelbuettel (2013a).

Risk analytics is another large area of application. An auto insurance company wants to identify drivers who are most likely to have accidents. A manufacturer is concerned about failure rates of new products. A retailer asks about the risk of losing a customer to another store. A financial services officer needs to identify consumers most likely to default on their loans—consumer financial histories and credit scores are utilized in predictive models in this area (Fishelson-Holstine 2004).

The objective in many risk analytics problems is classification, the prediction of a binary response. Logistic regression and machine learning classification methods are relevant here. Alternatively, we may want to predict how long a customer or client will stay with a particular product, service, or brand using survival or duration models.

Methods of financial modeling are reviewed by Benninga (2008). Useful references in R include Ruppert (2011) and Tsay (2013). Pfaff (2013) provides an extensive review of R packages and programming methods in finance. Mathematical programming methods are useful for portfolio optimization. Simulation methods are useful in financial modeling and risk analytics.

A.7 Social Network Analysis

"You talkin' to me?"

—Robert De Niro as Travis Bickle in *Taxi Driver* (1976)

Recognizing growth in the use of electronic social networks and intelligent mobile devices, organizations see opportunities for marketing communications and reference selling. Businesses, nonprofits, and governmental organizations (not to mention political campaigns) are interested in learning from the data of social media. The data sets are large but accessible. The possibilities are many.

There are the text data of social networks, including blog postings and 140-character Twitter messages. There are also the friends and followers links of social networks. We have discussed text analytics and sentiment analysis previously, and those methods apply to the text data of social networks. Let us focus on social network analysis here.

Social network analysis deals with relationships. It looks for patterns or regularities in relationships. Measurements of these relationships represent the structural variables in network models. Unlike many other studies in the social sciences, social network analysis works with relationships as the fundamental unit of analysis. Relationships imply interactions or linkages between actors. The actors may be people playing roles, organizations, firms, buyers and sellers in the marketplace, investors and entrepreneurs in the venture capital space, or nations in international commerce.

Social network analysis has been an active area of research in psychology, sociology, anthropology, and political science. The invention of the sociogram and concepts of social structure may be traced back more than eighty years (Moreno 1934; Radcliffe-Brown 1940). Research topics include isolation and popularity, prestige, power, and influence, social cohesion, subgroups and cliques, status and roles within organizations, balance and reciprocity, measures of betweenness, centrality, and marketplace relationships. There are the actors and the links between actors. The actors may be described in terms of their individual characteristics, the links by their strength and direction.

Social network data may be represented in a variety of ways, including graphs with nodes and links, points in multidimensional space, and dendrograms. Modeling techniques include multidimensional scaling, hierarchical cluster analysis, log linear modeling, and a variety of specialized methods.

We are living in a paparazzi world—privacy denied. While a few strident voices raise concerns about the loss of privacy and threats to the security of personal information (Rosen 2001; Turow 2013), the general populous seems quite willing to share the details of their lives and their personal associations. This makes the analysis of social network data a potentially lucrative enterprise.

An introduction to social networks is provided by Kadushin (2012). A comprehensive review of social network analysis is provided by Wasserman and Faust (1994). Log-linear models have been used extensively in this area of research. For an overview of log linear models, see Bishop, Fienberg, and Holland (1975), Christensen (1997), and Fienberg (2007). Application of log linear models in the analysis of social networks is discussed in Wasserman and Iacobucci (1986).

Berry and Browne (2005), and Langville and Meyer (2006) discuss technologies relevant to Web search engines, and Huberman (2001) and Clifton (2012) review patterns of Web user activities and Web analytics in general.

Programming in social network analysis is aided by a number of R packages (Barbera 2013; Butts 2013; Gentry 2013b; Gentry 2013a).

B

Measurement

"If you build it, he will come."

—Voice of Ray Liotta as Shoeless Joe Jackson
in *Field of Dreams* (1989)

As data scientists, we do more than work with existing data. Often we are asked to conduct primary research, design experiments, and conduct surveys, many of them relating to new products. Which is to say that modeling techniques in predictive analytics are often preceded by measurement.

The classic article by Campbell and Fiske (1959) provides a clear definition of reliability and validity: *Reliability is the agreement between two efforts to measure the same trait through maximally similar methods. Validity is represented in the agreement between two attempts to measure the same trait through maximally different methods.* (83)

The prototypical validation study involves a multitrait-multimethod matrix, as described by Campbell and Fiske (1959). This correlation matrix provides a structure for demonstrating construct validity. The matrix is partitioned by measurement methods. Within each method there are rows and columns associated with traits (attributes). Each element of the matrix represents a trait-method unit. The components of the matrix are the reliability diagonal, validity diagonals, heterotrait-monomethod triangles, and heterotrait-heteromethod triangles.

Suppose we want to demonstrate that extroverts rate comedies more highly than other types of movies. To carry out research in this area, we could develop measures of the personality trait *introversion-extroversion* and the consumer trait *preference for comedies*. Suppose further that we develop two measures for each trait, one based on a rating scale and the other on a text measure. With higher scores on measures of *introversion-extroversion* implying greater extroversion and higher scores on measures of *preference for comedies* indicating higher preference for comedies, we might expect to observe results such as those in figure B.1.

What do we want to observe in a multitrait-multimethod matrix? We would like to see high indices of internal consistency on the reliability diagonals. We want different measures of the same trait to correlate highly with one another, yielding high correlations on the validity diagonals. We want measures of the same trait to correlate more highly with one another than with measures of different traits. Accordingly, we should see higher correlations on the validity diagonals than in either the heterotrait-monomethod or the heterotrait-heteromethod triangles. How high is "high"? What precise pattern of correlations should we expect? To answer these questions, we refer to theory and to prior empirical research.

Campbell and Fiske (1959) talk about convergent validity and discriminant validity. Convergent validity refers to the notion that different measures of the same trait should converge. That is, different measures of the same trait or attribute should have relatively high correlations. Discriminant validity refers to the notion that measures of different traits should diverge. In other words, measures of different traits should have lower correlations than measures of the same trait. Convergent and discriminant validation are part of what we mean by construct validation. The meaning of a measure is defined in terms of its relationship to other measures.

Multitrait-multimethod matrices have been applied widely in the social sciences and consumer research (Bagozzi and Yi 1991). Cronbach (1995) talks about method variance and the fact that measures of different traits that utilize the same measurement technique can be correlated as a result of the way subjects respond to the technique itself. In other words, there can be individual differences in response style.

Figure B.1. *Hypothetical Multitrait-Multimethod Matrix*

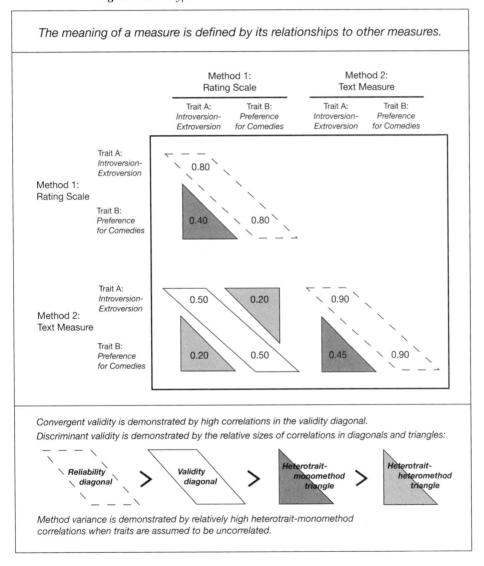

Validation is rarely easy. Low correlations between response and explanatory variables are common in social research. There are many variables to consider, many possible explanatory variables for every response. And there is considerable individual variability from one administration of a survey to the next and from one situation to the next.

Discussions of validity touch on fundamental issues in the philosophy of science, issues of theory construction, measurement, and testability. There are no easy answers here. If the theory is correct and the measures valid, then the pattern of relationships among the measures should be similar to the pattern predicted by theory. To the extent that this is true for observed data, we have partial confirmation of the theory and, at the same time, demonstration of construct validity. But what if the predictions do not pan out? Then we are faced with a dilemma: the theory could be wrong, one or more of the measures could be invalid, or we could have observed an event of low probability with correct theory and valid measures.

In consumer research there are times when we need to assess a person's thinking or decision-making process. We present detailed information and ask the respondent to rate or rank product profiles, make a choice, perform a calculation, or write an opinion. Through well designed surveys, we learn about price-quality, price-feature, and feature-by-feature trade-offs in consumer evaluation of new products. We learn how consumers feel about brands.

We touched on measurement issues in discussions of conjoint analysis and sentiment analysis. Let us consider a few alternative measurement methods, reviewing the rationale behind the methods.

Suppose we want to assess people's preferences for movies. Figure B.2 shows a conjoint measurement item. The consumer respondent is asked to rate a DVD movie product on a scale from 1 (low) to 7 (high). A brief description of the DVD movie is provided along with its price. This is a straightforward rating task. It would be used in conjunction with many other rating tasks. Respondent ratings will have meaningful magnitude, and the likely analysis is linear regression. This is an example of a traditional conjoint study item. Notice that price is included in this likelihood-to-purchase item.

Figure B.3 shows a more complicated task. A pair of movies is presented side-by-side, and the respondent is asked to compare them in terms of interest or preference. Degree of preference is on a sliding scale. Two measures are obtained from each item of this type, with the measures being conditional upon one another. The researcher is not forcing a choice between the movies as in a traditional paired comparison item.

A set of simple paired comparison items is shown in figure B.4. The respondent chooses one movie title from each pair, indicating preference. No description of the movies is provided. A paired comparison is simultaneously a ranking and a choice—a choice between two. An exhaustive set of paired comparisons across k movies would require $\frac{k(k-1)}{2}$ paired comparisons, with each movie being paired once with each other movie. It is not uncommon for paired comparison surveys to include hundreds of items. Fortunately, individual paired comparisons can be made quickly.

Marketing analysts can also present movies in sets of three or more in what are called multiple-rank-orders, as shown in figure B.5. Presented in sets of three movies, each multiple-rank-order item is equivalent to three paired comparisons. For a complete enumeration, then, multiple-rank-order triads require one-third as many items as paired comparisons. Each item, however, takes a little longer to complete.

Like multiple-rank-order items, best-worst items present objects in sets of three or more. For each item, the respondent is asked to choose a most preferred and least preferred object. A set of three-object best-worst items is equivalent to a set of multiple-rank-order triads, yielding a full set of paired comparisons. When presented in groups of four or more objects, however, best-worst items yield partial paired comparisons.

Figure B.6 shows a best-worst item with four movies. Notice how it is possible to extract five out of the possible six paired comparisons from this item. Best-worst surveys, sometimes called max-diff scaling, also have similarities to choice tasks. Instead of being asked to choose only the most preferred object in a set of objects, the respondent chooses two, the best and worst.

Figure B.2. *Conjoint Degree-of-Interest Rating*

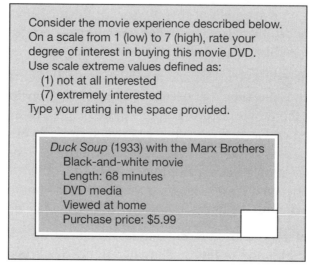

Consider the movie experience described below. On a scale from 1 (low) to 7 (high), rate your degree of interest in buying this movie DVD. Use scale extreme values defined as:
(1) not at all interested
(7) extremely interested
Type your rating in the space provided.

> *Duck Soup* (1933) with the Marx Brothers
> Black-and-white movie
> Length: 68 minutes
> DVD media
> Viewed at home
> Purchase price: $5.99

Figure B.3. *Conjoint Sliding Scale for Profile Pairs*

Below you see descriptions of two movies that you could watch. Use your mouse to move the slider along the scale, showing the degree to which you prefer one movie over the other.

Gorky Park (1983)

The film opens with the discovery of three mutilated bodies in the snow of Moscow's Gorky Park. The Chief Investigator of the Moscow Militia is assigned to unravel this horrific crime. The trail leads to Irina, a beautiful Soviet dissident who soon becomes his lover, and a rich businessman who will stop at nothing to corner the international sable market.

The Year of Living Dangerously (1982)

Guy Hamilton, an Australian reporter on assignment in politically unstable Indonesia, joins forces with a savvy photographer to expose government corruption. But it's Hamilton's connection to the beautiful Jill Bryant, an attaché with the British embassy, that complicates his life.

Strongly prefer movie at left   *No preference*   *Strongly prefer movie at right*

Figure B.4. *Paired Comparisons*

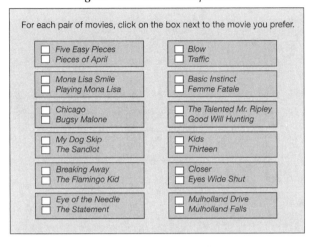

Figure B.5. *Multiple-Rank-Orders*

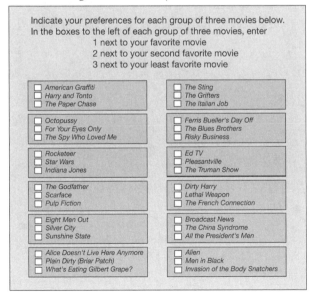

Figure B.6. *Best-worst Item Provides Partial Paired Comparisons*

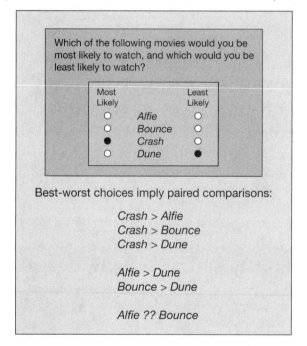

Obtaining interval measures from rank orders is a general way of thinking about scaling methods. We can use paired comparisons, rank orders, multiple-rank-orders, or best-worst responses from consumers to generate a paired-comparison preference matrix showing the proportion of times each object is ranked over each other object. And from a paired-comparison preference matrix, we can generate scale scores for the objects being compared. Interval measures convey more information than ranks. Seeing how consumer movie preferences fall along a real number line, for example, is much more informative than seeing the rank order of movies.

Many marketing analysts prefer choice tasks to assess consumer preferences and to make recommendations about product design and pricing. They argue that choice studies provide a straightforward approach to estimating market shares for products and brands. Furthermore, a well designed choice study bears a close resemblance to what consumers do in the marketplace. Consumers reveal their preferences in the choices they make.

The simplest of choice tasks is a paired comparison choice. Earlier we showed simple paired comparisons of movie titles. In figure B.7, we show a paired comparison choice task with more information about the movies to be compared. Paired comparisons are easy to make, even when there is extensive information about the objects being compared.[1]

Choice studies often present sets of three or four profiles, with each profile defined by a large number of attributes. Figure B.8 shows a choice task with three new movie ideas and profiles defined by six attributes. The consumer's task is to select one of the three hypothetical new movies. Choice tasks sometimes include a *none* option, permitting the consumer to move to the next item without making a choice.

Additional developments in preference measurement involve product configuration tasks and menu-based choice, as shown in figure B.9. When buying a computer or selecting meal items at a restaurant, we have many

---

[1] Paired comparisons are a convenient mechanism for obtaining choice and ratings data. Taste tests are commonly conducted as paired comparisons. One food is tasted. Water is drunk to clear the pallet. And then a second food is tasted. Asking which food tastes better or which food is preferred is a simple paired comparison. The optometrist asks us to compare two lenses in sequence. The patient looks through the first lens and then the second. Upon presenting the second lens, the optometrist asks a simple question, "Is this better or worse, or the same?" That is a paired comparison with three alternatives. Proximity in time is key to the comparison process, and using only one pair of lenses at a time simplifies the information processing task.

Figure B.7. *Paired Comparison Choice Task*

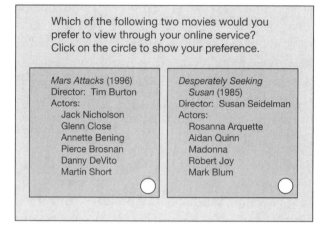

Figure B.8. *Choice Set with Three Product Profiles*

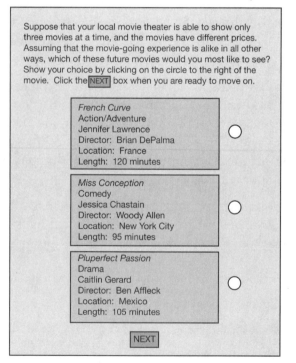

options from which to choose. We build a customized product instead of choosing from a set of preconfigured product profiles.

It is only fitting that the measurement techniques we use to assess consumer preferences reflect the way consumers purchase products. In most product categories, choice tasks reflect consumer behavior in the marketplace in a way that rankings and ratings do not. And in certain product categories, menus reflect consumer behavior in the marketplace in a way that choice tasks do not.

We can also assess consumer preferences through a sequence of choices in an elimination pick list. Figure B.10 shows an elimination pick list for a set of seven movies. Elimination pick list instructions ask the respondent to choose one movie at a time. A computer program records each choice as it is made and updates the screen image by eliminating the movie that has just been chosen. The consumer continues to pick movies until there are no more movies she wants to watch. The elimination pick list represents an enhanced choice task with a *none* alternative. It may also be thought of as a computer-assisted ranking task. [2]

Obtaining meaningful and accurate measures is a prerequisite to building predictive models we can trust. When designing consumer surveys, we need to use wording that is easy to understand and unambiguous. We need to provide choices that are distinct and clearly specified. We try to make tasks as simple and straightforward as possible, while presenting as much detail as is needed for the measurement objective.

---

[2] The elimination pick list, a technique introduced by Miller (2008a), is designed to be a faithful representation of consumer choice in the marketplace. We often choose more than one product, buy more than one thing at at time. The elimination pick list is simultaneously a ranking and a choice task. Compared to a ranking task, note that picking one alternative at a time is easier than ranking a set of alternatives, yet it accomplishes much the same purpose. The elimination pick list yields censored rank-order data with the possibility of tied ranks at the low end. Compared to a standard choice task, note that the pick list provides more information. We see not only the consumer's first choice—we see the consumer's entire consideration set. We get this information with a modicum of additional effort on the part of the consumer respondent. Item instructions, including information about products, is read prior to making the first choice, exactly as it would be in a standard choice task. There is no need for the respondent to read these instructions prior to making second or subsequent choices. The elimination pick list uses respondent time efficiently. The pick list is consistent with the way consumers evaluate and choose products in the marketplace. When faced with a set of choices, consumers would be unlikely to ask themselves about their most preferred and least preferred products, as in a best-worst choice task. Rather, consumer buyers focus at the top of the list, on their most preferred products. By providing direct evidence about consumer consideration sets, the elimination pick list has an advantage over other choice and ranking tasks.

Figure B.9. *Menu-based Choice Task*

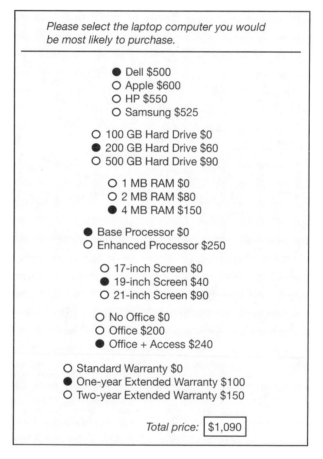

Adapted from Orme (2013) with permission of the publisher.

Figure B.10. *Elimination Pick List*

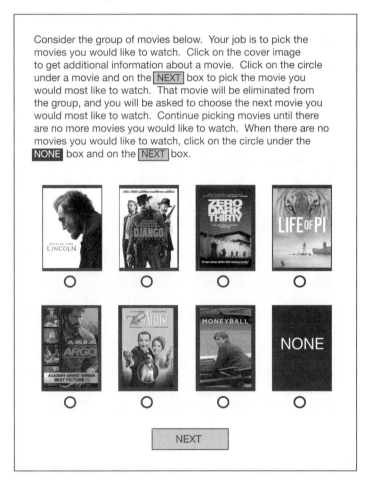

It is important to recognize the complexity of the task we present to consumer respondents. Paired comparisons are easier to make than multiple comparisons. Ranking a short list of alternatives is easier than ranking a long list of alternatives. Picking one alternative at a time is easier than ranking a set of alternatives. If we make a task similar to what consumers normally do in the marketplace, then consumers can more faithfully execute that task. This is the art and science of measurement.

Groves et al. (2009) provides a comprehensive review of survey research, including sampling, data collection modalities, data quality, nonresponse, and analysis issues. Lumley (2010) discusses sample survey design and analysis in the R programming environment. Miller (2008a) provides discussion of measurement, item formats, and alternative scales of measurement for business research. Scaling methods for obtaining interval measures from paired comparisons and rank orders are well documented in the psychometric literature (Guilford 1954; Torgerson 1958). Rounds, Miller, and Dawis (1978) review paired comparison and multiple-rank-order scaling, demonstrating a high degree of agreement between measurements obtained from these two methods. Louviere (1993) introduces best-worst scaling methods.

For references on measurement reliability and validity, we refer to the literature of psychometrics (Gulliksen 1950; Cronbach 1951; Ghiselli 1964; Nunnally 1967; Nunnally and Bernstein 1994; Lord and Novick 1968; Fiske 1971; Brown 1976). Betz and Weiss (2001) and Allen and Yen (2002) introduce concepts of measurement theory. Item response theory is discussed by Rogers, Swaminathan, and Hambleton (1991). Articles in the volume edited by Shrout and Fiske (1995) provide many examples of multitrait-multimethod matrices and review quantitative methods available for the analysis of such matrices. For R programming in psychometrics, see Revelle (2013).

C

Code and Utilities

"Well, here's another nice mess you've gotten me into!"

—OLIVER HARDY AS OLIVER IN *Sons of the Desert* (1933)

The code for the spine chart function in exhibit C.1, starting on page 268 and ending on page 276 shows how to construct a customized data visualization for conjoint studies. Using standard R graphics functions, the spine chart is built one point, line, and text string at a time. Market simulation utilities are provided in exhibit C.2 on page 276. These utilities are called by the programs in the chapter about brand and price.

Utilities for grid and ggplot2 graphics are provided in exhibits C.3 and C.4. The split-plotting utilities in exhibit C.3 (pages 277 and 279) are used in a number of chapters to render ggplot2 graphics objects with proper margins and multiple-plot layout. The wait-time ribbon plotting utility in exhibit C.4 (pages 280 through 291) is used in the chapter on operations management to plot wait-time ribbons for a call center example.

That common code is brought into the sentiment program using a source statement. The code is shown in exhibit C.5, beginning on page 292.

Utilities for computing distances between points defined by longitude and latitude are useful in spatial data analysis. These are provided in exhibit C.6 on page 296.

Exhibit C.1. *Conjoint Analysis Spine Chart*

```
# Conjoint Analysis Spine Chart

# spine chart accommodates up to 45 part-worths on one page
# |part-worth| <= 40 can be plotted directly on the spine chart
# |part-worths| > 40 can be accommodated through standardization

print.digits <- 2  # set number of digits on print and spine chart

# user-defined function for printing conjoint measures
if (print.digits == 2)
  pretty.print <- function(x) {sprintf("%1.2f",round(x,digits = 2))}
if (print.digits == 3)
  pretty.print <- function(x) {sprintf("%1.3f",round(x,digits = 3))}

# ----------------------------------------------------
# user-defined function for spine chart
# ----------------------------------------------------
spine.chart <- function(conjoint.results,
  color.for.part.worth.point = "blue",
  color.for.part.worth.line = "blue",
  left.side.symbol.to.print.around.part.worths = "(",
  right.side.symbol.to.print.around.part.worths = ")",
  left.side.symbol.to.print.around.importance = "",
  right.side.symbol.to.print.around.importance = "",
  color.for.printing.importance.text = "dark red",
  color.for.printing.part.worth.text = "black",
  draw.gray.background = TRUE,
  draw.optional.grid.lines = TRUE,
  print.internal.consistency = TRUE,
  fix.max.to.4 = FALSE,
  put.title.on.spine.chart = FALSE,
  title.on.spine.chart = paste("TITLE GOES HERE IF WE ASK FOR ONE",sep=""),
  plot.framing.box = TRUE,
  do.standardization = TRUE,
  do.ordered.attributes = TRUE) {

  # fix.max.to.4  option to override the range for part-worth plotting

  if(!do.ordered.attributes) effect.names <- conjoint.results$attributes
  if(do.ordered.attributes) effect.names <-
    conjoint.results$ordered.attributes

  number.of.levels.of.attribute <- NULL
  for(index.for.factor in seq(along=effect.names))
    number.of.levels.of.attribute <- c(number.of.levels.of.attribute,
      length(conjoint.results$xlevels[[effect.names[index.for.factor]]]))

  # total number of levels needed for vertical length of spine the spine plot
  total.number.of.levels <- sum(number.of.levels.of.attribute)
```

```
# define size of spaces based upon the number of part-worth levels to plot
 if(total.number.of.levels <= 20) {
  smaller.space <- 0.01
  small.space <- 0.02
  medium.space <- 0.03
  large.space <- 0.04
  }
if(total.number.of.levels > 20) {
  smaller.space <- 0.01 * 0.9
  small.space <- 0.02 * 0.9
  medium.space <- 0.03 * 0.9
  large.space <- 0.04 * 0.9
  }
if(total.number.of.levels > 22) {
  smaller.space <- 0.01 * 0.85
  small.space <- 0.02 * 0.85
  medium.space <- 0.03 * 0.825
  large.space <- 0.04 * 0.8
  }
if(total.number.of.levels > 25) {
  smaller.space <- 0.01 * 0.8
  small.space <- 0.02 * 0.8
  medium.space <- 0.03 * 0.75
  large.space <- 0.04 * 0.75
  }
if(total.number.of.levels > 35) {
  smaller.space <- 0.01 * 0.65
  small.space <- 0.02 * 0.65
  medium.space <- 0.03 * 0.6
  large.space <- 0.04 * 0.6
  }

# of course there is a limit to how much we can plot on one page
if (total.number.of.levels > 45)
  stop("\n\nTERMINATED: More than 45 part-worths on spine chart\n")

if(!do.standardization)
  part.worth.plotting.list <- conjoint.results$part.worths

if(do.standardization)
  part.worth.plotting.list <- conjoint.results$standardized.part.worths

# check the range of part-worths to see which path to go down for plotting
# initialize these toggles to start

max.is.less.than.40 <- FALSE
max.is.less.than.20 <- FALSE
max.is.less.than.10 <- FALSE
max.is.less.than.4 <- FALSE
max.is.less.than.2 <- FALSE
max.is.less.than.1 <- FALSE
```

```
if (max(abs(min(unlist(part.worth.plotting.list),na.rm=TRUE)),
    max(unlist(part.worth.plotting.list),na.rm=TRUE)) <= 40) {
  max.is.less.than.40 <- TRUE
  max.is.less.than.20 <- FALSE
  max.is.less.than.10 <- FALSE
  max.is.less.than.4 <- FALSE
  max.is.less.than.2 <- FALSE
  max.is.less.than.1 <- FALSE
  }
if (max(abs(min(unlist(part.worth.plotting.list),na.rm=TRUE)),
    max(unlist(part.worth.plotting.list),na.rm=TRUE)) <= 20) {
  max.is.less.than.40 <- FALSE
  max.is.less.than.20 <- TRUE
  max.is.less.than.10 <- FALSE
  max.is.less.than.4 <- FALSE
  max.is.less.than.2 <- FALSE
  max.is.less.than.1 <- FALSE
  }
if(max(abs(min(unlist(part.worth.plotting.list),na.rm=TRUE)),
    max(unlist(part.worth.plotting.list),na.rm=TRUE)) <= 10) {
  max.is.less.than.40 <- FALSE
  max.is.less.than.20 <- FALSE
  max.is.less.than.10 <- TRUE
  max.is.less.than.4 <- FALSE
  max.is.less.than.2 <- FALSE
  max.is.less.than.1 <- FALSE
  }
if (max(abs(min(unlist(part.worth.plotting.list),na.rm=TRUE)),
    max(unlist(part.worth.plotting.list),na.rm=TRUE)) <= 4) {
  max.is.less.than.40 <- FALSE
  max.is.less.than.20 <- FALSE
  max.is.less.than.4 <- TRUE
  max.is.less.than.10 <- FALSE
  max.is.less.than.2 <- FALSE
  max.is.less.than.1 <- FALSE
  }
if(max(abs(min(unlist(part.worth.plotting.list),na.rm=TRUE)),
    max(unlist(part.worth.plotting.list),na.rm=TRUE)) <= 2) {
  max.is.less.than.40 <- FALSE
  max.is.less.than.20 <- FALSE
  max.is.less.than.4 <- FALSE
  max.is.less.than.10 <- FALSE
  max.is.less.than.2 <- TRUE
  max.is.less.than.1 <- FALSE
  }
if(max(abs(min(unlist(part.worth.plotting.list),na.rm=TRUE)),
    max(unlist(part.worth.plotting.list),na.rm=TRUE)) <= 1) {
  max.is.less.than.40 <- FALSE
  max.is.less.than.20 <- FALSE
  max.is.less.than.4 <- FALSE
  max.is.less.than.10 <- FALSE
  max.is.less.than.2 <- FALSE
  max.is.less.than.1 <- TRUE
  }
```

```
# sometimes we override the range for part-worth plotting
# this is not usually done... but it is an option
if (fix.max.to.4) {
  max.is.less.than.40 <- FALSE
  max.is.less.than.20 <- FALSE
  max.is.less.than.10 <- FALSE
  max.is.less.than.4 <- TRUE
  max.is.less.than.2 <- FALSE
  max.is.less.than.1 <- FALSE
  }

if (!max.is.less.than.1 & !max.is.less.than.2 & !max.is.less.than.4 &
  !max.is.less.than.10 & !max.is.less.than.20 & !max.is.less.than.40)
    stop("\n\nTERMINATED: Spine chart cannot plot |part-worth| > 40")

# determine point positions for plotting part-worths on spine chart
if (max.is.less.than.1 | max.is.less.than.2 | max.is.less.than.4 |
  max.is.less.than.10 | max.is.less.than.20 | max.is.less.than.40) {
# begin if-block plotting when all part-worths in absolute value
# are less than one of the tested range values
# part-worth positions for plottting
# end if-block plotting when all part-worths in absolute value
# are less than one of the tested range values
# offsets for plotting vary with the max.is.less.than setting
  if(max.is.less.than.1) {
    list.scaling <- function(x) {0.75 + x/5}
    part.worth.point.position <-
      lapply(part.worth.plotting.list,list.scaling)
    }
  if(max.is.less.than.2) {
    list.scaling <- function(x) {0.75 + x/10}
    part.worth.point.position <-
      lapply(part.worth.plotting.list,list.scaling)
    }

  if(max.is.less.than.4) {
    list.scaling <- function(x) {0.75 + x/20}
    part.worth.point.position <-
      lapply(part.worth.plotting.list,list.scaling)
    }

  if(max.is.less.than.10) {
    list.scaling <- function(x) {0.75 + x/50}
    part.worth.point.position <-
      lapply(part.worth.plotting.list,list.scaling)
    }

  if(max.is.less.than.20) {
    list.scaling <- function(x) {0.75 + x/100}
    part.worth.point.position <-
      lapply(part.worth.plotting.list,list.scaling)
    }
```

```
  if(max.is.less.than.40) {
    list.scaling <- function(x) {0.75 + x/200}
    part.worth.point.position <-
      lapply(part.worth.plotting.list,list.scaling)
    }

  part.worth.point.position <- lapply(part.worth.plotting.list,list.scaling)
  }

if (plot.framing.box) plot(c(0,0,1,1),c(0,1,0,1),xlab="",ylab="",
  type="n",xaxt="n",yaxt="n")

if (!plot.framing.box) plot(c(0,0,1,1),c(0,1,0,1),xlab="",ylab="",
  type="n",xaxt="n",yaxt="n", bty="n")

if (put.title.on.spine.chart) {
  text(c(0.50),c(0.975),pos=3,labels=title.on.spine.chart,cex=01.5)
  y.location <- 0.925  # starting position with title
  }

if (!put.title.on.spine.chart) y.location <- 0.975  # no-title start

# store top of vertical line for later plotting needs
y.top.of.vertical.line <- y.location

x.center.position <- 0.75  # horizontal position of spine

# begin primary plotting loop
# think of a plot as a collection of text and symbols on screen or paper
# we are going to construct a plot one text string and symbol at a time
# (note that we may have to repeat this process at the end of the program)
for(k in seq(along=effect.names)) {
  y.location <- y.location - large.space
  text(c(0.4),c(y.location),pos=2,
    labels=paste(effect.name.map(effect.names[k])," ",sep=""),cex=01.0)
  text(c(0.525),c(y.location),pos=2,col=color.for.printing.importance.text,
  labels=paste(" ",left.side.symbol.to.print.around.importance,
  pretty.print(
    unlist(conjoint.results$attribute.importance[effect.names[k]])),"%",
    right.side.symbol.to.print.around.importance,sep=""),cex=01.0)

# begin loop for printing part-worths
  for(m in seq(1:number.of.levels.of.attribute[k])) {
    y.location <- y.location - medium.space
    text(c(0.4),c(y.location),pos=2,
    conjoint.results$xlevel[[effect.names[k]]][m],cex=01.0)
#   part.worth.label.data.frame[k,m],cex=01.0)

    text(c(0.525),c(y.location),pos=2,
    col=color.for.printing.part.worth.text,
    labels=paste(" ",left.side.symbol.to.print.around.part.worths,
    pretty.print(part.worth.plotting.list[[effect.names[k]]][m]),
    right.side.symbol.to.print.around.part.worths,sep=""),cex=01.0)
```

```
    points(part.worth.point.position[[effect.names[k]]][m],y.location,
      type = "p", pch = 20, col = color.for.part.worth.point, cex = 2)
    segments(x.center.position, y.location,
    part.worth.point.position[[effect.names[k]]][m], y.location,
      col = color.for.part.worth.line, lty = 1, lwd = 2)
    }
  }
y.location <- y.location - medium.space

# begin center axis and bottom plotting
y.bottom.of.vertical.line <- y.location  # store top of vertical line

below.y.bottom.of.vertical.line <- y.bottom.of.vertical.line - small.space/2

if (!draw.gray.background) {
# four optional grid lines may be drawn on the plot parallel to the spine
  if (draw.optional.grid.lines) {
    segments(0.55, y.top.of.vertical.line, 0.55,
      y.bottom.of.vertical.line, col = "black", lty = "solid", lwd = 1)
    segments(0.65, y.top.of.vertical.line, 0.65,
      y.bottom.of.vertical.line, col = "gray", lty = "solid", lwd = 1)
    segments(0.85, y.top.of.vertical.line, 0.85,
      y.bottom.of.vertical.line, col = "gray", lty = "solid", lwd = 1)
    segments(0.95, y.top.of.vertical.line, 0.95,
      y.bottom.of.vertical.line, col = "black", lty = "solid", lwd = 1)
    }
  }

# gray background for plotting area of the points
if (draw.gray.background) {
  rect(xleft = 0.55, ybottom = y.bottom.of.vertical.line,
    xright = 0.95, ytop = y.top.of.vertical.line, density = -1, angle = 45,
    col = "light gray", border = NULL, lty = "solid", lwd = 1)

# four optional grid lines may be drawn on the plot parallel to the spine
  if (draw.optional.grid.lines) {
    segments(0.55, y.top.of.vertical.line, 0.55,
      y.bottom.of.vertical.line, col = "black", lty = "solid", lwd = 1)

    segments(0.65, y.top.of.vertical.line, 0.65,
      y.bottom.of.vertical.line, col = "white", lty = "solid", lwd = 1)

    segments(0.85, y.top.of.vertical.line, 0.85,
      y.bottom.of.vertical.line, col = "white", lty = "solid", lwd = 1)

    segments(0.95, y.top.of.vertical.line, 0.95,
      y.bottom.of.vertical.line, col = "black", lty = "solid", lwd = 1)
    }
  }

# draw the all-important spine on the plot
segments(x.center.position, y.top.of.vertical.line, x.center.position,
  y.bottom.of.vertical.line, col = "black", lty = "dashed", lwd = 1)
```

```
# horizontal line at top
segments(0.55, y.top.of.vertical.line, 0.95, y.top.of.vertical.line,
    col = "black", lty = 1, lwd = 1)

# horizontal line at bottom
segments(0.55, y.bottom.of.vertical.line, 0.95, y.bottom.of.vertical.line,
    col = "black", lty = 1, lwd = 1)

# plot for ticks and labels
segments(0.55, y.bottom.of.vertical.line,
  0.55, below.y.bottom.of.vertical.line,
  col = "black", lty = 1, lwd = 1)   # tick line at bottom
segments(0.65, y.bottom.of.vertical.line,
  0.65, below.y.bottom.of.vertical.line,
  col = "black", lty = 1, lwd = 1)   # tick line at bottom
segments(0.75, y.bottom.of.vertical.line,
  0.75, below.y.bottom.of.vertical.line,
  col = "black", lty = 1, lwd = 1)   # tick line at bottom
segments(0.85, y.bottom.of.vertical.line,
  0.85, below.y.bottom.of.vertical.line,
  col = "black", lty = 1, lwd = 1)   # tick line at bottom
segments(0.95, y.bottom.of.vertical.line,
  0.95, below.y.bottom.of.vertical.line,
  col = "black", lty = 1, lwd = 1)   # tick line at bottom

# axis labels vary with the max.is.less.than range being used
if (max.is.less.than.1) text(c(0.55,0.65,0.75,0.85,0.95),
  rep(below.y.bottom.of.vertical.line,times=5),
  pos=1,labels=c("-1","-0.5","0","+0.5","+1"),cex=0.75)
if (max.is.less.than.2) text(c(0.55,0.65,0.75,0.85,0.95),
  rep(below.y.bottom.of.vertical.line,times=5),
  pos=1,labels=c("-2","-1","0","+1","+2"),cex=0.75)
if (max.is.less.than.4) text(c(0.55,0.65,0.75,0.85,0.95),
  rep(below.y.bottom.of.vertical.line,times=5),
  pos=1,labels=c("-4","-2","0","+2","+4"),cex=0.75)
if (max.is.less.than.10) text(c(0.55,0.65,0.75,0.85,0.95),
  rep(below.y.bottom.of.vertical.line,times=5),
  pos=1,labels=c("-10","-5","0","+5","+10"),cex=0.75)
if (max.is.less.than.20) text(c(0.55,0.65,0.75,0.85,0.95),
  rep(below.y.bottom.of.vertical.line,times=5),
  pos=1,labels=c("-20","-10","0","+10","+20"),cex=0.75)
if (max.is.less.than.40) text(c(0.55,0.65,0.75,0.85,0.95),
  rep(below.y.bottom.of.vertical.line,times=5),
  pos=1,labels=c("-40","-20","0","+20","+40"),cex=0.75)
y.location <- below.y.bottom.of.vertical.line - small.space

if(do.standardization)
  text(.75,y.location,pos=1,labels=c("Standardized Part-Worth"),cex=0.95)

if(!do.standardization) text(.75,y.location,pos=1,labels=c("Part-Worth"),
  cex=0.95)

y.location <- below.y.bottom.of.vertical.line - small.space
```

```
  if(do.standardization)
    text(0.75,y.location,pos=1,labels=c("Standardized Part-Worth"),cex=0.95)

  if(!do.standardization) text(0.75,y.location,pos=1,labels=c("Part-Worth"),
    cex=0.95)

  if(print.internal.consistency) {
    y.location <- y.location - medium.space
    text(c(0.525),c(y.location),pos=2,labels=paste("Internal consistency: ",
    pretty.print(conjoint.results$internal.consistency),
    sep=""))
    }

# if we have grid lines we may have plotted over part-worth points
# if we have a gray background then we have plotted over part-worth points
# so let us plot those all-important part-worth points and lines once again
if(draw.gray.background || draw.optional.grid.lines) {
  y.location <- y.top.of.vertical.line  # retreive the starting value

# repeat the primary plotting loop
for(k in seq(along=effect.names)) {
  y.location <- y.location - large.space
  text(c(0.4),c(y.location),pos=2,
    labels=paste(effect.name.map(effect.names[k])," ",sep=""),cex=01.0)
  text(c(0.525),c(y.location),pos=2,col=color.for.printing.importance.text,
    labels=paste(" ",left.side.symbol.to.print.around.importance,
    pretty.print(
    unlist(conjoint.results$attribute.importance[effect.names[k]])),"%",
    right.side.symbol.to.print.around.importance,sep=""),cex=01.0)

# begin loop for printing part-worths
    for(m in seq(1:number.of.levels.of.attribute[k])) {
        y.location <- y.location - medium.space
        text(c(0.4),c(y.location),pos=2,
        conjoint.results$xlevel[[effect.names[k]]][m],cex=01.0)
        text(c(0.525),c(y.location),
          pos=2,col=color.for.printing.part.worth.text,
          labels=paste(" ",left.side.symbol.to.print.around.part.worths,
          pretty.print(part.worth.plotting.list[[effect.names[k]]][m]),
          right.side.symbol.to.print.around.part.worths,sep=""),cex=01.0)

    points(part.worth.point.position[[effect.names[k]]][m],y.location,
      type = "p", pch = 20, col = color.for.part.worth.point, cex = 2)
    segments(x.center.position, y.location,
    part.worth.point.position[[effect.names[k]]][m], y.location,
      col = color.for.part.worth.line, lty = 1, lwd = 2)
    }
  }
}
}
# save spine.chart function for future work
save(spine.chart,file="mtpa_spine_chart.Rdata")
```

Exhibit C.2. *Market Simulation Utilities*

```
# Market Simulation Utilities

# user-defined function for first-choice simulation rule
first.choice.simulation.rule <- function(response, alpha = 1) {
  # begin function for first-choice rule
  # returns binary vector or response vector with equal division
  # of 1 across all locations at the maximum
  # use alpha for desired sum across respondents
  # alpha useful when the set of tested profiles is not expected to be one
  if(alpha < 0 || alpha > 1) stop("alpha must be between zero and one")
  response.vector <- numeric(length(response))
  for(k in seq(along=response))
    if(response[k] == max(response)) response.vector[k] <- 1
  alpha*(response.vector/sum(response.vector))
  }  # end first-choice rule function

# user-defined function for predicted choices from four-profile choice sets
choice.set.predictor <- function(predicted.probability) {
  predicted.choice <- length(predicted.probability)  # initialize
  index.fourth <- 0  # initialize block-of-four choice set indices
  while (index.fourth < length(predicted.probability)) {
    index.first  <- index.fourth + 1
    index.second <- index.fourth + 2
    index.third  <- index.fourth + 3
    index.fourth <- index.fourth + 4
    this.choice.set.probability.vector <-
      c(predicted.probability[index.first],
      predicted.probability[index.second],
      predicted.probability[index.third],
      predicted.probability[index.fourth])
    predicted.choice[index.first:index.fourth] <-
      first.choice.simulation.rule(this.choice.set.probability.vector)
    }
  predicted.choice <- factor(predicted.choice, levels = c(0,1),
    labels = c("NO","YES"))
  predicted.choice
  } # end choice.set.predictor function

# save market simulation utilities for future work
save(first.choice.simulation.rule,
  choice.set.predictor,
  file="mtpa_market_simulation_utilities.Rdata")
```

Exhibit C.3. *Split-plotting Utilities*

```
# Split-Plotting Utilities with grid Graphics

library(grid)  # grid graphics foundation of split-plotting utilities

# functions used with ggplot2 graphics to split the plotting region
# to set margins and to plot more than one ggplot object on one page/screen

vplayout <- function(x, y)
viewport(layout.pos.row=x, layout.pos.col=y)


# grid graphics utility plots one plot with margins
ggplot.print.with.margins <- function(ggplot.object.name,left.margin.pct=10,
  right.margin.pct=10,top.margin.pct=10,bottom.margin.pct=10)
{ # begin function for printing ggplot objects with margins
  # margins expressed as percentages of total... use integers
 grid.newpage()
pushViewport(viewport(layout=grid.layout(100,100)))
print(ggplot.object.name,
  vp=vplayout((0 + top.margin.pct):(100 - bottom.margin.pct),
  (0 + left.margin.pct):(100 - right.margin.pct)))
} # end function for printing ggplot objects with margins


# grid graphics utility plots two ggplot plotting objects in one column
special.top.bottom.ggplot.print.with.margins <-
  function(ggplot.object.name,ggplot.text.tagging.object.name,
  left.margin.pct=5,right.margin.pct=5,top.margin.pct=5,
  bottom.margin.pct=5,plot.pct=80,text.tagging.pct=10) {
# begin function for printing ggplot objects with margins
# and text tagging at bottom of plot
# margins expressed as percentages of total... use integers
  if((top.margin.pct + bottom.margin.pct + plot.pct + text.tagging.pct) != 100)
    stop(paste("function special.top.bottom.ggplot.print.with.margins()",
    "execution terminated:\n   top.margin.pct + bottom.margin.pct + ",
    "plot.pct + text.tagging.pct not equal to 100 percent",sep=""))
  grid.newpage()
  pushViewport(viewport(layout=grid.layout(100,100)))
  print(ggplot.object.name,
  vp=vplayout((0 + top.margin.pct):
    (100 - (bottom.margin.pct + text.tagging.pct)),
  (0 + left.margin.pct):(100 - right.margin.pct)))

  print(ggplot.text.tagging.object.name,
    vp=vplayout((0 + (top.margin.pct + plot.pct)):(100 - bottom.margin.pct),
    (0 + left.margin.pct):(100 - right.margin.pct)))
} # end function for printing ggplot objects with margins and text tagging
```

```
# grid graphics utility plots three ggplot plotting objects in one column
three.part.ggplot.print.with.margins <- function(ggfirstplot.object.name,
ggsecondplot.object.name,
ggthirdplot.object.name,
left.margin.pct=5,right.margin.pct=5,
top.margin.pct=10,bottom.margin.pct=10,
first.plot.pct=25,second.plot.pct=25,
third.plot.pct=30) {
# function for printing ggplot objects with margins and top and bottom plots
# margins expressed as percentages of total... use integers
if((top.margin.pct + bottom.margin.pct + first.plot.pct +
  second.plot.pct  + third.plot.pct) != 100)
    stop(paste("function special.top.bottom.ggplot.print.with.margins()",
        "execution terminated:\n  top.margin.pct + bottom.margin.pct",
        "+ first.plot.pct + second.plot.pct  + third.plot.pct not equal",
        "to 100 percent",sep=""))
grid.newpage()
pushViewport(viewport(layout=grid.layout(100,100)))

print(ggfirstplot.object.name, vp=vplayout((0 + top.margin.pct):
  (100 - (second.plot.pct  + third.plot.pct + bottom.margin.pct)),
  (0 + left.margin.pct):(100 - right.margin.pct)))

print(ggsecondplot.object.name,
  vp=vplayout((0 + top.margin.pct + first.plot.pct):
  (100 - (third.plot.pct + bottom.margin.pct)),
  (0 + left.margin.pct):(100 - right.margin.pct)))

print(ggthirdplot.object.name,
  vp=vplayout((0 + top.margin.pct + first.plot.pct + second.plot.pct):
  (100 - (bottom.margin.pct)),(0 + left.margin.pct):
  (100 - right.margin.pct)))
}

# grid graphics utility plots two ggplot plotting objects in one row
# primary plot graph at left... legend at right
special.left.right.ggplot.print.with.margins <-
  function(ggplot.object.name, ggplot.text.legend.object.name,
  left.margin.pct=5, right.margin.pct=5, top.margin.pct=5,
  bottom.margin.pct=5, plot.pct=85, text.legend.pct=5) {
# begin function for printing ggplot objects with margins
# and text legend at bottom of plot
# margins expressed as percentages of total... use integers
  if((left.margin.pct + right.margin.pct + plot.pct + text.legend.pct) != 100)
    stop(paste("function special.left.right.ggplot.print.with.margins()",
    "execution terminated:\n  left.margin.pct + right.margin.pct + ",
    "plot.pct + text.legend.pct not equal to 100 percent",sep=""))
  grid.newpage()
  pushViewport(viewport(layout=grid.layout(100,100)))
  print(ggplot.object.name,
  vp=vplayout((0 + top.margin.pct):(100 - (bottom.margin.pct)),
  (0 + left.margin.pct + text.legend.pct):(100 - right.margin.pct)))
```

```
   print(ggplot.text.legend.object.name,
      vp=vplayout((0 + (top.margin.pct)):(100 - bottom.margin.pct),
      (0 + left.margin.pct + plot.pct):(100 - right.margin.pct)))
} # end function for printing ggplot objects with margins and text legend

# save split-plotting utilities for future work
save(vplayout,
   ggplot.print.with.margins,
   special.top.bottom.ggplot.print.with.margins,
   three.part.ggplot.print.with.margins,
   special.left.right.ggplot.print.with.margins,
   file="mtpa_split_plotting_utilities.Rdata")
```

Exhibit C.4. *Wait-time Ribbon Plot*

```
# Wait-Time Ribbon Plot

wait.time.ribbon <- function(wait.service.data, title = "",
  wait.time.goal = 30, wait.time.max = 90,
  plotting.min = 0, plotting.max = 250,
  use.text.tagging = TRUE) {
# requires ggplot2 package
# data visualization for operations management
# wait.service.data is input data frame with the named columns as follows:
#   hour: integer hour of the day on 24-hour clock
#   wait: integer call wait time in seconds
#   service:  integer call service time in seconds (NA for no service)
#   server:  character string for server name or code
#            assumes that there is a distict character string for no server
#            this string is coded as NO_SERVER
# wait.time.goal:  desired maximum wait time (30 seconds default)
#                  represented as bottom of yellow region
# wait.time.max: when wait time becomes intolerable (90 seconds default)
#                represented as top of yellow region
# use.text.tagging default is TRUE for added text at bottom of plot
# set constants for ribbon plotting
MIN.SAMPLE <- 5  # min sample size for hourly calcuations
PERCENTILE.MIN <- 0.50  # used for bottom of acceptable wait time
PERCENTILE.MAX <- 0.90  # used for bottom of acceptable wait time
add_footnote_at_bottom_of_ribbon_plot <- TRUE
percentile.footnote <- paste("Bottom of ribbon = ",
  100*PERCENTILE.MIN, "th percentile of wait times",
  "   Top of ribbon = ", 100*PERCENTILE.MAX, "th percentile of wait times.",
  sep = "")

x.hour <- seq(from=0,to=23) # for horixontal axis scale

# code for ribbon region counts
calls.per.hour <- numeric(24)  # total calls initialized as zero
served.calls <- numeric(24)  # served calls initialized as zero
dropped.calls <- numeric(24)  # dropped/abandoned calls initialize as zero
ymin.percentile <- rep(NA,times=24)  # store for minimum percentile values
ymax.percentile <- rep(NA,times=24)  # store maximum percentile values

# compute number of calls per hour
# code more versatile than table command
# to accommodate hours with no calls
for(index.for.hour in 1:24) {
# begin for-loop for wait-time data call counts and percentile calculations
# 24-hour clock has first hour coded as zero in input data file
  coded.index.for.hour <- index.for.hour - 1
  temporary.vector <- na.omit(wait.service.data$hour)
  calls.per.hour[index.for.hour] <-
    sum(ifelse(temporary.vector==coded.index.for.hour,1,0))
    if(calls.per.hour[index.for.hour] >= MIN.SAMPLE) {
```

```r
# begin if-block for computing ymin and ymax values and number of servers
# when there are at least MIN.SAMPLE calls in the hour
    this.hour.wait.service.data <-
      wait.service.data[(wait.service.data$hour == coded.index.for.hour),]

    ymin.percentile[index.for.hour] <-
      quantile(this.hour.wait.service.data$wait,
      probs=c(PERCENTILE.MIN),na.rm = TRUE,names=FALSE,type=8)

    ymax.percentile[index.for.hour] <-
      quantile(this.hour.wait.service.data$wait,
      probs=c(PERCENTILE.MAX),na.rm = TRUE,names=FALSE,type=8)
    } # end if-block for computing ymin and ymax values

# if insufficient data we set min and max to be wait.time.goal
  if(calls.per.hour[index.for.hour] < MIN.SAMPLE) {
    ymin.percentile[index.for.hour] <- wait.time.goal
    ymax.percentile[index.for.hour] <- wait.time.goal
    }
  } # end for-loop for wait-time data call counts and percentile calculations


# compute number.of.servers data and served and dropped calls
number.of.servers <- numeric(24)  # initialize to zero
for(index.for.hour in 1:24) {
# begin for-loop for obtaining server data for the ribbon plot
# 24-hour clock has first hour coded as zero in input data file
  coded.index.for.hour <- index.for.hour - 1
  temporary.vector <- na.omit(wait.service.data$hour)
  calls.per.hour[index.for.hour] <-
    sum(ifelse(temporary.vector==coded.index.for.hour,1,0))
  this.hour.wait.service.data <-
      wait.service.data[(wait.service.data$hour == coded.index.for.hour),]

  served.calls[index.for.hour] <-
    nrow(subset(this.hour.wait.service.data, subset=(server != "NO_SERVER")))
  dropped.calls[index.for.hour] <-
    nrow(subset(this.hour.wait.service.data, subset=(server == "NO_SERVER")))

  if (nrow(this.hour.wait.service.data) > 0) {
# count is based upon the number of unique server names less NO_SERVER
    servers <-
      na.omit((unique(this.hour.wait.service.data$server)))
    valid.servers <- setdiff(servers, "NO_SERVER")
    number.of.servers[index.for.hour] <- length(valid.servers)
    }
  } # end for-loop for obtaining server data for the ribbon plot

greenmin <- rep(plotting.min, length=24)
greenmax <- rep(wait.time.goal, length=24)

yellowmin <- rep(wait.time.goal, length=24)
yellowmax <- rep(wait.time.max, length=24)
```

```
redmin <- rep(wait.time.max, length=24)
redmax <- rep(plotting.max, length=24)

ymax.topwhite <- rep(plotting.max,length=24)
ymin.topwhite <- ymax.percentile

ymax.bottomwhite <- ymin.percentile
ymin.bottomwhite <- rep(plotting.min,length=24)

# define data frame for plotting wait and service information for this day

call.center.plotting.frame <-
  data.frame(x.hour, ymin.percentile, ymax.percentile,
    calls.per.hour, number.of.servers,
    greenmin,greenmax,
    yellowmin,yellowmax,
    redmin,redmax,
    ymin.bottomwhite,ymax.bottomwhite,
    ymin.topwhite,ymax.topwhite)

#cat("\n\n","------------- ",title," -------------","\n")
#print(call.center.plotting.frame)

ggobject <- ggplot() +
geom_ribbon(data=call.center.plotting.frame,
mapping=aes(x=x.hour, ymin=greenmin, ymax=greenmax),
stat="identity",colour="white",fill="darkgreen") +
geom_ribbon(data=call.center.plotting.frame,
mapping=aes(x=x.hour, ymin=yellowmin, ymax=yellowmax),
stat="identity",colour="white",fill="yellow") +
geom_ribbon(data=call.center.plotting.frame,
mapping=aes(x=x.hour, ymin=redmin, ymax=redmax),
stat="identity",colour="white",fill="red") +
geom_ribbon(data=call.center.plotting.frame,
mapping=aes(x=x.hour, ymin=ymin.topwhite, ymax=ymax.topwhite),
stat="identity",colour="white",fill="white") +
geom_ribbon(data=call.center.plotting.frame,
mapping=aes(x=x.hour, ymin=ymin.bottomwhite, ymax=ymax.bottomwhite),
stat="identity",colour="white",fill="white") +
geom_hline(data=call.center.plotting.frame,
mapping=aes(yintercept=yellowmin[1])) +
geom_hline(data=call.center.plotting.frame,
mapping=aes(yintercept=redmin[1])) +
labs(title = title) + theme_bw(base_size = 12) +
scale_y_continuous(limits = c(greenmin[1], redmax[1])) +
xlab("Hour of Day (24-Hour Clock)") +
ylab("Wait Time (Seconds)")

# plotting with all default margins no text at bottom
if(!use.text.tagging) ggplot.print.with.margins(ggobject)
```

```r
# plotting with text tagging requires the creation of a ggplot text object
if (use.text.tagging) {
# define character data for the text taggging at bottom of plot
hour.title <- "Hour:"
hour.00 <- "00"
hour.01 <- "01"
hour.02 <- "02"
hour.03 <- "03"
hour.04 <- "04"
hour.05 <- "05"
hour.06 <- "06"
hour.07 <- "07"
hour.08 <- "08"
hour.09 <- "09"
hour.10 <- "10"
hour.11 <- "11"
hour.12 <- "12"
hour.13 <- "13"
hour.14 <- "14"
hour.15 <- "15"
hour.16 <- "16"
hour.17 <- "17"
hour.18 <- "18"
hour.19 <- "19"
hour.20 <- "20"
hour.21 <- "21"
hour.22 <- "22"
hour.23 <- "23"
calls.title <- "Calls:"
calls.00 <- as.character(calls.per.hour[1])
calls.01 <- as.character(calls.per.hour[2])
calls.02 <- as.character(calls.per.hour[3])
calls.03 <- as.character(calls.per.hour[4])
calls.04 <- as.character(calls.per.hour[5])
calls.05 <- as.character(calls.per.hour[6])
calls.06 <- as.character(calls.per.hour[7])
calls.07 <- as.character(calls.per.hour[8])
calls.08 <- as.character(calls.per.hour[9])
calls.09 <- as.character(calls.per.hour[10])
calls.10 <- as.character(calls.per.hour[11])
calls.11 <- as.character(calls.per.hour[12])
calls.12 <- as.character(calls.per.hour[13])
calls.13 <- as.character(calls.per.hour[14])
calls.14 <- as.character(calls.per.hour[15])
calls.15 <- as.character(calls.per.hour[16])
calls.16 <- as.character(calls.per.hour[17])
calls.17 <- as.character(calls.per.hour[18])
calls.18 <- as.character(calls.per.hour[19])
calls.19 <- as.character(calls.per.hour[20])
calls.20 <- as.character(calls.per.hour[21])
calls.21 <- as.character(calls.per.hour[22])
calls.22 <- as.character(calls.per.hour[23])
calls.23 <- as.character(calls.per.hour[24])
```

```
servers.title <- "Servers:"
servers.00 <- as.character(number.of.servers[1])
servers.01 <- as.character(number.of.servers[2])
servers.02 <- as.character(number.of.servers[3])
servers.03 <- as.character(number.of.servers[4])
servers.04 <- as.character(number.of.servers[5])
servers.05 <- as.character(number.of.servers[6])
servers.06 <- as.character(number.of.servers[7])
servers.07 <- as.character(number.of.servers[8])
servers.08 <- as.character(number.of.servers[9])
servers.09 <- as.character(number.of.servers[10])
servers.10 <- as.character(number.of.servers[11])
servers.11 <- as.character(number.of.servers[12])
servers.12 <- as.character(number.of.servers[13])
servers.13 <- as.character(number.of.servers[14])
servers.14 <- as.character(number.of.servers[15])
servers.15 <- as.character(number.of.servers[16])
servers.16 <- as.character(number.of.servers[17])
servers.17 <- as.character(number.of.servers[18])
servers.18 <- as.character(number.of.servers[19])
servers.19 <- as.character(number.of.servers[20])
servers.20 <- as.character(number.of.servers[21])
servers.21 <- as.character(number.of.servers[22])
servers.22 <- as.character(number.of.servers[23])
servers.23 <- as.character(number.of.servers[24])


served.title <- "Served:"
served.00 <- as.character(served.calls[1])
served.01 <- as.character(served.calls[2])
served.02 <- as.character(served.calls[3])
served.03 <- as.character(served.calls[4])
served.04 <- as.character(served.calls[5])
served.05 <- as.character(served.calls[6])
served.06 <- as.character(served.calls[7])
served.07 <- as.character(served.calls[8])
served.08 <- as.character(served.calls[9])
served.09 <- as.character(served.calls[10])
served.10 <- as.character(served.calls[11])
served.11 <- as.character(served.calls[12])
served.12 <- as.character(served.calls[13])
served.13 <- as.character(served.calls[14])
served.14 <- as.character(served.calls[15])
served.15 <- as.character(served.calls[16])
served.16 <- as.character(served.calls[17])
served.17 <- as.character(served.calls[18])
served.18 <- as.character(served.calls[19])
served.19 <- as.character(served.calls[20])
served.20 <- as.character(served.calls[21])
served.21 <- as.character(served.calls[22])
served.22 <- as.character(served.calls[23])
served.23 <- as.character(served.calls[24])
```

```
dropped.title <- "Dropped:"
dropped.00 <- as.character(dropped.calls[1])
dropped.01 <- as.character(dropped.calls[2])
dropped.02 <- as.character(dropped.calls[3])
dropped.03 <- as.character(dropped.calls[4])
dropped.04 <- as.character(dropped.calls[5])
dropped.05 <- as.character(dropped.calls[6])
dropped.06 <- as.character(dropped.calls[7])
dropped.07 <- as.character(dropped.calls[8])
dropped.08 <- as.character(dropped.calls[9])
dropped.09 <- as.character(dropped.calls[10])
dropped.10 <- as.character(dropped.calls[11])
dropped.11 <- as.character(dropped.calls[12])
dropped.12 <- as.character(dropped.calls[13])
dropped.13 <- as.character(dropped.calls[14])
dropped.14 <- as.character(dropped.calls[15])
dropped.15 <- as.character(dropped.calls[16])
dropped.16 <- as.character(dropped.calls[17])
dropped.17 <- as.character(dropped.calls[18])
dropped.18 <- as.character(dropped.calls[19])
dropped.19 <- as.character(dropped.calls[20])
dropped.20 <- as.character(dropped.calls[21])
dropped.21 <- as.character(dropped.calls[22])
dropped.22 <- as.character(dropped.calls[23])
dropped.23 <- as.character(dropped.calls[24])


# set up spacing and positioning for the table
y.current.level <- 1.0  # initialze position
y.large.space <- 0.175
y.medium.space <- 0.125
y.small.space <- 0.075


table.left.margin <- 0.1  # needed for row labels at left
horizontal.offset <- (1-table.left.margin)/24  # spacing in the text table


y.current.level <- y.current.level - y.medium.space

ggtextobject <- ggplot(data=data.frame(x = 0.5,y = y.current.level),
  aes(x=x,y=y,xmin=0,xmax=1,ymin=0,ymax=1),
  stat="identity", position="identity") + labs(x=NULL,y=NULL) +
geom_text(x = 0.025,y = y.current.level,label = hour.title,
aes(size=10.55),colour="black")  +
geom_text(x = (00*horizontal.offset + table.left.margin),
y = y.current.level,label = hour.00, aes(size=10.55),colour="black") +
geom_text(x = (01*horizontal.offset + table.left.margin),
y = y.current.level,label = hour.01, aes(size=10.55),colour="black") +
geom_text(x = (02*horizontal.offset + table.left.margin),
y = y.current.level,label = hour.02, aes(size=10.55),colour="black") +
geom_text(x = (03*horizontal.offset + table.left.margin),
y = y.current.level,label = hour.03, aes(size=10.55),colour="black") +
geom_text(x = (04*horizontal.offset + table.left.margin),
y = y.current.level,label = hour.04, aes(size=10.55),colour="black") +
```

```
geom_text(x = (05*horizontal.offset + table.left.margin),
y = y.current.level,label = hour.05, aes(size=10.55),colour="black") +
geom_text(x = (06*horizontal.offset + table.left.margin),
y = y.current.level,label = hour.06, aes(size=10.55),colour="black") +
geom_text(x = (07*horizontal.offset + table.left.margin),
y = y.current.level,label = hour.07, aes(size=10.55),colour="black") +
geom_text(x = (08*horizontal.offset + table.left.margin),
y = y.current.level,label = hour.08, aes(size=10.55),colour="black") +
geom_text(x = (09*horizontal.offset + table.left.margin),
y = y.current.level,label = hour.09, aes(size=10.55),colour="black") +
geom_text(x = (10*horizontal.offset + table.left.margin),
y = y.current.level,label = hour.10, aes(size=10.55),colour="black") +
geom_text(x = (11*horizontal.offset + table.left.margin),
y = y.current.level,label = hour.11, aes(size=10.55),colour="black") +
geom_text(x = (12*horizontal.offset + table.left.margin),
y = y.current.level,label = hour.12, aes(size=10.55),colour="black") +
geom_text(x = (13*horizontal.offset + table.left.margin),
y = y.current.level,label = hour.13, aes(size=10.55),colour="black") +
geom_text(x = (14*horizontal.offset + table.left.margin),
y = y.current.level,label = hour.14, aes(size=10.55),colour="black") +
geom_text(x = (15*horizontal.offset + table.left.margin),
y= y.current.level,label = hour.15, aes(size=10.55),colour="black") +
geom_text(x = (16*horizontal.offset + table.left.margin),
y = y.current.level,label = hour.16, aes(size=10.55),colour="black") +
geom_text(x = (17*horizontal.offset + table.left.margin),
y = y.current.level,label = hour.17, aes(size=10.55),colour="black") +
geom_text(x = (18*horizontal.offset + table.left.margin),
y = y.current.level,label = hour.18, aes(size=10.55),colour="black") +
geom_text(x = (19*horizontal.offset + table.left.margin),
y = y.current.level,label = hour.19, aes(size=10.55),colour="black") +
geom_text(x = (20*horizontal.offset + table.left.margin),
y = y.current.level,label = hour.20, aes(size=10.55),colour="black") +
geom_text(x = (21*horizontal.offset + table.left.margin),
y = y.current.level,label = hour.21, aes(size=10.55),colour="black") +
geom_text(x = (22*horizontal.offset + table.left.margin),
y = y.current.level,label = hour.22, aes(size=10.55),colour="black") +
geom_text(x = (23*horizontal.offset + table.left.margin),
y = y.current.level,label = hour.23, aes(size=10.55),colour="black")

y.current.level <- y.current.level - y.medium.space

ggtextobject <- ggtextobject + geom_text(x = 0.025,
y = y.current.level, label = servers.title,aes(size=10.55),colour="black") +
geom_text(x = (00*horizontal.offset + table.left.margin),
y = y.current.level, label = servers.00,aes(size=10.55),colour="black") +
geom_text(x = (01*horizontal.offset + table.left.margin),
y = y.current.level, label = servers.01,aes(size=10.55),colour="black") +
geom_text(x = (02*horizontal.offset + table.left.margin),
y = y.current.level, label = servers.02,aes(size=10.55),colour="black") +
geom_text(x = (03*horizontal.offset + table.left.margin),
y = y.current.level, label = servers.03,aes(size=10.55),colour="black") +
geom_text(x = (04*horizontal.offset + table.left.margin),
y = y.current.level, label = servers.04,aes(size=10.55),colour="black") +
```

```
geom_text(x = (05*horizontal.offset + table.left.margin),
y = y.current.level, label = servers.05,aes(size=10.55),colour="black") +
geom_text(x = (06*horizontal.offset + table.left.margin),
y = y.current.level, label = servers.06,aes(size=10.55),colour="black") +
geom_text(x = (07*horizontal.offset + table.left.margin),
y = y.current.level, label = servers.07,aes(size=10.55),colour="black") +
geom_text(x = (08*horizontal.offset + table.left.margin),
y = y.current.level, label = servers.08,aes(size=10.55),colour="black") +
geom_text(x = (09*horizontal.offset + table.left.margin),
y = y.current.level, label = servers.09,aes(size=10.55),colour="black") +
geom_text(x = (10*horizontal.offset + table.left.margin),
y = y.current.level, label = servers.10,aes(size=10.55),colour="black") +
geom_text(x = (11*horizontal.offset + table.left.margin),
y = y.current.level, label = servers.11,aes(size=10.55),colour="black") +
geom_text(x = (12*horizontal.offset + table.left.margin),
y = y.current.level, label = servers.12,aes(size=10.55),colour="black") +
geom_text(x = (13*horizontal.offset + table.left.margin),
y = y.current.level, label = servers.13,aes(size=10.55),colour="black") +
geom_text(x = (14*horizontal.offset + table.left.margin),
y = y.current.level, label = servers.14,aes(size=10.55),colour="black") +
geom_text(x = (15*horizontal.offset + table.left.margin),
y = y.current.level, label = servers.15,aes(size=10.55),colour="black") +
geom_text(x = (16*horizontal.offset + table.left.margin),
y = y.current.level, label = servers.16,aes(size=10.55),colour="black") +
geom_text(x = (17*horizontal.offset + table.left.margin),
y = y.current.level, label = servers.17,aes(size=10.55),colour="black") +
geom_text(x = (18*horizontal.offset + table.left.margin),
y = y.current.level, label = servers.18,aes(size=10.55),colour="black") +
geom_text(x = (19*horizontal.offset + table.left.margin),
y = y.current.level, label = servers.19,aes(size=10.55),colour="black") +
geom_text(x = (20*horizontal.offset + table.left.margin),
y = y.current.level, label = servers.20,aes(size=10.55),colour="black") +
geom_text(x = (21*horizontal.offset + table.left.margin),
y = y.current.level, label = servers.21,aes(size=10.55),colour="black") +
geom_text(x = (22*horizontal.offset + table.left.margin),
y = y.current.level, label = servers.22,aes(size=10.55),colour="black") +
geom_text(x = (23*horizontal.offset + table.left.margin),
y = y.current.level, label = servers.23,aes(size=10.55),colour="black")

# store line position for bottom of text segment of the visualization

y.level.divider.line <- y.current.level - y.medium.space
# temporary data frame needed to input to geom_hline later
middle.line.data <- data.frame(y.level.divider.line)

y.current.level <- y.level.divider.line - y.medium.space

ggtextobject <- ggtextobject +
geom_text(x = 0.025,y = y.current.level,
label = calls.title, aes(size=10.55),colour="black") +
geom_text(x = (00*horizontal.offset + table.left.margin),
y = y.current.level, label = calls.00, aes(size=10.55),colour="black") +
```

```
geom_text(x = (01*horizontal.offset + table.left.margin),
y = y.current.level, label = calls.01, aes(size=10.55),colour="black") +
geom_text(x = (02*horizontal.offset + table.left.margin),
y = y.current.level, label = calls.02, aes(size=10.55),colour="black") +
geom_text(x = (03*horizontal.offset + table.left.margin),
y = y.current.level, label = calls.03, aes(size=10.55),colour="black") +
geom_text(x = (04*horizontal.offset + table.left.margin),
y = y.current.level, label = calls.04, aes(size=10.55),colour="black") +
geom_text(x = (05*horizontal.offset + table.left.margin),
y = y.current.level, label = calls.05, aes(size=10.55),colour="black") +
geom_text(x = (06*horizontal.offset + table.left.margin),
y = y.current.level, label = calls.06, aes(size=10.55),colour="black") +
geom_text(x = (07*horizontal.offset + table.left.margin),
y = y.current.level, label = calls.07, aes(size=10.55),colour="black") +
geom_text(x = (08*horizontal.offset + table.left.margin),
y = y.current.level, label = calls.08, aes(size=10.55),colour="black") +
geom_text(x = (09*horizontal.offset + table.left.margin),
y = y.current.level, label = calls.09, aes(size=10.55),colour="black") +
geom_text(x = (10*horizontal.offset + table.left.margin),
y = y.current.level, label = calls.10, aes(size=10.55),colour="black") +
geom_text(x = (11*horizontal.offset + table.left.margin),
y = y.current.level, label = calls.11, aes(size=10.55),colour="black") +
geom_text(x = (12*horizontal.offset + table.left.margin),
y = y.current.level, label = calls.12, aes(size=10.55),colour="black") +
geom_text(x = (13*horizontal.offset + table.left.margin),
y = y.current.level, label = calls.13, aes(size=10.55),colour="black") +
geom_text(x = (14*horizontal.offset + table.left.margin),
y = y.current.level, label = calls.14, aes(size=10.55),colour="black") +
geom_text(x = (15*horizontal.offset + table.left.margin),
y = y.current.level, label = calls.15, aes(size=10.55),colour="black") +
geom_text(x = (16*horizontal.offset + table.left.margin),
y = y.current.level, label = calls.16, aes(size=10.55),colour="black") +
geom_text(x = (17*horizontal.offset + table.left.margin),
y = y.current.level, label = calls.17, aes(size=10.55),colour="black") +
geom_text(x = (18*horizontal.offset + table.left.margin),
y = y.current.level, label = calls.18, aes(size=10.55),colour="black") +
geom_text(x = (19*horizontal.offset + table.left.margin),
y = y.current.level, label = calls.19, aes(size=10.55),colour="black") +
geom_text(x = (20*horizontal.offset + table.left.margin),
y = y.current.level, label = calls.20, aes(size=10.55),colour="black") +
geom_text(x = (21*horizontal.offset + table.left.margin),
y = y.current.level, label = calls.21, aes(size=10.55),colour="black") +
geom_text(x = (22*horizontal.offset + table.left.margin),
y = y.current.level, label = calls.22, aes(size=10.55),colour="black") +
geom_text(x = (23*horizontal.offset + table.left.margin),
y = y.current.level, label = calls.23, aes(size=10.55),colour="black")

y.current.level <- y.current.level - y.medium.space

ggtextobject <- ggtextobject +
geom_text(x = 0.025,y = y.current.level,
label = served.title, aes(size=10.55),colour="black") +
```

```
geom_text(x = (00*horizontal.offset + table.left.margin),
y = y.current.level, label = served.00, aes(size=10.55),colour="black") +
geom_text(x = (01*horizontal.offset + table.left.margin),
y = y.current.level, label = served.01, aes(size=10.55),colour="black") +
geom_text(x = (02*horizontal.offset + table.left.margin),
y = y.current.level, label = served.02, aes(size=10.55),colour="black") +
geom_text(x = (03*horizontal.offset + table.left.margin),
y = y.current.level, label = served.03, aes(size=10.55),colour="black") +
geom_text(x = (04*horizontal.offset + table.left.margin),
y = y.current.level, label = served.04, aes(size=10.55),colour="black") +
geom_text(x = (05*horizontal.offset + table.left.margin),
y = y.current.level, label = served.05, aes(size=10.55),colour="black") +
geom_text(x = (06*horizontal.offset + table.left.margin),
y = y.current.level, label = served.06, aes(size=10.55),colour="black") +
geom_text(x = (07*horizontal.offset + table.left.margin),
y = y.current.level, label = served.07, aes(size=10.55),colour="black") +
geom_text(x = (08*horizontal.offset + table.left.margin),
y = y.current.level, label = served.08, aes(size=10.55),colour="black") +
geom_text(x = (09*horizontal.offset + table.left.margin),
y = y.current.level, label = served.09, aes(size=10.55),colour="black") +
geom_text(x = (10*horizontal.offset + table.left.margin),
y = y.current.level, label = served.10, aes(size=10.55),colour="black") +
geom_text(x = (11*horizontal.offset + table.left.margin),
y = y.current.level, label = served.11, aes(size=10.55),colour="black") +
geom_text(x = (12*horizontal.offset + table.left.margin),
y = y.current.level, label = served.12, aes(size=10.55),colour="black") +
geom_text(x = (13*horizontal.offset + table.left.margin),
y = y.current.level, label = served.13, aes(size=10.55),colour="black") +
geom_text(x = (14*horizontal.offset + table.left.margin),
y = y.current.level, label = served.14, aes(size=10.55),colour="black") +
geom_text(x = (15*horizontal.offset + table.left.margin),
y = y.current.level, label = served.15, aes(size=10.55),colour="black") +
geom_text(x = (16*horizontal.offset + table.left.margin),
y = y.current.level, label = served.16, aes(size=10.55),colour="black") +
geom_text(x = (17*horizontal.offset + table.left.margin),
y = y.current.level, label = served.17, aes(size=10.55),colour="black") +
geom_text(x = (18*horizontal.offset + table.left.margin),
y = y.current.level, label = served.18, aes(size=10.55),colour="black") +
geom_text(x = (19*horizontal.offset + table.left.margin),
y = y.current.level, label = served.19, aes(size=10.55),colour="black") +
geom_text(x = (20*horizontal.offset + table.left.margin),
y = y.current.level, label = served.20, aes(size=10.55),colour="black") +
geom_text(x = (21*horizontal.offset + table.left.margin),
y = y.current.level, label = served.21, aes(size=10.55),colour="black") +
geom_text(x = (22*horizontal.offset + table.left.margin),
y = y.current.level, label = served.22, aes(size=10.55),colour="black") +
geom_text(x = (23*horizontal.offset + table.left.margin),
y = y.current.level, label = served.23, aes(size=10.55),colour="black")

y.current.level <- y.current.level - y.medium.space

ggtextobject <- ggtextobject +
```

```
geom_text(x = 0.025,y = y.current.level,
label = dropped.title, aes(size=10.55),colour="black") +
geom_text(x = (00*horizontal.offset + table.left.margin),
y = y.current.level, label = dropped.00, aes(size=10.55),colour="black") +
geom_text(x = (01*horizontal.offset + table.left.margin),
y = y.current.level, label = dropped.01, aes(size=10.55),colour="black") +
geom_text(x = (02*horizontal.offset + table.left.margin),
y = y.current.level, label = dropped.02, aes(size=10.55),colour="black") +
geom_text(x = (03*horizontal.offset + table.left.margin),
y = y.current.level, label = dropped.03, aes(size=10.55),colour="black") +
geom_text(x = (04*horizontal.offset + table.left.margin),
y = y.current.level, label = dropped.04, aes(size=10.55),colour="black") +
geom_text(x = (05*horizontal.offset + table.left.margin),
y = y.current.level, label = dropped.05, aes(size=10.55),colour="black") +
geom_text(x = (06*horizontal.offset + table.left.margin),
y = y.current.level, label = dropped.06, aes(size=10.55),colour="black") +
geom_text(x = (07*horizontal.offset + table.left.margin),
y = y.current.level, label = dropped.07, aes(size=10.55),colour="black") +
geom_text(x = (08*horizontal.offset + table.left.margin),
y = y.current.level, label = dropped.08, aes(size=10.55),colour="black") +
geom_text(x = (09*horizontal.offset + table.left.margin),
y = y.current.level, label = dropped.09, aes(size=10.55),colour="black") +
geom_text(x = (10*horizontal.offset + table.left.margin),
y = y.current.level, label = dropped.10, aes(size=10.55),colour="black") +
geom_text(x = (11*horizontal.offset + table.left.margin),
y = y.current.level, label = dropped.11, aes(size=10.55),colour="black") +
geom_text(x = (12*horizontal.offset + table.left.margin),
y = y.current.level, label = dropped.12, aes(size=10.55),colour="black") +
geom_text(x = (13*horizontal.offset + table.left.margin),
y = y.current.level, label = dropped.13, aes(size=10.55),colour="black") +
geom_text(x = (14*horizontal.offset + table.left.margin),
y = y.current.level, label = dropped.14, aes(size=10.55),colour="black") +
geom_text(x = (15*horizontal.offset + table.left.margin),
y = y.current.level, label = dropped.15, aes(size=10.55),colour="black") +
geom_text(x = (16*horizontal.offset + table.left.margin),
y = y.current.level, label = dropped.16, aes(size=10.55),colour="black") +
geom_text(x = (17*horizontal.offset + table.left.margin),
y = y.current.level, label = dropped.17, aes(size=10.55),colour="black") +
geom_text(x = (18*horizontal.offset + table.left.margin),
y = y.current.level, label = dropped.18, aes(size=10.55),colour="black") +
geom_text(x = (19*horizontal.offset + table.left.margin),
y = y.current.level, label = dropped.19, aes(size=10.55),colour="black") +
geom_text(x = (20*horizontal.offset + table.left.margin),
y = y.current.level, label = dropped.20, aes(size=10.55),colour="black") +
geom_text(x = (21*horizontal.offset + table.left.margin),
y = y.current.level, label = dropped.21, aes(size=10.55),colour="black") +
geom_text(x = (22*horizontal.offset + table.left.margin),
y = y.current.level, label = dropped.22, aes(size=10.55),colour="black") +
geom_text(x = (23*horizontal.offset + table.left.margin),
y = y.current.level, label = dropped.23, aes(size=10.55),colour="black")

y.level.divider.line <- y.current.level - y.medium.space
```

```
# temporary data frame needed to input to geom_hline later
bottom.line.data <- data.frame(y.level.divider.line)

y.current.level <- y.level.divider.line - y.medium.space

# add footnote centered at bottom of plot if requested
if (add_footnote_at_bottom_of_ribbon_plot)
  ggtextobject <- ggtextobject +
  geom_text(x = 0.5,y = y.current.level,
  label = percentile.footnote, aes(size=10.55), colour="black")

# finish up the plot with background definition and divider lines
ggtextobject <- ggtextobject + geom_hline(aes(yintercept=1)) +
geom_hline(data=bottom.line.data,
  mapping = aes(yintercept = y.level.divider.line)) +
geom_hline(data=middle.line.data,
  mapping = aes(yintercept = y.level.divider.line)) +
theme(legend.position = "none")  +
theme(panel.grid.minor = element_blank()) +
theme(panel.grid.major = element_blank())  +
theme(panel.background = element_blank()) +
theme(axis.ticks = element_blank()) +
scale_y_continuous(breaks=c(0,1),label=c("","")) +
scale_x_continuous(breaks=c(0,1),label=c("",""))

# user-defined function plots with text annotation/tagging at the bottom
special.top.bottom.ggplot.print.with.margins(ggobject,ggtextobject,
plot.pct=55,text.tagging.pct=35)
}
} # end of wait-time ribbon function

# save wait-time ribbon utility for future work
save(wait.time.ribbon,
  file="mtpa_wait_time_ribbon_utility.Rdata")
```

Exhibit C.5. *Word Scoring Code for Sentiment Analysis*

```
# -------------------------------------
# Word/item analysis method
# -------------------------------------
# develop simple counts for working.corpus
# for each of the words in the sentiment list
# these new variables will be given the names of the words
# compute the number of words that match each word
amazing <- integer(length(names(working.corpus)))
beautiful <- integer(length(names(working.corpus)))
classic <- integer(length(names(working.corpus)))
enjoy <- integer(length(names(working.corpus)))
enjoyed <- integer(length(names(working.corpus)))
entertaining <- integer(length(names(working.corpus)))
excellent <- integer(length(names(working.corpus)))
fans <- integer(length(names(working.corpus)))
favorite <- integer(length(names(working.corpus)))
fine <- integer(length(names(working.corpus)))
fun <- integer(length(names(working.corpus)))
humor <- integer(length(names(working.corpus)))
lead <- integer(length(names(working.corpus)))
liked <- integer(length(names(working.corpus)))
love <- integer(length(names(working.corpus)))
loved <- integer(length(names(working.corpus)))
modern <- integer(length(names(working.corpus)))
nice <- integer(length(names(working.corpus)))
perfect <- integer(length(names(working.corpus)))
pretty <- integer(length(names(working.corpus)))
recommend <- integer(length(names(working.corpus)))
strong <- integer(length(names(working.corpus)))
top <- integer(length(names(working.corpus)))
wonderful <- integer(length(names(working.corpus)))
worth <- integer(length(names(working.corpus)))
bad <- integer(length(names(working.corpus)))
boring <- integer(length(names(working.corpus)))
cheap <- integer(length(names(working.corpus)))
creepy <- integer(length(names(working.corpus)))
dark <- integer(length(names(working.corpus)))
dead <- integer(length(names(working.corpus)))
death <- integer(length(names(working.corpus)))
evil <- integer(length(names(working.corpus)))
hard <- integer(length(names(working.corpus)))
kill <- integer(length(names(working.corpus)))
killed <- integer(length(names(working.corpus)))
lack <- integer(length(names(working.corpus)))
lost <- integer(length(names(working.corpus)))
miss <- integer(length(names(working.corpus)))
murder <- integer(length(names(working.corpus)))
mystery <- integer(length(names(working.corpus)))
plot <- integer(length(names(working.corpus)))
poor <- integer(length(names(working.corpus)))
sad <- integer(length(names(working.corpus)))
scary <- integer(length(names(working.corpus)))
```

```
slow <- integer(length(names(working.corpus)))
terrible <- integer(length(names(working.corpus)))
waste <- integer(length(names(working.corpus)))
worst <- integer(length(names(working.corpus)))
wrong <- integer(length(names(working.corpus)))

reviews.tdm <- TermDocumentMatrix(working.corpus)

for(index.for.document in seq(along=names(working.corpus))) {
  amazing[index.for.document] <-
    sum(termFreq(working.corpus[[index.for.document]],
    control = list(dictionary = "amazing")))
  beautiful[index.for.document] <-
    sum(termFreq(working.corpus[[index.for.document]],
    control = list(dictionary = "beautiful")))
  classic[index.for.document] <-
    sum(termFreq(working.corpus[[index.for.document]],
    control = list(dictionary = "classic")))
  enjoy[index.for.document] <-
    sum(termFreq(working.corpus[[index.for.document]],
    control = list(dictionary = "enjoy")))
  enjoyed[index.for.document] <-
    sum(termFreq(working.corpus[[index.for.document]],
    control = list(dictionary = "enjoyed")))
  entertaining[index.for.document] <-
    sum(termFreq(working.corpus[[index.for.document]],
    control = list(dictionary = "entertaining")))
  excellent[index.for.document] <-
    sum(termFreq(working.corpus[[index.for.document]],
    control = list(dictionary = "excellent")))
  fans[index.for.document] <-
    sum(termFreq(working.corpus[[index.for.document]],
    control = list(dictionary = "fans")))
  favorite[index.for.document] <-
    sum(termFreq(working.corpus[[index.for.document]],
    control = list(dictionary = "favorite")))
  fine[index.for.document] <-
    sum(termFreq(working.corpus[[index.for.document]],
    control = list(dictionary = "fine")))
  fun[index.for.document] <-
    sum(termFreq(working.corpus[[index.for.document]],
    control = list(dictionary = "fun")))
  humor[index.for.document] <-
    sum(termFreq(working.corpus[[index.for.document]],
    control = list(dictionary = "humor")))
  lead[index.for.document] <-
    sum(termFreq(working.corpus[[index.for.document]],
    control = list(dictionary = "lead")))
  liked[index.for.document] <-
    sum(termFreq(working.corpus[[index.for.document]],
    control = list(dictionary = "liked")))
  love[index.for.document] <-
    sum(termFreq(working.corpus[[index.for.document]],
    control = list(dictionary = "love")))
```

```
loved[index.for.document] <-
  sum(termFreq(working.corpus[[index.for.document]],
  control = list(dictionary = "loved")))
modern[index.for.document] <-
  sum(termFreq(working.corpus[[index.for.document]],
  control = list(dictionary = "modern")))
nice[index.for.document] <-
  sum(termFreq(working.corpus[[index.for.document]],
  control = list(dictionary = "nice")))
perfect[index.for.document] <-
  sum(termFreq(working.corpus[[index.for.document]],
  control = list(dictionary = "perfect")))
pretty[index.for.document] <-
  sum(termFreq(working.corpus[[index.for.document]],
  control = list(dictionary = "pretty")))
recommend[index.for.document] <-
  sum(termFreq(working.corpus[[index.for.document]],
  control = list(dictionary = "recommend")))
strong[index.for.document] <-
  sum(termFreq(working.corpus[[index.for.document]],
  control = list(dictionary = "strong")))
top[index.for.document] <-
  sum(termFreq(working.corpus[[index.for.document]],
  control = list(dictionary = "top")))
wonderful[index.for.document] <-
  sum(termFreq(working.corpus[[index.for.document]],
  control = list(dictionary = "wonderful")))
worth[index.for.document] <-
  sum(termFreq(working.corpus[[index.for.document]],
  control = list(dictionary = "worth")))
bad[index.for.document] <-
  sum(termFreq(working.corpus[[index.for.document]],
  control = list(dictionary = "bad")))
boring[index.for.document] <-
  sum(termFreq(working.corpus[[index.for.document]],
  control = list(dictionary = "boring")))
cheap[index.for.document] <-
  sum(termFreq(working.corpus[[index.for.document]],
  control = list(dictionary = "cheap")))
creepy[index.for.document] <-
  sum(termFreq(working.corpus[[index.for.document]],
  control = list(dictionary = "creepy")))
dark[index.for.document] <-
  sum(termFreq(working.corpus[[index.for.document]],
  control = list(dictionary = "dark")))
dead[index.for.document] <-
  sum(termFreq(working.corpus[[index.for.document]],
  control = list(dictionary = "dead")))
death[index.for.document] <-
  sum(termFreq(working.corpus[[index.for.document]],
  control = list(dictionary = "death")))
evil[index.for.document] <-
  sum(termFreq(working.corpus[[index.for.document]],
  control = list(dictionary = "evil")))
```

```r
hard[index.for.document] <-
  sum(termFreq(working.corpus[[index.for.document]],
  control = list(dictionary = "hard")))
kill[index.for.document] <-
  sum(termFreq(working.corpus[[index.for.document]],
  control = list(dictionary = "kill")))
killed[index.for.document] <-
  sum(termFreq(working.corpus[[index.for.document]],
  control = list(dictionary = "killed")))
lack[index.for.document] <-
  sum(termFreq(working.corpus[[index.for.document]],
  control = list(dictionary = "lack")))
lost[index.for.document] <-
  sum(termFreq(working.corpus[[index.for.document]],
  control = list(dictionary = "lost")))
miss[index.for.document] <-
  sum(termFreq(working.corpus[[index.for.document]],
  control = list(dictionary = "miss")))
murder[index.for.document] <-
  sum(termFreq(working.corpus[[index.for.document]],
  control = list(dictionary = "murder")))
mystery[index.for.document] <-
  sum(termFreq(working.corpus[[index.for.document]],
  control = list(dictionary = "mystery")))
plot[index.for.document] <-
  sum(termFreq(working.corpus[[index.for.document]],
  control = list(dictionary = "plot")))
poor[index.for.document] <-
  sum(termFreq(working.corpus[[index.for.document]],
  control = list(dictionary = "poor")))
sad[index.for.document] <-
  sum(termFreq(working.corpus[[index.for.document]],
  control = list(dictionary = "sad")))
scary[index.for.document] <-
  sum(termFreq(working.corpus[[index.for.document]],
  control = list(dictionary = "scary")))
slow[index.for.document] <-
  sum(termFreq(working.corpus[[index.for.document]],
  control = list(dictionary = "slow")))
terrible[index.for.document] <-
  sum(termFreq(working.corpus[[index.for.document]],
  control = list(dictionary = "terrible")))
waste[index.for.document] <-
  sum(termFreq(working.corpus[[index.for.document]],
  control = list(dictionary = "waste")))
worst[index.for.document] <-
  sum(termFreq(working.corpus[[index.for.document]],
  control = list(dictionary = "worst")))
wrong[index.for.document] <-
  sum(termFreq(working.corpus[[index.for.document]],
  control = list(dictionary = "wrong")))
}
```

Exhibit C.6. *Utilities for Spatial Data Analysis*

```
# Utilities for Spatial Data Analysis

# user-defined function to convert degrees to radians
# needed for lat.long.distance function
degrees.to.radians <- function(x) {
  (pi/180)*x
  } # end degrees.to.radians function

# user-defined function to calculate distance between two points in miles
# when the two points (a and b) are defined by longitude and latitude
lat.long.distance <- function(longitude.a,latitude.a,longitude.b,latitude.b) {
  radius.of.earth <- 24872/(2*pi)
  c <- sin((degrees.to.radians(latitude.a) -
    degrees.to.radians(latitude.b))/2)^2 +
    cos(degrees.to.radians(latitude.a)) *
    cos(degrees.to.radians(latitude.b)) *
    sin((degrees.to.radians(longitude.a) -
    degrees.to.radians(longitude.b))/2)^2
  2 * radius.of.earth * (asin(sqrt(c)))
  } # end lat.long.distance function

save(degrees.to.radians,
  lat.long.distance,
  file = "mtpa_spatial_distance_utilities.R")
```

Bibliography

Adler, J. 2010. *R in a Nutshell: A Desktop Quick Reference*. Sebastopol, Calif.: O'Reilly.

Agrawal, R., H. Mannila, R. Srikant, H. Toivonen, and A. I. Verkamo 1996. Fast discovery of association rules. In U. M. Fayyad, G. Piatetsky-Shapiro, P. Smyth, and R. Uthurusamy (eds.), *Handbook of Data Mining and Knowledge Discovery*, Chapter 12, pp. 307–328. Menlo Park, Calif. and Cambridge, Mass.: American Association for Artificial Intelligence and MIT Press.

Aizaki, H. 2012, September 22. Basic functions for supporting an implementation of choice experiments in R. *Journal of Statistical Software, Code Snippets* 50(2):1–24. http://www.jstatsoft.org/v50/c02.

Aizaki, H. 2013. *support.CEs: Basic Functions for Supporting an Implementation of Choice Experiments*. Comprehensive R Archive Network. 2013. http://cran.r-project.org/web/packages/support.CEs/support.CEs.pdf.

Ajmani, V. B. 2009. *Applied Econometrics Using the SAS System*. New York: Wiley.

Akaike, H. 1973. Information theory and an extension of the maximum likelihood principle. In B. N. Petrov and F. Csaki (eds.), *Second International Symposium on Information Theory*, pp. 267–281. Budapest: Akademiai Kiado.

Aksin, Z., M. Armony, and V. Mehrotra 2007, November–December. The modern call center: A multi-disciplinary perspective on operations management research. *Production and Operations Management* 16(6):665–688.

Alamar, B. C. 2013. *Sports Analytics: A Guide for Coaches, Managers, and Other Decision Makers*. New York: Columbia University Press.

Albert, J. H., J. Bennett, and J. J. Cochran (eds.) 2005. *Anthology of Statistics in Sports*. Alexandria, Va.: ASA-SIAM.

Albert, J. H. and J. Bennett 2003. *Curve Ball: Baseball, Statistics, and the Role of Chance in the Game*. New York: Springer.

Albert, J. H. 2003. *Teaching Statistics Using Baseball*. Washington D.C.: The Mathematical Association of America.

Albert, J. 2009. *Bayesian Computation with R*. New York: Springer.

Alfons, A., M. Templ, and P. Filzmoser 2010, November 16. An object-oriented framework for statistical simulation: The R package simFrame. *Journal of Statistical Software* 37(3):1–36. http://www.jstatsoft.org/v37/i03.

Alfons, A., M. Templ, and P. Filzmoser 2013. *An Object-Oriented Framework for Statistical Simulation: The R Package simFrame*. Comprehensive R Archive Network. 2013. http://cran.r-project.org/web/packages/simFrame/vignettes/simFrame-intro.pdf.

Alfons, A. 2013a. *cvTools: Cross-Validation Tools for Regression Models*. Comprehensive R Archive Network. 2013. http://cran.r-project.org/web/packages/cvTools/cvTools.pdf.

Alfons, A. 2013b. *simFrame: Simulation Framework*. Comprehensive R Archive Network. 2013. http://cran.r-project.org/web/packages/simFrame/simFrame.pdf.

Allen, M. J. and W. M. Yen 2002. *Introduction to Measurement Theory*. Prospect Heights, Ill.: Waveland Press.

Andersen, P. K., Ø. Borgan, R. D. Gill, and N. Keiding 1993. *Statistical Models Based on Counting Processes*. New York: Springer.

Anscombe, F. J. 1973, February. Graphs in statistical analysis. *The American Statistician* 27: 17–21.

Armstrong, J. S. (ed.) 2001. *Principles of Forecasting: A Handbook for Researchers and Practitioners*. Boston: Kluwer.

Asur, S. and B. A. Huberman 2010. Predicting the future with social media. In *Proceedings of the 2010 IEEE/WIC/ACM International Conference on Web Intelligence and Intelligent Agent Technology - Volume 01*, WI-IAT '10, pp. 492–499. Washington, DC, USA: IEEE Computer Society. http://dx.doi.org/10.1109/WI-IAT.2010.63.

Athanasopoulos, G., R. A. Ahmed, and R. J. Hyndman 2009. Hierarchical forecasts for Australian domestic tourism. *International Journal of Forecasting* 25:146–166.

Avery, C. and J. Chevalier 1999. Identifying investor sentiment from price paths: The case of football betting. *Journal of Business* 72(4):493–521.

Baayen, R. H. 2008. *Analyzing Linguistic Data: A Practical Introduction to Statistics with R*. Cambridge, UK: Cambridge University Press.

Bacon, L. D. 2002. Marketing. In W. Klösgen and J. M. ytkow (eds.), *Handbook of Data Mining and Knowledge Discovery*, Chapter 34, pp. 715–725. Oxford: Oxford University Press.

Baeza-Yates, R. and B. Ribeiro-Neto 1999. *Modern Information Retrieval*. New York: ACM Press.

Bagozzi, R. P. and Y. Yi 1991. Multitrait-multimethod matrices in consumer research. *Journal of Consumer Research* 17:426–439.

Barbera, P. 2013. *streamR: Access to Twitter Streaming API via R*. Comprehensive R Archive Network. 2013. http://cran.r-project.org/web/packages/streamR/streamR.pdf.

Barndorff-Nielsen, O. E., J. L. Jensen, and W. S. Kendall (eds.) 1993. *Networks and Chaos— Statistical Procedures and Probabilistic Aspects*. London: Chapman and Hall.

Bar-Eli, M., S. Avugos, and M. Raab 2006. Twenty years of "hot hand" research: Review and critique. *Journal of Sport and Exercise* 7:525–553.

Bates, D. M. and D. G. Watts 2007. *Nonlinear Regression Analysis and Its Applications*. New York: Wiley.

Bates, D. and M. Maechler 2013. *Matrix: Sparse and Dense Matrix Classes and Methods*. Comprehensive R Archive Network. 2013. http://cran.r-project.org/web/packages/support.CEs/support.CEs.pdf.

Baumohl, B. 2008. *The Secrets of Economic Indicators: Hidden Clues to Future Economic Trends and Investment Opportunities* (second ed.). Upper Saddle River, N.J.: Pearson.

Becker, R. A., J. M. Chambers, and A. R. Wilks 1988. *S: An Interactive Environment for Data Analysis and Graphics*. Pacific Grove, Calif.: Wadsworth & Brooks/Cole. Champions of S, S-Plus, and R call this "the blue book.".

Becker, R. A. and J. M. Chambers 1984. *S: An Interactive Environment for Data Analysis and Graphics*. Belmont, CA: Wadsworth. Champions of S, S-Plus, and R call this "the brown book.".

Becker, R. A. and W. S. Cleveland 1996. *S-Plus Trellis^{TM} Graphics User's Manual*. Seattle: MathSoft, Inc.

Becker, R. A., A. R. Wilks, R. Brownrigg, and T. P. Minka 2013. *maps: Draw Geographical Maps*. Comprehensive R Archive Network. 2013. http://cran.r-project.org/web/packages/maps/maps.pdf.

Beleites, C. 2013. *arrayhelpers: Convenience Functions for Arrays*. Comprehensive R Archive Network. 2013.
http://cran.r-project.org/web/packages/arrayhelpers/arrayhelpers.pdf.

Belew, R. K. 2000. *Finding Out About: A Cognitive Perspective on Search Engine Technology and the WWW*. Cambridge: Cambridge University Press.

Belsley, D. A., E. Kuh, and R. E. Welsch 1980. *Regression Diagnostics: Identifying Influential Data and Sources of Collinearity*. New York: Wiley.

Benninga, S. 2008. *Financial Modeling* (third ed.). Cambridge, Mass.: MIT Press.

Ben-Akiva, M. and S. R. Lerman 1985. *Discrete Choice Analysis: Theory and Application to Travel Demand*. Cambridge: MIT Press.

Berkelaar, M. 2013. *lpSolve: Interface to Lp_solve v.5.5 to solve linear/integer programs*. Comprehensive R Archive Network. 2013.
http://cran.r-project.org/web/packages/lpSolve/lpSolve.pdf.

Berk, R. A. 2008. *Statistical Learning from a Regression Perspective*. New York: Springer.

Berndt, E. R. 1991. *The Practice of Econometrics*. Reading, Mass.: Addison-Wesley.

Berri, D. J. and M. B. Schmidt 2010. *Stumbling on Wins: Two Economists Expose the Pitfalls on the Road to Victory in Professional Sports*. Upper Saddle River, N.J.: FT Press/Pearson.

Berry, D. A. 1996. *Statistics: A Bayesian Perspective*. Belmont, Calif.: Duxbury.

Berry, M. W. and M. Browne 2005. *Google's Page Rank and Beyond: The Science of Search Engine Rankings* (second ed.). Philadelphia: SIAM.

Betz, N. E. and D. J. Weiss 2001. Validity. In B. Bolton (ed.), *Handbook of Measurement and Evaluation in Rehabilitation* (third ed.)., pp. 49–73. Gaithersburg, Md.: Aspen Publishers.

Bishop, C. M. 1995. *Neural Networks for Pattern Recognition*. Oxford: Oxford University Press.

Bishop, Y. M. M., S. E. Fienberg, and P. W. Holland 1975. *Discrete Multivariate Analysis: Theory and Practice*. Cambridge: MIT Press.

Bivand, R. A., E. J. Pebesma, and V. Gómez-Rubio 2008. *Applied Spatial Data Analysis with R*. New York: Springer.

Bivand, R. and D. Yu 2013. *spgwr: Geographically Weighted Regression*. Comprehensive R Archive Network. 2013.
http://cran.at.r-project.org/web/packages/spgwr/spgwr.pdf.

Bivand, R. 2013. *Geographically Weighted Regression*. Comprehensive R Archive Network. 2013. http://cran.at.r-project.org/web/packages/spgwr/vignettes/GWR.pdf.

Bollen, J., H. Mao, and X. Zeng 2011. Twitter mood predicts the stock market. *Journal of Computational Science* 2:1–8.

Borenstein, M., L. V. Hedges, J. P. T. Higgins, and H. R. Rothstein 2009. *Introduction to Meta-Analysis*. New York: Wiley.

Borg, I. and P. J. F. Groenen 2010. *Modern Multidimensional Scaling: Theory and Applications* (second ed.). New York: Springer.

Boser, B. E., I. M. Guyon, and V. N. Vapnik 1992. A training algorithm for optimal margin classifiers. In *Proceedings of the Fifth Conference on Computational Learning Theory*, pp. 144–152. Association for Computing Machinery Press.

Bowman, A. W. and A. Azzalini 1997. *Applied Smoothing Techniques for Data Analysis*. Oxford: Oxford University Press.

Box, G. E. P. and D. R. Cox 1964. An analysis of transformations. *Journal of the Royal Statistical Society, Series B (Methodological)* 26(2):211–252.

Box, G. E. P., W. G. Hunter, and J. S. Hunter 2005. *Statistics for Experimenters: Design, Innovation, and Discovery* (second ed.). New York: Wiley.

Box, G. E. P., G. M. Jenkins, and G. C. Reinsel 2008. *Time Series Analysis: Forecasting and Control* (fourth ed.). New York: Wiley.

Bozdogan, H. (ed.) 2004. *Statistical Data Mining and Knowledge Discovery*. Boca Raton, Fla.: CRC Press.

Boztug, Y. and T. Reutterer 2008. A combined approach for segment-specific market basket analysis. *European Journal of Operational Research* 187(1):294–312.

Braun, W. J. and D. J. Murdoch 2007. *A First Course in Statistical Programming with R*. Cambridge, UK: Cambridge University Press.

Breiman, L., J. H. Friedman, R. A. Olshen, and C. J. Stone 1984. *Classification and Regression Trees*. New York: Chapman & Hall.

Breiman, L. 2001a. Random forests. Technical report from the Statistics Department of the University of California at Berkeley.

Breiman, L. 2001b. Statistical modeling: The two cultures. *Statistical Science* 16(3):199–215.

Brown, F. G. 1976. *Principles of Educational and Psychological Testing* (Second ed.). New York: Holt, Rinehart, and Winston.

Brown, L., N. Gans, A. Mandelbaum, A. Sakov, H. Shen, S. Zeltyn, and L. Zhao 2005. Statistical analysis of a telephone call center: A queueing-science perspective. *Journal of the American Statistical Association* 100(469):36–50.

Bruzzese, D. and C. Davino 2008. Visual mining of association rules. In S. Simoff, M. H. Böhlen, and A. Mazeika (eds.), *Visual Data Mining: Theory, Techniques and Tools for Visual Analytics*, pp. 103–122. New York: Springer.

Buchta, C. and M. Hahsler 2013. *arulesSequences: Mining Frequent Sequences*. Comprehensive R Archive Network. 2013. http://cran.r-project.org/web/packages/arulesSequences/arulesSequences.pdf.

Burnham, K. P. and D. R. Anderson 2002. *Model Selection and Multimodel Inference: A Practical Information-Theoretic Approach* (second ed.). New York: Springer-Verlag.

Burns, P. 2011, April. *The R Inferno*.
http://www.burns-stat.com/pages/Tutor/R_inferno.pdf.

Butts, C. T. 2013. *sna: Tools for Social Network Analysis*. Comprehensive R Archive Network. 2013. http://cran.r-project.org/web/packages/sna/sna.pdf.

Buvač, V. and P. J. Stone 2001, April 2. The General Inquirer user's guide. Software developed with the support of Harvard University and The Gallup Organization.

Cameron, A. C. and P. K. Trivedi 1998. *Regression Analysis of Count Data*. Cambridge: Cambridge University Press.

Campbell, D. T. and D. W. Fiske 1959. Convergent validity and discriminant validity by the multitrait-multimethod matrix. *Psychological Bulletin* 56:81–105.

Campbell, D. T. and J. C. Stanley 1963. *Experimental and Quasi-Experimental Designs for Research*. Skokie, IL: Rand McNally.

Canadilla, P. 2013. *queueing: Analysis of Queueing Networks and Models*. Comprehensive R Archive Network. 2013.
http://cran.r-project.org/web/packages/queueing/queueing.pdf.

Carlin, B. P. and T. A. Louis 1996. *Bayes and Empirical Bayes Methods for Data Analysis*. London: Chapman & Hall.

Carlin, B. P. 1996, February. Improved NCAA basketball tournament modeling via point spread and team strength information. *The American Statistician* 50(1):39–43.

Carroll, B., P. Palmer, J. Thorn, and D. Pietrusza (eds.) 1998. *The Hidden Game of Football: The Next Edition*. Kingston, N.Y.: Total Sports.

Carroll, J. D. and P. E. Green 1995. Psychometric methods in marketing research: Part I, conjoint analysis. *Journal of Marketing Research* 32:385–391.

Carroll, J. D. and P. E. Green 1997. Psychometric methods in marketing research: Part II, multidimensional scaling. *Journal of Marketing Research* 34:193–204.

Carr, D. B., R. J. Littlefield, W. L. Nicholson, and J. S. Littlefield 1987. Scatterplot matrix techniques for large N. *Journal of the American Statistical Association* 83:424–436.

Carr, D. B. 1991. Looking at large data sets using binned data plots. In A. Buja and P. Tukey (eds.), *Computing and Graphics in Statistics*, pp. 7–39. New York: Springer-Verlag.

Carr, D., N. Lewin-Koh, and M. Maechler 2013. *hexbin: Hexagonal Binning Routines*. Comprehensive R Archive Network. 2013. http://cran.r-project.org/web/packages/hexbin/hexbin.pdf.

Caudill, M. and C. Butler 1990. *Naturally Intelligent Systems*. Cambridge: MIT Press.

Cespedes, F. V., J. P. Dougherty, and B. S. Skinner, III 2013, Winter. How to identify the best customers for your business. *MIT Sloan Management Review* 54(2):53–59.

Chambers, J. M., W. S. Cleveland, B. Kleiner, and P. A. Tukey 1983. *Graphical Methods for Data Analysis*. Belmont, Calif.: Wadsworth.

Chambers, J. M. and T. J. Hastie (eds.) 1992. *Statistical Models in S*. Pacific Grove, Calif.: Wadsworth & Brooks/Cole. Champions of S, S-Plus, and R call this "the white book." It introduced statistical modeling syntax using S3 classes.

Chambers, J. M. 1998. *Programming with Data: A Guide to the S Language*. New York: Springer-Verlag. We could call this "the green book." Original documentation for S4 classes in S, S-Plus, and R.

Chambers, J. M. 2008. *Software for Data Analysis: Programming in R*. New York: Springer.

Chang, W. 2013. *R Graphics Cookbook*. Sebastopol, Calif.: O'Reilly.

Charniak, E. 1993. *Statistical Language Learning*. Cambridge: MIT Press.

Chatfield, C. (ed.) 2003. *The Analysis of Time Series: An Introduction* (sixth ed.). New York: CRC Press.

Chatterjee, S. and A. S. Hadi 2012. *Regression Analysis by Example* (fifth ed.). New York: Wiley.

Chau, M. and H. Chen 2003. Personalized and focused Web spiders. In N. Zhong, J. Liu, and Y. Yao (eds.), *Web Intelligence*, Chapter 10, pp. 198–217. New York: Springer.

Chen, D.-G. and K. E. Peace 2013. *Applied Meta-Analysis with R*. Boca Raton, Fla.: Chapman Hall/CRC.

Chen, H., M. Chau, and D. Zeng 2002. CI Spider: A tool for competitive intelligence on the Web. *Decision Support Systems* 34:1–17.

Chen, H. and M. Chau 2004. Web mining: Machine learning for Web applications. In B. Cronin (ed.), *Annual Review of Information Science and Technology*, Volume 38, Chapter 6, pp. 289–329. Medford, N.J.: Information Today.

Cherkassky, V. and F. Mulier 1998. *Learning from Data: Concepts, Theory, and Methods*. New York: Wiley.

Chihara, L. and T. Hesterberg 2011. *Mathematical Statistics with Resampling and R*. New York: Wiley.

Christensen, R. 1997. *Log-Linear Models and Logistic-Regression* (second ed.). New York: Springer.

Christianini, N. and J. Shawe-Taylor 2000. *Support Vector Machines and Other Kernel-Based Learning Methods*. Cambridge, UK: Cambridge University Press.

Cleveland, W. S. 1993. *Visualizing Data*. Murray Hill, N.J.: AT&T Bell Laboratories. Initial documentation for trellis graphics in S-Plus.

Cleveland, W. S. 1994. *The Elements of Graphing Data*. Murray Hill, N.J.: AT&T Bell Laboratories.

Clifton, B. 2012. *Advanced Web Metrics with Google Analytics* (third ed.). New York: Wiley.

Cochran, W. G. and G. M. Cox 1957. *Experimental Designs* (Second ed.). New York: Wiley.

Cochran, W. G. 1977. *Sampling Techniques*. New York: Wiley.

Cohen, J. 1960, April. A coefficient of agreement for nominal data. *Educational and Psychological Measurement* 20(1):37–46.

Commandeur, J. J. F. and S. J. Koopman (eds.) 2007. *An Introduction to State Space Time Series Analysis*. Oxford: Oxford University Press.

Congdon, P. 2001. *Bayesian Statistical Modeling*. New York: Wiley.

Congdon, P. 2003. *Applied Bayesian Modeling*. New York: Wiley.

Conway, D. and J. M. White 2012. *Machine Learning for Hackers* (third ed.). Sebastopol, Calif.: O'Reilly.

Cook, R. D. and S. Weisberg 1999. *Applied Regression Including Computing and Graphics*. New York: Wiley.

Cook, R. D. 1998. *Regression Graphics: Ideas for Studying Regressions through Graphics*. New York: Wiley.

Cook, R. D. 2007. Fisher lecture: Dimension reduction in regression. *Statistical Science* 22: 1–26.

Cook, T. D. and D. T. Campbell 1979. *Quasi-Experimentation: Design & Analysis Issues for Field Settings*. Boston: Houghton Mifflin.

Cooper, L. G. and M. Nakanishi 1988. *Market-Share Analysis*. Norwell, Mass.: Kluwer.

Cooper, L. G. 1999. Market share models. In J. Eliashberg and G. L. Lilien (eds.), *Handbook of Operations Research and Management Science: Vol. 5, Marketing*, Chapter 1, pp. 259–314. New York: Elsevier North Holland.

Cowpertwait, P. S. P. and A. V. Metcalfe 2009. *Introductory Time Series with R*. New York: Springer.

Cox, D. R. 1958. *Planning of Experiments*. New York: Wiley.

Cox, D. R. 1970. *Analysis of Binary Data*. London: Chapman and Hall.

Cox, T. F. and M. A. A. Cox 1994. *Multidimensional Scaling*. London: Chapman & Hall.

Craddock, J. (ed.) 2012. *VideoHound's Golden Movie Retriever 2013: The Complete Guide to Movies on All Home Entertainment Formats*. Farmington Hills, Mich.: Gale.

Cranor, L. F. and B. A. LaMacchia 1998. Spam! *Communications of the ACM* 41(8):74–83.

Cressie, N. and C. K. Wikle 2011. *Statistics for Spatio-Temporal Data*. New York: Wiley.

Cressie, N. 1993. *Statistics for Spatial Data* (revised ed.). New York: Wiley.

Cristianini, N. and J. Shawe-Taylor 2000. *An Introduction to Support Vector Machines and Other Kernel-Based Learning Methods*. Cambridge: Cambridge University Press.

Croissant, Y. 2013. *mlogit: Multinomial Logit Model*. Comprehensive R Archive Network. 2013. http://cran.r-project.org/web/packages/mlogit/mlogit.pdf.

Cronbach, L. J. 1951. Coefficient alpha and the internal structure of tests. *Psychometrika* 16:297–334.

Cronbach, L. J. 1995. Giving method variance its due. In P. E. Shrout and S. T. Fiske (eds.), *Personality Research, Methods, and Theory: A Festschrift Honoring Donald W. Fiske*, Chapter 10, pp. 145–157. Hillsdale, N.J.: Lawrence Erlbaum Associates.

Cumming, G. 2012. *Understanding the New Statistics: Effect Sizes, Confidence Intervals, and Meta-Analysis*. New York: Routledge.

Daconta, M. C., L. J. Obrst, and K. T. Smith 2003. *The Semantic Web: A Guide to the Future of XML, Web Services, and Knowledge Management*. New York: Wiley.

Dalgaard, P. 2002. *Introductory Statistics with R*. New York: Springer-Verlag.

Dantzig, G. B. 1954. A comment on Edie's "Traffic Delays at Toll Booths". *Operations Research* 2(2):107–108.

Davenport, T. H., J. G. Harris, and R. Morison 2010. *Analytics at Work: Smarter Decisions, Better Results*. Boston: Harvard Business School Press.

Davenport, T. H. and J. G. Harris 2007. *Competing on Analytics: The New Science of Winning*. Boston: Harvard Business School Press.

Davison, A. C. and D. V. Hinkley 1997. *Bootstrap Methods and their Application*. Cambridge: Cambridge University Press.

Davison, M. L. 1992. *Multidimensional Scaling*. Melbourne, Fla.: Krieger.

Dean, J. and S. Ghemawat 2004. MapReduce: Simplifed Data Processing on Large Clusters. Retrieved from the World Wide Web at http://static.usenix.org/event/osdi04/tech/full_papers/dean/dean.pdf.

Dehuri, S., M. Patra, B. B. Misra, and A. K. Jagadev (eds.) 2012. *Intelligent Techniques in Recommendation Systems*. Hershey, Pa.: IGI Global.

Delen, D., R. Sharda, and P. Kumar 2007. Movie forecast guru: A Web-based DSS for Hollywood managers. *Decision Support Systems* 43(4):1151–1170.

Deming, W. E. 1950. *Some Theory of Sampling*. New York: Wiley. Republished in 1966 by Dover Publications, New York.

Dickson, P. R. 1997. *Marketing Management* (second ed.). Orlando, Fla.: Harcourt Brace & Company.

Diggle, P. J., K.-Y. Liang, and S. L. Zeger 1994. *Analysis of Longitudinal Data*. Oxford: Oxford University Press.

Dippold, K. and H. Hruschka 2013. Variable selection for market basket analysis. *Computational Statistics* 28(2):519–539. http://dx.doi.org/10.1007/s00180-012-0315-3. ISSN 0943-4062.

Draper, N. R. and H. Smith 1998. *Applied Regression Analysis* (third ed.). New York: Wiley.

Dubins, L. E. and L. J. Savage 1965. *Inequalities for Stochastic Processes: How to Gamble If You Must*. New York: Dover.

Duda, R. O., P. E. Hart, and D. G. Stork 2001. *Pattern Classification* (second ed.). New York: Wiley.

Dumais, S. T. 2004. Latent semantic analysis. In B. Cronin (ed.), *Annual Review of Information Science and Technology*, Volume 38, Chapter 4, pp. 189–230. Medford, N.J.: Information Today.

Durbin, J. and S. J. Koopman 2012. *Time Series Analysis by State Space Methods* (second ed.). New York: Oxford University Press.

Eddelbuettel, D. 2013a. *CRAN Task View: Empirical Finance*. Comprehensive R Archive Network. 2013. http://cran.r-project.org/web/views/Finance.html.

Eddelbuettel, D. 2013b. *CRAN Task View: High-Performance and Parallel Computing with R*. Comprehensive R Archive Network. 2013. http://cran.r-project.org/web/views/HighPerformanceComputing.html.

Eden, S. 2013, March 4. Meet the world's top NBA gambler. *ESPN The Magazine*. Analytics issue of *ESPN The Magazine*. Retrieved from the World Wide Web at http://espn.go.com/blog/playbook/dollars/post/_/id/2935/meet-the-worlds-top-nba-gambler.

Efron, B. and R. Tibshirani 1993. *An Introduction to the Bootstrap*. London: Chapman and Hall.

Efron, B. 2012. *Large-Scale Inference: Empirical Bayes Methods of Estimation, Testing, and Prediction* (reprint ed.). Cambridge, UK: Cambridge University Press.

Elff, M. 2013. *mclogit: Mixed Conditional Logit*. Comprehensive R Archive Network. 2013. http://cran.r-project.org/web/packages/mclogit/mclogit.pdf.

Eliashberg, J. and G. L. Lilien (eds.) 1993. *Handbooks in Operations Research and Management Science: Volume 5 Marketing*. New York: North Holland.

Enders, W. 2010. *Applied Econometric Time Series* (third ed.). New York: Wiley.

Ernst, A. T., H. Jiang, M. Krishnamoorthy, and D. Sier 2004. Staff scheduling and rostering: A review of applications, methods, and models. *European Journal of Operations Research* 153:3–27.

Everitt, B. S., S. Landau, M. Leese, and D. Stahl 2011. *Cluster Analysis* (fifth ed.). New York: Wiley.

Everitt, B. and G. Dunn 2001. *Applied Multivariate Data Analysis* (second ed.). New York: Wiley.

Everitt, B. and S. Rabe-Hesketh 1997. *The Analysis of Proximity Data*. London: Arnold.

Everitt, B. 2005. *R and S-Plus Companion to Multivariate Analysis*. New York: Springer.

Fader, P. S. and B. G. S. Hardie 1996, November. Modeling consumer choice among SKUs. *Journal of Marketing Research* 33:442–452.

Fader, P. S. and B. G. S. Hardie 2002. A note on an integrated model of consumer buying behavior. *European Journal of Operational Research* 139(3):682–687.

Faraway, J. J. 2004. *Linear Models with R*. Boca Raton, Fla.: Chapman & Hall/CRC.

Fawcett, T. 2003, January 7. ROC graphs: Notes and practical considerations for researchers. http://www.hpl.hp.com/techreports/2003/HPL-2003-4.pdf.

Fayyad, U. M., G. Piatetsky-Shapiro, P. Smyth, and R. Uthurusamy (eds.) 1996. *Advances in Knowledge Discovery and Data Mining*. Cambridge: MIT Press.

Feinerer, I., K. Hornik, and D. Meyer 2008, 3 31. Text mining infrastructure in R. *Journal of Statistical Software* 25(5):1–54. http://www.jstatsoft.org/v25/i05. ISSN 1548-7660.

Feinerer, I. and K. Hornik 2013a. *tm: Text Mining Package*. Comprehensive R Archive Network. 2013. http://cran.r-project.org/web/packages/tm/tm.pdf.

Feinerer, I. and K. Hornik 2013b. *wordnet: WordNet Interface*. Comprehensive R Archive Network. 2013. http://cran.r-project.org/web/packages/wordnet/wordnet.pdf.

Feinerer, I. 2012. *Introduction to the wordnet Package*. Comprehensive R Archive Network. 2012. http://cran.r-project.org/web/packages/wordnet/vignettes/wordnet.pdf.

Feinerer, I. 2013. *Introduction to the tm Package*. Comprehensive R Archive Network. 2013. http://cran.r-project.org/web/packages/tm/vignettes/tm.pdf.

Feldman, D. M. 2002a, Winter. The pricing puzzle. *Marketing Research*:14–19.

Feldman, R., Y. Aumann, Y. Liberzon, K. Ankori, J. Schler, and B. Rosenfeld 2001. A domain independent environment for creating information extraction modules. In *Proceedings of the tenth international conference on Information and knowledge management*, pp. 586–588. ACM Press. ISBN 1-58113-436-3.

Feldman, R. and H. Hirsh 1997. Exploiting background information in knowledge discovery from text. *Journal of Intelligent Information Systems* 9(1):83–97. ISSN 0925-9902.

Feldman, R. 1999. Mining unstructured data. In *Tutorial notes of the fifth ACM SIGKDD international conference on Knowledge discovery and data mining*, pp. 182–236. ACM Press. ISBN 1-58113-171-2.

Feldman, R. 2002b. Text mining. In W. Klösgen and J. M. ytkow (eds.), *Handbook of Data Mining and Knowledge Discovery*, Chapter 38, pp. 749–757. Oxford: Oxford University Press.

Fellbaum, C. 1998. *WordNet: An Electronic Lexical Database*. Cambridge, Mass.: MIT Press.

Feller, W. 1968. *An Introduction to Probability Theory and Its Applications* (third ed.), Volume I. New York: Wiley.

Feller, W. 1971. *An Introduction to Probability Theory and Its Applications*, Volume 2. New York: Wiley.

Fellows, I. 2013a. *wordcloud: Word Clouds*. Comprehensive R Archive Network. 2013. http://cran.r-project.org/web/packages/wordcloud/wordcloud.pdf.

Fellows, I. 2013b. wordcloud makes words less cloudy. Retrieved from the World Wide Web at http://blog.fellstat.com/.

Fenzel, D., J. Hendler, H. Lieberman, and W. Wahlster (eds.) 2003. *Spinning the Semantic Web: Bringing the World Wide Web to Its Full Potential*. Cambridge: MIT Press.

Few, S. 2009. *Now You See It: Simple Visualization Techniques and Quantitative Analysis*. Oakland, Calif.: Analytics Press.

Fienberg, S. E. 2007. *Analysis of Cross-Classified Categorical Data* (second ed.). New York: Springer.

Firth, D. 1991. Generalized linear models. In D. Hinkley and E. Snell (eds.), *Statistical Theory and Modeling: In Honour of Sir David Cox, FRS*, Chapter 3, pp. 55–82. London: Chapman and Hall.

Fishelson-Holstine, H. 2004, February. The role of credit scoring in increasing homeownership for underserved populations. Joint Center for Housing Studies Working Paper. Retrieved from the World Wide Web at http://jchs.harvard.edu/sites/jchs.harvard.edu/files/babc_04-12.pdf.

Fisher, R. A. 1970. *Statistical Methods for Research Workers* (fourteenth ed.). Edinburgh: Oliver and Boyd. First edition published in 1925.

Fisher, R. A. 1971. *Design of Experiments* (ninth ed.). New York: Macmillan. First edition published in 1935.

Fiske, D. W. 1971. *Measuring the Concepts of Personality*. Chicago: Aldine.

Fogel, D. B. 2001. *Blondie24: Playing at the Edge of AI*. San Francisco: Morgan Kaufmann.

Fotheringham, A. S., C. Brunsdon, and M. Charlton 2002. *Geographically Weighted Regression: The Analysis of Spatially Varying Relationships*. New York: Wiley.

Fox, J. and S. Weisberg 2011. *An R Companion to Applied Regression* (second ed.). Thousand Oaks, Calif.: Sage.

Fox, J. 2002, January. Robust regression: Appendix to an R and S-PLUS companion to applied regression. Retrieved from the World Wide Web at http://cran.r-project.org/doc/contrib/Fox-Companion/appendix-robust-regression.pdf.

Fox, J. 2013. *car: Companion to Applied Regression*. Comprehensive R Archive Network. 2013. http://cran.r-project.org/web/packages/car/car.pdf.

Franks, B. 2012. *Taming the Big Data Tidal Wave: Finding Opportunities in Huge Data Streams with Advanced Analytics*. Hoboken, N.J.: Wiley.

Frees, E. W. and T. W. Miller 2004. Sales forecasting with longitudinal data models. *International Journal of Forecasting* 20:99–114.

Friedl, J. E. F. 2006. *Mastering Regular Expressions* (third ed.). Sebastopol, Calif.: O'Reilly.

Friedman, J. H. 1991. Multivariate adaptive regression splines (with discussion). *The Annals of Statistics* 19(1):1–141.

Friendly, M. 1994. Mosaic displays for multi-way contingency tables. *Journal of the American Statistical Association* 89:17–23.

Friendly, M. 2000. *Visualizing Categorical Data*. Cary, N.C.: SAS Institute.

Gabriel, K. R. 1971. The biplot graphical display of matrices with application to principal component analysis. *Biometrika* 58:453–467.

Garey, M. R. and D. S. Johnson 1979. *Computers and Intractability: A Guide to the Theory of NP-Completeness*. New York: W. H. Freeman.

Geisler, C. 2004. *Analyzing Streams of Language: Twelve Steps to the Systematic Coding of Text, Talk, and Other Verbal Data*. New York: Pearson Education.

Geisser, S. and W. O. Johnson 2006. *Modes of Parametric Statistical Inference*. New York: Wiley.

Geisser, S. 1993. *Predictive Inference: An Introduction*. New York: Chapman Hall.

Gelman, A., J. B. Carlin, H. S. Stern, and D. B. Rubin 1995. *Bayesian Data Analysis*. London: Chapman & Hall.

Gelman, A. and J. Hill 2007. *Data Analysis Using Regression and Mulitlevel/Hierarchical Models*. Cambridge, UK: Cambridge University Press.

Gentle, J. E. 2002. *Elements of Computational Statistics*. New York: Springer.

Gentle, J. E. 2003. *Random Number Generation and Monte Carlo Methods* (second ed.). New York: Springer.

Gentry, J. 2013a. *twitteR: R based Twitter Client*. Comprehensive R Archive Network. 2013. http://cran.r-project.org/web/packages/twitteR/twitteR.pdf.

Gentry, J. 2013b. *Twitter Client for R*. Comprehensive R Archive Network. 2013. http://cran.r-project.org/web/packages/twitteR/vignettes/twitteR.pdf.

Ghiselli, E. E. 1964. *Theory of Psychological Measurement*. New York: McGraw-Hill.

Glickman, M. E. and H. S. Stern 1998. A state-space model for national football league scores. *Journal of the American Statistical Association* 93(441):25–35.

Gnanadesikan, R. 1997. *Methods for Statistical Data Analysis of Multivariate Observations* (second ed.). New York: Wiley.

Goldman, S. (ed.) 2005. *Mind Game: How the Boston Red Sox got Smart, Won a World Series, and Created a New Blueprint for Winning*. New York: Workman Publishing.

Gordon, A. D. 1999. *Classification* (second ed.). Boca Raton, Fla.: Chapman & Hall/CRC.

Gower, J. C. and D. J. Hand 1996. *Biplots*. London: Chapman & Hall.

Gower, J. C. 1971. A general coefficient of similarity and some of its properties. *Biometrics* 27:857–871.

Granger, C. W. 1969. Investigating causal relations by econometric models and cross-spectral methods. *Econometrica* 37:424–438.

Graybill, F. A. 1961. *Introduction to Linear Statistical Models, Volume 1*. New York: McGraw-Hill.

Graybill, F. A. 2000. *Theory and Application of the Linear Model*. Stamford, Conn.: Cengage Learning.

Greene, W. H. 2012. *Econometric Analysis* (seventh ed.). Upper Saddle River, N.J.: Pearson Prentice Hall.

Gries, S. T. 2009. *Quantitative Corpus Linguistics with R: A Practical Introduction*. New York: Routledge.

Gries, S. T. 2013. *Statistics for Linguistics with R: A Pratical Introduction* (second revised ed.). Berlin: De Gruyter Mouton.

Grolemund, G. and H. Wickham 2011, April 7. Dates and times made easy with lubridate. *Journal of Statistical Software* 40(3):1–25. http://www.jstatsoft.org/v40/i03.

Grolemund, G. and H. Wickham 2013. *lubridate: Make Dealing with Dates a Little Easier*. Comprehensive R Archive Network. 2013. http://cran.r-project.org/web/packages/lubridate/lubridate.pdf.

Gross, D., J. F. Shortle, J. M. Thompson, and C. M. Harris 2008. *Fundamentals of Queueing Theory* (fourth ed.). New York: Wiley.

Grothendieck, G. 2013a. *gsubfn: Utilities for Strings and Function Arguments*. Comprehensive R Archive Network. 2013. http://cran.r-project.org/web/packages/gsubfn/gsubfn.pdf.

Grothendieck, G. 2013b. *gsubfn: Utilities for Strings and Function Arguments (Vignette)*. Comprehensive R Archive Network. 2013. http://cran.r-project.org/web/packages/gsubfn/vignettes/gsubfn.pdf.

Groves, R. M., F. J. Fowler, Jr., M. P. Couper, J. M. Lepkowski, E. Singer, and R. Tourangeau 2009. *Survey Methodology* (second ed.). New York: Wiley.

Guilford, J. P. 1954. *Psychometric Methods* (second ed.). New York: McGraw-Hill. First edition published in 1936.

Gulliksen, H. 1950. *Theory of Mental Tests*. New York: Wiley.

Gustafsson, A., A. Herrmann, and F. Huber (eds.) 2000. *Conjoint Measurement: Methods and Applications*. New York: Springer-Verlag.

Hahsler, M., C. Buchta, B. Grün, and K. Hornik 2013a. *arules: Mining Association Rules and Frequent Itemsets*. Comprehensive R Archive Network. 2013. http://cran.r-project.org/web/packages/arules/arules.pdf.

Hahsler, M., C. Buchta, B. Grün, and K. Hornik 2013b. *Introduction to arules: A Computational Environment for Mining Association Rules and Frequent Itemsets*. Comprehensive R Archive Network. 2013. http://cran.r-project.org/web/packages/arules/vignettes/arules.pdf.

Hahsler, M., C. Buchta, and K. Hornik 2008. Selective association rule generation. *Computational Statistics* 23:303–315.

Hahsler, M., S. Chelluboina, K. Hornik, and C. Buchta 2011. The arules R-package ecosystem: Analyzing interesting patterns from large transaction data sets. *Journal of Machine Learning Research* 12:2021–2025.

Hahsler, M. and S. Chelluboina 2013a. *arulesViz: Visualizing Association Rules and Frequent Itemsets*. Comprehensive R Archive Network. 2013. http://cran.r-project.org/web/packages/arulesViz/arulesViz.pdf.

Hahsler, M. and S. Chelluboina 2013b. *Visualizing Association Rules: Introduction to the R-extension Package arulesViz*. Comprehensive R Archive Network. 2013. http://cran.r-project.org/web/packages/arulesViz/vignettes/arulesViz.pdf.

Hahsler, M., B. Grün, and K. Hornik 2005, September 29. arules: A computational environment for mining association rules and frequent item sets. *Journal of Statistical Software* 14(15):1–25. http://www.jstatsoft.org/v14/i15.

Hahsler, M., K. Hornik, and T. Reutterer 2006. Implications of probabilistic data modeling for mining association rules. In M. Spiliopoulou, R. Kruse, C. Borgelt, A. Nuernberger, and W. Gaul (eds.), *Data and Information Analysis to Knowledge Engineering, Studies in Classification, Data Analysis, and Knowledge Organization*, pp. 598–605. New York: Springer.

Hahsler, M. 2013a. *arulesNBMiner: Mining NB-Frequent Itemsets and NB-Precise Rules*. Comprehensive R Archive Network. 2013. http://cran.r-project.org/web/packages/arulesNBMiner/arulesNBMiner.pdf.

Hahsler, M. 2013b. *recommenderlab: A Framework for Developing and Testing Recommendation Algorithms*. Comprehensive R Archive Network. 2013. http://cran.r-project.org/web/packages/recommenderlab/vignettes/recommenderlab.pdf.

Hahsler, M. 2013c. *recommenderlab: Lab for Developing and Testing Recommender Algorithms*. Comprehensive R Archive Network. 2013. http://cran.r-project.org/web/packages/recommenderlab/recommenderlab.pdf.

Hakes, J. K. and R. D. Sauer 2006. An economic evaluation of the "Moneyball" hypothesis. *Journal of Economic Perspectives* 20(3):173–185.

Hamilton, J. D. 1994. *Time Series Analysis*. Princeton, N.J.: Princeton University Press.

Hand, D. J. 1997. *Construction and Assessment of Classification Rules*. New York: Wiley.

Hand, D., H. Mannila, and P. Smyth 2001. *Principles of Data Mining*. Cambridge: MIT Press.

Hanssens, D. M., L. J. Parsons, and R. L. Schultz 2001. *Market Response Models: Econometric and Time Series Analysis* (second ed.). Boston: Kluwer.

Han, J., M. Kamber, and J. Pei 2011. *Data Mining: Concepts and Techniques* (third ed.). San Francisco: Morgan Kaufmann.

Harrell, Jr., F. E. 2001. *Regression Modeling Strategies*. New York: Springer.

Hartigan, J. A. and B. Kleiner 1984. A mosaic of television ratings. *The American Statistician* 38(1):32–35.

Hart, R. P. 2000a. *Campaign Talk: Why Elections Are Good for Us*. Princeton, N.J.: Princeton University Press.

Hart, R. P. 2000b. *DICTION 5.0: The Text Analysis Program*. Thousand Oaks, Calif.: Sage.

Hart, R. P. 2001. Redeveloping Diction: theoretical considerations. In M. D. West (ed.), *Theory, Method, and Practice in Computer Content Analysis*, Chapter 3, pp. 43–60. Westport, Conn.: Ablex.

Hastie, T. J. and R. Tibshirani 1990. *Generalized Additive Models*. London: Chapman and Hall.

Hastie, T. J. 1992a. Generalized additive models. In J. M. Chambers and T. J. Hastie (eds.), *Statistical Models in S*, Chapter 7, pp. 249–307. Pacific Grove, Calif.: Wadsworth & Brooks/Cole.

Hastie, T. J. 1992b. Generalized linear models. In J. M. Chambers and T. J. Hastie (eds.), *Statistical Models in S*, Chapter 6, pp. 195–247. Pacific Grove, Calif.: Wadsworth & Brooks/Cole.

Hastie, T., R. Tibshirani, and J. Friedman 2009. *The Elements of Statistical Learning: Data Mining, Inference, and Prediction* (second ed.). New York: Springer.

Hausser, R. 2001. *Foundations of Computational Linguistics: Human-Computer Communication in Natural Language* (second ed.). New York: Springer-Verlag.

Haykin, S. 2008. *Neural Networks and Learning Machines* (third ed.). Upper Saddle River, N.J.: Prentice Hall.

Hearst, M. A. 1997. Texttiling: Segmenting text into multi-paragraph subtopic passages. *Computational Linguistics* 23(1):33–64.

Hearst, M. A. 1999, June 20–26. Untangling text data mining. In *Proceedings of ACL'99: The 37th Annual Meeting of the Association for Computational Linguistics*. Retrieved from the World Wide Web on March 20, 2004, at: http://www.sims.berkeley.edu/hearst.

Hearst, M. A. 2003, October 17. What is text mining? Retrieved from the World Wide Web on March 20, 2004, at: http://www.sims.berkeley.edu/hearst.

Heer, J., M. Bostock, and V. Ogievetsky 2010, May 1. A tour through the visualization zoo: A survey of powerful visualization techniques, from the obvious to the obscure. *acmqueue: Association for Computing Machinery*:1–22. Retrieved from the World Wide Web at http://queue.acm.org/detail.cfm?id=1805128.

Heer, J., N. Kong, and M. Agrawala 2009. Sizing the horizon: The effects of chart size and layering on the graphical perception of time series visualizations. In *Proceedings of the SIGCHI Conference on Human Factors in Computing Systems*, CHI '09, pp. 1303–1312. New York: ACM. http://doi.acm.org/10.1145/1518701.1518897.

Heiberger, R. M. and B. Holland 2004. *Statistical Analysis and Data Display: An Intermediate Course*. New York: Springer.

Hemenway, K. and T. Calishain 2004. *Spidering Hacks: 100 Industrial-Strength Tips & Tools*. Sabastopol, Calif.: O'Reilly.

Hensher, D. A. and L. W. Johnson 1981. *Applied Discrete-Choice Modeling*. New York: Wiley.

Hensher, D. A., J. M. Rose, and W. H. Greene 2005. *Applied Choice Analysis: A Primer*. Cambridge: Cambridge University Press.

Hinkelmann, K. and O. Kempthorne 1994. *Design and Analysis of Experiments: Volume I. Introduction to Experimental Design*. New York: Wiley. Revision of Kempthorne (1952).

Hinkley, D. V., N. Reid, and E. J. Snell (eds.) 1991. *Statistical Theory and Modeling*. London: Chapman and Hall.

Hlavac, M. 2013. *stargazer: LaTeX Code for Well Formatted Regression and Summary Statistics Tables*. Cambridge, USA: Comprehensive R Archive Network and Harvard University. 2013. http://CRAN.R-project.org/package=stargazer.

Hoffmann, T. 2013. *batch: Batching Routines in Parallel and Passing Command-Line Arguments to R*. Comprehensive R Archive Network. 2013. http://cran.r-project.org/web/packages/batch/batch.pdf.

Hoff, P. D. 2009. *A First Course in Bayesian Statistical Methods*. New York: Springer.

Holden, K., D. A. Peel, and J. L. Thompson 1990. *Economic Forecasting: An Introduction*. Cambridge, UK: Cambridge University Press.

Hollis, N. 2005, Fall. Branding unmasked: Expose the mysterious consumer purchase process. *Marketing Research* 17(3):24–29.

Hornik, K. 2013a. *RWeka: R/Weka Interface*. Comprehensive R Archive Network. 2013. http://cran.r-project.org/web/packages/RWeka/RWeka.pdf.

Hornik, K. 2013b. *RWeka Odds and Ends*. Comprehensive R Archive Network. 2013. http://cran.r-project.org/web/packages/RWeka/vignettes/RWeka.pdf.

Hosmer, D. W., S. Lemeshow, and R. X. Sturdivant 2013. *Applied Logistic Regression* (third ed.). New York: Wiley.

Hothorn, T., K. Hornik, and A. Zeileis 2013. *party: A Laboratory for Recursive Partytioning*. Comprehensive R Archive Network. 2013. http://cran.r-project.org/web/packages/party/vignettes/party.pdf.

Hothorn, T., A. Zeileis, R. W. Farebrother, C. Cummins, G. Millo, and D. Mitchell 2013. *lmtest: Testing Linear Regression Models.* Comprehensive R Archive Network. 2013. http://cran.r-project.org/web/packages/lmtest/lmtest.pdf.

Hothorn, T. and A. Zeileis 2013a. *partykit: A Toolkit for Recursive Partytioning.* Comprehensive R Archive Network. 2013. http://cran.r-project.org/web/packages/partykit/partykit.pdf.

Hothorn, T. and A. Zeileis 2013b. *partykit vignette: A Toolkit for Recursive Partytioning.* Comprehensive R Archive Network. 2013. http://cran.r-project.org/web/packages/partykit/vignettes/partykit.pdf.

Hothorn, Leisch, Zeileis, and Hornik 2005, September. The design and analysis of benchmark experiments. *Journal of Computational and Graphical Statistics* 14(3):675–699.

Huberman, B. A. 2001. *The Laws of the Web: Patterns in the Ecology of Information.* Cambridge: MIT Press.

Huber, J. and K. Zwerina 1996. The importance of utility balance in efficient choice designs. *Journal of Marketing Research* 33:307–317.

Huber, P. J. and E. M. Ronchetti 2009. *Robust Statistics* (second ed.). New York: Wiley.

Hu, M. and B. Liu 2004, August 22–25. Mining and summarizing customer reviews. *Proceedings of the ACM SIGKDD International Conference on Knowledge Discovery Data Mining (KDD-2004).* Full paper available from the World Wide Web at http://www.cs.uic.edu/ liub/publications/kdd04-revSummary.pdf Original source for opinion and sentiment lexicon, available from the World Wide Web at http://www.cs.uic.edu/ liub/FBS/sentiment-analysis.htmllexicon.

Hyndman, R. J., R. A. Ahmed, G. Athanasopoulos, and H. L. Shang 2011. Optimal combination forecasts for hierarchical time series. *Computational Statistics and Data Analysis* 55:2579–2589.

Hyndman, R. J., R. A. Ahmed, and H. L. Shang 2013. *hts: Hierarchical and Grouped Time Series.* Comprehensive R Archive Network. 2013. http://cran.r-project.org/web/packages/hts/hts.pdf.

Hyndman, R. J., G. Athanasopoulos, S. Razbash, D. Schmidt, Z. Zhou, and Y. Khan 2013. *forecast: Forecasting Functions for Time Series and Linear Models.* Comprehensive R Archive Network. 2013. http://cran.r-project.org/web/packages/forecast/forecast.pdf.

Hyndman, R. J., A. B. Koehler, J. K. Ord, and R. D. Snyder 2008. *Forecasting with Exponential Smoothing: The State Space Approach.* New York: Springer.

Ihaka, R., P. Murrell, K. Hornik, J. C. Fisher, and A. Zeileis 2013. *colorspace: Color Space Manipulation.* Comprehensive R Archive Network. 2013. http://cran.r-project.org/web/packages/colorspace/colorspace.pdf.

Indurkhya, N. and F. J. Damerau (eds.) 2010. *Handbook of Natural Language Processing* (second ed.). Boca Raton, Fla.: Chapman and Hall/CRC.

Inselberg, A. 1985. The plane with parallel coordinates. *The Visual Computer* 1(4):69–91.

Izenman, A. J. 2008. *Modern Multivariate Statistical Techniques: Regression, Classification, and Manifold Learning.* New York: Springer.

James, B. 2010. *The New Bill James Historical Baseball Abstract.* New York: Free Press.

Janssen, A. J. E. M., J. S. H. van Leeuwaarden, and B. Zwart 2011, November–December. Refining square-root safety staffing by expanding Erlang C. *Operations Research* 59 (6):1512–1522.

Johnson, K. 2008. *Quantitative Methods in Linguistics*. Malden, Mass.: Blackwell Publishing.

Johnson, M. E. 1987. *Multivariate Statistical Simulation*. New York: Wiley.

Johnson, R. A. and D. W. Wichern 1998. *Applied Multivariate Statistical Analysis* (fourth ed.). Upper Saddle River, N.J.: Prentice Hall.

Joula, P. 2008. *Authorship Attribution*. Hanover, Mass.: Now Publishers.

Judge, G. G., W. E. Griffiths, R. C. Hill, H. Lütkepohl, and T.-C. Lee 1985. *The Theory and Practice of Econometrics* (second ed.). New York: Wiley.

Jurafsky, D. and J. H. Martin 2009. *Speech and Language Processing: An Introduction to Natural Language Processing, Computational Linguistics, and Speech Recognition* (second ed.). Upper Saddle River, N.J.: Prentice Hall.

Kadushin, C. 2012. *Understanding Social Networks*. New York: Oxford University Press.

Kahin, B. and H. R. Varian (eds.) 2000. *Internet Publishing: The Economics of Digital Information and Intellectual Property*. Cambridge, Mass.: MIT Press.

Kahn, L. M. 2000. The sports business as a labor market laboratory. *Journal of Economic Perspectives* 14(3):75–94.

Kaluzny, S. P., S. C. Vega, T. P. Cardoso, and A. A. Shelly 1998. *S+ Spatial Statistics: User's Manual for Windows and UNIX*. New York: Springer-Verlag.

Kaplan, D. T. 2012. *Statistical Modeling: A Fresh Approach* (second ed.). St. Paul, Minn.: Project Mosaic.

Kaplan, E. H. and S. J. Garstka 2001. March madness and the office pool. *Management Science* 47(3):369–382.

Kass, R. E. and A. E. Raftery 1995. Bayes factors. *Journal of the American Statistical Association* 90:773–795.

Kaufman, L. and P. J. Rousseeuw 1990. *Finding Groups in Data: An Introduction to Cluster Analysis*. New York: Wiley.

Keller, J. B. 1994. A characterization of the Poisson distribution and the probability of winning a game. *The American Statistician* 48(4):294–298.

Kelly, E. F. and P. J. Stone (eds.) 1975. *Computer Recognition of English Word Senses*. Amsterdam: North-Holland.

Kempthorne, O. 1952. *The Design and Analysis of Experiments*. New York: Wiley. Also see Hinkelmann and Kempthorne (1994).

Kennedy, P. 2008. *A Guide to Econometrics* (sixth ed.). New York: Wiley.

Keppel, G. and T. D. Wickens 2004. *Design and Analysis: A Researcher's Handbook* (fourth ed.). Upper Saddle River: N.J.: Pearson.

Keri, J. (ed.) 2006. *Baseball Between the Numbers: Why Everything You Know About the Game is Wrong*. New York: Basic Books.

Kirk, R. E. 2013. *Experimental Design: Procedures for the Behavioral Sciences* (fourth ed.). Thousand Oaks, Calif.: Sage.

Kleiber, C. and A. Zeileis 2008. *Applied Econometrics*. New York: Springer.

Kleinrock, L. 2009. *Queueing Systems: Computer Systems Modeling Fundamentals Volume 1.* New York: Wiley.

Klösgen, W. and J. M. ytkow (eds.) 2002. *Handbook of Data Mining and Knowledge Discovery.* Oxford: Oxford University Press.

Kohonen, T. 2008. *Self-Organizing Maps* (third ed.). New York: Springer-Verlag.

Kolari, P. and A. Joshi 2004. Web mining research and practice. *IEEE Computing Science and Engineering* 6(4):49–53.

Koller, M. and W. A. Stahel 2011. Sharpening Wald-type inference in robust regression for small samples. *Computational Statistics and Data Analysis* 55(8):2504–2515.

Koller, M. 2013. *Simulations for Sharpening Wald-type Inference in Robust Regression for Small Samples.* Comprehensive R Archive Network. 2013. http://cran.r-project.org/web/packages/robustbase/vignettes/lmrob$_s$imulation.pd$f$.

Konik, M. 2006. *The Smart Money: How the World's Best Sports Bettors Beat the Bookies Out of Millions.* New York: Simon & Schuster.

Kotler, P. and K. L. Keller 2012. *Marketing Management* (fourteenth ed.). Upper Saddle River, N.J.: Prentice Hall.

Kotsiantis, S. and D. Kanellopoulos 2006. Association rules mining: A recent overview. *GESTS International Transactions on Computer Science and Engineering* 32(1):71–82. Retrieved from the World Wide Web at http://www.csis.pace.edu/ ctappert/dps/d861-13/session2-p1.pdf.

Krippendorff, K. H. 2012. *Content Analysis: An Introduction to Its Methodology* (third ed.). Thousand Oaks, Calif.: Sage.

Krishnamurthi, L. 2001. Pricing strategies and tactics. In D. Iacobucci (ed.), *Kellogg on Marketing,* Chapter 12, pp. 279–301. Wiley.

Kuhfeld, W. F., R. D. Tobias, and M. Garratt 1994. Efficient experimental design with marketing research applications. *Journal of Marketing Research* 31:545–557.

Kuhn, M. and K. Johnson 2013. *Applied Predictive Modeling.* New York: Springer.

Kuhn, M. 2013. *caret: Classification and Regression Training.* Comprehensive R Archive Network. 2013. http://cran.r-project.org/web/packages/caret/caret.pdf.

Kutner, M. H., C. J. Nachtsheim, J. Neter, and W. Li 2004. *Applied Linear Statistical Models* (fifth ed.). Boston: McGraw-Hill.

Lam, W. and K.-Y. Lai 2001. A meta-learning approach for text categorization. In *Proceedings of the 24th annual international ACM SIGIR conference on Research and development in information retrieval,* pp. 303–309. ACM Press. ISBN 1-58113-331-6.

Langley, P. 1996. *Elements of Machine Learning.* San Francisco: Morgan Kaufmann.

Langville, A. N. and C. D. Meyer 2006. *Google's Page Rank and Beyond: The Science of Search Engine Rankings.* Princeton, N.J.: Princeton University Press.

Langville, A. N. and C. D. Meyer 2012. *Who's 1?: The Science of Rating and Ranking.* Princeton, N.J.: Princeton University Press.

Larsen, B. and C. Aone 1999. Fast and effective text mining using linear-time document clustering. In *Proceedings of the fifth ACM SIGKDD international conference on Knowledge discovery and data mining,* pp. 16–22. ACM Press. ISBN 1-58113-143-7.

Laursen, G. H. N. and J. Thorlund 2010. *Business Analytics for Managers: Taking Business Intelligence Beyond Reporting.* Hoboken, N.J.: Wiley.

Lawrence, S. and C. L. Giles 1998. Searching the World Wide Web. *Science* 280(3):98–100.

Lebart, L. 1998. Visualizations of textual data. In J. Blasius and M. Greenacre (eds.), *Visualizing of Categorical Data*, Chapter 11, pp. 133–147. San Diego: Academic Press.

Leeflang, P. S. H., D. R. Wittink, M. Wedel, and P. A. Naert 2000. *Building Models for Marketing Decisions*. Boston: Kluwer.

Leetaru, K. 2011. *Data Mining Methods for Content Analysis: An Introduction to the Computational Analysis of Content*. New York: Routledge.

Lee, C.-H. and H.-C. Yang 1999. A Web text mining approach based on self-organizing map. In *Proceedings of the second international workshop on Web information and data management*, pp. 59–62. ACM Press. ISBN 1-58113-221-2.

Leisch, F. and B. Gruen 2013. *CRAN Task View: Cluster Analysis   Finite Mixture Models*. Comprehensive R Archive Network. 2013. http://cran.r-project.org/web/views/Cluster.html.

Lemke, R. J., M. Leonard, and K. Tlhokwane 2010. Estimating attendance at major league baseball games for the 2007 season. *Journal of Sports Economics* 11(3):316–348.

Leonard, A. 2013, February 1. How Netflix is turning viewers into puppets. *Salon*. Retrieved from the World Wide Web at: http://www.salon.com/2013/02/01/how_netflix_is_turning_viewers_into_puppets/.

Levy, P. S. and S. Lemeshow 2008. *Sampling of Populations: Methods and Applications* (fourth ed.). New York: Wiley.

Lewin-Koh, N. 2013. *Hexagon Binning: an Overview*. Comprehensive R Archive Network. 2013.
http://cran.r-project.org/web/packages/hexbin/vignettes/hexagon_binning.pdf.

Lewis, M. 2003. *Moneyball: The Art of Winning an Unfair Game*. New York: W. W. Norton & Company.

Le, C. T. 1997. *Applied Survival Analysis*. New York: Wiley.

Le, C. T. 1998. *Applied Categorical Data Analysis*. New York: Wiley.

Liaw, A. and M. Wiener 2013. *randomForest: Breiman and Cutler's Random Forests for Classification and Regression*. Comprehensive R Archive Network. 2013. http://cran.r-project.org/web/packages/randomForest/randomForest.pdf.

Ligges, U. 2005. *Programmieren mit R*. Berlin and Heidelberg: Springer.

Lilien, G. L., P. Kotler, and K. S. Moorthy 1992. *Marketing Models*. Englewood Cliffs, N.J.: Prentice-Hall.

Lilien, G. L. and A. Rangaswamy 2003. *Marketing Engineering: Computer-Assisted Marketing Analysis and Planning* (second ed.). Upper Saddle River, N.J.: Prentice Hall.

Lindsey, J. K. 1997. *Applying Generalized Linear Models*. New York: Springer.

Little, J. D. C. 1970. Models and managers: The concept of a decision calculus. *Management Science* 16(8):B466–B485.

Little, R. J. A. and D. B. Rubin 1987. *Statistical Analysis with Missing Data*. New York: Wiley.

Liu, B. 2010. Sentiment analysis and subjectivity. In N. Indurkhya and F. J. Damerau (eds.), *Handbook of Natural Language Processing* (second ed.)., pp. 627–665. Boca Raton, Fla.: Chapman and Hall/CRC.

Liu, B. 2011. *Web Data Mining: Exploring Hyperlinks, Contents, and Usage Data*. New York: Springer.

Liu, B. 2012. *Sentiment Analysis and Opinion Mining*. San Rafael, Calif.: Morgan Claypool.

Lloyd, C. D. 2010. *Spatial Data Analysis: An Introduction for GIS Users*. Oxford, UK: Oxford University Press.

Lloyd, C. J. 1999. *Statistical Analysis of Categorical Data*. New York: Wiley.

Lord, F. M. and M. R. Novick 1968. *Statistical Theories of Mental Test Scores*. Reading, Mass.: Addison-Wesley.

Louviere, J. J., D. A. Hensher, and J. D. Swait 2000. *Stated Choice Methods: Analysis and Application*. Cambridge: Cambridge University Press.

Louviere, J. J. 1993. The best-worst or maximum difference measurement model: Applications to behavioral research in marketing. Paper presented at the American Marketing Association Behavioral Research Conference, Phoenix.

Luce, D. and J. Tukey 1964. Simultaneous conjoint measurement: A new type of fundamental measurement. *Journal of Mathematical Psychology* 1:1–27.

Lumley, T. 2004, June. Programmers' Niche: A simple class, in S3 and S4. *R News* 4(1): 33–36. http://CRAN.R-project.org/doc/Rnews/.

Lumley, T. 2010. *Complex Surveys: A Guide to Analysis Using R*. New York: Wiley.

Lyon, D. W. 2000. Pricing research. In C. Chakrapani (ed.), *Marketing Research: State-of-the-Art Perspectives*, Chapter 19, pp. 551–582. American Marketing Association.

Lyon, D. W. 2002, Winter. The price is right (or is it)? *Marketing Research*:8–13.

Maas, A. L., R. E. Daly, P. T. Pham, D. Huang, A. Y. Ng, and C. Potts 2011, June. Learning word vectors for sentiment analysis. In *Proceedings of the 49th Annual Meeting of the Association for Computational Linguistics: Human Language Technologies*, pp. 142–150. Portland, Ore.: Association for Computational Linguistics. Retrieved from the World Wide Web at http://ai.stanford.edu/ amaas/papers/wvSent_acl2011.pdf.

Maechler, M. 2013a. *Package cluster*. Comprehensive R Archive Network. 2013. http://cran.r-project.org/web/packages/cluster/cluster.pdf.

Maechler, M. 2013b. *robustbase: Basic Robust Statistics*. Comprehensive R Archive Network. 2013. http://cran.r-project.org/web/packages/robustbase/robustbase.pdf.

Maindonald, J. and J. Braun 2003. *Data Analysis and Graphics Using R: An Example-Based Approach*. Cambridge: Cambridge University Press.

Makridakis, S., S. C. Wheelwright, and R. J. Hyndman 2005. *Forecasting Methods and Applications* (third ed.). New York: Wiley.

Mallows, C. L. 1973. Some comments on C_p. Technometrics 15:661–675.

Mani, I. and M. T. Maybury (eds.) 1999. *Advances in Automatic Text Summarization*. Cambridge: MIT Press.

Manly, B. F. J. 1992. *The Design and Analysis of Research Studies*. Cambridge: Cambridge University Press.

Manly, B. F. J. 1994. *Multivariate Statistical Methods: A Primer* (second ed.). London: Chapman & Hall.

Manning, C. D. and H. Schütze 1999. *Foundations of Statistical Natural Language Processing*. Cambridge: MIT Press.

Marder, E. 1997. *The Laws of Choice: Predicting Consumer Behavior*. New York: Free Press.

Maronna, R. A., D. R. Martin, and V. J. Yohai 2006. *Robust Statistics Theory and Methods*. New York: Wiley.

Marshall, P. and E. T. Bradlow 2002. A unified approach to conjoint analysis methods. *Journal of the American Statistical Association* 97(459):674–682.

Matloff, N. 2011. *The Art of R Programming*. San Francisco: no starch press.

Maybury, M. T. (ed.) 1997. *Intelligent Multimedia Information Retrieval*. Menlo Park, Calif./ Cambridge: AAAI Press / MIT Press.

McCallum, Q. E. and S. Weston 2012. *Parallel R*. Sebastopol, Calif.: O'Reilly.

McCullagh, P. and J. A. Nelder 1989. *Generalized Linear Models* (second ed.). New York: Chapman and Hall.

McFadden, D. 2001. Economic choices. *American Economic Review* 91:351–378.

McIlroy, D., R. Brownrigg, T. P. Minka, and R. Bivand 2013. *mapproj: Map Projections*. Comprehensive R Archive Network. 2013.
http://cran.r-project.org/web/packages/mapproj/mapproj.pdf.

Meadow, C. T., B. R. Boyce, and D. H. Kraft 2000. *Text Information Retrieval Systems* (second ed.). San Diego: Academic Press.

Merkl, D. 2002. Text mining with self-organizing maps. In W. Klösgen and J. M. ytkow (eds.), *Handbook of Data Mining and Knowledge Discovery*, Chapter 46.9, pp. 903–910. Oxford: Oxford University Press.

Meyer, D., E. Dimitriadou, K. Hornik, A. Weingessel, and F. Leisch 2013. *e1071: Misc Functions of the Department of Statistics (e1071), TU Wien*. Comprehensive R Archive Network. 2013. http://cran.r-project.org/web/packages/e1071/e1071.pdf.

Meyer, D., A. Zeileis, K. Hornik, and M. Friendly 2013b. *Residual-Based Shadings in vcd*. Comprehensive R Archive Network. 2013. http://cran.r-project.org/web/packages/vcd/vignettes/residual-shadings.pdf.

Meyer, D., A. Zeileis, K. Hornik, and M. Friendly 2013a. *vcd: Visualizing Categorical Data*. Comprehensive R Archive Network. 2013.
http://cran.r-project.org/web/packages/vcd/vcd.pdf.

Meyer, D., A. Zeileis, and K. Hornik 2006, October 19. The strucplot framework: Visualizing multi-way contingency tables with vcd. *Journal of Statistical Software* 17(3):1–48. http://www.jstatsoft.org/v17/i03.

Meyer, D. 2013a. *Proximity Measures in the proxy Package for R*. Comprehensive R Archive Network. 2013.
http://cran.r-project.org/web/packages/proxy/vignettes/overview.pdf.

Meyer, D. 2013b. *proxy: Distance and Similarity Measures*. Comprehensive R Archive Network. 2013. http://cran.r-project.org/web/packages/proxy/proxy.pdf.

Meyer, D. 2013c. *Support Vector Machines*. Comprehensive R Archive Network. 2013. http://cran.r-project.org/web/packages/e1071/vignettes/svmdoc.pdf.

Milborrow, S. 2013. *rpart.plot: Plot rpart models. An Enhanced Version of plot.rpart*. Comprehensive R Archive Network. 2013.
http://cran.r-project.org/web/packages/rpart.plot/rpart.plot.pdf.

Miller, G. A. 1995. Wordnet: A lexical database for english. *Communications of the ACM* 38 (11):39–41.

Miller, T. W. 2005. *Data and Text Mining: A Business Applications Approach*. Upper Saddle River, N.J.: Pearson Prentice Hall. http://www.pearsonhighered.com/educator/product/Data-and-Text-Mining-A-Business-Applications-Approach/9780131400856.page.

Miller, T. W. 2008a. *Research and Information Services: An Integrated Approach to Business*. Glendale, Calif.: Research Publishers LLC. http://research-publishers.com/rp/rais.htm.

Miller, T. W. 2008b. *Without a Tout: How to Pick a Winning Team*. Glendale, Calif.: Research Publishers LLC. http://research-publishers.com/rp/wat.html.

Moreno, J. L. 1934. Who shall survive?: Foundations of sociometry, group psychotherapy, and sociodrama. Reprinted in 1953 (second edition) and in 1978 (third edition) by Beacon House, Inc., Beacon, N.Y.

Moskowitz, T. J. and L. J. Wertheim 2011. *Scorecasting: The Hidden Influences Behind How Sports Are Played and Games Are Won*. New York: Crown Archetype.

Mosteller, F., R. E. K. Rourke, and G. B. Thomas, Jr. 1970. *Probability with Statistical Applications* (second ed.). Reading, Mass.: Addison-Wesley.

Mosteller, F. and J. W. Tukey 1977. *Data Analysis and Regression*. Reading, Mass.: Addison-Wesley.

Mosteller, F. and D. L. Wallace 1984. *Applied Bayesian and Classical Inference: The Case of "The Federalist" Papers* (second ed.). New York: Springer. Earlier edition published in 1964 by Addison-Wesley, Reading, Mass. The previous title was *Inference and Disputed Authorship: "The Federalist"*.

Mosteller, F. 1965. *Fifty Challenging Problems in Probability with Solutions*. Reading, Mass.: Addison-Wesley.

Mosteller, F. 1997. Lessons from sports statistics. *The American Statistician* 51(4):305–310.

Moustafa, R. and E. Wegman 2006. Multivariate continuous data—parallel coordinates. In A. Unwin, M. Theus, and H. Hoffman (eds.), *Graphics of Large Databases: Visualizing a Million*, Chapter 7, pp. 143–155. New York: Springer.

Murrell, P. 2011. *R Graphics* (second ed.). Boca Raton, Fla.: CRC Press.

Nagle, T. T. and J. Hogan 2005. *The Strategy and Tactics of Pricing: A Guide to Growing More Profitably* (fourth ed.). Upper Saddle River, N.J.: Prentice Hall.

National Bureau of Economic Research 2010, September 20. Business cycle dating committee report. Available at http://www.nber.org/cycles/sept2010.html.

Neal, W. D. 2000. Market segmentation. In C. Chakrapani (ed.), *Marketing Research: State-of-the-Art Perspectives*, Chapter 1, pp. 375–399. American Marketing Association.

Nelson, W. B. 2003. *Recurrent Events Data Analysis for Product Repairs, Disease Recurrences, and Other Applications*. Series on Statistics and Applied Probability. Philadelphia and Alexandria, Va.: ASA-SIAM.

Neuendorf, K. A. 2002. *The Content Analysis Guidebook*. Thousand Oaks, Calif.: Sage.

Nielsen, A. 1979. Marketing research at the checkout. *Marketing Trends* 1:1–3.

Nunnally, J. C. and I. H. Bernstein 1994. *Psychometric Theory* (third ed.). New York: McGraw-Hill.

Nunnally, J. C. 1967. *Psychometric Theory*. New York: McGraw-Hill.

O'Hagan, A. 2010. *Kendall's Advanced Theory of Statistics: Bayesian Inference*, Volume 2B. New York: Wiley.

Oliver, D. 2004. *Basketball on Paper: Rules and Tools of Performance Analysis*. Dulles, Va.: Brassey's Press.

Orme, B. K. 2013. *Getting Started with Conjoint Analysis: Strategies for Product Design and Pricing Research* (third ed.). Glendale, Calif.: Research Publishers LLC. http://research-publishers.com/rp/gsca.htm.

Osgood, C., G. Suci, and P. Tannenbaum (eds.) 1957. *The Measurement of Meaning*. Urbana, Ill.: University of Illinois Press.

Osgood, C. 1962. Studies in the generality of affective meaning systems. *American Psychologist* 17:10–28.

Pace, R. K. and R. Barry 1997. Sparse spatial autoregressions. *Statistics and Probability Letters* 33:291–297.

Pang, B. and L. Lee 2008. Opinion mining and sentiment analysis. *Foundations and Trends in Information Retrieval* 2(1–2):1–135.

Pebesma, E. 2013. *CRAN Task View: Handling and Analyzing Spatio-Temporal Data*. Comprehensive R Archive Network. 2013.
http://cran.r-project.org/web/views/SpatioTemporal.html.

Peppers, D. and M. Rogers 1993. *The One to One Future: Building Relationships One Customer at a Time*. New York: Doubleday.

Petris, G. and W. Gilks 2013. *dlm: Bayesian and Likelihood Analysis of Dynamic Linear Models*. Comprehensive R Archive Network. 2013. http://cran.r-project.org/web/packages/dlm/dlm.pdf.

Petris, G., S. Petrone, and P. Campagnoli 2009. *Dynamic Linear Models with R*. New York: Springer.

Petris, G. 2010, October 13. An R package for dynamic linear models. *Journal of Statistical Software* 36(12):1–16. http://www.jstatsoft.org/v36/i12.

Pfaff, B. 2013. *Financial Risk Modeling and Portfolio Optimization with R*. New York: Wiley.

Piatetsky-Shapiro, G. and W. Frawley (eds.) 1991. *Knowledge Discovery in Databases*. Menlo Park, Calif.: AAAI Press.

Pindyck, R. and D. Rubinfeld 2012. *Microeconomics* (eighth ed.). Upper Saddle River, N.J.: Pearson.

Pinheiro, J. C. and D. M. Bates 2009. *Mixed-Effects Models in S and S-PLUS*. New York: Springer-Verlag.

Pinker, S. 1994. *The Language Instinct*. New York: W. Morrow and Co.

Pinker, S. 1997. *How the Mind Works*. New York: W.W. Norton & Company.

Pinker, S. 1999. *Words and Rules: The Ingredients of Language*. New York: HarperCollins.

Pollard, R. 1973, June. Collegiate football scores and the negative binomial distribution. *Journal of the American Statistical Association* 68(342):351–352.

Popping, R. 2000. *Computer-Assisted Text Analysis*. Thousand Oaks, Calif.: Sage.

Potts, C. 2011. On the negativity of negation. In *Proceedings of Semantics and Linguistic Theory 20*, pp. 636–659. CLC Publications. Retrieved from the World Wide Web at http://elanguage.net/journals/salt/article/view/20.636/1414.

Press, S. J. 2004. The role of Bayesian and frequentist multivariate modeling in statistical data mining. In H. Bozdogan (ed.), *Statistical Data Mining and Knowledge Discovery*, Chapter 1, pp. 1–14. Boca Raton, Fla.: CRC Press.

Pyle, D. 1999. *Data Preparation for Data Mining*. San Francisco: Morgan Kaufmann.

Quinlan, J. R. 1993. *C4.5: Programs for Machine Learning*. San Mateo, Calif.: Morgan Kaufmann.

Radcliffe-Brown, A. R. 1940. On social structure. *Journal of the Royal Anthropological Society of Great Britain and Ireland* 70:1–12.

Radev, D., W. Fan, H. Qi, H. Wu, and A. Grewal 2002. Probabilistic question answering on the Web. In *Proceedings of the Eleventh International Conference on World Wide Web*, pp. 408–419. ACM Press. ISBN 1-58113-449-5.

Rastogi, R. and K. Shim 1999. Scalable algorithms for mining large databases. In *Tutorial notes of the fifth ACM SIGKDD International Conference on Knowledge Discovery and Data Mining*, pp. 73–140. ACM Press. ISBN 1-58113-171-2.

Ratner, B. 2011. *Statistical and Machine-Learning Data Mining: Techniques for Better Predictive Modeling and Analysis of Big Data* (second ed.). Boca Raton, Fla.: CRC Press.

Reed, R. D. and R. J. Marks, II 1999. *Neural Smithing: Supervised Learning in Feedforward Artificial Neural Networks*. Cambridge: MIT Press.

Reep, C., R. Pollard, and B. Benjamin 1971. Skill and chance in ball games. *Journal of the Royal Statistical Society, Series A (General)* 134(4):623–629.

Reis, A. and J. Trout 2001. *Positioning: The Battle for Your Mind*. New York: McGraw-Hill.

Revelle, W. 2013. *psych: Procedures for Psychological, Psychometric, and Personality Research*. Comprehensive R Archive Network. 2013. http://cran.r-project.org/web/packages/psych/psych.pdf.

Ricci, F., L. Rokach, B. Shapira, and P. B. Kantor (eds.) 2011. *Recommender Systems Handbook*. New York: Springer.

Ripley, B. D. 1996. *Pattern Recognition and Neural Networks*. Cambridge: Cambridge University Press.

Roberts, C. W. (ed.) 1997. *Text Analysis for the Social Sciences: Methods for Drawing Statistical Inferences from Texts and Transcripts*. Mahwah, N.J.: Lawrence Erlbaum Associates.

Robert, C. P. and G. Casella 2009. *Introducing Monte Carlo Methods with R*. New York: Springer.

Robert, C. P. 2007. *The Bayesian Choice: From Decision Theoretic Foundations to Computational Implementation* (second ed.). New York: Springer.

Rogers, H. . J., H. Swaminathan, and R. K. Hambleton 1991. *Fundamentals of Item Response Theory*. Newbury Park, Calif.: Sage.

Romer, D. 2006. Do firms maximize? Evidence from professional football. *Journal of Political Economy* 114(2):340–365.

Rosenbaum, P. R. 1995. *Observational Studies*. New York: Springer.

Rosen, J. 2001. *The Unwanted Gaze: The Destruction of Privacy in America*. New York: Vintage.

Rossi, P. E., G. M. Allenby, and R. McCulloch 2005. *Bayesian Statistics and Marketing*. New York: Wiley.

Rossi, P. E. and G. M. Allenby 2003. Bayesian statistics and marketing. *Marketing Science* 22(3):304–328.

Rossi, P. 2013. *bayesm: Bayesian Inference for Marketing/Micro-econometrics.* Comprehensive R Archive Network. 2013.
http://cran.r-project.org/web/packages/bayesm/bayesm.pdf.

Ross, S. M. 2006. *Introduction to Probability Models* (tenth ed.). New York: Academic Press.

Rounds, J. B., T. W. Miller, and R. V. Dawis 1978. Comparability of multiple rank order and paired comparison methods. *Applied Psychological Measurement* 2(3):415–422.

Rousseeuw, P. J. 1987. Silhouettes: A graphical aid to the interpretation and validation of cluster analysis. *Journal of Computational and Applied Mathematics* 20:53–65.

Rubin, D. B. 1987. *Multiple Imputation for Nonresponse in Surveys.* New York: Wiley.

Ruppert, D. 2011. *Statistics and Data Analysis for Financial Engineering.* New York: Springer.

Ryan, J. A. 2013. *quantmod: Quantitative Financial Modelling Framework.* Comprehensive R Archive Network. 2013.
http://cran.r-project.org/web/packages/quantmod/quantmod.pdf.

Ryan, T. P. 2008. *Modern Regression Methods* (second ed.). New York: Wiley.

Salsburg, D. 2001. *The Lady Tasting Tea: How Statistics Revolutionized Science in the Twentieth Century.* New York: Henry Holt and Company.

Sarkar, D. and F. Andrews 2013. *latticeExtra: Extra Graphical Utilities Based on Lattice.* Comprehensive R Archive Network. 2013.
http://cran.r-project.org/web/packages/latticeExtra/latticeExtra.pdf.

Sarkar, D. 2008. *Lattice: Multivariate Data Visualization with R.* New York: Springer.

Sarkar, D. 2013. *lattice: Lattice Graphics.* Comprehensive R Archive Network. 2013.
http://cran.r-project.org/web/packages/lattice/lattice.pdf.

Sauer, R. D. 1998, December. The economics of wagering markets. *Journal of Economic Literature* 36:2021–2064.

Schafer, J. L. 2000. *Analysis of Incomplete Multivariate Data.* London: Chapman and Hall.

Schauerhuber, M., A. Zeileis, D. Meyer, and K. Hornik 2008. Benchmarking open-source tree learners in R/RWeka. In C. Preisach, H. Burkhardt, L. Schmidt-Thieme, and R. Decker (eds.), *Data Analysis, Machine Learning, and Applications,* pp. 389–396. New York: Springer.

Schrott, P. R. and D. J. Lanoue 1994. Trends and perspectives in content analysis. In I. Borg and P. Mohler (eds.), *Trends and Perspectives in Empirical Social Research,* pp. 327–345. Berlin: Walter de Gruyter.

Schwarz, A. 2004. *The Numbers Game: Baseball's Lifelong Fascination with Statistics.* New York: St. Martin's Griffin.

Schwarz, G. 1978. Estimating the dimension of a model. *Annals of Statistics* 6:461–464.

Schwertman, N. C., T. A. McCready, and L. Howard 1991, February. Probability models for the NCAA regional basketball tournaments. *The American Statistician* 45(1):35–38.

Schwertman, N. C., K. L. Schenk, and B. C. Holbrook 1996, February. More probability models for the NCAA regional basketball tournaments. *The American Statistician* 50(1):34–38.

Sebastiani, F. 2002. Machine learning in automated text categorization. *ACM Computing Surveys* 34(1):1–47.

Seber, G. A. F. 2000. *Multivariate Observations*. New York: Wiley. Originally published in 1984.

Sermas, R. 2013. *ChoiceModelR: Choice Modeling in R*. Comprehensive R Archive Network. 2013.
http://cran.r-project.org/web/packages/ChoiceModelR/ChoiceModelR.pdf.

Shapiro, C. and H. R. Varian 1999. *Information Rules: A Strategic Guide to the New Economy*. Boston: Harvard Business School Press.

Sharda, R. and D. Delen 2006. Predicting box office success of motion pictures with neural networks. *Expert Systems with Applications* 30:243–254.

Sharma, S. 1996. *Applied Multivariate Techniques*. New York: Wiley.

Shrout, P. E. and S. T. Fiske (eds.) 1995. *Personality Research, Methods, and Theory: A Festschrift Honoring Donald W. Fiske*. Hillsdale, N.J.: Lawrence Erlbaum Associates.

Siegel, E. 2013. *Predictive Analytics: The Power to Predict Who Will Click, Buy, Lie, or Die*. Hoboken, N.J.: Wiley.

Silver, N. 2012. *The Signal and the Noise: Why So Many Predictions Fail—But Some Don't*. New York: The Penguin Press.

Simonoff, J. S. 1996. *Smoothing Methods in Statistics*. New York: Springer-Verlag.

Simon, H. A. 2002. Foreward: enhancing the intelligence of discovery systems. In W. Klösgen and J. M. ytkow (eds.), *Handbook of Data Mining and Knowledge Discovery*, p. xvii. Oxford: Oxford University Press.

Sing, T., O. Sander, N. Beerenwinkel, and T. Lengauer 2005. ROCR: Visualizing classifier performance in R. *Bioinformatics* 21(20):3940–3941.

Snedecor, G. W. and W. G. Cochran 1989. *Statistical Methods* (eighth ed.). Ames, Iowa: Iowa State University Press. First edition published by Snedecor in 1937.

Socher, R., J. Pennington, E. H. Huang, A. Y. Ng, and C. D. Manning 2011. Semi-Supervised Recursive Autoencoders for Predicting Sentiment Distributions. In *Proceedings of the 2011 Conference on Empirical Methods in Natural Language Processing (EMNLP)*.

Spector, P. 2008. *Data Management with R*. New York: Springer.

Srivastava, A. N. and M. Sahami (eds.) 2009. *Text Mining: Classification, Clustering, and Applications*. Boca Raton, Fla.: CRC Press.

Stahel, W. and S. Weisberg (eds.) 1991. *Directions in Robust Statistics and Diagnostics*, Volume 34 of *IMA Volumes in Mathematics and Its Applications*. New York: Springer-Verlag.

Sternthal, B. and A. M. Tybout 2001. Segmentation and targeting. In D. Iacobucci (ed.), *Kellogg on Marketing*, Chapter 1, pp. 3–30. Wiley.

Stern, H. S. 1991, December. On the probability of winning a football game. *The American Statistician* 45(3):179–183.

Stigler, G. J. 1987. *The Theory of Price* (fourth ed.). New York: Macmillan.

Stone, P. J., D. C. Dunphy, M. S. Smith, and D. M. Ogilvie 1966. *The General Inquirer: A Computer Approach to Content Analysis*. Cambridge: MIT Press.

Stone, P. J. 1997. Thematic text analysis: New agendas for analyzing text content. In C. W. Roberts (ed.), *Text Analysis for the Social Sciences: Methods for Drawing Statistical Inferences from Texts and Transcripts*, Chapter 2, pp. 35–54. Mahwah, N.J.: Lawrence Erlbaum Associates.

Stuart, A., K. Ord, and S. Arnold 2010. *Kendall's Advanced Theory of Statistics: Classical Inference and the Linear Model*, Volume 2A. New York: Wiley.

Suess, E. A. and B. E. Trumbo 2010. *Introduction to Probability Simulation and Gibbs Sampling with R*. New York: Springer.

Sullivan, D. 2001. *Document Warehousing and Text Mining: Techniques for Improving Business Operations, Marketing, and Sales*. New York: Wiley.

Szymanski, C. 2013. *dlmodeler: Generalized Dynamic Linear Modeler*. Comprehensive R Archive Network. 2013.
http://cran.r-project.org/web/packages/dlmodeler/dlmodeler.pdf.

Taddy, M. 2013a. Measuring political sentiment on Twitter: factor-optimal design for multinomial inverse regression. Retrieved from the World Wide Web at http://arxiv.org/pdf/1206.3776v5.pdf.

Taddy, M. 2013b. Multinomial inverse regression for text analysis. Retrieved from the World Wide Web at http://arxiv.org/pdf/1012.2098v6.pdf.

Taddy, M. 2013c. *textir: Inverse Regression for Text Analysis*. 2013. http://cran.r-project.org/web/packages/textir/textir.pdf.

Tango, T. M., M. G. Lichtman, and A. E. Dolphin 2007. *The Book: Playing the Percentages in Baseball*. Dulles, Va.: Potomac Books.

Tanner, M. A. 1996. *Tools for Statistical Inference: Methods for the Exploration of Posterior Distributions and Likelihood Functions* (third ed.). New York: Springer.

Tan, P.-N., M. Steinbach, and V. Kumar 2005. *Introduction to Data Mining*. Boston: Addison-Wesley.

Therneau, T. M. and P. M. Grambsch 2000. *Modeling Survival Data: Extending the Cox Model*. New York: Springer.

Therneau, T., B. Atkinson, and B. Ripley 2013. *rpart: Recursive Partitioning*. Comprehensive R Archive Network. 2013.
http://cran.r-project.org/web/packages/rpart/rpart.pdf.

Therneau, T. and C. Crowson 2013. *Using Time Dependent Covariates and Time Dependent Coefficients in the Cox Model*. Comprehensive R Archive Network. 2013.
http://cran.r-project.org/web/packages/survival/vignettes/timedep.pdf.

Therneau, T. 2013. *survival: Survival Analysis*. Comprehensive R Archive Network. 2013.
http://cran.r-project.org/web/packages/survival/survival.pdf.

Thompson, M. 1975. On any given Sunday: Fair competitor orderings with maximum likelihood methods. *Journal of the American Statistical Association* 70(351):536–541.

Thorn, J. and P. Palmer 1985. *The Hidden Game of Baseball: A Revolutionary Approach to Baseball and Its Statistics* (revised and updated ed.). New York: Doubleday.

Thurman, W. N. and M. E. Fisher 1988. Chickens, eggs, and causality, or which came first? *American Journal of Agricultural Economics* 70(2):237–238.

Thurstone, L. L. 1927. A law of comparative judgment. *Psychological Review* 34:273–286.

Tong, S. and D. Koller 2001. Support vector machine active learning with applications to text classification. *Journal of Machine Learning Research* 2:45–66.

Torgerson, W. S. 1958. *Theory and Methods of Scaling*. New York: Wiley.

Train, K. E. 1985. *Qualitative Choice Analysis*. Cambridge, Mass.: MIT Press.

Train, K. E. 2003. *Discrete Choice Methods with Simulation*. Cambridge: Cambridge University Press.

Train, K. and Y. Croissant 2013. *Kenneth Train's exercises using the mlogit Package for R*. Comprehensive R Archive Network. 2013.
http://cran.r-project.org/web/packages/mlogit/vignettes/Exercises.pdf.

Trybula, W. J. 1999. Text mining. In M. E. Williams (ed.), *Annual Review of Information Science and Technology*, Volume 34, Chapter 7, pp. 385–420. Medford, N.J.: Information Today, Inc.

Tsay, R. S. 2013. *An Introduction to Analysis of Financial Data with R*. New York: Wiley.

Tufte, E. R. 1990. *Envisioning Information*. Cheshire, Conn.: Graphic Press.

Tufte, E. R. 1997. *Visual Explanations: Images and Quantities, Evidence and Narrative*. Cheshire, Conn.: Graphic Press.

Tufte, E. R. 2004. *The Visual Display of Quantitative Information* (second ed.). Cheshire, Conn.: Graphics Press.

Tufte, E. R. 2006. *Beautiful Evidence*. Cheshire, Conn.: Graphics Press.

Tukey, J. W. and F. Mosteller 1977. *Data Analysis and Regression: A Second Course in Statistics*. Reading, Mass.: Addison-Wesley.

Tukey, J. W. 1977. *Exploratory Data Analysis*. Reading, Mass.: Addison-Wesley.

Turney, P. D. 2002, July 8–10. Thumbs up or thumbs down? Semantic orientation applied to unsupervised classification of reviews. *Proceedings of the 40th Annual Meeting of the Association for Computational Linguistics (ACL '02)*:417–424. Available from the National Research Council Canada publications archive.

Turow, J. 2013. *The Daily You: How the New Advertising Industry Is Defining Your Identity and Your Worth*. New Haven, Conn.: Yale University Press.

Tybout, A. M. and B. Sternthal 2001. Brand positioning. In D. Iacobucci (ed.), *Kellogg on Marketing*, Chapter 2, pp. 31–57. Wiley.

Unwin, A., M. Theus, and H. Hofmann (eds.) 2006. *Graphics of Large Datasets: Visualizing a Million*. New York: Springer.

Vapnik, V. N. 1998. *Statistical Learning Theory*. New York: Wiley.

Vapnik, V. N. 2000. *The Nature of Statistical Learning Theory* (second ed.). New York: Springer.

Varian, H. R. 2005. *Intermediate Microeconomics: A Modern Approach* (seventh ed.). New York: Norton.

Velleman, P. F. and L. Wilkinson 1993, February. Nominal, ordinal, interval, and ratio typologies are misleading. *The American Statistician* 47(1):65–72.

Venables, W. N. and B. D. Ripley 2000. *S Programming*. New York: Springer-Verlag.

Venables, W. N. and B. D. Ripley 2002. *Modern Applied Statistics with S* (fourth ed.). New York: Springer-Verlag. Champions of S, S-Plus, and R call this "the mustard book.".

Venables, W. N., D. M. Smith, and R Development Core Team 2001. *An Introduction to R*. Bristol, UK: Network Theory Limited.

Wainer, H. 1997. *Visual Revelations: Graphical Tales of Fate and Deception from Napoleon Bonaparte to Ross Perot*. New York: Springer-Verlag.

Wasserman, L. 2010. *All of Statistics: A Concise Course in Statistical Inference*. New York: Springer.

Wasserman, S. and K. Faust 1994. *Social Network Analysis: Methods and Applications*. Cambridge, UK: Cambridge University Press.

Wasserman, S. and D. Iacobucci 1986. Statistical analysis of discrete relational data. *British Journal of Mathematical and Statistical Psychology* 39:41–64.

Wassertheil-Smoller, S. 1990. *Biostatistics and Epidemiology: A Primer for Health Professionals*. New York: Springer.

Wedel, M. and W. Kamakura 2000. *Market Segmentation: Conceptual and Methodological Foundations* (second ed.). Boston: Kluwer.

Wegman, E. J. 1990. Hyperdimensional data analysis using parallel coordinates. *Journal of the American Statistical Association* 85:664–675.

Weisberg, S. 2005. *Applied Linear Regression* (third ed.). New York: Wiley.

Weiss, S. M., N. Indurkhya, and T. Zhang 2010. *Fundamentals of Predictive Text Mining*. New York: Springer.

Wei, Y. 2013. Colors in R. Retrieved from the World Wide Web at http://www.stat.columbia.edu/ tzheng/files/Rcolor.pdf.

West, B. T. 2006. A simple and flexible rating method for predicting success in the NCAA basketball tournament. *Journal of Quantitative Analysis in Sports* 2(3):1–14.

West, M. D. (ed.) 2001. *Theory, Method, and Practice in Computer Content Analysis*. Westport, Conn.: Ablex.

Wickham, H. and W. Chang 2013. *ggplot2: An Implementation of the Grammar of Graphics*. Comprehensive R Archive Network. 2013. http://cran.r-project.org/web/packages/ggplot2/ggplot2.pdf.

Wickham, H. 2009. *ggplot2: Elegant Graphics for Data Analysis*. New York: Springer.

Wickham, H. 2010. stringr: Modern, consistent string processing. *The R Journal* 2(2):38–40.

Wickham, H. 2011, April 7. The split-apply-combine strategy for data analysis. *Journal of Statistical Software* 40(1):1–29. http://www.jstatsoft.org/v40/i01.

Wickham, H. 2013a. *plyr: Tools for Splitting, Applying and Combining Data*. Comprehensive R Archive Network. 2013. http://cran.r-project.org/web/packages/plyr/plyr.pdf.

Wickham, H. 2013b. *stringr: Make It Easier to Work with Strings*. Comprehensive R Archive Network. 2013. http://cran.r-project.org/web/packages/stringr/stringr.pdf.

Wilkinson, L. 2005. *The Grammar of Graphics* (second ed.). New York: Springer.

Williams, H. P. 1999. *Model Building in Mathematical Programming* (fourth ed.). New York: Wiley.

Winer, B. J., D. R. Brown, and K. M. Michels 1991. *Statistical Principles in Experimental Design* (third ed.). New York: McGraw-Hill.

Winston, W. L. 2009. *Mathletics: How Gamblers, Managers, and Sports Enthusiasts Use Mathematics in Baseball, Basketball, and Football*. Princeton, N.J.: Princeton University Press.

Witten, I. H., E. Frank, and M. A. Hall 2011. *Data Mining: Practical Machine Learning Tools and Techniques*. Burlington, Mass.: Morgan Kaufmann.

Witten, I. H., A. Moffat, and T. C. Bell 1999. *Managing Gigabytes: Compressing and Indexing Documents and Images* (second ed.). San Francisco: Morgan Kaufmann.

Yao, K. 2007. *Weighing the Odds in Sports Betting*. Las Vegas, Nev.: Pi Yee Press.

Yates, F. 1980. *Sampling Methods for Censuses and Surveys* (fourth ed.). New York: Macmillan. First edition published by Griffin in London in 1949.

Yau, N. 2011. *Visualize This: The FlowingData Guide to Design, Visualization, and Statistics*. New York: Wiley.

Yau, N. 2013. *Data Points: Visualization That Means Something*. New York: Wiley.

Ye, N. (ed.) 2003. *The Handbook of Data Mining*. Mahwah, N.J.: Lawrence Erlbaum.

Youmans, G. 1990. Measuring lexical style and competence: The type-token vocabulary curve. *Style* 24(4):584–599.

Youmans, G. 1991. A new tool for discourse analysis: The vocabulary management profile. *Language* 67(4):763–789.

ZaÔane, O. R. and M.-L. Antonie 2002. Classifying text documents by associating terms with text categories. In *Proceedings of the Thirteenth Australasian Conference on Database Technologies*, pp. 215–222. Australian Computer Society, Inc. ISBN 0-909925-83-6.

Zeileis, A., K. Hornik, and P. Murrell 2009, July. Escaping RGBland: Selecting colors for statistical graphics. *Computational Statistics and Data Analysis* 53(9):3259–3270.

Zeileis, A., K. Hornik, and P. Murrell 2013. *HCL-Based Color Palettes in R*. Comprehensive R Archive Network. 2013.
http://cran.r-project.org/web/packages/colorspace/vignettes/hcl-colors.pdf.

Zeileis, A., T. Hothorn, and K. Hornik 2013. *party with the mob: Model-Based Recursive Partitioning in R*. Comprehensive R Archive Network. 2013. http://cran.r-project.org/web/packages/party/vignettes/MOB.pdf.

Zhang, H. and B. Singer 1999. *Recursive Partitioning in the Health Sciences*. New York: Springer-Verlag.

Zhong, N., J. Liu, and Y. Yao (eds.) 2003. *Web Intelligence*. New York: Springer-Verlag.

Zipf, H. 1949. *Human Behavior and the Principle of Least Effort*. Cambridge, Mass.: Addison-Wesley.

Zivot, E. and J. Wang 2003. *Modeling Financial Time Series with S-PLUS*. Seattle: Insightful Corporation.

Zwerina, K. 1997. *Discrete Choice Experiments in Marketing: Use of Priors in Efficient Choice Designs and Their Application to Individual Preference Measurement*. New York: Physica-Verlag.

Index

A

advertising, 15–29
Akaike information criterion (AIC), 5
ARIMA model, *see* time series analysis
association rule, 40–42

B

bag-of-words approach, *see* text analytics
bar chart, *see* data visualization
Bayes information criterion (BIC), 5
Bayesian statistics, 5, 178, 191, 233, 248
benchmark study, *see* simulation
best-worst scaling, 260
biclustering, 248
big data, 231–235
biplot, *see* data visualization
block clustering, *see* biclustering
bootstrap, 8
box plot, *see* data visualization
brand equity research, 173–209
bubble chart, *see* data visualization

C

call center scheduling, *see* workforce scheduling
choice study, 29
    menu-based, 264
classical statistics, 5
classification, 2, 12, 113, 122, 240
    accuracy, 240, 241
classification tree, *see* tree-structured model
cluster analysis, 99, 248, 251
coefficient of determination, 239
collaborative filtering, 243
computational linguistics, *see* text analytics, natural language processing
conjoint analysis, 33, 258
content analysis, 126

corpus, *see* text analytics
correlation heat map, *see* data visualization, heat map
credit scoring, 249
cross-sectional study, *see* data organization
cross-validation, 6, 240

D

data mining, *see* data-adaptive research
data organization, 5, 58
data science, 1–14
data visualization, 8–13
    bar chart, 41, 43
    biplot, 90
    box plot, 16, 18
    bubble chart, 45
    density plot, 180, 182
    diagnostics, 22, 239
    dot chart, 124, 217
    heat map, 164, 165, 212, 213
    histogram, 86, 157, 160, 162, 163
    horizon plot, 54, 56, 57, 91, 92
    lattice plot, 11, 16, 19, 21, 22
    line graph, 72, 75
    mosaic plot, 178, 179
    multiple time series plot, 55
    network diagram, 47
    parallel coordinates, 183, 185
    ribbon plot, 68–71, 280
    scatter plot, 44
    scatter plot matrix, 212, 214
    spine chart, 30, 31, 33, 34, 268
    strip plot, 16, 21
    ternary plot, 180, 181
    time series plot, 59, 60
    tree diagram, 125, 216
data-adaptive research, 3, 4
density plot, *see* data visualization
dependent variable, *see* response

discrete event simulation, *see* simulation, process simulation
dot chart, *see* data visualization
duration analysis, *see* survival analysis

E

economic analysis, 53–66
    indexing, 54
elimination pick list, 265
empirical Bayes, 233, *see* Bayesian statistics
Erlang C, *see* queueing model
explanatory variable, 2, 3, 238
exploratory data analysis, 16

F

financial data analysis, 249
forecasting, 58–61, 218
four Ps, *see* marketing mix model

G

game-day simulation, *see* simulation, game-day
General Inquirer, 126
generalized least-squares, 239
generalized linear model, 239
generative grammar, *see* text analytics
geographically weighted regression, 216
graphics, *see* data visualization
group filtering, *see* collaborative filtering

H

hierarchical Bayes, *see* Bayesian statistics
hierarchical models, 233
histogram, *see* data visualization
horizon plot, *see* data visualization
hybrid model, 216

I

independent variable, *see* explanatory variable
integer programming, *see* mathematical programming
item analysis, psychometrics, 121

K

Kappa, *see* classification, accuracy

L

lattice plot, *see* data visualization
leading indicator, 54, 61
least-squares regression, *see* regression
lexical table, *see* text analytics, terms-by-documents matrix

line graph, *see* data visualization
linear discriminant analysis, 240
linear least-squares regression, *see* regression
linear model, 238, 239
linear predictor, 238
linguistics, *see* text analytics, natural language processing
log-linear models, 251
logical empiricism, 1
logistic regression, 121, 238
longitudinal study, *see* data organization

M

machine learning, *see* data-adaptive research
market basket analysis, 37–52
market response model, 25
market segmentation, *see* segmentation
market simulation, *see* simulation
marketing mix model, 24
mathematical programming, 67, 75, 249
    integer programming, 74
    sensitivity testing, 75
matrix bubble chart, *see* data visualization, bubble chart
mean-squared error (MSE), *see* root mean-squared error (RMSE)
measurement, 253–266
    construct validity, 253
    content validity, 127
    convergent validity, 254
    discriminant validity, 254
    face validity, 127
    multitrait-multimethod matrix, 253, 255
    reliability, 253
meta-analysis, 234
metadata, *see* text analytics
model-dependent research, 3, 4
morphology, *see* text analytics
mosaic plot, *see* data visualization
multidimensional scaling, 87, 89, 99, 244, 245, 251
multilevel models, *see* hierarchical models
multiple time series plot, *see* data visualization, time series plot
multivariate methods, 99, 244

N

natural language processing, *see* text analytics
nearest-neighbor model, 218, 219, 243
network diagram, *see* data visualization
neural network, 240

O

operations management, 67–83
optimization, constrained, 74
organization of data, *see* data, organization

P

paired comparisons, 259, 262
parallel coordinates plot, *see* data visualization
parsing, *see* text analytics, text parsing
perceptual map, *see* data visualization
philosophy, 1
Poisson regression, 238
predictive analytics, 1–14
    definition, 2
predictor, *see* explanatory variable
preference scaling, 245
preference study, 29
pricing research, 173–209
principal component analysis, 244
privacy, 251
probability
    binomial distribution, 159
    negative binomial distribution, 159, 161, 164
    Poisson distribution, 159, 161, 164
probability heat map, *see* data visualization, heat map
process simulation, *see* simulation
product positioning, 244–245
promotion, 15–29

Q

queueing model, 67, 68, 73

R

R package
    arules, 50
    arulesViz, 50
    car, 26
    caret, 129, 197
    ChoiceModelR, 197
    cluster, 101
    cvTools, 220
    e1071, 129
    forecast, 62
    ggplot2, 77, 101, 129, 197
    grid, 77, 101, 129
    lattice, 26, 197, 220
    latticeExtra, 62, 101, 129
    lmtest, 62
    lpSolve, 77
    lstringr, 129
    lubridate, 62, 77
    lvcd, 197
    mapproj, 220
    maps, 220
    quantmod, 62
    queueing, 77
    randomForest, 129, 220
    RColorBrewer, 50
    rpart, 129, 220
    rpart.plot, 129, 220
    spgwr, 220
    stringr, 101
    tm, 101, 129
    wordcloud, 101
R-squared, 239
random forest, 122–124, 212, 217
recommender systems, 242–243
regression, 2, 12, 20, 23, 24, 121, 212, 215, 238–239
    robust methods, 239
    time series regression, 58
regression tree, *see* tree-structured model
reliability, *see* measurement
response, 2, 238
ribbon plot, *see* data visualization
risk analytics, 249
robust methods, *see* regression
ROC curve, *see* classification, accuracy
root mean-squared error (RMSE), 239

S

sales forecasting, *see* forecasting
scatter plot, *see* data visualization
scatter plot matrix, *see* data visualization
segmentation, 246–248
semantics, *see* text analytics
sentiment analysis, 113–148
simulation, 151, 152, 155, 240, 249
    benchmark study, 122, 216, 240
    game-day, 150, 152, 155, 156
    market simulation, 183, 186, 187
    process simulation, 67, 68, 75, 76
    what-if analysis, 12
site selection, 218, *see* spatial data analysis
social filtering, *see* collaborative filtering
social network analysis, 250–251
spatial data analysis, 209–230
spatio-temporal model, 210, 219
spine chart, *see* data visualization
sports analytics, 149–172
state space model, *see* time series analysis
statistical experiment, *see* simulation
statistical graphics, *see* data visualization
statistical learning, *see* data-adaptive research
statistical simulation, *see* simulation

strip plot, *see* data visualization
supervised learning, 97, 248
support vector machines, 122, 240
survey research, 266
survival analysis, 238, 249
syntax, *see* text analytics

T

tag, *see* text analytics, metadata
target marketing, 246–248
terms-by-documents matrix, *see* text analytics
ternary plot, *see* data visualization
text analytics, 83–113
    bag-of-words approach, 86, 91
    corpus, 87
    generative grammar, 93, 94
    metadata, 85
    morphology, 94
    natural language processing, 86, 91, 93, 128
    semantics, 94
    stemming, 95
    syntax, 94
    terms-by-documents matrix, 87, 95, 96
    text parsing, 85, 93
    text summarization, 97
text measure, 85, 86, 91, 126, 127
text mining, *see* text analytics
thematic analysis, 126

time series analysis, 53
    ARIMA model, 58
    multiple time series, 55
    state space model, 58
time series plot, *see* data visualization
traditional research, 3
training-and-test regimen, 6–8, 20
tree diagram, *see* data visualization
tree-structured model
    classification, 123, 125
    regression, 212, 216
trellis plot, *see* data visualization, lattice plot
triplot, *see* data visualization, ternary plot

U

unsupervised learning, 97, 248

V

validity, *see* measurement

W

wait-time ribbon, *see* data visualization, ribbon plot
Web analytics, 251
Weka, 49, 240
what-if analysis, *see* simulation
workforce scheduling, 67–83